At the Feet of *Jesus*

Daily Devotions
to Nurture
a Mary Heart

JOANNA
WEAVER

Compiled with Angela Howard

WATERBROOK
PRESS

At the Feet of Jesus
Published by WaterBrook Press
12265 Oracle Boulevard, Suite 200
Colorado Springs, Colorado 80921

Includes previously published material from *Having a Mary Heart in a Martha World, Having a Mary Spirit,* and *Lazarus Awakening.* Some entries have been edited for space and/or context.

Personal stories appearing in this book are used by permission. In some instances the names or details have been changed to protect the privacy of the persons involved.

ISBN 978-0-307-73100-5
ISBN 978-0-307-73102-9 (electronic)

Copyright © 2012 by Joanna Weaver

Cover design by Mark D. Ford

Published in association with the literary agency of Janet Kobobel Grant, Books & Such, 52 Mission Circle, Suite 122, PMB 170, Santa Rosa, CA 95409.

Published in the United States by WaterBrook Multnomah, an imprint of the Crown Publishing Group, a division of Random House Inc., New York.

WaterBrook and its deer colophon are registered trademarks of Random House Inc.

Cataloging-in-Publication Data is on file with the Library of Congress.

Printed in the United States of America
2012—First Edition

10 9 8 7 6 5 4 3 2 1

Special Sales
Most WaterBrook Multnomah books are available at special quantity discounts when purchased in bulk by corporations, organizations, and special-interest groups. Custom imprinting or excerpting can also be done to fit special needs. For information, please e-mail SpecialMarkets@WaterBrookMultnomah.com or call 1-800-603-7051.

To my dear friend and writing companion,
Angela Howard:
Thank you for loving God and loving people in such
a passionate yet winsome way!
This book would not have been possible without you.

And to Patty Strellnauer:
You have been Jesus to me, my sweet sister.
Your wise friendship has sheltered my heart
as well as challenged my soul.
I am forever grateful.

CONTENTS

A Note from Joanna...

At the feet of Jesus.

I don't know what those words do to your heart, but they stir something deep within me. My spirit longs for time with the Lord, but life often interferes. So many responsibilities to take care of. So many duties to be done.

Sitting at Jesus's feet was a choice Mary had to make the day He came to her family's home in Bethany (Luke 10:38–42). It is a choice you and I must make as well. Laying aside our busyness—even our busyness for God—so that we might focus our hearts on spending time alone with Him.

I hope you will find this devotional a helpful companion on your journey into God's presence. I've interwoven excerpts from my three Bethany books: *Having a Mary Heart in a Martha World*, *Having a Mary Spirit*, and *Lazarus Awakening*. I've also included previously unpublished material that didn't make it into my original books, each of which I've labeled "outtake." A "Read and Reflect" section will help you dig into the life-changing Word of God for yourself, giving you opportunity to find the "better part" Mary enjoyed and the "one thing" I believe her sister Martha discovered as she received the rebuke of the Lord and found life for her soul.

Sprinkled throughout the year are "Going Deeper" sidebars to help you develop a daily quiet time, and in the back of the book you'll find a unique one-year Bible reading guide that takes you back and forth between the Old Testament and the New (check out the downloadable format at www.becominghis.com). It is my prayer that you'll fall in love with God's Word in a brand-new way as you discover the message of grace woven throughout the Bible from beginning to end.

Down at the feet of Jesus. That's where it all begins.

*L*ord Jesus, I give You my life.
I invite You to have Your way in me.
Take me and break me. Shake me and make me.
Fill me and spill me. Change me and rearrange me.
But whatever You do, Lord, don't leave me the same.
Spirit of wisdom and revelation, I welcome Your work.
Open my eyes so I can see… my ears so I can hear…
I choose truth over comfort, challenge over complacency.
Lord, make me forever Yours.
And most of all, make me like You.

     Amen.

Teach us to number our days aright,
that we may gain a heart of wisdom.
PSALM 90:12

January 1

I've always dreamed of being much more than I am. More organized, more disciplined, more loving...much more "much more," if you know what I mean! Each January I set out on a new self-improvement program.

This year I'll get in shape.

This year I'll keep my house clean.

This year I'll send out birthday cards. On time.

This year—really—I'll be the loving, forgiving, obedient woman of God I long to be instead of the willful, stubborn, disobedient Christian I sometimes see staring back at me in the mirror.

All noble goals. Truth be told, I am much more at peace when my house is clean. And I believe that if you really love people, you ought to care enough to send the very best—or at least one of those ninety-nine-cent cards from Wal-Mart! And I know that genuine happiness only comes from living close to God and obeying Him.

I really do want to be different. I want to be changed.

As the saying goes, "There's a skinny woman inside me just struggling to get out." Unfortunately—as the saying continues—"I can usually sedate her with four or five cupcakes."

Maybe you've discovered, as I have, that most New Year's resolutions have little effect on day-to-day life except to add a burden of guilt and a feeling of failure. Continually striving, yet never arriving.

I'm so glad we have a Savior who loves us just as we are, but loves us too much to leave us that way. Jesus will do whatever it takes to return to us the glory of God that we were meant to reflect in the world. So that, through our lives, people might see who God really is.

—Having a Mary Spirit

READ: Hebrews 4:14–16

REFLECT: What does it mean to know that you have a high priest who understands your weaknesses?

January 2

May [God] give you the Spirit of wisdom and revelation, so that you may know him better. EPHESIANS 1:17

Perhaps no passage of Scripture better describes the conflict we feel as women than the one we find in the gospel of Luke. Just mention the names *Mary* and *Martha* around a group of Christian women and you'll get knowing looks and nervous giggles. We've all felt the struggle. We want to worship like Mary, but the Martha inside keeps bossing us around.

Here's a refresher course in case you've forgotten the story. It's the tale of two sisters. It's the tale of you and me.

> As Jesus and his disciples were on their way, he came to a village where a woman named Martha opened her home to him. She had a sister called Mary, who sat at the Lord's feet listening to what he said. But Martha was distracted by all the preparations that had to be made. She came to him and asked, "Lord, don't you care that my sister has left me to do the work by myself? Tell her to help me!"
>
> "Martha, Martha," the Lord answered, "you are worried and upset about many things, but only one thing is needed. Mary has chosen what is better, and it will not be taken away from her." (Luke 10:38–42)

Instead of applauding Martha, Jesus gently rebukes her, telling her Mary has chosen "what is better." Or, as another translation puts it, "Mary has chosen the better part" (NRSV).

"The better part?" Martha must have echoed incredulously.

"The better part!" I say to God in the midst of my own whirl of activity. "You mean there's more? I have to do more?"

No, no, comes the answer to my tired heart. Jesus's words in Luke 10 are incredibly freeing to those of us on the performance treadmill of life.

It isn't "more" He requires of us.

In fact, it may be less.

—Having a Mary Heart

READ: Matthew 23:1–4

REFLECT: What do you struggle with most—the burden of expectations put on you by others or those you put on yourself?

January 3

I'll never forget crying in the darkness one night many years ago. My husband was an associate pastor at a large church, and our lives were extremely busy. The size of the church meant there were always people in need. I would go to bed at night worried about all the things I didn't accomplish and should have, about all the things I'd accomplished but not very well.

I remember clinging to my husband that night as he tried to comfort me. "What's wrong, honey?" he asked, caressing my hair. But I couldn't explain. I was completely overwhelmed.

The only thing that came out between sobs was a broken plea. "Tell me the good news," I begged him. "I honestly can't remember… Tell me the good news."

Perhaps you have felt the same way. You've known the Lord your whole life, and yet you haven't found the peace and fulfillment you've always longed for. So you've stepped up the pace, hoping that in offering more service, somehow you will merit more love.

Or perhaps you've withdrawn from service. You've gone the route I've described above and, frankly, you've had it. You've stopped volunteering, stopped saying yes. You're out of the loop and glad for it. And yet the peace and quiet holds no peace and quiet. The stillness hasn't led to the closer walk with God you'd hoped for, just a sense of resentment. You go to church; you go through the motions of worship, then leave and go home the same. And at night, sometimes you wonder, "What is the good news? Can someone tell me? I can't remember."

If you're struggling to remember what makes the gospel so priceless, so precious, bring your questions to Jesus. You have a Savior who stands ready to share the good news of hope for your weary heart.

—Having a Mary Heart

Read: Matthew 11:28

Reflect: How would your life be different if you took Jesus up on His offer of rest?

January 4

He chose us...to the praise of the glory of His grace, by which He made us accepted in the Beloved. EPHESIANS 1:4, 6, NKJV

The good news is woven through the New Testament in a grace-filled strand that shines especially bright in the gospel stories of Mary and Martha. The message is this: salvation isn't about what I do; it's about what Jesus did.

The cross did more than pay for my sins; it set me free from the bondage of the "shoulds" and "if onlys" and "what might have beens." And Jesus's words to Martha are the words He wants to speak to your heart and mine: "You are worried and upset about many things, but only one thing is needed" (Luke 10:41–42).

The "one thing" is not found in doing more.

It's found by sitting at His feet.

Catch that: Mary sat at His feet. She didn't move a muscle. She listened. She didn't come up with clever responses or a doctrinal thesis. Her gift was availability. (In the end, I believe that was Martha's gift as well.)

The only requirement for a deeper friendship with God is showing up with a heart open and ready to receive. Jesus invites us to come and rest, to spend time with Him in Living Room Intimacy. Intimacy that allows us to be honest in our complaints, bold in our approach, and lavish in our love. Intimacy that allows us to hear our Father's voice and discern our Father's will. Intimacy that so fills us with His love and His nature that it spills out to our dry, thirsty world in Kitchen Service.

In the Living Room. That's where it all begins. Down at His feet.

—*Having a Mary Heart*

READ: Jeremiah 29:12–13

REFLECT: What does God promise will happen when we seek Him?

God did this so that men would seek him and perhaps reach out for him and find him, though he is not far from each of us. Acts 17:27

January 5

Intimacy with God. What does it mean to you—and how do you achieve it? Is it some mystical level of consciousness attainable only by the deeply devout?

Some religions say that it is. According to Hinduism, a religion based on the *karma* of good works, one lifetime isn't enough for the soul to achieve spiritual enlightenment. Hindu mathematicians calculate it takes 6.8 million rotations through reincarnation for justice to mete out enough punishment that it finally balances the wrongs we have done so that we can receive the ultimate spiritual level of nirvana.[1]

In the Far East, during religious festivals, men often have hooks inserted under the skin of their backs. These hooks are then tied to wagonloads of rocks, which the men drag through the streets, hoping to obtain forgiveness for their sins. In certain areas of Mexico, the devout crawl miles on their knees in pilgrimage.

All over the world, people go to unimaginable lengths to find God—which is sad when you consider the unimaginable lengths God has already gone to find *us*.

We don't need millions of lifetimes in order to be pure enough to see God. We don't need to stick hooks in our backs or tear the flesh off our knees in order to earn God's favor.

All we really need is Jesus. For He is all the evidence we need. The Father actually *wants* us close and is willing to do whatever is necessary to make sure it happens.

—*Having a Mary Heart*

READ: Romans 6:23
REFLECT: Consider the difference between a wage and a gift. What kind of gift does God offer?

January 6

I will be your God and you will be my people. JEREMIAH 7:23

I imagine there must have been a quiet restlessness about Yahweh for some time. A far-off look now and then revealed a yearning, a longing. Almost a sadness. Perhaps, then, it wasn't such a surprise when the Uncreated declared His desire to create.

"Let us make man in our image," said the Creator, stooping down to fill His hands with dust. With great care the Eternal One shaped His work. Then, bending over, He gently breathed into the lifeless clay, and a man was created... then a woman. The two were handsome enough, the angels thought, though a bit ordinary, especially when measured against all that had been created before. Yet God seemed quite pleased.

Perhaps, the angels pondered, this creation had some special talent they were unaware of, some unique quality that would make them useful to the kingdom. So they waited to see these humans perform.

But soon it became evident that all God's previous work—the soaring mountains, the lush green valleys, the glorious sunrises, and the watercolor sunsets—had been made for the pleasure and delight of man and woman, His last created works.

But not just for their pleasure. The shimmering world was a backdrop. A stage upon which the angels would watch creation's true purpose unfold. For all of it had been made to facilitate God's passionate pursuit of relationship with humankind.

—*Lazarus Awakening*

READ: 1 Peter 2:9–10
REFLECT: How does it make you feel to realize you've been chosen by God?

*Jesus Christ…gave himself…to purify
for himself a people that are his very
own.* Titus 2:13–14

January 7

Perhaps you've never considered how much your heavenly Father longs to know you and be known by you. We've been told that we were born with a God-shaped hole—a spiritual vacuum that can't be filled by anything or anyone except God Himself. But have you ever considered that God might have a *you*-shaped hole, an emptiness that only you can fill?

That's the overarching implication of the biblical message. From the book of Genesis to the Song of Solomon, from Ecclesiastes to Malachi, from Matthew to Revelation, the entire Bible records an epic story of the ever-reaching, always-pursuing, tenaciously tender love of God. I appreciate the way The Message expresses Ephesians 1:4–8:

> Long before he laid down earth's foundations, [God] had us in mind,
> had settled on us as the focus of his love, to be made whole and holy by
> his love. Long, long ago he decided to adopt us into his family through
> Jesus Christ. (What pleasure he took in planning this!) He wanted us
> to enter into the celebration of his lavish gift-giving by the hand of his
> beloved Son.
>
> Because of the sacrifice of the Messiah, his blood poured out on
> the altar of the Cross, we're a free people—free of penalties and punish-
> ments chalked up by all our misdeeds. And not just barely free, either.
> Abundantly free! He thought of everything, provided for everything we
> could possibly need.

Amazing, isn't it? God's gifts are all ours, just waiting to be received. The riches of heaven, the love of our Father, and a Savior who's obliterated the power of sin.

—Lazarus Awakening

READ: Ephesians 1:4–8
REFLECT: Underline key phrases in these verses that speak most to you, then
read these verses aloud, emphasizing those phrases.

The Invitation

There is no more important question than the one asked by a Philippian jailer over two thousand years ago: "What must I do to be saved?" (Acts 16:30).

Jesus answered that question once and for all by taking the punishment for our sins upon Himself. We simply have to accept the free gift of salvation He offers. How do we do that? The Billy Graham Evangelistic Association outlines four steps for receiving Christ:

- Admit your need. (I am a sinner.)
- Be willing to turn from your sins (repent).
- Believe that Jesus Christ died for you on the cross and rose from the grave.
- Pray a prayer like this: Dear Lord Jesus, I know that I am a sinner, and I ask for Your forgiveness. I believe You died for my sins and rose from the dead. I turn from my sins and invite You to come into my heart and life. I want to trust and follow You as my Lord and Savior. In Your Name, amen.[2]

In John 1:12, the Bible promises that "to all who received him, to those who believed in his name, he gave the right to become children of God." What an incredible offer! What an amazing gift.

We simply have to accept it. For Jesus has done everything else.

—Lazarus Awakening

And everyone who calls on the name
of the Lord will be saved.

ACTS 2:21

Be still, and know that I am God.
PSALM 46:10

January 8

After hearing several hundred sermons about Mary and Martha of Bethany and their story found in Luke 10:38–42, I assumed the meaning was fairly straightforward. Mary was the heroine. Martha was the villain. And, unfortunately, too much of the time I was Martha! I felt the Lord convicting me of my tendency to rush around, busy with "many things" while ignoring the "one thing" that was needed—to sit at Jesus's feet.

But as I studied the rest of the sisters' story in John 11 and 12, I discovered something so beautiful, so amazing, that I felt compelled to share it in *Having a Mary Heart in a Martha World.* For I saw two women change before my eyes, both of them experiencing a holy makeover when they encountered the living Lord.

Perhaps the most comforting thing I learned was that none of us has it all together. Even on our best days and with our best intentions, we all eventually blow it. We start out operating in our gifts and talents—excited to be serving the Messiah—only to have our efforts morph into a full-blown pity party when we don't get enough help, or we aren't appreciated, or someone else gets the attention we know we deserve.

But what stood out most to me was the fact that when Jesus scolded Martha about her busyness, He wasn't condemning her efficiency and hard work or her can-do personality. He wasn't telling her she had to be just like Mary to please Him. Jesus simply didn't want Martha to be so caught up in Kitchen Service *for* Him that she missed out on the joy of Living Room Intimacy *with* Him.

Jesus offers the same invitation to you and me today.

—*Having a Mary Spirit*

READ: Luke 10:38–42
REFLECT: Which sister do you relate to most, and why?

January 9

Whatever you do, work at it with all your heart, as working for the Lord, not for men. COLOSSIANS 3:23

The story is told of a man who met God in a lovely valley one day.[3] "Is there anything I can do for You?" the man asked.

"Yes, there is," God said. "I have a wagon with three stones in it, and I need someone to pull it up the hill for Me. Are you willing?"

"Yes, I'd love to do something for You. Those stones don't look very heavy, and the wagon's in good shape. I'd be happy to do that."

God gave the man specific instructions, sketching a map in the dust at the side of the road. "Go through the woods and up the road that winds up the side of the hill. Once you get to the top, just leave the wagon there. Thank you for your willingness to help Me today."

"No problem!" the man replied and set off cheerfully. The wagon pulled a bit behind him, but the burden was an easy one. *What a joy to be able to help the Lord,* he thought, enjoying the beautiful day.

Just around the third bend, he walked into a small village. A man there asked what he was doing. "Well, God gave me a job this morning. I'm delivering these three stones to the top of the hill."

"My goodness! I was just praying this morning about how I was going to get this rock to the top of the mountain," the man told him. "Could you take it up there for me? It would be such an answer to prayer."

The man said, "Of course. I don't suppose God would mind. Just put it with the other stones." Then he set off with three stones and a rock rolling behind him....

—*Having a Mary Heart*

READ: Galatians 6:2
REFLECT: As Christians, what are we called to do?

This is love for God: to obey his commands. And his commands are not burdensome. 1 JOHN 5:3

January 10

...The wagon seemed a bit heavier. The man could feel the jolt of each bump, and the wagon seemed to pull to one side a bit. The man stopped to adjust the load as he sang a hymn of praise, pleased to be helping out a brother as he served God. He soon reached another small village where a good friend lived.

"You're going to the top of the hill?" his oldest friend asked.

"Yes! I am so excited. Can you imagine, God gave me something to do!"

"Hey!" said his friend. "I need this bag of pebbles taken up. I've been so worried that it might not get taken care of since I haven't any time to do it myself. But you could fit it in right between the three stones here in the middle." With that, he placed his burden in the wagon.

"Shouldn't be a problem," the man said. "I think I can handle it." He waved good-bye and began to pull the wagon back onto the road.

The wagon was definitely tugging on his arm now, but it wasn't uncomfortable. As he started up the incline, he began to feel the weight of the three stones, the rock, and the pebbles. Certainly God would be proud of how energetic and helpful he'd been.

One little stop followed another, and the wagon grew fuller and fuller. The sun was hot above the man pulling it, and his shoulders ached with the strain. The songs of praise and thanksgiving that had filled his heart had long since left his lips as resentment began to build inside. Surely this wasn't what he had signed up for that morning. God had given him a burden heavier than he could bear....

—*Having a Mary Heart*

READ: Matthew 11:29–30
REFLECT: How does Jesus describe the yoke and burden He invites us to share?

January 11

For each one should carry his own load.
GALATIANS 6:5

…The wagon lumbered and swayed over the ruts in the road. Frustrated, the man wanted to give up. "This is it!" he fumed as the load of obligations collided with the back of his legs. "Oh God," he wailed. "I thought You were behind this trip, but I am overcome by the heaviness of it. You'll have to get someone else to do it."

As he prayed, God came to his side. "Sounds like you're having a hard time," God said as He looked into the wagon. "What is this?" He held up the bag of pebbles.

"That belongs to John, my good friend. He didn't have time to bring it up himself. I thought I would help."

"And this?" God tumbled two pieces of shale over the side of the wagon as the man tried to explain. God continued to unload the wagon, removing both light and heavy items. They dropped to the ground, the dust swirling up around them. The man who had hoped to help God grew silent.

"If you will be content to let others take their own burdens," God told him, "I will help you with your task."

"But I promised I would help! I can't leave these things lying here."

"Let others shoulder their own belongings," God said gently. "I know you were trying to help, but when you are weighted down with all these cares, you cannot do what I have asked of you."

The man jumped to his feet, suddenly realizing the freedom God was offering. "You mean I only have to take the three stones after all?" he asked.

"That is what I asked you to do." God smiled. "My yoke is easy, and my burden is light. I will never ask you to carry more than I will give you the strength to bear."

—Having a Mary Heart

READ: Galatians 6:2–5

REFLECT: What burden-bearing insight do these verses provide when considered together?

Be very careful, then, how you live—not as unwise but as wise. Ephesians 5:15

January 12

Nothing is harder to bear than a burden we're not called to carry. While God does call us to bear one another's burdens, He has not asked us to step in and do what people are not willing to do themselves. And while there are many needs, God has not asked us to meet every one.

In fact we, like Martha, may be surprised by how little God actually requires.

When my friend Tricia started feeling overwhelmed by her too-busy life, she and her husband, John, decided to dump some rocks from their overloaded wagons. Here's the simple process they followed. Maybe you'll find it helpful, too.

1. They made a list of all the activities they were involved in (children, work, church, etc.).
2. They prayed over and prioritized the activities as to importance, assigning each one a number from one to four.
3. Then they eliminated all the fours.

While this process may sound overly simplistic, it really helped John and Tricia lighten their load. "It was hard to see things we enjoyed go out the door!" Tricia says. "But the freedom and the peace we've gained have been more than worth it."

Can you imagine how your perspective—not to mention your life!—would change if your own load were lightened? How much more energy you would have for the things that matter most—especially more time with Jesus?

—Having a Mary Heart

READ: Proverbs 16:9

REFLECT: Take a moment and make a list of the things that are currently in your wagon. Then, with this verse in mind, ask God what should stay and what should go.

January 13

But seek first his kingdom and his righteousness, and all these things will be given to you as well. MATTHEW 6:33

In his book *First Things First,* Stephen Covey tells the story of a man teaching a time-management seminar. In order to make a point, the man picked up some fist-sized rocks and put them in a wide-mouthed gallon jar. Then he looked out at the class and asked, "Is the jar full?"

Some of the students blurted out, "Yes." The teacher laughed gently and said, "No, it's not." He pulled out a bucket of pea gravel and began to pour it in the jar. The class watched as the pea gravel filtered down between the rocks until it reached the top.

"Now, is the jar full?"

The class was a bit reticent to answer. After all, they'd been wrong before. The man poured a bucket of sand down among the pea gravel and the large rocks. He shook the jar gently to let the sand settle, then added more. He asked again, "Is the jar full?" They said, "Probably not."

Now the teacher poured a pitcher of water in the jar. It filtered down until it was running over. "Is the jar full?" the time-management consultant asked. The class answered, "We think it is."

"Okay, class," he said. "What is the lesson in this visual aid?"

Somebody said, "No matter how busy your life is, there is always room for more!"

"No," the teacher said as the class broke into laughter. "That's not it! The point is this: if you don't put the big rocks in first you'll never get them in later."[4]

It sounds like the same point Jesus made when He said, "Seek first his kingdom...and all these things will be given to you as well" (Matthew 6:33).

—*Having a Mary Heart*

READ: 2 Chronicles 1:7–12

REFLECT: What did Solomon set as his highest priority, and what was the result of that choice?

This is love: not that we loved God, but that he loved us. 1 JOHN 4:10

Getting God's love from our heads to our hearts may be the most difficult—yet the most important—thing we ever attempt to do.

"I need to talk," Lisa whispered in my ear. A committed Christian with a deep passion for the Lord, my friend had tears pooling in her dark eyes.

"I don't know what's wrong with me," she said, as she looked down at her feet. "I could go to the worst criminal, look them in the eye, and tell them, 'Jesus loves you!' and mean it from the bottom of my heart.

"But, Joanna," she said, gripping my hand, "I can't seem to look in the mirror and convince myself."

I'd felt that same terrible disconnect early in my walk with the Lord. Hoping He loved me but never really knowing for sure. Sadly, I've heard a sense of lonely detachment echoed by hundreds of women I've talked to around the country. Beautiful women. Plain women. Strong Christian women, deep in the Word and active in their church, as well as women brand new to their faith. Personal attributes or IQs seem to matter little. Whether they were raised in a loving home or an abusive situation, it doesn't seem to change what one friend calls an epidemic among Christian women (and many men as well): a barren heart condition I call love-doubt.

"Jesus loves me—this I know, for the Bible tells me so."[5] Many of us have sung the song since we were children. But do we really believe it? Or has Christ's love remained more of a fairy tale than a reality we've experienced for ourselves in the only place we can really know for sure?

Our hearts.

—*Lazarus Awakening*

READ: Romans 5:6–8

REFLECT: Describe what God has done to prove His love for you.

January 15

When [Satan] lies, he speaks his native language, for he is a liar and the father of lies. JOHN 8:44

Because Satan hates God so much, he hates God's children. His favorite pastime is whispering lies to us. Lies that tell us we're enough on our own...or that God could never love us.

And—the worst lie of all—the insinuation that our transformation itself is a fairy tale.

For Satan loves to twist our salvation stories and insist that, while for a moment our pumpkins may have become carriages and our rags glistening gowns, midnight has tolled, and it's time we face reality. He insists we're nothing more than barefoot Cinderellas, beggar girls trying to find our way back home, with no happily-ever-after to close our stories and no handsome Prince to call our own. That no matter how we wish and hope and dream, we will never experience lasting change. Not here on this earth, at any rate.

Nothing could be further from the truth. Yet that doesn't change the fact that many of us are living far more like paupers than princesses. Like slave girls rather than daughters of the King.

I read an unsettling statistic reported by researcher George H. Gallup Jr. According to his poll, while 42 percent of Americans claim to be born-again Christians, only 10 percent of those polled can point to a transforming encounter with Christ.[6]

In other words, nine out of ten Christians report that, while they may be going to heaven, nothing much has changed for them here on earth. They may have secured an eternal fire-insurance policy, but they haven't experienced the life change Christ came to give. And while occasionally they may get spiritual warm fuzzies, they can't point to any noticeable reconstruction going on in their lives.

I know I've felt like that before. But perhaps instead of focusing on how far we have yet to go, we should spend a little more time looking back. Gratefully considering how far God has brought us by His sweet, sustaining grace.

—*Having a Mary Spirit*

READ: Psalm 77:11–12

REFLECT: List the changes you've experienced over the years, no matter how small. Give thanks and welcome God's continued work.

Your enemy the devil prowls around like a roaring lion looking for someone to devour. 1 PETER 5:8

January 16

I've come to realize that Satan is not nearly as disappointed at losing me from his kingdom as he is determined to keep me from being effective in God's kingdom. If Satan can't make me fall away from God's grace, he will do everything he can to keep me from fully embracing God's grace. Satan wants me—and he wants you!—to be so constantly preoccupied with what we're not that we never get around to realizing all that God is. Our enemy wants to keep us so consumed with our inadequacies that we never get around to appropriating the love and transforming power God has made available to us through His Son.

And in reality, when you look at all the evidence, Satan is right. Because of the Fall, we are unworthy of salvation. Unlikely candidates for anything but destruction. Wanting to do what is right one minute only to do what is wrong the next (Romans 7:15). The only appropriate response we—like Paul—can give is an anguished cry: "Oh, what a miserable person I am!" (verse 24, NLT).

But then Paul continues. "Thank God!" he writes in verse 25 (NLT). "The answer is in Jesus Christ our Lord."

Woohoo! Preach it, brother! I love a happy ending.

The trouble is, Paul doesn't end the verse there. Instead, he reiterates that, though in our hearts and minds we want to obey God's laws, our "sinful nature" makes us slaves to sin.

Wait a minute! Let's go back to the victory-in-Jesus part. I thought we were new creations when we got saved. I thought the old had gone and the new had come (2 Corinthians 5:17). I thought we'd signed on for a holy makeover.

Well, yes, we are. And, yes, it has. And, yes, you did.

But Flesh Woman doesn't know it yet.

—Having a Mary Spirit

READ: 2 Corinthians 5:17
REFLECT: Write this verse on a note card, and place it where you can declare it out loud several times a day. Memorize it and make it a part of your arsenal when the enemy attacks.

January 17

Oh, that my ways were steadfast in obeying your decrees! PSALM 119:5

It's a shock, I tell you. I had no idea she lived inside of me. For a very nice, exceptionally sweet (well, sometimes) Christian girl like me to have the likes of her not only as a neighbor but as an actual roommate, well, the discovery was nearly more than I could bear. "You have to leave," I told her. But she simply ignored my efforts to evict her.

Finally, I had to face the truth. Though I'd heard it said and read it in the Bible, the complete reality of my predicament hit me for the first time.

Paul was right. "In me (that is, in my flesh,) dwelleth no good thing" (Romans 7:18, KJV).

My sister, Linda, knew it all along. "They all think you're so wonderful," she sneered when we were teens, her blue eyes narrowing. "If they only knew what you're really like."

My sister had me. I knew she was right. The way I lived at home didn't always match up with my at-church-and-out-in-public persona. Cross me at church and I did my best to be nice about it. Cross me at home—and watch out! I turned into an Emmy award–winning drama queen. Whining. Complaining. Fighting for my rights. Insisting everyone follow my agenda.

Nobody knows the trouble I've been—I mean, seen!

Not that I meant to be a hypocrite. Nor did I set out purposely to deceive. It was just so hard lining up what I knew I ought to be with what I actually was. My heart agreed with God's law, but other parts of me seemed to have a rebellious streak.

All I could do was pray that the outside world never found out what I was really like. Because I wasn't certain I could be any different.

—*Having a Mary Spirit*

READ: Psalm 51:10

REFLECT: Where do you sense the biggest disconnect between what you want to be and what you are? Read this verse out loud as a prayer.

January 18

I'll never forget the relief I felt when we studied Romans 7 in youth group one night. The apostle Paul writes:

> I don't understand myself at all, for I really want to do what is right, but I don't do it. Instead, I do the very thing I hate. I know perfectly well that what I am doing is wrong, and my bad conscience shows that I agree that the law is good. But I can't help myself, because it is sin inside me that makes me do these evil things.
>
> I know I am rotten through and through so far as my old sinful nature is concerned. No matter which way I turn, I can't make myself do right. I want to, but I can't. When I want to do good, I don't. And when I try not to do wrong, I do it anyway. But if I am doing what I don't want to do, I am not really the one doing it; the sin within me is doing it.
>
> It seems to be a fact of life that when I want to do what is right, I inevitably do what is wrong. I love God's law with all my heart. But there is another law at work within me that is at war with my mind.... Who will free me from this life that is dominated by sin? (Romans 7:15–24, NLT 1996)

Finally! Someone had put into words the wretched wrestling I had felt in my heart for so long. It was as if two people lived inside of me—one bad, one good. As if I were caught in an unholy tug of war, the outcome of which felt strangely like a matter of life or death.

Because, of course, it was.

—Having a Mary Spirit

READ: Romans 7:24–8:4

REFLECT: List what Christ came to do, according to Romans 8:1–4. How does that reality change your perspective toward your sinful nature?

January 19

Flesh gives birth to flesh, but the Spirit gives birth to spirit. JOHN 3:6

Whether we realize it or not, we all have a little Dr. Jekyll and Ms. Hyde going on inside. No matter how sweet and compliant we may seem, we all feel the influence of Flesh Woman—that unholy roommate Paul identifies in Romans 7:18: "For I know that in me (that is, in my flesh) nothing good dwells" (NKJV). Flesh Woman lives inside all of us. She's that contrary, rebellious, incredibly self-centered version of ourselves who shows up when things don't go the way we planned and life seems habitually unfair.

I must warn you, however, that on the surface Flesh Woman doesn't always appear so bad. Instead of wearing leather and tattoos, my Flesh Woman prefers lace and carefully coiffured hair. She goes to great lengths to be respectable because she feeds on people's praise and applause.

You see, Flesh Woman doesn't need dark alleys and smoky bars to work her worst. I'm discovering she may flourish most in religious surroundings, carefully disguised in church-lady clothes.

You know the kind of outfits I mean. The critical attitude we call *discernment.* The righteous indignation we use to justify our not-so-righteous anger. The flattery we pour on in order to secure coveted positions. The false humility in which we cloak ourselves while secretly hoping to be admired.

Unfortunately, we rarely pause to wonder if what we're doing is wrong, for it feels so right. And that's just as Flesh Woman wants it to be. For if you were to pull off her mask, you'd know what she's really up to. Her main goal is not your benefit, but her power base. Though Flesh Woman would never admit it, she's determined to do whatever it takes to remain in control of your life.

—Having a Mary Spirit

READ: Galatians 5:17–21

REFLECT: What "acts of the sinful nature" are listed in verses 19–21? What other less obvious acts does your Flesh Woman seem to enjoy?

*How long must I wrestle with my
thoughts?... How long will my enemy
triumph over me?* PSALM 13:2

January 20

The battlefield is the mind when it comes to the enemy's attempt to derail our Christianity, so I'm learning to train my mind for battle by practicing the following disciplines:

1. ***Take every thought captive*** (2 Corinthians 10:5). Try not to let your mind wander indiscriminately. If the thought takes you away from God, consciously bring it to Jesus and leave it there.

2. ***Resist vain imaginations*** (Romans 1:21, KJV). When you feel yourself getting caught up in a cycle of fear, worry, or regret, stop! Consciously rein in your imagination, and shift your focus to Christ as the source of your peace (Isaiah 26:3).

3. ***Refuse to agree with the devil.*** When thoughts of condemnation or fear come to mind, remind yourself that God is bigger than your biggest problem and stronger than your greatest weakness (Philippians 4:13).

4. ***Bless those who curse you*** (Luke 6:26–28). If you carry a grudge in your heart, it will consume your mind. When resentment arises against someone, begin praying for, not against, that person.

5. ***Renew your mind with the Word of God*** (Romans 12:2; Ephesians 5:26). Get into the Word daily, and allow it to transform your thinking. Find a scripture that speaks to your particular situation, then memorize it.

6. ***Speak truth to yourself*** (John 8:32). Consciously counter demeaning self-talk and other negative ideas by repeating God's truth to yourself. Declare what you know to be greater than what you feel.

7. ***Develop an attitude of gratitude.*** Purposefully think about things that are of "good report" (Philippians 4:8, KJV). Make a list if you need to. Don't give voice to negativity. Instead, declare out loud your thankfulness to God (1 Thessalonians 5:18).

—*Lazarus Awakening*

READ: Philippians 4:8
REFLECT: Write the above verse on a card. Consider memorizing it as a checklist for your thought life.

January 21

My dwelling place will be with them.
EZEKIEL 37:27

Of all the gifts we mortals try to offer, the only thing God really wants is a companion—a counterpart like the one He created for Adam. Someone to share life with, both the laughter and the tears. Someone to love who chooses to love Him in return.

I think that's why Jesus was so attracted to the home and family He found in Bethany. With Mary, Martha, and Lazarus, Jesus could be Himself. Though there was never anything false about Christ—no pretense or facade put on for the public—it must have been nice to have an oasis, a place where little was required except His presence. After being constantly surrounded by so many people needing so many things, to simply relax in Martha's home must have been a treat, especially when Martha finally learned to do the same!

While I'm sure Jesus enjoyed her cooking and the family's hospitality, I believe something more drew the Bread of Life to the family's table. It was the open arms of three people who received the Lord unreservedly and loved Him without demand, meeting the gift of His acceptance with their own.

I've always prayed that my heart would be a Bethlehem, a place for Christ to be birthed afresh and anew every day. But I'm beginning to pray that it would also be a Bethany, a safe place for God to lay His head, a haven in the midst of a needy world where Christ can come and be ministered unto rather than always ministering to.

—Outtake from *Lazarus Awakening*

READ: Jeremiah 24:7
REFLECT: Describe what God wants to give us and how the gift He offers could change your life.

Lord, the one you love is sick. JOHN 11:3

January 22

I can only imagine how Mary and Martha must have felt when their brother, Lazarus, fell ill. Everything had been going so well. Since Jesus had come to visit them, nothing had been the same. There was a new peace. A new joy. A new sense of love that permeated the whole household. The incident recorded in Luke 10:38–42 had been more than just a couple of small paragraphs. That meeting had completely rewritten the story of their lives. But now, it seemed, the plot was taking a puzzling turn.

Perhaps it all started with a fever. "A little bit of my chicken soup, a good night's sleep, and you'll feel just fine," Martha probably told her brother matter-of-factly as she spooned the tasty broth into his waiting lips. Mary probably nodded and smiled as she sat beside him with a wet cloth, cooling his brow.

"I'm sure you're right, Martha," Lazarus may have said, gratefully sinking back into his pillow and the capable ministrations of his sisters. "I'll be fine."

But as you probably already know, Lazarus wasn't.

John 11:1 doesn't go into detail about his ailment, telling us only that there was a man named Lazarus who was sick.

But through the account that follows, it's obvious Lazarus must have been a very special man. He was dearly loved—not only by his sisters, but also by Jesus. The message sent by Mary and Martha said it all: "Lord, the *one you love* is sick" (11:3, emphasis mine). Their relationship must have been exceptionally close. This wasn't a stranger. This was a friend.

As believers, you and I are counted among His friends as well. When we face difficult times as the family from Bethany did, we can trust Jesus—even though there are many things we just don't understand.

—Having a Mary Heart

READ: John 11:1–3 and Jeremiah 29:11

REFLECT: How can the realization that God has good plans for our lives give us hope, even in the midst of trials?

January 23

When [Jesus] heard that Lazarus was sick, he stayed where he was two more days. JOHN 11:6

"Do you see anything yet?" I imagine Martha asking quietly as she joins her sister on the front porch. "Jesus should have been here by now, don't you think?"

But Mary doesn't answer. She can't. Turning away instead to hide her tears, she goes back into the house to check on their brother.

"Where are You, Lord?" Martha whispers as she gazes down the dirt road, looking for shapes on the horizon or, at the very least, a lone figure coming back with news of Jesus's pending arrival. But there is nothing—only one bird calling to another in the distance and the sun beating down on her head.

"Where are You?" Martha groans softly.

Suddenly a loud wail comes from the house behind her, and Martha knows her brother is gone. After a final desperate glance down the road, she rushes to find her sister collapsed at Lazarus's bedside, stroking and kissing his lifeless hand as tears course down her cheeks.

Why? The depth of sorrow in Mary's eyes magnifies Martha's own pain as her sister pleads for help to make sense of it all. "Why didn't Jesus come?" she asks. "Why did Lazarus have to die?"

But there are no answers—none that make sense. So the two sisters find comfort where they can. In each other's arms.

And in their pain we find echoes of our own confusion. As well as questions—so very many questions.

What are we to do when God doesn't behave the way we thought He should, the way we were taught He would? What are we to feel when our Savior seemingly pulls a no-show, leaving us to wrestle with the pain on our own?

—*Lazarus Awakening*

READ: John 11:4–6 and Hebrews 10:35–36

REFLECT: What should our response be as we wait for God to act?

"For my thoughts are not your thoughts, neither are your ways my ways," declares the LORD. ISAIAH 55:8

January 24

"The hardest problem I have to handle as a Christian," pastor and author Ray C. Stedman once said, "is what to do when God does not do what I have been taught to expect him to do; when God gets out of line and does not act the way I think he ought. What do I do about that?"[7]

These are the hard questions we must wrestle with in the story of Lazarus. Why would Jesus allow such sorrow to come to a family who loved Him so much? Why would He withhold His power to heal when He'd healed so often before?

These aren't easy subjects to understand. They're not easy realities to endure. I realize that you may be reading this while aching over more tragedy and pain than I can even imagine. Perhaps you've lost a child. Maybe you are facing a diagnosis you've always dreaded. Or you may have experienced a broken marriage and are now facing life alone.

Why? There are no easy answers. The fact is, we may not know the purpose behind our pain until we see Jesus face to face. Even then, we aren't guaranteed any explanations. We are given only a promise: "He will wipe every tear from their eyes. There will be no more death or mourning or crying or pain, for the old order of things has passed away" (Revelation 21:4).

—*Having a Mary Heart*

READ: Psalm 56:8. "You keep track of all my sorrows. You have collected all my tears in your bottle. You have recorded each one in your book" (NLT).

REFLECT: What difference does it make in your perspective to know God cares so deeply about your pain?

January 25

In this world you will have trouble.
But...I have overcome the world.
John 16:33

Because we live in this world, trapped in the old order of things, tragedy will touch our lives. That's simply a fact—for Christians and non-Christians alike. We will all lose loved ones. We will all eventually die. Romans 8:28 is often distorted to mean "only good things will happen to those who love God." But Paul means just the opposite. In the very next paragraph he spells out the kinds of "things" we can expect in this world:

> Who shall separate us from the love of Christ? Shall trouble or hardship or persecution or famine or nakedness or danger or sword?... For I am convinced that neither death nor life, neither angels nor demons, neither the present nor the future, nor any powers, neither height nor depth, nor anything else in all creation, will be able to separate us from the love of God that is in Christ Jesus our Lord. (Romans 8:35, 38–39)

Trials are real. We who are Christians don't escape life, Paul says. We overcome life: "In all these things we are more than conquerors through him who loved us" (8:37).

This promise anchors our all-too-shaky world to His unshakeable kingdom.

And so do the lessons of Lazarus. For while life may shake, rattle, and roll, this rock-solid truth from John 11:5 remains: "Jesus *loved* Martha and her sister and Lazarus" (emphasis mine).

Love. That's a dependable anchor. Go ahead. Put your name in the blank: "Jesus loves _____."

And you can cling to that love, for it will hold you.

—Having a Mary Heart

Read: Lamentations 3:21–23
Reflect: Read these verses out loud, meditating on the phrases and emphasizing the ones that mean the most to you.

Study to shew thyself approved unto God,…rightly dividing the word of truth. 2 Timothy 2:15, KJV

January 26

As I've spent time in God's Word, I've run across a number of thoughts and ideas in Scripture that seem to contradict one another. For instance, Paul teaches that salvation comes solely by faith (Romans 3:22–26). Yet James says that faith without works is dead (2:17). Paul tells us that our flesh has been crucified with Christ—past tense! But then he urges us to "put to death the deeds of the body" (Romans 8:13, NKJV) on an ongoing basis.

So which one is it? you may ask. *Which is true? Which one do I do?*

The answer, I believe, is often…both. Both are true. And we must do both.

In eastern Montana, farmers and ranchers often plant trees as windbreaks. But in order for a young tree to survive the winter blasts as well as summer heat of the prairie wind, the farmer has to stake off the tree. So he ties four strings to the trunk and then drives stakes deep in the ground at four corners—east, west, north, and south. Then the wind can howl, but the little tree, held secure by the tension between the four strings, won't fall.

I believe God has built the same kind of four-cornered "holy tension" into His Word. Because we humans tend toward extremes, swinging too far in one direction and then veering way too far in the other, God wrote balance points into Scripture. Principles that appear contradictory at first glance, but—when followed—help us grow straight and tall, strong and deep.

As I continue to live the mystery of these scriptural paradoxes, I'm beginning to find they make perfect sense. More important, the very contradictions that stretch my mind are the ones that change me most deeply.

And isn't change the whole point?

—Having a Mary Spirit

READ: Philippians 2:12–13

REFLECT: What two-sided holy tension do you find in these verses?

January 27

The LORD has anointed me to preach good news. ISAIAH 61:1

I don't think we can begin to imagine how radical Christ's New Testament message of grace sounded to a people who had been living under the Law for thousands of years. The thought that there might be a different way to approach God—a better way—was appealing to some Jews but threatening to many others.

For those who kept stumbling over the rules and regulations set up by the religious elite—never quite measuring up to the yardstick of the Law—the idea that God might love them apart from what they did must have been incredibly liberating.

But for the Jewish hierarchy who had mastered the Law and felt quite proud of it, Jesus's words surely posed a threat. His message pierced their religious facades, revealing the darkness of their hearts and, quite frankly, making them mad. Rather than running to the grace and forgiveness He offered, they kept defaulting to the yardstick—using it to justify themselves one minute, wielding it as a weapon against Jesus the next.

"You come from Nazareth?" His critics said, pointing the yardstick. "Nothing good comes from Nazareth." *That's one whack for you.* "You eat with tax collectors and sinners?" the Pharisees ridiculed. "That's even worse." *Whack, whack.* "You heal on the Sabbath?" they screamed, waving their rules and regulations. *"Off with Your head!"*

The Sadducees and Pharisees had no room in their religion for freedom. As a result, they had no room for Christ. They were people of the yardstick.

Unfortunately, we tend to favor the yardstick as well—using it to measure ourselves and others against our personal ideas of holiness. Wielding it as an instrument of punishment, rather than a tool intended to help us recognize our deep, endless need for grace.

—*Lazarus Awakening*

READ: Matthew 5:17

REFLECT: Do you tend to be more grace oriented or law oriented? What did Jesus come to do?

January 28

Even though Jesus kept insisting He hadn't come to "abolish the Law or the Prophets...but to fulfill them" (Matthew 5:17), the religious just wouldn't listen. Like little children they plugged their ears and kept singing the same old tune, though a New Song had been sent from heaven.

Which is so very sad. Especially when you consider that the Law they were so zealous for had been intended to *prepare* them for the Messiah rather than *keep* them from acknowledging Him.

After all, God established His original covenant with Abraham long before He gave Moses the Law—430 years before, to be exact (Galatians 3:17). The love the Father extended to Abraham and to all those who came after him had no strings attached. It was based on the recipient's acceptance of grace from beginning to end.

But somehow Israel fell in love with the Law rather than in love with their God. And we are in danger of doing the same thing. Exalting rules as the pathway to heaven. Embracing formulas as our salvation. Worshiping our own willpower rather than allowing the power of God to work in us to transform our lives.[8]

Such self-induced holiness didn't work for the Jews, and it doesn't work for us. That's why Jesus had to come.

—*Lazarus Awakening*

READ: Galatians 3:10–11

REFLECT: According to these verses, what is the danger of relying on our ability to keep the Law? What are we to rely upon instead?

January 29

For what the law was powerless to do…God did by sending his own Son.
ROMANS 8:3

The Law had originally been given "to show people their sins," Galatians 3:19 tells us. But it was "designed to last only until the coming of the child who was promised" (NLT). Though the yardstick of the Law helped keep us in line, it was never intended to save us. Only Christ could do that.

And oh may I tell you how that comforts my soul?

I'll never forget the day I handed Jesus my yardstick. I had been saved since childhood, but I was almost thirty before the message of grace finally made the trip from my head to my heart, setting me "free from the law of sin and death" (Romans 8:2). As the light of the good news finally penetrated the darkness of my self-condemning mind, the "perfect love" 1 John 4:18 speaks of began to drive out my insecurity, which had always been rooted in fear of punishment.

When I finally laid down my Pharisee pride and admitted that in myself I would never be—could never be—enough, I experienced a breakthrough that has radically changed my life. For as I surrendered my yardstick—the tool of comparison that had caused so much mental torment and a sense of separation from God—Jesus took it from my hands. Then, with a look of great love, He broke it over His knee and turned it into a cross, reminding me that He died so I wouldn't have to.

That the punishment I so fully deserve has already been paid for.

That the way has been made for everyone who will believe in Jesus not only to come to Him but to come back home to the heart of God.

—*Lazarus Awakening*

READ: Luke 23:44–46 and Hebrews 10:19–23

REFLECT: What significant thing happened at the cross and what does it mean for your relationship with God?

Lord, you have been our dwelling place throughout all generations. PSALM 90:1

January 30

The same friendship Mary found at Jesus's feet is available to you and me. His presence is a place where we can be comfortable, where we can kick off our shoes and let down our hair. It's a place of transparency and vulnerability; a place where we are completely known yet completely loved. It is truly a place called home.

If we love Him and obey His teachings, Jesus says in John 14:23, God will actually come and live with us. "My Father will love him," He said of those who follow Him, "and we will come to him and *make our home* with him" (emphasis mine).

But Jesus not only wants to be at home in us; He also wants us to make our home in Him, as Max Lucado writes in *The Great House of God:*

> He has no interest in being a weekend getaway or a Sunday bungalow or a summer cottage. Don't consider using God as a vacation cabin or an eventual retirement home. He wants you under his roof now and always. He wants to be your mailing address, your point of reference; he wants to be your home.[9]

What a beautiful, gracious offer from the Lord of hosts. It's hard to imagine saying no to the opportunity to live in God and rest in Him. But we can— and so often we do.

When we refuse God's offer of grace-filled rest in the Living Room, the only alternative is the tyranny of works. We will be driven to do more and more, trying to win God's approval. And still we will fail, because what the Father really wants is for us to find our identity—our "mailing address" as Lucado puts it—in Him and Him alone.

—Having a Mary Heart

READ: Psalm 84:1–4

REFLECT: How does your heart respond to the thought of making your "nest" near God's altar?

January 31

Give me an undivided heart, that I may fear your name. PSALM 86:11

In his book *Crazy Love,* Francis Chan invites us to invite God to help us love Him more.

> If you merely pretend that you enjoy God or love Him, He knows. You can't fool Him; don't even try.
>
> Instead, tell Him how you feel. Tell Him that He isn't the most important thing in this life to you, and that you're sorry for that. Tell Him that you've been lukewarm, that you've chosen _____ over Him time and again. Tell Him that you want Him to change you, that you long to genuinely enjoy Him. Tell Him how you want to experience true satisfaction and pleasure and joy in your relationship with Him. Tell Him you want to love Him more than anything on this earth. Tell Him you want to treasure the kingdom of heaven so much that you'd willingly sell everything in order to get it. Tell Him what you like about Him, what you appreciate, and what brings you joy.
>
> *Jesus, I need to give myself up. I am not strong enough to love You and walk with You on my own. I can't do it, and I need You. I need You deeply and desperately. I believe You are worth it, that You are better than anything else I could have in this life or the next. I want You. And when I don't, I want to want You. Be all in me. Take all of me. Have Your way with me.*[10]

I've found that amazing things happen when I get honest like this with God. My heart softens and my perspective changes as He responds to my cry to know Him more.

—*Lazarus Awakening*

READ: Ezekiel 11:19
REFLECT: Consider anything that might be hindering your love for God. Fill in the blank above as you work through the suggested prayer prompts, asking God to give you an undivided heart.

Jesus Christ laid down his life for us. And we ought to lay down our lives for our brothers. 1 JOHN 3:16

My father-in-law is a great guy. He's the kind of person whom laughter follows everywhere he goes. He's always joking, always having fun. And yet, a sweet spirituality seems to constantly surround him. *Humble.* That's how people describe him. And though it pains me a bit (just kidding, Dad!), I have to agree.

I remember storming into his office one day when we served on staff at his church. I was steamed, really mad. Someone had done something totally out of line, and I was determined to give that person a piece of my mind. Dad just listened to my complaint. He let me spill out my hurt and disappointment, my angry words and defensiveness.

He waited until I was through, then with great tenderness, he spoke words I've never been able to forget: "Joanna, when you said yes to the ministry, you laid your life down. In a sense, you said yes to being stepped on."

That was it. Dad didn't take sides; he didn't call in the lousy jerk for church discipline. He didn't even try to set up mediation to solve the situation. With Spirit-led discernment, Dad's words put the finger on my real problem—an infectious pride that had been festering deep down in my heart, affecting the rest of my life.

Mercifully, Dad didn't elaborate. He didn't mention the hard edge in my voice lately or my inflexibility when things didn't go the way I thought they should. He just said a simple sentence and let the Lord do the rest.

I wanted to argue. I wanted to demand justice on my behalf.

But inside, I knew he was right.

—Outtake from *Having a Mary Heart*

READ: John 10:17–18a
REFLECT: What lessons can we learn from Jesus's example in these verses?

February 2

Learn from me, for I am gentle and humble in heart, and you will find rest for your souls. MATTHEW 11:29

The world has had enough of the up-and-comers, the pushers and the shovers, the proud and the confident who would sooner walk over someone than help them up. What the world is looking for is authentic Christianity. The heart of a Savior, willing to lay down His life...exemplified by a humble and generous people who are willing to lay down their own agendas and love the world back to God. What does that kind of life look like? I like the way Andrew Murray puts it:

> Humility is perfect quietness of heart. It is to expect nothing, to wonder at nothing that is done to me, to feel nothing done against me. It is to be at rest when nobody praises me, and when I am blamed or despised. It is to have a blessed home in the Lord, where I can go in and shut the door, and kneel to my Father in secret, and am at peace as in a deep sea of calmness, when all around and above is trouble.[11]

As a result of this restful peace, our lives become full of the "aroma of Christ" which, according to the apostle Paul, *"through us* spreads everywhere the fragrance of the knowledge of him" (2 Corinthians 2:14–15, emphasis mine).

When we willingly bend and bow, when we embrace God's breaking as our making, when we make ourselves of no reputation, the life of Christ is released in us. And the fragrance...well, it is intoxicatingly attractive. It turned the world upside down two thousand years ago, and God wants to use the fragrance of Christ to do so again. But it only comes through brokenness, through the genuine beauty of true humility.

—Having a Mary Spirit

READ: 1 Peter 2:23

REFLECT: What is the secret of quietness found in Jesus's response to difficulty?

February 3

One of the most precious ways God expresses His love for us is through His Word, the Bible. The Hebrew word for *Bible* is *mikra,* which means "the calling out of God."[12]

Isn't that wonderful? We don't have to wonder what God thinks, what He feels about certain topics, because to a large extent He has already told us through Scripture. Better yet, we don't have to wonder whether He loves us or not. According to my dictionary, the Old English word for *gospel* is *godspell.* God spells out His love for the whole world to see. It's right there in His Word.

"Fear not, for I have redeemed you," the Lord tells us in Isaiah 43:1, 4. "I have summoned you by name.... You are precious and honored in my sight... because I love you." We are a chosen people. Made holy. Deeply and dearly loved by God. How do I know that? I hear God's voice telling me, "calling out" to me, every time I open His Word.

I love the way Kent Hughes describes the intimate impact of spending time with God. "Think of it this way," he writes. "Our lives are like photographic plates, and prayer is like a time exposure to God. As we expose ourselves to God for a half hour, an hour, perhaps two hours a day, his image is imprinted more and more upon us. More and more we absorb the image of his character, his love, his wisdom, his way of dealing with life and people."[13]

That's what I want. That's what I need. And that's what I receive when I spend time in God's Word and in prayer. I get more of Jesus and, in the process, a little less of me.

—Having a Mary Heart

READ: Proverbs 2:1–11
REFLECT: List the benefits of seeking God through prayer and the Word.

February 4

Satisfy us in the morning with your unfailing love, that we may sing for joy and be glad all our days. PSALM 90:14

King David must have been a morning person when it came to time alone with God. "In the morning, O LORD, you hear my voice; in the morning I lay my requests before you and wait in expectation" (Psalm 5:3). Jesus tended toward morning as well, according to Mark 1:35: "Very early in the morning, while it was still dark, Jesus got up, left the house and went off to a solitary place, where he prayed."

As for myself, I've fluctuated between morning and night, but when it comes to my devotions, I have finally settled for morning once again. Not only is it easier for me to find uninterrupted time then, but I've found it is a wonderful way to start the day.

But again, it's not really that important *when* I choose to meet God every day. What really matters is that I show up regularly—and to be honest, that's where I've always fallen short. Because of my all-or-nothing temperament, missing a day or two of devotions was enough to throw me off track for days, even weeks. I'm ashamed to admit there were entire months when I went without having a sit-down-with-my-Bible-and-pray alone time with God.

But consistency, after all, doesn't mean perfection; it simply means refusing to give up trying. So with a huge amount of God's grace and a stubborn will to keep trying, I've been able to get back on track with my quiet times. Through those times, I have felt myself grow closer to the Lord. Steadily, consistently closer. And also, in the process, more filled with His presence. More calm and serene. More practically centered.

It's amazing what a little consistent time-out can do for you. Especially when you spend that time with Jesus.

—Having a Mary Heart

READ: Psalm 105:1–5

REFLECT: What aspects of this psalm could you incorporate into your quiet time with the Lord?

Choose this day whom you will serve.
JOSHUA 24:15, RSV

February 5

When John Michael and Jessica were small, I used an analogy I'd heard to try to explain the dilemma that even little children feel. "It's like you have a good dog and a bad dog inside you," I explained one night as I tucked them into bed after a particularly difficult day.

"The good dog belongs to Jesus, and the bad dog belongs to the devil. They fight and fight. And they'll keep on fighting until you decide which one you want to win. If you feed the good dog, the good dog will win. But if you feed the bad dog, the bad dog will win."

We were in the car a few days later, when I noticed John Michael glance over at his sleeping sister as though he was trying to figure something out. "What's the matter, Michael?" I asked, catching his eye in the rearview mirror.

"I think I got the bad dog inside me, Mom," he said in all seriousness. "He wants to hit Jessica *so* bad!"

Don't you wish we outgrew such inner turmoil? Oh, we may no longer have a desire to hit our sister (except when she really deserves it!), but we may struggle with feelings of envy and resentment when someone else gets something we've wanted—like the promotion we deserve or the new car we need. We may smile on the outside and offer our congratulations, but inside the bad dog howls as Flesh Woman stalks the halls of our hearts, ranting and raving at the injustice of it all.

And left to ourselves, this is our destiny. But this torment is exactly what Jesus came to save us from.

—*Having a Mary Spirit*

READ: Romans 6:12–14
REFLECT: According to these verses, what can we do to settle the Good Dog/Bad Dog battles we sometimes face?

February 6

For the wrath of man does not produce the righteousness of God.
JAMES 1:20, NKJV

I've felt Flesh Woman's influence more times than I care to recall. Just put me in a position where I feel treated unfairly, forgotten, or left out—and you'll hear my case. Again and again and again. Because nothing brings out the worst in me more than injustice.

I'm often reminded of Kathy Bates's character in the movie *Fried Green Tomatoes*. After a couple of snotty bimbo Barbie dolls steal her parking space, saying, "Face it, lady. We're younger and faster," Bates takes matters into her own hands, awakening what she calls the "Twanda Amazon Woman" inside her. She stands up for herself and takes control.

Well, she takes control, all right. She repeatedly smashes their Volkswagen's rear end with her midsize sedan, then tells the upset Barbies, "Face it, girls, I'm older and I have more insurance."[14]

The movie struck a deep chord in women everywhere. The problem is, it was just a movie. Kathy Bates's character never had to address the painful consequences of unleashing Twanda on the world. For how do you turn off that selfish I'll-get-mine-no-matter-what attitude once you've released it? How do you handle the guilt, the wrecked relationships, and the ongoing frustration when tantrums don't solve anything? And what do you do with the reality that the Twanda inside of you has very little interest in following God?

You see, what Kathy Bates's character calls "Twanda," the Bible calls "flesh"—and Scripture makes it clear that the Flesh Woman in each of us is energetically opposed to the kind of transformation God wants for us.

—*Having a Mary Spirit*

READ: Ephesians 4:25–5:2
REFLECT: As Christ-followers, what lower-nature practices are we to get rid of? What qualities of Jesus should we imitate instead?

May...the God of peace sanctify you through and through...spirit, soul and body. 1 THESSALONIANS 5:23

February 7

Ray Stedman's book *Authentic Christianity*[15] has helped me understand the struggle between my flesh and my own best intentions—and why, though I really am a new creature in Christ, an ongoing war still seems to rage "in my members," as Paul puts it in the King James Version of Romans 7:23.

You see, God created each one of us as a three-part person: body, soul, and spirit. The *body* is the physical, outermost part of us, the tent of skin and bone we live in that makes contact with the world around us. The *soul* is our inner person—thoughts, emotions, and will. It is the part of us that reasons, feels, and makes choices, allowing us to know and love God in a practical way.

But it is the innermost part of us, our *spirits,* that are awakened only by salvation. Previously dead because of sin and the Fall of man, the spirit is the hidden place where the Holy Spirit takes up residence when we invite Christ into our lives. When the Spirit comes, He throws open the shutters that have darkened our spiritual understanding and turns on the lights, filling us with God's presence, with His sparkling joy and peace. At that very moment, in our spirits, we become new creatures in Christ (2 Corinthians 5:17). We comprehend truth as never before. And our holy makeover—that is, our perfecting by grace—begins.

However, we must cooperate with that makeover. "Live by the Spirit, and you will not gratify the desires of the sinful nature," Paul reminds us in Galatians 5:16. With the Lord's help, we can have victory in the ongoing conflict between the Spirit and the flesh. But that victory is determined by whose side we take.

—Having a Mary Spirit

READ: Titus 2:11–12

REFLECT: According to these verses, how are you and I changed by grace?

February 8

You are not your own; you were bought at a price. 1 Corinthians 6:19–20

Do you ever feel yourself holding back parts of your life, wondering how much you can give and still have something left? Like Mary, you feel the call to total abandonment, but surrender like that makes you afraid. If you've felt that way, you're not alone. I think every one of us comes to a crossroads in our relationship with God where we're faced with the dilemma of total or partial surrender.

I remember the day God brought me to that crossroads. For nearly a month He had been dealing with my heart, asking me to sell out to Him. Jesus had been my Savior, but He wasn't yet my Lord. He was telling me it was time to surrender.

I wanted to obey, but I was so afraid. I was a young teenager with a lot of plans and dreams. If I gave myself completely to Him, would He take them all away and make me go to Africa? At the time, that was the worst fate I could imagine. But instead of answering my questions and calming my fears, the Lord kept pressing me for a decision. *"Will you give Me your all?"* He asked. No negotiations. No promised stock options. Total abandonment was what He demanded, and nothing less.

I stood there shivering in the darkness, my arms clasped around all my hopes and my dreams, and I realized there was no turning back. It was all my heart or nothing. To walk away from this decision would mean, for me, walking away from God. And that I could not, would not do. So I closed my eyes and took a breath and flung myself out into the dark unknown.

"I'm Yours, Lord," my heart cried. "All of me! Nothing held back."

—*Having a Mary Heart*

Read: Mark 8:34–36

Reflect: What does Jesus say we must do in order to follow Him, and why should we do it?

She has done a beautiful thing to me....
She did what she could. MARK 14:6, 8

February 9

Because of my own pivotal moment of surrender, I think I know a little bit of what Mary must have felt that day she knelt at Jesus's feet. As she held her precious ointment, she must have trembled inside. Perhaps she'd stared at the alabaster bottle in the night. *Can I? Should I? Will I?* Until she said, "Yes, Lord. I'll give my all."

So when she broke the bottle and poured the ointment, Mary didn't stop to count the cost or calculate how much of the ointment was actually needed. She spilled it all out. Lavishly. Extravagantly. Until her treasure ran down over Jesus's feet and soaked into the floor.

Then she did something I find disconcerting. She unbound her headpiece and wiped Jesus's feet with her hair. By that act, she laid down her glory and, in essence, stood naked before her Lord. For in that culture, no proper woman ever let her hair down in public. A woman's hair was her glory, her identity, her ultimate sign of femininity, an intimate gift meant only for her husband. But for Mary, nothing was too extravagant for Jesus; she was even willing to risk her reputation. Like a lover before her beloved, she made herself vulnerable and fragile, open for rejection or rebuke.

But neither came. Only the tender, silent approval of a Bridegroom for His bride. Jesus watched as Mary dried His feet, and I'm sure there were tears in His eyes.

The extravagance might be misunderstood by the others, but not by the One she loved. "She has done a beautiful thing for me," Jesus said in the face of His disciples' disapproval.

Leave her alone. She belongs to Me.

—*Having a Mary Heart*

READ: 2 Samuel 24:21–24
REFLECT: What do David's words mean to you?

February 10

Let the beloved of the LORD rest secure in him. DEUTERONOMY 33:12

Ah, the indescribable joy of being loved!

My little Romeo of a son can't seem to do enough to show how much he adores me. His attentions come complete with dandelions and stick-figure cards and lots and lots of verbal declarations.

It's not just the words that make my heart go pitter-patter; it is the *way* he says them. He doesn't throw them flippantly over his shoulder as he goes outside to play. Nor does he use his affection to win his own way. Not yet, anyway. For now, at least, his professions of love are just pure adoration. And lately, for whatever reason, Josh infuses these three syllables with such ardor and emotion they take my breath away.

"Mom," he says, looking intently in my eyes. Then, in a slow, sweet drawl marked by his speech impediment, he draws out the middle word to give it extra emphasis. "I wuuuuv you."

Suddenly, all is right with my world.

My heart captures a snapshot with a scribbled caption describing the joy of being loved. Not for what I've done, not even for who I am. But simply because the mere sight of me causes such intense emotion that words are required.

Why am I telling you this? To make you wish you'd had an unexpected pregnancy at age forty that resulted in an amazing little boy like mine?

No, though I could wish no greater gift for anyone.

I'm telling you this because Joshua is teaching me about the kind of relationship Christ longs to have with me. The love affair I'm enjoying with my six-year-old[16] is the kind of love affair God wants to enjoy with all His children. The intermingling of hearts He has longed for since the foundation of the world.

—Lazarus Awakening

READ: Ephesians 3:17–19

REFLECT: How does verse 19 describe God's love, and what happens when we come to know it?

If anyone loves me...we will come to him and make our home with him.
JOHN 14:23

February 11

Robert Boyd Munger's article "My Heart Christ's Home" changed forever how I viewed my quiet time with the Lord. Through the simple analogy he suggested, I discovered what it meant to have a Mary heart toward God. Suddenly, my eyes were open to what true devotion is.

It is not a duty. It is a delight.

It is not an exercise in piety. It is a privilege.

And it is not so much a visit as it is a homecoming.

"Without question one of the most remarkable Christian doctrines is that Jesus Christ Himself through the presence of the Holy Spirit will actually enter a heart, settle down and be at home there," Munger says. "[Jesus] came into the darkness of my heart and turned on the light. He built a fire in the cold hearth and banished the chill. He started music where there had been stillness and He filled the emptiness with His own loving, wonderful fellowship."

Munger goes on to tell how he showed Christ around the house of his heart, inviting him to "settle down and be perfectly at home," welcoming Him room by room. Together they visited the library of his mind—"a very small room with very thick walls." They peered into the dining room of his appetites and desires. They spent a little time in the workshop where his talents and skills were kept, and the rumpus room of "certain associations and friendships, activities and amusements." They even poked their heads into the hall closet filled with dead, rotting things he had managed to hoard.[17]

All of them were places that needed a Savior's touch. The kind of touch each one of us needs....

—Having a Mary Heart

READ: Isaiah 1:15–18

REFLECT: Take a moment to clean out your "hall closet" with repentance, and invite Jesus to be at home in your heart.

February 12

Behold, I stand at the door and knock. If anyone hears My voice and opens the door, I will come in. REVELATION 3:20, NKJV

…As Pastor Munger went on, his descriptions reflected the rooms of my heart as well. But it was his depiction of the drawing room that would forever change the way I viewed my time with the Lord. Especially when I considered the picture of friendship with God he portrayed.

> We walked next into the drawing room. This room was rather intimate and comfortable. I liked it. It had a fireplace, overstuffed chairs, a bookcase, sofa, and a quiet atmosphere.
>
> He also seemed pleased with it. He said, "This is indeed a delightful room. Let us come here often. It is secluded and quiet and we can have fellowship together."
>
> Well, naturally, as a young Christian I was thrilled. I could not think of anything I would rather do than have a few minutes apart with Christ in intimate comradeship.
>
> He promised, "I will be here every morning early. Meet with Me here and we will start the day together." So, morning after morning, I would come downstairs to the drawing room and He would take a book of the Bible from the bookcase. He would open it and then we would read together. He would tell me of its riches and unfold to me its truths. He would make my heart warm as he revealed his love and grace toward me. They were wonderful hours together. In fact, we called the drawing room the "withdrawing room." It was a period when we had our quiet time together.…[18]

—Having a Mary Heart

READ: Psalm 40:1–3

REFLECT: What happens when we "wait patiently for the Lord"?

I live in a high and holy place, but also with him who is contrite. Isaiah 57:15

February 13

...Robert Munger continues:

> But little by little, under the pressure of many responsibilities, this time began to be shortened.... I began to miss a day now and then.... I would miss it two days in a row and often more.
>
> I remember one morning when I was in a hurry.... As I passed the drawing room, the door was ajar. Looking in I saw a fire in the fireplace and the Lord sitting there.... "Blessed Master, forgive me. Have You been here all these mornings?"
>
> "Yes," He said, "I told you I would be here every morning to meet with you." Then I was even more ashamed. He had been faithful in spite of my faithlessness. I asked His forgiveness and He readily forgave me....
>
> He said, "The trouble with you is this: You have been thinking of the quiet time, of the Bible study and prayer time, as a factor in your own spiritual progress, but you have forgotten that this hour means something to Me also."[19]

What an amazing thought—that Christ wants to spend quality time with me. That He looks forward to our time together and misses me when I don't show up. Once that message started sinking into my heart, I started looking at my devotional time in a whole new way—not as a ritual, but as a relationship.

And a relationship doesn't just happen. It has to be nurtured, protected, and loved.

—Having a Mary Heart

Read: Colossians 2:6–7

Reflect: Why is it important to learn more about Jesus?

45

February 14

I trust in your unfailing love; my heart rejoices in your salvation. PSALM 13:5

I don't know why Jesus chose me to love. Really, I don't. Perhaps you don't understand why He chose you. But He did. Really, He did.

When my husband proposed marriage so many years ago, I didn't say, "Wait a minute, John. Do you have any idea what you're getting into?" I didn't pull out a list of reasons why he couldn't possibly love me or a rap sheet detailing my inadequacies to prove why he shouldn't—although there were and are many.

No way! I just threw my arms open wide and accepted his love. I would have been a fool to turn down an offer like that.

I wonder what would happen in our lives if we stopped resisting God's love and started receiving it? What if we just accepted the altogether-too-good-to-be-true news that the yardstick has been broken and the cross has opened a door to intimacy with our Maker?

For if we are ever to be His beloved, we must be willing to *be* loved.

Maybe it's time to go look in the mirror and start witnessing to ourselves.

Maybe it's time we stop living by what we feel and start proclaiming what our spirits already know. "I have been chosen by God. Whether or not I feel loved or believe I deserve it, from this moment on I choose to be loved."

You may have to force yourself to say the words. Today your emotions may not correspond with what you've just declared. It is likely you may have to repeat the same words tomorrow. And do it again the next day. And the next.

Until the message gets through your thick head to your newly tender heart. Until you finally come to believe what's been true all along.

Shh…listen. Do you hear it?

It's Love.

And He's calling your name.

—*Lazarus Awakening*

READ: Song of Solomon 7:10

REFLECT: Step to a mirror and inform your heart, "I am my beloved's, and his desire is toward me" (Song of Solomon 7:10, NKJV). Ask God to help you receive the love He offers.

Now is the time of God's favor, now is the day of salvation. 2 CORINTHIANS 6:2

February 15

For the first sixteen years of my life, Grandma Nora lived with us. She helped raise us kids while my mother worked, and I have so many wonderful memories of my times with her. Cheeseburgers and Pepsi at Woolworth's soda fountain. Taking turns spending the night tucked in her big iron bed. Grandma Nora blessed us with a rich legacy of love.

When she passed away, my brother and sister and I sat around sharing all that Grandma Nora had meant to us. "I feel kind of bad," Steve said. "I hope you guys weren't mad that I was her favorite."

I looked at him in amazement. "What do you mean?" I asked. "I was her favorite."

Linda looked at both of us and shook her head. "No way! *I* was her favorite!"

We all stared at each other in disbelief and then dissolved in laughter and wonderment. To experience such depth of love and attention that all three of us would secretly consider ourselves loved the most—wow! I want to love like that.

I think this experience might explain what happened to John, the disciple of Jesus. I've always found it odd how, rather than using his name in the gospel he authored, John refers to himself, again and again, as "the disciple whom Jesus loved" (for example, John 13:23). Scholars have all sorts of explanations as to why John did that, but I have a feeling it's because John had an encounter with Christ that left him forever changed.

Instead of defining himself, John let Jesus define him. But rather than diminishing the love Christ had for others, John's bold declaration increases the astounding possibility that Jesus might love the rest of us just as much.

So much that we, too, will never be able to look at ourselves—let alone define who we are—the same way again.

—Having a Mary Spirit

READ: 1 John 3:1–3

REFLECT: What is the result of the Father's lavish love?

February 16

Keep your heart with all diligence,
for out of it spring the issues of life.
PROVERBS 4:23, NKJV

A favorite of tourists, the quaint little village lay nestled high in the Austrian Alps. In the center of town lay a glistening pond fed by mountain streams, and each summer, beautiful white swans floated across its sparkling depths as townsfolk and visitors sat on its grassy banks. The whole place was paradise, some said. Absolute paradise.

But one evening, as the town council met to review its budget, one member pointed to an expense no one had noticed before. "Keeper of the Spring," a councilman read. "What's that?"

"Just an old man who lives up the mountain," another answered. "Not quite sure what he does. Something to do with the spring and the city's water supply."

Perhaps this was an area they could save money, they reasoned. And so they sent word that the old man's services would no longer be needed.

At first, nothing seemed to change. But by the following spring, when the swans didn't return, several commented. Others wondered about the yellowish-brown tint of the water and the odor that wafted up when the weather was just right. But no one thought anything about the old man on the mountain— until the day a curious few hiked up to the source of the spring.

Along the way, they noticed rocks and debris blocking the water's flow, but the real problem lay at the spring itself. Its once bubbling depths were now still and dark, clogged with rotting leaves and forest litter—the very things the old man had spent his summers working so faithfully to remove.

And that's when everyone realized.

No one was more important to the town than the Keeper of the Spring.[20]

—Having a Mary Spirit

READ: Proverbs 4:20–27

REFLECT: Reword these verses as your personal prayer to God: "Lord, I will pay attention to what You say…"

Hold on to instruction, do not let
it go; guard it well, for it is your life.
PROVERBS 4:13

February 17

"Above all else, guard your heart," King Solomon wrote in Proverbs 4:23, "for it is the wellspring of life." Intended as advice to his son, this was a lesson Solomon himself should have heeded. For although he started out as the wisest man who ever lived, Solomon ended his life in disgrace and ruin. All because he didn't guard his heart.

From the beginning of his reign, Solomon began to compromise God's principles. At first it was small things like worshiping the Lord on high places—a practice Yahweh had clearly forbidden (see 1 Kings 3:3 and Numbers 33:51–52). But that seemingly insignificant compromise led to larger concessions. By the end of his life, Solomon had not only built temples to his wives' pagan gods, but he had bowed down and worshiped them himself (1 Kings 11:3–6).

This mixing and mingling of the holy with the unholy is a temptation God's followers still face today. It didn't work then, and it won't work now. Not because God is unreasonable in His demands, but because He knows such compromise will eventually destroy not only us, but everything He wants to do through us. For even a little sin in our wellspring has the power to pollute and corrupt the very essence of who we are.

If King Solomon were here today, I think he would warn us: Guard your heart! Whatever you allow into your life will eventually be revealed—both the good and the bad.

—Having a Mary Spirit

READ: 1 Kings 11:1–11
REFLECT: Note key things that caused Solomon to lose his kingdom. What warnings do you see for your life?

February 18

Do not fret—it leads only to evil.
PSALM 37:8

I come from a long line of Swedish worriers.

"Käre mej," my Grandma Anna used to say over and over. "Dear me, dear me." Too high, too fast. Too much, too little. With all the potential danger in the world, there seemed to be only one response—worry.

I remember lying in bed at night going over my list of fears. Somehow, as a young teenager, I had determined that the secret for avoiding trouble was to worry about it. In fact, I worried if I forgot to worry about something.

When Mom and Dad went to Hawaii for their fifteenth anniversary, I spent most of the week trying to think of everything that might go wrong. What if the plane crashed? What if a tidal wave wiped out Waikiki? Anything could happen. Rotten pineapples. Bad sushi. Salmonella poisoning from coconut milk left out overnight. I'd be left an orphan, sob. I'd be left to raise my little brother and sister alone. Big, big sobs.

Of course, my parents returned home safe and sound, healthy and tan. But in some twisted way, this merely confirmed my thesis: worry so it won't happen. And so, little by little, worry become my mode of operation.

What about you? Has worry become a dominating factor in your life?

If so, please know you have a Savior who has promised to be your Burden Bearer. You were never meant to live this life alone. Cast your cares on Jesus. For He cares for you (1 Peter 5:7, NKJV).

—Having a Mary Heart

 READ: Luke 12:22–31
REFLECT: What things have you been worried about that God has already promised to supply?

An anxious heart weighs a man down.
PROVERBS 12:25

February 19

Dr. Edward Hallowell, author of *Worry: Controlling It and Using It Wisely,*[21] provides a checklist to help you decide if worry is a problem in your life. If you recognize yourself in these descriptions, chances are you have a problem with worry.

___ You find you spend much more time in useless, nonconstructive worry than other people you know.

___ People around you comment on how much of a worrier you are.

___ You feel that is bad luck or tempting fate not to worry.

___ Worry interferes with your work—you miss opportunities, fail to make decisions, perform at lower than optimal level.

___ Worry interferes with your close relationships—your spouse and/or friends sometimes complain that your worrying is a drain on their energy and patience.

___ You know that many of your worries are unrealistic or exaggerated, yet you cannot seem to control them.

___ Sometimes you feel overwhelmed by worry and even experience physical symptoms such as rapid heart rate, rapid breathing, shortness of breath, sweating, dizziness, or trembling.

___ You feel a chronic need for reassurance even when everything is fine.

___ You feel an exaggerated fear of certain situations that other people seem to handle with little difficulty.

___ Your parents or grandparents were known as great worriers, or they suffered from an anxiety disorder.[22]

Whether your worry is inherited or simply part of your nature, Jesus wants to set you free. He can change your heart and rewire your soul as you choose to trust God rather than give way to fear.

—Having a Mary Heart

READ: Joshua 1:9
REFLECT: We all worry on one level or another; take the things you've discovered about yourself in the test above to God in prayer.

February 20

Do not be afraid or discouraged…for there is a greater power with us than with him. 2 CHRONICLES 32:7

We all get sidetracked by distraction, dipping down now and then into discouragement and doubt. The secret is not to stay there. Here are several ways you can beat the downward spiral of the Deadly Ds in your life.

- *Allow for rest stops.* Discouragement is often our body's way of saying, "Stop! I need rest." Try taking a nap or getting to bed a little earlier. It's amazing how different things will look in the light of morning (Exodus 34:21).

- *Get a new point of view.* Take a few steps back and ask God to help you see His perspective on your situation. Often what seems to be an impassable mountain in our eyes is only a steppingstone in His (Isaiah 33:17).

- *Have patience.* It's easy to get discouraged when things don't go the way you planned. But if you've committed your concerns to the Lord, you can be sure He is at work, even when you don't see His hand (Romans 8:28).

- *Mingle.* Discouragement feeds off isolation. Get out of the house! Go visit some friends. It's amazing how good old-fashioned fellowship can lift our spirits and chase away the blues (Psalm 133:1).

- *Set the timer.* Okay. So things aren't so good. I've found it helpful to set the oven timer and allow ten minutes for a good cry. But when the buzzer sounds, I blow my nose, wipe my eyes, and surrender my situation to the Lord so I can move on (Ecclesiastes 3:4).

—Having a Mary Heart

READ & REFLECT: Read each of the verses mentioned above. Which one do you need most today?

February 21

Of all the ailments in all the world, no illness has caused as much pain or as much destruction as the widespread but often misdiagnosed inner plague called *S-I-N.*

In these three little letters, we find the DNA of a supervirus that has destroyed more careers, more marriages, more families, more churches, more men, women, boys, and girls than all of earth's diseases put together.

Try as we might, we can't get away from it, for it is interwoven in the fabric of our humanity. Passed down through generation after generation of both good men and bad, gentle mothers and raging lunatics, noble kings and evil tyrants. It rests inside me, and it abides in you as well. For it might be said of each of us: "Lord, the one you love is sick" (John 11:3).

We might not be ax murderers. Yet the slander that slips so easily off our tongues murders more than we know. We might not be scam artists or child abusers, prostitutes or thugs, but the envy and lust and anger and pride that lurk inside us trouble the heart of God just as much as any of our darker pastimes.

Because sin—all sin—destroys. It maims and it cuts us off from the life we need.

And if we're honest with ourselves, we know it. We feel it. We are, every one of us, sin-sick—there is no other way to describe it. And our transgressions, if not confessed and dealt with, separate us from God, causing the love-doubt that haunts our nights and clouds our days.

But we don't have to live that way. Because if we'll simply agree with the diagnosis, Jesus has already provided the cure.

—Lazarus Awakening

READ: Romans 4:7–8

REFLECT: If you have unconfessed sin in your life, ask Jesus to forgive you. Then repeat these verses aloud in a prayer of gratitude.

February 22

You have been set free from sin.
ROMANS 6:18

Of the forty-five times the word *sin* appears in Romans, it is used as a noun in every instance except one. This has radical implications for my life—and yours.

Too often we think of sin as something we do—wrong thoughts, wrong attitudes, wrong behavior. But according to Romans chapters 5 through 8, sin is an active entity, a force at work within us. An unholy spirit, if you will. And this active entity—sin "at work in the members of my body" (Romans 7:23)—manipulates me, as well as my flesh, to do the wrong things.

Before I met Christ, sin was fully in charge. It pulled my strings like an evil puppet master, causing me to dance like a helpless marionette. Enslaved to his dark choreography, I flopped here and there, going through the motions of life. On the outside I appeared as though I was in control, but in reality I was a powerless captive. A slave. Addicted to self-love, pain avoidance, and pleasure, I did sin's bidding—beating myself up for my failures and slapping myself on the back for my accomplishments. I was a one-person Punch and Judy show.

Then Jesus came. When I said yes to Him, the Puppet Master, He cut the soul-strings that tied my soul to sin and allowed me to truly live. I was no longer a wooden Pinocchio wishing and longing to be real. Christ breathed His breath of life into me and set me free to be all I was created to be.

—Having a Mary Spirit

READ: Galatians 5:1
REFLECT: What does Paul tell us to do about the "yoke of slavery"?

Through Christ I've been set free.

Free to live. Free to move. And free to remain in bondage if I wish.

Strangely it is possible for me to belong to Christ and still act as if I'm controlled by sin. To actually believe I'm controlled by sin, although the strings—that is, the bonds of sin—have been severed by Jesus's death and resurrection.

Teacher and author Anabel Gillham explains it like this: "The patterns in your life become so deeply entrenched that you perform them habitually—not even recognizing that you are exhibiting un-Christlike behavior…or that you have a choice to resist."

"That's just the way I am," we tell ourselves.

No, Anabel says, "that's just the way you've learned."[23]

So how do we change those entrenched muscle-memory patterns that keep us fighting sin and the flesh even after we've been set free from their influence? The apostle Paul suggests two things we must do.

First, we must *reckon ourselves dead to sin*—choosing to rest our faith completely in what Christ has done for us. Then we must continue to *put to death* the residue of our earthly nature which remains even after Flesh Woman has been crucified.

When Paul writes in Romans 6:11, "Likewise you also, reckon yourselves to be dead indeed to sin, but alive to God in Christ Jesus our Lord" (NKJV), he's not asking us to suppose anything. He's just telling us to do the math. Stop making things difficult—just add it up!

Because of all that Jesus did, the debt you owed was canceled—"Paid in full!" Sin no longer owns you. You are no longer obligated to obey its commands.

—*Having a Mary Spirit*

READ: Romans 12:2

REFLECT: What "patterns of this world" do find yourself returning to again and again? Fill in the blank with your pattern: "Lord, I reckon myself dead to _____ and alive to Christ."

February 24

Let us examine our ways…let us return to the Lord. Lamentations 3:40

"Create in me a clean heart, O God," David wrote in Psalm 51:10–11, "and renew a right spirit within me. Cast me not away from thy presence; and take not thy holy Spirit from me" (KJV). No one has prayed this prayer with as much heartfelt sincerity as the man who wrote it.

King David, you see, was a man found out. All his dirty little secrets—his lust for Bathsheba, his plot to have her husband killed, his willingness to lie about it—had been exposed by God through the prophet Nathan.

When he finally faced the reality of who he was and what he'd done, David went to the only appropriate place any of us can go when our inner darkness is finally revealed: he poured out his heart to God.

He did the same in Psalm 139:23–24: "Search me, O God, and know my heart…. See if there is any offensive way in me."

An important prayer for all of us. Because we live such surface lives, we find we can gloss over sin just as we cover our kids' crayon marks with a coat of paint. It is possible to become so adept at leading the "unexamined life" as Socrates called it, that even the author of the psalms could steal another man's wife, have him murdered, father an illegitimate child, and justify it all in his mind.

But God never deals in deception—or denial. In His mercy, He confronts what we ignore and reveals what we are much too willing to hide. Though we may put our fingers in our ears and hum loudly like a rebellious child, God will still find a way to put the truth in front of us.

—*Having a Mary Spirit*

READ: Psalm 51:6

REFLECT: What do you think God means by "truth in the inner parts"?

*Blessed is the man you discipline,
O LORD.* PSALM 94:12

February 25

What happens when we refuse to listen to God and act on what He says?

The Bible is clear that God, like a loving parent, will administer the appropriate correction in our lives. "For whom the LORD loves He reproves," states Proverbs 3:12, "even as a father *corrects* the son in whom he delights" (NASB).

The level of the discipline we receive depends mostly on the level of our teachability. When my mother was small, all her father had to do was look disappointed with her and she'd be in his arms, melting with tears, begging for his forgiveness. Suffice it to say, it required a little more force on my dad's part when it came to his eldest child. I was not only well raised, I was also well "reared." And quite often, come to think of it.

Spiritually, the same is true. If we are teachable, we come around quickly to obedience. As a consequence, the level of discipline is fairly minor, sometimes even painless. But if we are unteachable, if we refuse God's rebuke, the level of discipline increases in severity, just like my "rearing" did. Not because God is ruthless, but because our hearts are rebellious. Our loving Father will do whatever it takes to break that rebellion before that rebellion breaks us.

"Before I was afflicted I went astray," the psalmist writes, "but now I obey your word" (Psalm 119:67). Before you think God cruel, read on. This is no trembling, abused child. This is a chastened son who, like me, can look back and say to His Father with full assurance: "You are good, and what you do is good; teach me your decrees" (119:68).

—*Having a Mary Heart*

 READ & REFLECT: Look up the word *discipline* in a concordance or Bible website. Choose one or two verses to meditate on.

February 26

*Every word of God is flawless; he is a
shield to those who take refuge in him.*
PROVERBS 30:5

A few years back I looked at my relationship with God and realized that my quiet-time communication style involved a series of monologues with very little dialogue. I would read about what God thought. Then I'd spend a few minutes telling God what I thought. But I never allowed us to get to the point of conversation, of give-and-take discourse, of the questions and answers that bring life to a relationship.

But that changed when I began to read the Bible as God's love letter to me. I started to hear His voice calling out to me in the pages of Scripture, and I began to respond to it from my heart. I started a Bible-reading highlights journal in which I recorded what I felt the Lord was saying to me from His Word.

Instead of the two or three chapters of Bible reading I'd tried to cram in before, I read smaller portions this time, usually one chapter. Instead of simply reading a passage, I'd meditate on it, underlining important verses as I went. Then I'd choose the verse that spoke most clearly to me and respond to the verse in my journal. Sometimes I would paraphrase it into my own words. Sometimes I asked questions. But usually the verse became a prayer as I asked the Lord to apply the truth of His Word to my life and my heart.

I wasn't just reading through the Bible; the Bible was getting through to me. My prayer life, too, took on fresh life. No longer was I just presenting God with my wish list and some suggestions about how I thought He should handle it. I was conversing with God—both talking and listening.

Gradually, duty turned into delight and ritual transformed into relationship—the very thing for which each of us were made.

—Having a Mary Heart

READ: Psalm 19:7–11
REFLECT: Describe what God's Word does for us.

Journal the Journey

When I started journaling what God spoke to me through His Word, the Bible became alive for me. No longer did I walk away, forgetting what I saw (James 1:23–24); instead, the Word was actually changing me as I applied it to my own life. I invite you to try the approach[24] I've found most helpful:

1. Using a Bible translation that you enjoy and understand, ask the Holy Spirit to quicken your heart to hear what He wants to say to you through His Word.

2. Read slowly through a chapter until something sticks out to you, then meditate on that portion. Here are a few places you might begin to read:

   | Psalm 23 | John 1 | Philippians 2 |
   | Psalm 139 | James 1 | Colossians 3 |

   Proverbs (with 31 chapters, there is one for each day of the month)

3. As you read, mark key words or phrases in one or more of the following ways:

   Underline   (Circle)   [Bracket]
   /Diagonal Lead-in and out/   Highlighter (the nonbleed kind)

4. Use the following template to journal your Bible reading highlights:

   Date: _____ Portion I read today: _____

   Best thing I marked: *Reference:* _____

   *Scripture:*_____

   How it impressed me: _____

   _____

   _____

   _____

   —Having a Mary Heart

Let God transform you into a new person
by changing the way you think.

Romans 12:2, nlt

February 27

See how much he loved him.
JOHN 11:36, TLB

Though we don't have a lot of background on Lazarus, we can still learn some important things about this man from Scripture.

First, Jesus loved Lazarus.

Second, that love translated into a close relationship between the two.

The first point may seem obvious and somewhat unimportant. After all, Jesus loves everyone. And yet the narrator of the biblical account highlights their closeness several times to make sure we know that this was not just a generic acquaintance.

In John 11:3, for instance, Lazarus's sisters send word: "Lord, the one you *love* is sick."

Later, in verse 5, John reiterates: "Jesus *loved* Martha and her sister and Lazarus."

Even the Jews who later gathered at Lazarus's funeral must have been aware of this extra-special relationship between Christ and the man they mourned, for when they saw Jesus weeping at the tomb, they said, "See how he *loved* him!" (verse 36).

Though He knew how the story would end, when Jesus arrived in Bethany and saw Mary weeping, John 11:33 tells us "he was deeply moved in spirit and troubled." So troubled, in fact, that He may have literally groaned out loud. The Greek word for "deeply moved," *embrimaomai,* comes from the root word that means "to snort with anger; to have indignation."[25] Jesus didn't take the family's pain lightly. For Lazarus was much more than a follower.

When referring to Mary and Martha's brother, Jesus used a term that seems generic but is far more intimate than that—not to mention powerful. And it can change our relationship with our Maker if we will seek to be named by it as well.

When talking about Lazarus, Jesus called him "friend" (John 11:11).

—Lazarus Awakening

 READ: Proverbs 17:17

REFLECT: In what ways has Jesus proven Himself both a friend and a brother to you?

60

February 28

What does it mean to be a friend of God? I'm talking about an honest-to-goodness, true-blue, when-the-chips-are-down kind of friend.

I've felt the Lord challenging me with this very question. I'd like to think Jesus considers me a friend. But am I really? Am I someone He can feel safe with? Is my heart a place with plenty of room for Him to spread out and relax? Is *mi casa* truly His *casa*?

It isn't easy finding a friend like that. Just ask any Hollywood celebrity who is hounded by friends who seem sincere but are really out for what they can get.

In his book on the psychology of fame and the problems of celebrity, author David Giles describes the loneliness that often stalks famous people. Even as far back as 60 BC, Giles notes, the Greek philosopher Cicero "complained that, despite the 'droves of friends' surrounding him, he was unable to find one with whom he could 'fetch a private sigh.'"[26]

I wonder if God ever feels like that. Does His heart hurt when He realizes most people hang around Him for what they can get?

For the contacts they can make. For the warm fuzzies they feel. For the benefits and perks that come with Christianity—peace, joy, provision. Or for the rewards they expect when they offer God a calculated gift of service.

Such a self-centered, result-oriented relationship must grieve the heart of the Almighty. It certainly causes us to miss out on the intimacy He intends.

—Lazarus Awakening

READ: John 15:13–15

REFLECT: According to these verses, what kind of friendship does Jesus want to have with you?

February 29

Whom have I in heaven but you? And earth has nothing I desire besides you.
PSALM 73:25

Have you ever considered what you will do when you get to heaven? Will you kneel adoringly at Jesus's feet…or sit close to talk? Will you run to Him like a child and climb up on His lap…or look deep in His eyes before falling to your knees in worship? Just imagine how wonderful that is going to be.

Then let me ask you, are you doing that here?

Are you drawing as close to Jesus as you can possibly get while you live for Him here on earth? First Corinthians 13:12 (KJV) seems to suggest that we will be known in heaven as we are known on earth. And that, I believe, should have radical implications on how we live our lives each day. I don't want to wait until I get to heaven to know Jesus. I want to snuggle up close to Him today.

I want to lay my head on His chest and hear His heart beat as the disciple John did (John 21:20, KJV). I want to lay my greatest treasures down at His feet as Mary did. I want to serve the Lord wholeheartedly yet respond to His rebuke and change as Martha did.

Most of all I want to laugh like Lazarus—laugh aloud with pure wonder that I belong to Jesus and He belongs to me.

In AD 890, when the supposed tomb of Mary and Martha's brother was discovered on Cyprus, the marble sarcophagus they found was marked with a simple inscription: "Lazarus…friend of Christ."[27]

I can't think of a better way to be defined—in life or in death. Both *here* on earth as well as *there* someday. For this world is not our home. We're just passing through.

—Lazarus Awakening

READ: Revelation 22:4–5
REFLECT: Describe the relationship we will enjoy with God when we get to heaven.

Could you men not keep watch with me for one hour? MATTHEW 26:40

March 1

Making room for the Better Part in our lives isn't easy. Many great men and women of God have struggled to hammer out time alone with their Savior. J. Sidlow Baxter describes his battle to reestablish a regular devotional time after a "velvety little voice told him to be practical…that he wasn't of the spiritual sort, that only a few people could be like that."

He writes:

> As never before, my will and I stood face to face. I asked my will the straight question, "Will, are you ready for an hour of prayer?" Will answered, "Here I am, and I'm quite ready, if you are." So Will and I linked arms and turned to go for our time of prayer. At once all the emotions began pulling the other way and protesting, "We're not coming." I saw Will stagger just a bit, so I asked, "Can you stick it out, Will?" and Will replied, "Yes, if you can." So Will went, and we got down to prayer.… It was a struggle all the way through. At one point… one of those traitorous emotions had snared my imagination and had run off to the golf course; and it was all I could do to drag the wicked rascal back.…
>
> At the end of that hour, if you had asked me, "Have you had a 'good time'?" I would have had to reply, "No, it has been a wearying wrestle with contrary emotions and a truant imagination from beginning to end." What is more, that battle with the emotions continued for between two and three weeks…[28]

—Having a Mary Heart

READ: Psalm 63:1–8

REFLECT: Using the words of this psalm, ask God to give you the kind of spiritual hunger David had.

March 2

My heart says of you, "Seek his face!"
Your face, LORD, I will seek. PSALM 27:8

Describing his battle to have a regular quiet time with God, J. Sidlow Baxter continues:

> …if you had asked me at the end of that period, "Have you had a 'good time' in your daily praying?" I would have had to confess, "No, at times it has seemed as though the heavens were brass, and God too distant to hear, and the Lord Jesus strangely aloof, and prayer accomplishing nothing."
>
> Yet something was happening. For one thing, Will and I really taught the emotions that we were completely independent of them.… About two weeks after the contest began…I overheard one of the emotions whisper to the other, "Come on, you guys, it's no use wasting any more time resisting: they'll [pray] just the same."…
>
> Then, another couple of weeks later, what do you think happened?
>
> During one of our prayer times, when Will and I were no more thinking of the emotions than of the man in the moon, one of the most vigorous of the emotions unexpectedly sprang up and shouted, "Hallelujah!" at which all the other emotions exclaimed, "Amen!" And for the first time the whole of my being—intellect, will, and emotions—was united in one coordinated prayer-operation. All at once, God was real, heaven was open, the Lord Jesus was luminously present, the Holy Spirit was indeed moving through my longings, and prayer was surprisingly vital.[29]

When I first read Baxter's words, they unlocked something deep within my soul. So I wasn't alone! Suddenly I felt hope—hope that I, too, could experience the joy of the Better Part. I didn't have to wait until I felt spiritual to spend time with God. I just had to make a decision of the will, and the spiritual feelings would eventually come around.

—Having a Mary Heart

READ: Colossians 1:9

REFLECT: Begin a list of needs—both yours and others'—to pray for each day, keeping Colossians 1:9 in mind. Mark and date answers to prayer as they come.

Exercise yourself toward godliness.
1 Timothy 4:7, NKJV

We have a Savior who understands that we are caught in a human body of contradictions. Wanting God one minute and chasing the world the next. Desiring holiness, yet settling for compromise. Hungering for the divine, yet willing to trade it for a bowl of stale porridge and a nap in the shade.

Jesus not only understands our weaknesses, He has the power and the know-how to help us change. However, let me warn you. The process of transformation is not nearly as passive as that statement makes it sound. Instead of speaking a word and instantly changing our lives, God asks us to partner with Him in our own transformation.

I like how author Andrea Wells Miller describes this process. Too often, she says, when confronted with the challenge to change,

> I spiritually lie down on the operating table, grab the ether mask, and get ready for surgery and the healing that will follow, saying "Okay, Lord, here I am…'yielded and still, mold me and make me after thy will.'"
>
> It's as if the Lord says, "First, fold your arms across your chest."
>
> "Great!" I answer.
>
> But then he says, "Now, sit up and lie back down 100 times."

"That's *not* what I had in mind!" Miller concludes.[30] But it is what God had in mind when He made us. The Lord knows that we need the process as much as we need the product. For it isn't just our holiness God is after. He also wants to make us wholly His.

—Having a Mary Spirit

Read: 1 Corinthians 9:24
Reflect: What effort should we put forth, and why?

March 4

Wake up, O sleeper. Ephesians 5:14

Throughout the Bible sleep is synonymous with death. Ironically, as with Snow White, a poisoned fruit caused Adam and Eve to fall into a spiritual unconsciousness that still affects you and me today. When God told the first couple not to eat from the forbidden tree, when He said, "You will surely die" (Genesis 2:17), He wasn't kidding. The moment they disobeyed, the center of their beings fell asleep. The part of them that had communed best with their Creator—that is, their spirits—died.[31]

Likewise, our spirits remain locked in death-sleep until we meet Jesus Christ as our personal Savior. Until the Prince of Peace wakens our slumbering hearts with a tender kiss and the sprinkling of His shed blood, the most important part of our beings will remain lifeless and dead. Only Christ can perform the spiritual CPR we so desperately need.

But it's important to realize that even after we commit our lives to Jesus, the danger of spiritual slumber is never far away. Even though we are no longer dead in our spirits, it's still possible for us to be lulled back to sleep in our souls. Suffering from a type of spiritual narcolepsy and sleepwalking through life, we remain loved by Jesus—just as Lazarus was—but in desperate need of being awakened by an encounter with the living God.

How is it possible that Christians could fall into such slumber? In most cases it doesn't happen suddenly. Nodding off to the things of God is usually an incremental process. A slow numbing of the heart. A drifting and dreaming of our souls as they follow other pursuits.

But such slumber never rejuvenates, it only exhausts us. Causing us to miss out on more than we know.

—Lazarus Awakening

Read: Proverbs 24:30–34

Reflect: Describe how spiritual laziness might lead to spiritual poverty.

I have come…so that no one who believes in me should stay in darkness.
JOHN 12:46

March 5

In my case spiritual slumber usually starts with a lullaby. A compromising tune hummed by the deceiver one day. A long ballad of self-pity sung by Satan the next. There are as many different lyrics as there are listening ears. Music to make us doubt God's goodness. Tunes to make us cease to care. Lullabies intended to lull us bye-bye to the point we're blind to the enemy's devices and deaf to the Spirit's voice. And deeply, desperately in need of a wake-up call.

Years ago, I was staying at a hotel in Houston, Texas. When I called the front desk to schedule a wake-up call, they promised to do just that and more.

"If you don't answer the phone, we'll knock at the door," the man on the line said. "If you don't answer the door, we will come in and shake you until you get up."

Now that's what I call service! A bit unsettling but, still, service!

I believe God would love to do the same for us if we'd just give Him permission. He knows how easily we sleep through spiritual alarm clocks. He's watched us consistently shrug off His stirrings when He's tried to revive us. But our heavenly Father is willing to do whatever it takes to revive us if we will only listen and respond to Him.

We're asleep, Lord Jesus. Wake us up! should be our daily prayer. *Wake us up to Your loving mercy. Wake us up to Your goodness and Your power to save.*

—*Lazarus Awakening*

READ: Mark 13:35–37
REFLECT: Why is it so important that we be wide-awake Christians?

March 6

Woe to those who call evil good and good evil. ISAIAH 5:20

I wonder sometimes if we've surgically removed the heart of the good news in order to make it more palatable. For some reason we find it easier to believe in a Cosmic Grandfather who winks at our sin as if to say, "Boys will be boys, but I still love them," than in a God who was so grieved over our sin that He climbed up on a cross to ransom us from the slavery of sin.

We'd rather believe that humanity is basically good, and God basically forgetful. But "do not be deceived" the Bible says in Galatians 6:7. "God cannot be mocked. A man reaps what he sows." Sin, by nature, always yields a consequence. You can't go against God's Law without suffering the repercussions; perhaps you won't see them right away, but eventually, inevitably, they will come.

Just ask the fifty-something woman trying to restore relationships with her children after taking off to find herself in her midthirties. Or ask the man trying to put back together the pieces of his marriage after a casual one-night stand. Or ask the couple facing bankruptcy after gambling their weekends away at the local casino. It all seemed like not-quite-innocent fun, an exotic escape that somehow turned into a trap.

But it isn't just the big sins we need rescuing from. Careless words, greedy looks, and negative thoughts hold consequences as well. Just consider the friendship severed by thoughtless gossip or the discontentment created by envy or the job lost by a critical tongue.

We are each bound by sin and captive to its consequences. We need a Savior, not a grandpa. We need a Rescuer, not an enabler. We need a God who can set us free, not a God who simply looks the other way.

—Outtake from *Lazarus Awakening*

READ: 1 Timothy 4:1–2

REFLECT: Are you allowing things in your life that have seared your conscience? What will you do about them?

The ancient city of Sardis sat proudly upon a rock citadel high above a river valley in Asia Minor. A seemingly impenetrable fortress, it was considered one of the greatest cities in the world. Its king, Croesus, once led his troops against Cyrus of Persia, only to be severely beaten back to the refuge of his city. Cyrus followed him and laid siege to Sardis for fourteen days, but soon realized Croesus would never surrender. So the Persian king offered a reward to anyone who could find entry into the city.

Meanwhile, Croesus assigned only a few guards to the city walls before retiring to his palace. He wasn't worried. His fortress could not be taken.

But when a Sardinian sentry dropped his helmet, a Persian soldier named Hyeroeades noticed the guard slip out from the base of the cliff, reclaim his gear, and go back into a hidden fold in the mountain. With that careless mistake the sentry revealed a crack in the seemingly unbreachable wall of rock.

That evening a party of Cyrus's troops crept up the same crevice and captured the city without a struggle.[32]

Like the citadel of Sardis, we all have fault lines that run through our souls. Weak spots in our psyches that may go undetected—or simply ignored—for years. These are the very places Satan searches for when he prowls around "like a roaring lion looking for someone to devour" (1 Peter 5:8). Sin crouches at our doors, looking for points of entry into our hearts and souls. Which is why it's so important to allow God to expose and confront the cracks in our characters.

—Having a Mary Spirit

READ: Genesis 4:1–7
REFLECT: What seems to be Cain's fault line? How does God suggest he deal with it?

March 8

Teach me to do your will, for you are my God; may your good Spirit lead me on level ground. PSALM 143:10

As long as I'm alive, I will probably struggle with my need for approval. God has been so kind to heal me in many ways. His unconditional love and acceptance continue to fill the gap that runs through my soul. Yet I believe I will always be vulnerable to sin in this particular area. Not as vulnerable as I was before God revealed it, but vulnerable all the same.

That might sound like a lack of faith, but I prefer to call it wisdom. For even though I am far less needy than I used to be, I still have days where—as Brennan Manning puts it—"my ravenous insecurities [make] my sense of self-worth rise and fall like a sailboat on the winds of another's approval or disapproval."[33]

Being realistic about my weakness has prompted me to post a guard at that spot. With the Holy Spirit's help, I have recognized several warning signs that indicate the enemy is trying to exploit my weakness. Recognizing and responding appropriately to those warnings has protected me more times than I can count.

My own careless words, for example, have become a warning sign for me. Whenever I begin to tout my opinions as gospel truth, I know trouble isn't far away. I've also learned to watch out for self-pity. In my case, "poor-me" thoughts are a one-way ticket to depression, as well as a sign that I don't trust God's provision in my life. And my tendency toward self-promotion is a real red flag. Whenever I make "me" and my accomplishments the topic of a conversation, I know I'm treading on dangerous ground. I'm much better off making others my focus.

—Having a Mary Spirit

READ: Luke 3:4–6
REFLECT: These words were spoken by John the Baptist of the coming Messiah. What valleys and crooked places in your life need healing?

I confess my iniquity; I am troubled by my sin. PSALM 38:18

March 9

Here's something I'm learning to do on a regular basis—something I've found that makes a big difference in the level of intimacy I enjoy with Christ.

I call it "spiritual housekeeping."

We tend to suffer from dropsy around our house. You know the affliction? We come in the door and drop whatever we have on the floor. On the next trip, we drop some more. This makes for a quite messy house and a very frustrated housekeeper. Which is me.

But spiritually speaking, I tend to do the same thing. I'll drop an unkind word here, spill a negative attitude there, let a resentment lie where it fell in a corner. It isn't long before the clutter of sin is knee high and my heart paralyzed, not knowing where to start cleaning up the mess.

Not a great way to live. But I'm learning. I'm getting better.

Now, instead of letting sin pile up, I try to do my housekeeping every day. My goal is obedience—avoiding sin by following God's commands. But when I mess up, I try to choose repentance. I tell God I'm sorry and look for ways to make amends for any damage I've caused. I consciously give the Lord those things I just can't fix, and resolve to do better, depending on God to make it possible.

Conscious repentance leads to unconscious holiness. That phrase, gleaned from the writings of Oswald Chambers, has done incredible things in my walk with God. Not to mention my spiritual housekeeping. But while repenting is easy, I must never forget my forgiveness cost Jesus His very life.

—Having a Mary Heart

READ: 1 John 1:9
REFLECT: What does God promise to do if we'll confess our sins?

March 10

Every year or five, I get the urge to spring clean. The clutter finally overwhelms me, and I know it's time to act. And so, armed with a trash bag, I go through the house doing what FlyLady calls the "27 Fling Boogie."

Now, you might be wondering, who is she and what in the world is that?

The 27 Fling Boogie is one of the tactics author Marla Cilley, a.k.a. Fly-Lady, suggests for cleaning out the clutter that dominates so much of our lives. It's really simple: "Grab a garbage bag and boogie!" Set a timer for fifteen minutes and run through your house, quickly picking twenty-seven items to throw away. After throwing that bag in the trash, set the timer again and pick out twenty-seven things to give away.[34]

Easy, right? Well, it's a little harder than it sounds, because most of us get attached to our physical junk.

Unfortunately, we get accustomed to the clutter in our spiritual lives as well. Like an overstuffed closet, our hearts are often filled with piles of bad habits and unforgiven grievances and fears; our minds a jumbled mess of impure thoughts and baggage from the past. I've found that if I don't make a point of regularly cleaning out all the lower-nature junk from my spiritual closet, I will usually default to the easiest and most familiar responses.

But those are rarely the responses of a Christlike heart.

—Having a Mary Spirit

READ: 2 Corinthians 7:1

REFLECT: Tomorrow we'll consider a list of unspiritual things we need to get rid of, but why not start by getting rid of some household clutter today? Follow Cilley's advice above: grab a garbage bag, set a timer, and start to "boogie"!

Therefore, get rid of all moral filth and the evil that is so prevalent and humbly accept the word planted in you, which can save you. JAMES 1:21

March 11

In light of yesterday's entry, it's time for the 27 Fling Spiritual Boogie! Reread 2 Corinthians 7:1 and reflect on how to declutter your life of the following:

1. ***Jealousy.*** (You are all you get to be—enjoy it!)
2. ***Perfectionism.*** (Desire to do your best but then accept it as enough.)
3. ***Regrets.*** (You can't undo mistakes, but you can learn from them.)
4. ***Shame.*** (If you've truly repented, accept that you've been forgiven!)
5. ***Blame.*** (Stop pointing the finger at everyone else.)
6. ***Coarse joking.*** (Crude humor rarely uplifts; it only demeans.)
7. ***Self-hatred.*** (Forgive yourself and move on. God has!)
8. ***Gossip.*** (If it can't be said in front of the person, don't say it.)
9. ***Fear.*** (Stop and pray before fear takes hold.)
10. ***Short temper.*** (Count to ten or give yourself a time-out.)
11. ***Fantasies.*** (Don't miss life by habitually checking out.)
12. ***Envy.*** (Learn to want what you have.)
13. ***Lies.*** (Discard the habit of half-truths, exaggerations, and deception.)
14. ***Swearing.*** (Eliminate even sugarcoated words like *gosh* and *heck*!)
15. ***Complaining.*** (Don't nurse it or rehearse it…disperse it.)
16. ***Guilt trips.*** (Don't book travel for yourself and don't send others.)
17. ***Ingratitude.*** (Look for things to be thankful for—express it aloud.)
18. ***Comparison.*** (Accept yourself and appreciate others.)
19. ***Impatience.*** (Develop long-suffering without the whine.)
20. ***Careless words.*** (Ask, "Does this really need to be said?")
21. ***Passivity.*** (Tie up loose ends by taking action.)
22. ***Laziness.*** (Do one thing today you don't want to do.)
23. ***Worry.*** (Add "Dear Jesus" to your fear and turn it into prayer.)
24. ***Greed.*** (Give something you love away.)
25. ***Negativity.*** (Train yourself to look for the good in situations.)
26. ***Self-pity.*** (Cry for five minutes if you must, then blow your nose and move on!)
27. ***Lust.*** (Eliminate the I-must-have-it-now desire for people and things.)

—Having a Mary Spirit

March 12

Resentment kills a fool, and envy slays the simple. JOB 5:2

The story is told of a priest who served a small parish in an obscure countryside. He loved his people, and he was doing God's work quite effectively—so effectively, in fact, that two demons were assigned by Satan to derail his ministry. They tried every method in their bag of tricks, but to no avail. The placid priest seemed beyond their reach. Finally, they called for a conference with the devil himself.

"We've tried everything," the demons explained, listing their efforts. Satan listened, then offered this advice. "It's quite easy," he hissed. "Bring him news that his brother has been made bishop."

The demons looked at one another. It seemed too simple. They had expected something more diabolical. But it was worth a try. Nothing else had worked.

Several weeks later they returned gleefully. The old priest hadn't taken the happy news of his brother's promotion well at all. The man's former joy had been turned to moping. His encouraging words had been replaced with grumbling and gloom. In a short time, the man's vibrant ministry had been destroyed by the green worm of envy and the black cloud of disappointment—the bitter conclusion that "it just wasn't fair."

We can all fall prey to the same satanic trick if we're not careful. Snares and traps surround us. For the enemy of our soul knows that if he can sidetrack us from God's purposes by getting our eyes on others, he can keep us circling the cul-de-sac of comparison, overwhelmed by envy and bitterness. Off track and out of sorts. Racking up miles on our odometers, but never arriving at the destination for which we were made.

—Having a Mary Heart

READ: Proverbs 14:30

REFLECT: Describe a time when envy and/or disappointment knocked you off course.

Throughout time, Satan has resorted to "Three Deadly Ds of Destruction" to bring down God's best and brightest:

- Distraction
- Discouragement
- Doubt

The underlying strategy is fairly simple: Get people's eyes off God and on their circumstances. Make them believe that their "happiness" lies in the "happenings" that surround them. Or send them good news—about somebody else. When they're thoroughly discouraged, tell them God doesn't care. Then sit back and let doubt do its work.

When Jesus met Martha that day in Bethany, she was "distracted." That's where Satan usually begins. He knows if we're overly worried and bogged down by duties, chances are good our hearts will not hear the Savior's call to come. While distraction may not win the battle for our soul, getting our eyes off of what is important certainly makes us more vulnerable to attack.

Martha's pursuits were far from trivial. That's important to recognize. In fact, the "preparations" Martha pursued were described by Luke as *diakonia*—the New Testament word for "ministry." "But even pure ministry for Jesus can become a weight we drag around," says pastor and author Dutch Sheets. "It's called the 'treadmill anointing,' and it isn't from God."[35]

I've experienced the treadmill anointing in ministry far more often than I'd like to admit. Even on those days when I have the best of motives, my heart can be pulled away from doing things "as unto the Lord" and settle for simply getting things done.

—Having a Mary Heart

Read: 2 Corinthians 1:8–9
Reflect: What benefit did Paul find in the difficulties and discouragement he faced?

March 14

*Give me relief from my distress; be
merciful to me and hear my prayer.*
PSALM 4:1

When discouragement breaks down our perspective and dismantles our defenses, it causes us to say and do things we would never consider saying or doing otherwise. Though we may have just completed great things for God, weary discouragement tells us we're useless, hopeless, and abandoned.

Elijah felt that kind of discouragement. Having just won a mighty victory over the prophets of Baal (1 Kings 18), Elijah had been flying high. But when Jezebel took out a contract on Elijah's life, the wicked queen's haughty words brought the mighty prophet back to earth with a *thud.* Less than a day after holy fire fell from heaven—proving once and for all that God was God—Elijah was running for his life.

"Don't you care?" Elijah asked God as he sat trembling under the broom tree in the desert. "I have had enough, LORD," he whimpered in 1 Kings 19:4. "Take my life." Just let me die.

Have you spent much time under the broom tree of self-pity? I have. It's easy to find a shady spot and feel sorry for ourselves when we're distracted and discouraged. Especially when we run up against unexpected opposition. Especially when it feels like we're running for our lives.

In the dictionary you'll find *self-pity* stuck between *self-perpetuating* and *self-pollinating.* I had to laugh when I saw it, because it's so true. I happen to be an expert on the subject. Being quite the hostess myself, I throw pity parties fairly regularly. Trouble is, no one wants to come. Self-pity is a lonely occupation.

—Having a Mary Heart

READ: 1 Samuel 30:1–6
REFLECT: Like Elijah, David faced a terrible, not-so-good day. Rather than giving into self-pity, what did David do?

I am afraid that just as Eve was deceived by the serpent's cunning, your minds may somehow be led astray.
2 CORINTHIANS 11:3

March 15

Throughout history, Satan has found that trying to make humanity question God's existence is futile. As Paul writes in Romans 1:19–20, God's existence is written upon man's heart. Time and time again, over the course of history, agnosticism and atheism have fallen before the bedrock belief: *God is.* In our lifetime, we've seen a century of atheistic unbelief crumble along with the Soviet Union and the Berlin Wall. Contrary to Communist prediction, belief in God has definitely not died. In fact, the rise of atheistic states in the twentieth century actually spurred the growth of religion.

Since atheism has been less than effective, Satan has returned to another lie in his bag of tricks. If he can't make us doubt God's existence, Satan will do his best to make us doubt God's love. After he has distracted us…after he has discouraged us…Satan's final tactic is disillusionment and doubt.

You're on your own, baby, he whispers to our loneliness. *See? God doesn't really care, or He would have shown up by now.*

Nothing could be further from the truth, of course. And yet, Satan continues to use this deception with great success. Even against God's own children.

I'm ashamed to say my heart has sometimes listened to Satan's siren song. The words of doubt and notes of disillusionment echo the frustration and confusion I feel inside. A countermelody to faith, the mournful tune arises during those times when God neither acts the way I think He should nor loves me the way I want to be loved. Like two songs being played in different keys, the dissonance of what I *feel* clashes with what I *know* and threatens to drown out the anthem of God's eternal love.

In the end, I have to choose. Which song will I listen to?

—Having a Mary Heart

READ: Genesis 3:1–5
REFLECT: What lie(s) does Satan use most often in his attempt to make you doubt God's love?

March 16

Jesus reached out and touched him.
"I am willing," he said. "Be healed!"
MATTHEW 8:3, NLT

In first grade, I sat in front of a little girl with shoulder-length brown hair and pretty blue eyes. I don't remember her name, as I was only in her class for about three months. But I do remember her heartrending cries. She suffered from a rare skin disorder that made a simple touch burn like fire.

She couldn't play with the rest of us during recess. Most of the time she kept to herself, rarely talking, cringing when anyone came near. I had given my heart to Jesus the year before in kindergarten, and something inside told me this little girl needed a friend. Slowly, a friendship developed between us. I'd help her paste and cut (because holding the scissors hurt too much), and she helped me with math problems I couldn't understand.

We moved away midyear, and I never saw that girl again. I've often wondered what happened to her. I pray that she was healed. I can't imagine going through life without the comfort of a touch. The blessing of an embrace.

It is one of the things I love most about Jesus. Over and over, you see His hands reaching out, caressing a child, touching and healing a leper. Hands that shaped eternity ruffle a little boy's hair. Hands that formed life out of dust now use mud to heal a blind man. Freshly nail-scarred hands fix breakfast for a ragtag bunch of beloved men exhausted from a night of frustrated fishing.

You and I have the privilege of being Jesus's hands to this world, reaching out to the wounded, the outcasts, the ones who fear touch but need it so much.

"Oh to be His hand extended," the old song says. "Reaching out to the oppressed. Let me touch Him, let me touch Jesus. So that others may know and be blessed."[36]

—Outtake from *Having a Mary Heart*

READ: Matthew 25:34–40

REFLECT: Why is it important to minister in practical ways to those around us?

Whatever you do, do it all for the glory of God. 1 Corinthians 10:31

March 17

After experiencing a spiritual awakening at the age of eighteen, Nicholas Herman had one goal: "to walk as in God's presence." He joined a monastery in Paris in 1666 and served there until he died at eighty years of age, "full of love and years and honored by all who knew him."

Perhaps you'd recognize Nicholas by his Carmelite name: Brother Lawrence. In his collection of letters, *The Practice of the Presence of God,* he explains that it's not just what we do for Christ that matters, but how we go about it.

When Brother Lawrence joined the monastery, he had expected to spend his days in prayer and meditation. Instead, he was assigned to cooking and cleanup. Yet once Brother Lawrence decided to "do everything there for the love of God, and with prayer...for his grace to do his work well," he found his Kitchen Service a joy and an avenue to a closer walk with God. He writes:

> The time of business does not with me differ from the time of prayer, and in the noise and clatter of my kitchen, while several persons are at the same time calling for different things, I possess God in as great tranquility as if I were upon my knees at the blessed sacrament.[37]

What a goal! To be so in tune with the presence of God that washing dishes becomes an act of worship and the mundane moments of our lives become aflame with the divine.

Service without spirituality is exhausting and hopeless. But spirituality without service is barren and selfish. When we unite the two something wonderful happens to our work in the kitchen. Sinks turn into sanctuaries. Mops swab holy ground. And daily chores that used to bore us or wear us down become opportunities to express our gratitude—selfless avenues for His grace.

—Having a Mary Heart

Read: Colossians 3:22–24

Reflect: What should be our attitude towards work and acts of service?

March 18

*When words are many, sin is not absent,
but he who holds his tongue is wise.*
PROVERBS 10:19

There is nothing like difficult situations and adversity to reveal what we're made of. In fact, I'm convinced that trouble and stress are one of the most common ways God shows us the weakness of our flesh and the futility of our self-efforts. In His mercy, He often allows stress to build up until the weak areas in our lives begin to give way under pressure.

That is exactly what happened with me.

When I experienced a rift in my dearest friendships, God used it to open my eyes to a fault line in my life—my hunger for approval. Though I'd felt small rumblings before, it took an 8.5 earthquake on my emotional Richter scale before I finally acknowledged that I had a problem. A problem I no longer wanted to hide and, more important, a core issue I needed God to deal with.

It all started so innocently—with a difference of opinion between me and a group of friends at church. Talking off the top of my head, I got on one of my opinionated soapboxes, and a flippant remark landed like a spark on my most treasured relationships. These were women I dearly loved (and still love), women who had supported me through the most demanding year of my life. Women who, like me, were exhausted and slightly on edge.

I had no idea how damaging my thoughtless comment would prove to be. Like a tourist flicking a cigarette out a car window on the way through Yellowstone, I threw out my careless, self-important words. And suddenly our forest was on fire.

No wonder the Bible warns us over and over about the danger of an untamed tongue....

—*Having a Mary Spirit*

READ: James 3:2–6
REFLECT: According to these verses, what is the benefit of a controlled tongue and the danger of an uncontrolled one?

Don't have anything to do with foolish…
arguments, because you know they
produce quarrels. 2 TIMOTHY 2:23

March 19

…When my friends and I tried to put out the fire my words had started, it only grew worse. The misunderstanding spread. Resentments flared. Smoldering hurts from the past burst into flame again. No matter what any of us of tried, we couldn't seem to get the situation under control.

At the risk of sounding melodramatic, I believe Satan had taken out a contract on our friendships and perhaps our very lives. But God had another plan.

Don't you love those words? *But God…* All through the Word (sixty-one times, to be precise) we read that little phrase right before God intervenes in a situation, taking what Satan meant for evil and turning it for good. And God still intervenes today.

But please note. While God may intervene, He doesn't necessarily interrupt. In fact, He may prolong the painful circumstances and injustice in order to work out His perfect purpose in our lives. He may allow us to experience the consequences of our sins in order to wean us from their deceptive embrace. For He is a wise Father and He knows what we need. Even when we question His ways.

"How long, O LORD?" David asks repeatedly in the psalms. How long must all this go on? I, too, asked questions. So many important people in my life, it seemed, were upset with me. But I know now, after the fact, that they felt just as wounded, isolated, and abandoned as I did. For Satan doesn't waste his fiery darts on just one person when he has the chance to ruin multiple lives.

But be assured God doesn't waste opportunities either.…

—*Having a Mary Spirit*

READ: Romans 8:28
REFLECT: What does "*all*" things" (emphasis mine) mean to you? Is the plural form of the word "those" significant?

March 20

I will thoroughly purge away your dross and remove all your impurities.
Isaiah 1:25

…I can look back on that painful time with my friends and see that God was hemming me in. I love Psalm 139:5: "You have hedged me behind and before, and laid Your hand upon me" (NKJV). It still comforts me to think of God cradling me in His hands, keeping me safe and still in the midst of the darkest storm. But at that particular time I felt pressed, as if God was narrowing my life rather than nurturing it. Nearly a year into the experience, I finally figured out an analogy to describe what I was going through

"I know what God's doing!" I told a friend as I slapped my hands together and held them tight. "He's got me in a ten-month mammogram!"

And what it revealed wasn't very pretty. Flesh. Lots and lots of flesh—and one very ugly weak spot.

It was as if the Great Physician had placed the results of the mammogram on a screen so I could finally see what He'd known all along. There, down the center of my being, ran a dark streak of self-centered preoccupation with how I was perceived and what other people thought of me. A desperate hunger for compliments and affirmation, achievement and praise. A tendency to look to people rather than to God for life and meaning.

Now, years later, I can see the Lord's handiwork all over that dark night of my soul. Had God not used the removal of approval, had He not confounded my idolatry of people's opinions, I would have missed the joy of finding all I need in Him alone.

—*Having a Mary Spirit*

READ: Proverbs 25:4

REFLECT: Why is it important to allow God to remove any impurities from our lives?

Take heed to yourselves, lest your heart be deceived, and you turn aside and serve other gods. DEUTERONOMY 11:16, NKJV

March 21

Back in Old Testament times, Satan's game plan was to litter the world with thousands of counterfeit gods. Because we are innately wired to worship something or someone bigger than ourselves, the enemy has implanted into every culture a belief in mythical beings or a system of pathways to obscure and distant gods.

The Greeks had Zeus. The Hindus have *karma*. The Buddhists follow the Eightfold Path. Even natives of isolated, remote jungles and islands have come up with religious systems. But, according to God, all were poor counterfeits, usurpers of His rightful place in the hearts of His created.

"You shall have no other gods before me," Yahweh commanded in Deuteronomy 5:7. "You shall not bow down to them or worship them; for I, the LORD your God, am a jealous God" (verse 9). And He wasn't kidding. Sending fire from heaven to scatter the prophets of Baal. Toppling the Philistine's god, Dagon, so the statue lay prostrate before the ark of the Lord.

At times God even required what appeared to be extreme measures—the utter destruction of neighboring kingdoms in order to protect His people from the idolatrous pull of those nations' gods.

It seems to me that idolatry today has become more personal than cultural. Rather than adopting foreign gods to bow down to, we tend to carve our own. "*Any*thing in life can serve as an idol," Timothy Keller writes in his book *Counterfeit Gods.* Even good things.

According to Keller, an idol "is anything more important to you than God, anything that absorbs your heart and imagination more than God, anything you seek to give you what only God can give."[38]

It's no wonder that idolatry of any kind has always been, and will always be, a slap in the face of God.

—Outtake from *Lazarus Awakening*

READ: Deuteronomy 32:15–18

REFLECT: Considering the progression of Israel's idolatry, can you see parallels in our culture today?

March 22

Without the shedding of blood there is no forgiveness. HEBREWS 9:22

It's ludicrous to think that God would have gone to so much trouble to send His own Son, Jesus Christ, to suffer and die if there had been any other way to reconcile you and me to His heart and to restore the relationship that fell apart when Eve took that first bite.

And it's absurd to think that Jesus would have agreed to go through such torment had there been an easier path. Why come and take the form of man if you and I could be made perfect through a few million cycles of Hindu reincarnation? Why suffer disgrace and public ridicule, the cross and all its shame, if all that heaven required was enough good works on our part to outweigh the bad?

The answer is simple: Jesus came and died and rose again because the ransom had to be paid; the debt we owed had to be satisfied; the power of sin and death that ruled over humanity from the beginning of time had to be broken. But in order for that to happen, blood had to be spilled. For without it, there is no forgiveness of sin (Hebrews 9:22).

Only one spotless Lamb could satisfy the requirement. And only one Lion of Judah could break all our chains.

God is love. Oh yes, He is. But love is Jesus. And if we want one, we must accept the Other.

For until we walk through the doorway that Jesus opened on the cross, we will never find the center-of-God's-heart relationship we need and the incredible love for which we were made.

—Outtake from *Lazarus Awakening*

READ: Colossians 1:19–23

REFLECT: What did Jesus's blood purchase for us, and what should be our response?

Picture with me a liturgical church service taking place during Lent—the six-week period leading up to Easter that commemorates Christ's journey to the cross. On this day, the congregants remember one event in particular—the night Jesus knelt to wash His disciples' feet.

A few in the chapel shift uncomfortably in their pews. Women smooth skirts down over naked knees, while men cough nervously, trying to remember whether they washed between their toes. The time has come to celebrate one of Christ's final acts. One of His most tender, humble offerings.

The priest gives instructions as bowls of water and linen towels are brought before the people. Then two by two, the act is performed. One person kneels while the other bends to remove his shoes. Both feel awkward. The kneeling one cringes slightly as he considers where the feet before him have walked and the residue they might bear. The one being washed trembles inwardly as he allows his most unattractive feature to be put on public display.

But as the warm water caresses callused skin, something special happens. A tender vulnerability stretches around the room and pulls people in, tying them together in a mutual bond that comes from yielding. It is palpable, and it is sacred.

The feet are dried and shoes replaced. Here and there, all over the sanctuary, the roles are quietly reversed and the act repeated. The served becomes a servant, and the servant becomes the served. And through it all and in it all, Jesus is remembered.

Christ is glorified.

—Outtake from *Having a Mary Heart*

READ: Philippians 2:3–8

REFLECT: In order to be like Jesus, what qualities should you cultivate?

March 24

Love your neighbor as yourself.
MATTHEW 19:19

Somehow the humble sacrament of foot washing has been forgotten by most churches, yet it was ordained by Christ Himself. "Now that I, your Lord and Teacher, have washed your feet, you also should wash one another's feet," Jesus told His disciples at the Last Supper in John 13:14–15. "I have set you an *example* that you should do as I have done for you" (emphasis mine).

There is more to this passage than we find in John. When we turn to the parallel account in Luke 22:24, we find that "a dispute [had arisen] among them as to which of them was considered to be greatest." Even in the shadow of the cross, the disciples still argued for position.

What a poignant picture. I can almost see the disciples as they talk around the Passover table. Perhaps it starts out as friendly banter, but before long, the teasing turns to flaunting, and the taunting to outright anger. In the midst of all this, Jesus quietly rises, takes off His outer garments, and wraps a towel around His waist. He pours water into a basin and carries it to the table. One disciple abandons the argument, then another; until only two sounds remain. The sloshing of water in a bowl, and the rubbing of towel against feet.

The act is familiar—startlingly so. The disciples had witnessed a similar scene in Bethany. They didn't understand Mary's extravagant act then, and they struggle to understand the meaning of Christ's humble act now. But one thing they do know: this is love. Receiving them and then washing them. At the point of their deepest need.

Just as Jesus receives you and me.

—Outtake from *Having a Mary Heart*

READ: 1 John 3:16–20
REFLECT: What is involved in loving as Jesus loved, and what are the benefits?

Dear children, let's not merely say that we love each other; let us show the truth by our actions. 1 JOHN 3:18, NLT

March 25

A woman I once met at a retreat was coming out of years of addiction. You could tell she felt a little out of place in the midst of four hundred Christian women, but she had come with a friend. The same friend who had helped bring her back to life with a simple kiss of acceptance.

"I was so afraid to tell her who I was and what I had done," the woman told me. "But I knew I'd found a true friend when I told her I was a heroin addict and she didn't flinch."

Then she smiled. "And believe me, I was watching."

Wow. What power lies in the gift of acceptance. The Good Samaritan didn't flinch at the mess before him. He didn't pull back when he saw the victim was his enemy—one of the hated race who hated him. Instead, he moved closer and pressed in.

What would happen if we stopped judging one another and just got down to the business of loving one another? Easy to say and harder to do. Believe me, I know. It's a struggle to really love to the point of action—to truly be *moved* with compassion as Jesus was—especially when many times people seem to have created most of their problems.

And yet, in order to be truly Christlike, we must love people when they least expect it and least deserve it. As I once heard a speaker say, we are to "grace them, don't shame them."

In most cases we do that best by opening our hearts and opening our ears.

Then opening our arms with unconditional love and welcoming them in just as they are.

—Outtake from *Lazarus Awakening*

READ: John 8:3–11

REFLECT: Describe a time when someone graced you rather than shamed you. How did it affect your life?

March 26

It is God who arms me with strength and makes my way perfect. 2 SAMUEL 22:33

I started praying the prayer early in our ministry, and I meant it from the bottom of my heart: "Lord, make me perfect by the time I'm thirty."

My inadequacies and imperfections were causing a lot of problems. Certainly God would honor my prayer and deliver me from myself.

I tried to enlist a couple of friends to pray on my behalf, but they just howled with laughter. "Yeah, right!" they said. "Perfect by thirty? Like that's going to happen."

Okay, perhaps I was a little naive. But the idea wasn't mine. Jesus had said it in His Word: "Be perfect, therefore, as your heavenly Father is perfect" (Matthew 5:48). If God required perfection, I reasoned, certainly He would give me the tools to accomplish it.

And, in many ways, He has. God has not only provided the tools for my transformation, but His Holy Spirit has also been at work in me, actively moving me toward the perfect wholeness God intended for my life. For this is what *perfect* means in the Bible.

Teleios. Mature. Complete.[39]

However, that process of moving toward perfection hasn't happened nearly as quickly as I'd hoped. In fact, at times I've felt that heaven itself was working against my best efforts. And perhaps it was—because God's plans for making us like His Son have very little to do with mere self-improvement.

You see, I assumed that Christian perfection was an outer work *I* had to do. A cleaning up and purifying of my words, my life, and my actions. But in my heartfelt desire to serve and honor the Lord, I fell prey to the same lie that deceived the Pharisees so long ago.

The lie that holiness is all up to us.

—*Having a Mary Spirit*

READ: Galatians 2:21
REFLECT: If holiness could be gained through our own self-effort, then what would be true?

The Pharisees were godly men, at least on the outside. Their sole purpose in life was to obey all of God's commands, so they made up hundreds of rules and regulations, known as the *Mishnah.* Translated into English, it is a book of almost eight hundred pages. Later, Jewish scholars added commentaries on how to fulfill the *Mishnah.* Known collectively as the *Talmud,* these commentaries fill at least twelve volumes.

Yet even the Jews recognized the hypocrisy that sometimes accompanied the Pharisees' pious attempts at religious perfection. The *Talmud* itself distinguishes seven different kinds of Pharisees:

1. The *Shoulder Pharisee,* who followed the Law but wore his good deeds on his shoulder to be seen of men.
2. The *Wait-a-Little Pharisee,* always able to offer a valid excuse to put off a good deed.
3. The *Bruised* or *Bleeding Pharisee,* so intent on avoiding evil that whenever a woman approached he would close his eyes and therefore run into things.
4. The *Humpbacked* or *Tumbling Pharisee,* so determined to look humble that he bent completely over and often tripped over obstacles.
5. The *Ever-Reckoning* or *Compounding Pharisee,* forever counting up his good deeds in the belief that each one put God further in his debt.
6. The *Timid* or *Fearing Pharisee,* constantly cleansing the outside of the cup and the platter to escape God's wrath.
7. Finally, the *God-fearing Pharisee,* defined by the Jews themselves as truly loving God.[40]

Only one out of seven was admired as a man who found delight rather than drudgery in obeying God's Law, no matter how difficult it might be.

—Having a Mary Spirit

Read: Romans 10:2–3

Reflect: Which of the Pharisaical tendencies listed above do you struggle with most?

March 28

Let us fix our eyes on Jesus, the author and perfecter of our faith. HEBREWS 12:2

I've been a Pharisee of one kind or another more often than I care to admit. For no matter how pure my intent, the only result of making outward purity my goal has been an unhealthy self-obsession and a self-worth that swings wildly between feelings of inordinate pride or overwhelming failure—depending on how well I think I've done that day.

Oswald Chambers warns against this dangerous preoccupation with our own "personal whiteness," as he calls it; referring to the unhealthy kind of introspection that focuses on our inadequacies rather than on God's power to redeem and change our lives.

"As long as our eyes are upon our own personal whiteness," he writes in *My Utmost for His Highest,* "we shall never get near the reality of Redemption." Later he adds, "The continual grubbing on the inside to see whether we are what we ought to be generates a self-centered, morbid type of Christianity, not the robust, simple life of the child of God."[41]

Over and over in the New Testament, Christ confronted those who had succumbed to the whitewashed-tomb syndrome—the dangerous belief that we can somehow make ourselves presentable to God through our own human effort. Not only were such efforts pointless and even dangerous, Jesus said, but they were no longer necessary. God had a better plan.

The Sin Bearer had come.

—Having a Mary Spirit

READ: Matthew 23:27–28
REFLECT: What did Jesus warn the Pharisees about, and why?

Then Mary…poured it on Jesus' feet and wiped his feet with her hair. And the house was filled with the fragrance of the perfume. JOHN 12:3

March 29

No one can know what took place in Mary's heart when she anointed Jesus on His way to the cross. However, the sweet sadness and the sense of destiny surrounding this final trip to Jerusalem seem evident. We know that Jesus had "set [His] face like flint" (Isaiah 50:7) toward the Holy City. Toward certain arrest and certain death.

According Matthew 26:2, Jesus had told the disciples what awaited Him: "The Son of Man will be handed over to be crucified." He had kept no secrets, but still the disciples seemed unable to comprehend fully what was happening. Of all the people surrounding Him, only Mary appeared to understand, for only she seemed moved to take the appropriate action.

This story found in John 12:1–8 is the last time the Bible mentions Mary, Martha, and Lazarus. Though religious tradition places all three at the cross, Scripture doesn't specify their presence there. It's clear, however, this family deeply loved the Lord, and He loved them. This trio from Bethany had provided something Jesus needed after leaving Nazareth three and a half years before.

They had given Him a home. A family. A place to lay His head.

The treasure Mary poured out that day was more than an expensive perfume. She was pouring out her very life in love and sacrificial service.

To those who secretly criticized such extravagance, Jesus said, "I tell you the truth, wherever the gospel is preached throughout the world, what she has done will also be told, in memory of her" (Mark 14:9).

Imagine the impact on the world if each one of us laid down our lives as well.

—Having a Mary Heart

 READ: John 12:3 and Matthew 6:19–21

REFLECT: What treasure are you storing up? Consider what God might be able to do with that treasure if, like Mary, you gave it all to Him.

March 30

By one sacrifice he has made perfect forever those who are being made holy.
HEBREWS 10:14

After the raising of Lazarus, Jesus was gaining a lot of notoriety—not to mention followers.

"If we let him go on like this," the chief priests and some of the Pharisees had argued before the Jewish governing authority, the Sanhedrin (John 11:48), "everyone will believe in him, and then the Romans will come and take away both our place and our nation."

Loss of position. Loss of power. Loss of influence. At this point in the game, that was a risk the Jewish leaders were not prepared to take—especially not after they had worked so hard to secure just those things.

The Sanhedrin had only recently negotiated an uneasy truce with the Roman procurator, Pilate, and after a rocky beginning it was finally working well. Until Jesus showed up, that is.

"You know nothing at all!" Caiaphas, the high priest, erupted during the meeting. "You do not realize that it is better for you that one man die for the people than that the whole nation perish" (11:49–50).

But it was Caiaphas who hadn't a clue. Unbeknownst to him, he had just "prophesied that Jesus would die for the Jewish nation," John writes in verses 51–52, "and not only for that nation but also for the scattered children of God, to bring them together and make them one."

So while the religious establishment plotted Jesus's downfall, God's plan to bring all humanity back to Him was gathering speed. Heaven's gates began to open, ready to receive all who would come in through Jesus Christ the Son.

Eternity's song began to play. The Lamb "slain from the creation of the world" (Revelation 13:8) was about to die so you and I could know God.

—Having a Mary Heart

READ: Isaiah 53:3–6
REFLECT: Read this passage slowly out loud as you consider all Christ has done for you.

For Christ died for sins once for all, the righteous for the unrighteous, to bring you to God. 1 PETER 3:18

March 31

It's hard to imagine the Creator of the universe wanting to know us. We feel so unworthy. That's why many of us persist in thinking that we must earn our way to heaven, that only the superspiritual can really know God.

Burdened with the weight of our own spirituality, we struggle beneath a load of self-imposed obligations: "I have to do this…" or "I can't really know God until I do that…" We can spend so much of our lives trying to get ready to know God or backing away out of fear of displeasing God that we never get around to enjoying the Living Room Intimacy Jesus came to provide.

And yet intimacy with God was indeed the very point of Jesus's coming and of His dying. "You who once were far away have been brought near through the blood of Christ," Paul writes in Ephesians 2:13. For when Jesus died, His cross bridged the great chasm of sin that separated us from God. With His last breath, Jesus blew aside the curtain that had kept sinful humans from touching a holy God. Now we could come into God's very presence, clean and approved, not by our works, but by His grace. Jesus "destroyed the barrier, the dividing wall of hostility" (verse 14) that had separated humanity from God.

When we couldn't reach up to heaven, heaven came down to us and welcomed us into the Living Room through the doorway of Jesus Christ.

That is the good news of the gospel.

The way has been made. The price has been paid. All we need to do is come.

—Having a Mary Heart

READ: Ephesians 3:12
REFLECT: Perhaps it's been awhile since you approached the Lord with freedom and confidence. Do it now, thanking Him for all He's done.

*Going Deeper*_____

Tools for Transformation

God has used many practices and experiences to shape my life. I've found that the following spiritual disciplines have helped me grow in my relationship with the Lord and become more like Jesus. I recommend them all to you.

Developing a Quiet Time. Carving out a regular time and place to hear from God has truly transformed my life. As I sit quietly before Him, read my Bible and other devotional materials, write in my journal, and pray, I am led in the way I should go.

Memorizing Scripture. When I'm struggling in a certain area, I've found that memorizing verses on that topic is especially helpful. Hiding God's Word in my heart not only changes my thinking; it stores up spiritual provision for future need. (See "Memorizing Scripture" on page 147.)

Listening to Others. I'm thankful for the Christian wisdom I glean from books, sermons, Bible studies, and godly friends—faithful mentors who proclaim, "This is the way, walk ye in it" (Isaiah 30:21, KJV).

Journaling the Journey. It isn't enough for me to see my face in the mirror of God's Word; I must respond with obedience. I've found that regular journaling—keeping track of both my own thoughts and what I perceive the Lord is saying to me—reminds me of God's faithfulness and keeps me accountable. (See "Journal the Journey" on page 59.)

Gathering with the Body. I pursue every opportunity to meet with God's people—from prayer groups to church services to retreats and conferences. When two or more are gathered together, God is there and we are changed (Matthew 18:20).

Altar-ing My Ego. Responding to God by going to the altar has changed my life. Whether I'm at home or at church, bowing my knee as well as my heart nails down my commitment to follow and obey what He is speaking to my heart.

—*Having a Mary Spirit*

The Spirit of the LORD will come upon you in power,...
and you will be changed into a different person.

1 SAMUEL 10:6

April 1

The story is told of a young man who left the Old Country and sailed to America to make a new life in the New World. Before he left, his father pressed some money in his hand and his mother handed him a box of food for the journey. Then they kissed and hugged and tearfully said good-bye.

On the boat, the young man gave his ticket to the porter and found his way to the tiny cabin he'd share with several others during the month-long voyage. That evening at mealtime, the young man went topside and unwrapped a sandwich his mother had made. He ate silently as he watched the other passengers file into a large room crowded with tables. He listened to their chatty laughter and watched as waiters brought plates filled with hot, steaming food. But he just smiled, enjoying his mother's fresh homemade bread and the crisp apple his brother had picked that morning. *Bless my family,* he prayed.

As the days went by, the young man's box of food quickly dwindled. But meals such as they offered in the dining room were certain to cost a lot. He'd need that money later.

He ate alone in his cabin now. The smell from the dining hall made his stomach wrench with hunger. He allowed himself a few crackers and some cheese each day, whispering a prayer of thanks before scraping the mold off the hard lump. A shriveled apple and the tepid rainwater he'd collected in a can completed his meager meal....

—Having a Mary Heart

READ: Psalm 107:4–9

REFLECT: Have you ever felt like the kind of wanderer the psalmist describes? What does God do for us when we cry out to Him?

April 2

He has filled the hungry with good things. LUKE 1:53

…Nearly a month into the transatlantic voyage, and just three days out of New York, the last of the young man's food was gone except for a wormy apple. The young man could take no more. Pale and weak, he asked the porter in broken English, "How much?" The porter looked confused. "Food," the young man said as he held out some coins and pointed to the dining room. "How much?"

Finally the ship steward understood. He smiled and shook his head. "It costs nothing," he said, closing the immigrant's hand back around his money. "You are free to eat! The cost of food was included in the price of passage."

This story means a lot to me. For years I lived like a pauper instead of a princess. I'd settled for stale cheese and shriveled apples instead of enjoying the rich table God had prepared for me. I kept waiting for the day I'd be worthy to sit at His table, never realizing that the cost of such fellowship was included in the price Christ paid for my passage.

The price has been paid. Please hear this simple truth. If you have accepted Jesus Christ as your Savior, the price has been paid for you. The "dividing wall of hostility" (Ephesians 2:14) has been torn down, at least on God's side. But there may need to be a bit of demolition work on your end, because the enemy of our souls keeps quite busy building barriers to block spiritual intimacy.

And unfortunately, we tend to help him along. Allowing cherished sins as well as heart-dividing pastimes to come between us and the love we need.

—Having a Mary Heart

READ: Isaiah 55:1–2

REFLECT: What invitation does God give to all who will come?

April 3

I wonder what it was like for Lazarus when he heard Jesus's voice from inside his tomb. Was it a far-off echo he first heard? A familiar yet distant voice calling him back from the holding cell of death?

I wonder what happened in Lazarus's body at the sound of his name. Did his heart suddenly start beating again? Was there a great intake of air as he drew his first breath in days? Did he awaken slowly, or did energy come like a sudden lightning bolt, sitting him up straight before propelling him out of the tomb?

Either way, once he was fully conscious, Lazarus was faced with a choice. Just as we are. To go back to sleep and remain where he was, or to get up from the grave and walk out into new life.

Because when Love calls our name, we can ignore His voice, or we can respond. We can pull back into the dark familiarity of what we've known, or we can step out into the light, ready to embrace what God has waiting for us. Though His voice may seem faint and distant, He is calling us out of our tombs just as surely as He called Lazarus.

So what should we do when we hear Him speak?

Only one response has helped me, and I offer it to you as well: Choose to move closer. Answer His cry with your own. Shuffle toward the light, and you'll find the Light becoming brighter. His voice growing louder. His words becoming clearer.

All because you've chosen to listen and respond, tuning your heart to the voice of your Savior.

—Lazarus Awakening

Read: Isaiah 43:1

Reflect: How does it feel to know God calls you by name?

April 4

What a wretched man I am! Who will rescue me...? ROMANS 7:24

Sadly, I fear too many Christians accept a zombie-like existence as their fate. We're living resurrected—sort of. But we know our lives should be more joyful. More peaceful. We know we should be loving, kind, forgiving. But instead, too often we're anxious, selfish, and cruel. The odor of our not-yet-decomposed lower nature seems to hang around our lives continually, no matter how many disinfectants we try or room fresheners we plug in.

If you find yourself in this situation, may I ask you a question? Have you ever considered dying? Have you ever considered climbing upon the cross and staying there until Christ's life is able to have its way in you?

Though the Bible is clear that what Jesus did on Calvary was enough to purchase your salvation and mine, a sanctifying work still needs to be done—a holy transaction that requires a kind of death.

Until we "put to death...whatever belongs to [our] earthly nature," as Colossians 3:5 commands, we will never be able to emerge from our tombs and actually "practice resurrection" as Wendell Berry describes it.[42]

"If anyone would come after me," Jesus said in Mark 8:34, "he must deny himself and take up his cross and follow me." But may I submit that it isn't enough just to pick up the cross. We must allow the cross to have its way in us. Continually walking down the Via Dolorosa yet never allowing ourselves to reach Golgotha is not what Jesus meant when He said, "Follow me."

For without a crucifixion, there can be no resurrection.

—*Lazarus Awakening*

READ: Colossians 3:5–10

REFLECT: What things must we put to death and rid ourselves of?

Put off your old self, which is being corrupted by its deceitful desires.
EPHESIANS 4:22

The *how* of putting to death our earthly nature is a question we each must consider. What does "dying to live" look like on a practical level?

For me, it involves rejecting the influence of anything that is in direct opposition to the rule and reign of Christ in my heart, including...

- my desire to control and direct my own life (and the lives of others),
- my right to be treated fairly at all times (and in all ways),
- my need to be well thought of (and thought of frequently), and
- my insatiable appetite for escape (whether through food, television, books, or other avenues).

Did you notice that all these are me-centered desires? Which is exactly the problem. For in order to facilitate Christ's life-changing invasion of the kingdoms in my heart, I must dethrone my lower nature by dying to self and my flesh—the "sinful nature" Paul writes so much about.

"Don't you realize that you become the slave of whatever you choose to obey?" Paul reminds us in Romans 6:16 (NLT). "You can be a slave to sin, which leads to death, or you can choose to obey God, which leads to righteous living."

While I am not my sin, thank the Lord, only I decide whether or not I will be controlled by it. That's why it's so important that I keep saying no to my self-centeredness.

And my tendency toward self-protection and self-pity.

And my natural inclination to be self-absorbed and self-promoting, self-actualizing and self-relying.

The list can go on and on. Just put *self* before nearly anything, and we've got a problem that can only be cured by a crucifixion.

—*Lazarus Awakening*

READ: Psalm 139:23–24

REFLECT: What "me-centered" desires do you struggle with? Take a moment and give God access to those kingdoms in your heart that refuse to bow to His Lordship.

April 6

Therefore, if anyone is in Christ, he is a new creation. 2 Corinthians 5:17

My favorite scene in *The Passion of the Christ* comes as Jesus struggles up the road to Calvary. Though He's bloody, beaten, and nearly dead on His feet, the soldiers whip Him to make Him go on. Trying to reach her Son, Mary fights the crowd, but she can't get to Him. Then, somehow, just as Jesus crumples under the weight of the cross, their paths meet, and for a moment they seem entirely alone.

As blood mixed with the sweat of exhaustion drips from His body, Jesus lifts His face and looks at His mother. Then, with an intensity that still reverberates in my heart today, He speaks these words: "Behold, I make all things new."[43]

"Don't look at what you see," Jesus is telling her. "Remember what you know. Remember what the angel said. Remember the prophecies. Don't forget that I was born to die. For I am the final sacrifice. I lay the path to eternal life upon this road to death. And because I die, you—and all who come afterward—will live. I make all things new. And that includes you."

God's ways rarely make sense to our finite human minds. And if we aren't careful, we will spend most of our life arguing with God rather than embracing His ways.

Doubting His word rather than trusting His power.

Resisting His love rather than resting in His arms.

Remaining the same for fear of the cost of being made new.

—*Having a Mary Spirit*

READ: Matthew 27:15–44

REFLECT: In verses 38–44, the mockers at the cross demanded signs to prove Jesus was God's Son. Do you ever find yourself doing the same thing?

"It is finished," Jesus said just before He died (John 19:30). And with those words came the great exchange. His death became ours so that our lives could become His. Three days later tragedy turned into triumph as the Lamb came bursting forth from the tomb like a Lion. Silencing hell's laughter, Jesus snatched the keys of death and the grave and shattered Satan's schemes, redeeming you and me and causing all the destruction the enemy had perpetrated against us to boomerang back on his deceiving, thieving, troublemaking head.

Christ still does the same recycling work today, taking the garbage of people's lives and fashioning masterpieces of grace. Reclaiming prostitutes and murderers, lepers and beggars, greedy executives and desperate housewives and transforming them into life-size trophies of His love.

This is the power of the gospel. This is the centerpiece of the good news!

"Christ did not come to make bad men good," Ravi Zacharias points out, "but to make dead men alive."[44] For our heavenly Father knew we needed more than a renovation. We needed a resurrection. And that's what Jesus came to bring.

"This sickness will not end in death," Jesus reassured the disciples concerning Lazarus in John 11:4, and He whispers the same hope to you and me today.

Go ahead and fill in the blank with your situation. "Lord, the one You love is _____." Diagnosed with cancer, facing bankruptcy, losing a marriage— the list can go on and on. But not one of those problems is too big for God.

This sickness, this heartache, this life-altering situation will not end in death, Jesus promises. Instead, if we'll respond to His invitation and leave the tombs of our sin and even our doubt, our lives will declare the truth of His next statement: "It is for God's glory."

—*Lazarus Awakening*

READ: Matthew 27:45–54

REFLECT: In light of Jesus's words on the cross, describe a time you felt forsaken but later realized God was working on your behalf all the time.

April 8

The Son of Man must…be crucified and on the third day be raised again.
LUKE 24:7

Philip wasn't like the other children at church. Though he was a pleasant, happy boy, he struggled with things that came easily to other kids. He looked different, too, and everyone knew it was because he had Down syndrome. His Sunday school teacher worked hard to get the third-grade class to play together, but Philip's disability made it difficult for him to fit in.

Easter was just around the corner, and the teacher had a wonderful idea for his class. He gathered the big plastic eggs that pantyhose used to come in and gave one to each child. Then, together, they went outside into a beautiful spring day.

"I want each of you to find something that reminds you of Easter—of new life," the teacher explained. "Put it in the egg, and when we get inside we'll share what we found."

The search was glorious. It was confusing. It was wild. The boys and girls ran all over the church grounds gathering their symbols until finally, breathlessly, the eight-year-olds were ready to return inside.

They put their eggs on the table, then one by one the teacher began to open them. The children stood around the table watching.

He opened one, and there was a flower. Everybody oohed and aahed.

He opened another and found a butterfly. "Beautiful," the girls all said.

But when the teacher opened the last egg, the group fell silent. "There's nothing there!" said one child. "Somebody didn't do it right."[45]…

—*Having a Mary Heart*

READ: Matthew 27:57–66

REFLECT: After Jesus's death, what extra precaution did the chief priests take, and why?

…As the class looked at the empty egg that should have held a memento of Easter, the teacher felt a tug on his shirt and turned to see Philip standing beside him. "It's mine," Philip said.

The children said, "You don't ever do things right, Philip. There's nothing there!"

"I did so," Philip said. "I did do it right. It's empty. *The tomb is empty!*"

There was another silence. A very deep, unlike-eight-year-olds kind of silence. And at that moment a miracle happened. Philip became a part of that third-grade Sunday school class. They took him in.

Three months later, Philip died. His family had known since the time he was born that he wouldn't live out a full life span. An infection that most children would have quickly shrugged off took the life out of his body.

The day of the funeral, the church was filled with people mourning Philip's death. But it was the sight of nine third-graders walking down the aisle with their Sunday school teacher that brought tears to most eyes.

The children didn't bring flowers. Instead, they marched right up to the altar, and placed on it an empty egg—an empty, old, discarded pantyhose egg.[46]

We will all die. Lazarus eventually did. Little Philip did. You and I will.

But never forget: The end is not the end. It is only the beginning. When we belong to Jesus, we simply leave our empty shells behind and go to glory. "Where, O death, is your victory?" Paul writes to remind us in 1 Corinthians 15:55. "Where, O death, is your sting?"

—*Having a Mary Heart*

READ: Matthew 28:1–20

REFLECT: What does Jesus's promise in the last part of verse 20 mean to you?

April 10

I am the resurrection and the life. He who believes in me will live. JOHN 11:25

My prayer is that we will discover afresh and anew the incredible, life-bringing power of Jesus Christ. Not just in theory. Not by intellect or mere head knowledge, but by the work of the Holy Spirit.

Resurrection life! For you and for me. Not someday when Christ returns, but today. Right now. Right here. In your heart and mine.

What a big prayer. What a huge expectation! But that's exactly what Jesus made possible for you and me. He died and rose again so that we could know beyond any shadow of a doubt that we are loved, that we are accepted, that we are fully and completely forgiven.

Jesus died so we could experience new life. He didn't allow Himself to be stripped naked and beaten nearly to death so we could experience spiritual ecstasies now and then. He didn't go through the pain and humiliation of the cross so we could sit in church Sunday after Sunday blandly singing about His sacrifice but never experiencing His resurrection power. He didn't go to hell and snatch the keys of death and the grave from Satan's icy grip just so we could write volumes of theological debate to fill shelves or make us wiser than the next guy.

Our Savior died and He rose again from the grave so that you and I could be born again. So that we could have a fresh start and a clean heart every single day of our lives. He did it all to prove His love. So you and I could know that there is nothing—absolutely nothing!—that can separate us from the love of God that is in Christ Jesus.

—Outtake from *Lazarus Awakening*

READ: Romans 8:38–39
REFLECT: Write out this passage, and post it somewhere you will see it often. Consider memorizing it.

I have come that they may have life, and have it to the full. John 10:10

April 11

Many months behind on my *Lazarus Awakening* deadline, an invitation to speak at a church event in California stirred something in my heart, and I agreed to go.

I had no idea the location was Lazarusville.

The host church, birthed out of the 1970s Jesus movement, was filled with resurrection stories. Everywhere I turned, I met yet another person who had been spiritually dead and now lived again. After getting saved, my former-hippie hostess answered God's call to go back home and love her parents. She did. Not just in word but also in deed.

So drastic was the change in her that both of her parents accepted the Lord. "I gave birth to my daughter," her dear mama told me, eyes all alight, "and she gave birth to me!"

One woman I met was brought to Jesus through her little boy. After years of looking for love in all the wrong places, Robin finally encountered the love of God through a memory verse her son had learned in Sunday school. "[Cast] all your care upon Him, for He cares for you," the little boy recited to his mother (1 Peter 5:7, NKJV).

"Who's 'Him'?" she asked sarcastically.

"Jesus, Mama," he said solemnly. "Jesus cares for you."

Those four little words broke something hard inside Robin. Though she was too proud to take her son to church that Sunday, she followed the bus and slipped in a side door. There she found the Love she'd been looking for her whole life.

Transformation. It was all around me that weekend. The sound of butterfly wings and souls metamorphosing in the presence of the Lord. Lazaruses and Lazarellas—every one of them.

—Lazarus Awakening

READ: 1 Corinthians 1:4–6

REFLECT: Turn this portion of Scripture into a prayer, asking that the "testimony about Christ" be confirmed within you.

April 12

To this end I labor, struggling with all his energy, which so powerfully works in me. Colossians 1:29

In her devotional classic *Springs in the Valley,* Lettie B. Cowman tells the story of a naturalist who spotted a large butterfly fluttering frantically as if in distress. It appeared to be caught on something. The man reached down, took hold of its wings, and set it free. The butterfly flew only a few feet before falling to the ground, dead.

Under a magnifying glass in his lab, the naturalist discovered blood flowing from tiny veins in the lovely creature's wings. He realized that inadvertently he had interrupted something very important. The butterfly's frantic fluttering had really been an attempt to emerge from its chrysalis—a strength-building process designed by God. If allowed to struggle long enough, the butterfly would have come forth ready for long and wide flight. Early release, however, ended that beautiful dream.

So it is with God's children, Mrs. Cowman writes.

How the Father wishes for them wide ranges in experience and truth. He permits us to be fastened to some form of struggle. We would tear ourselves free. We cry out in our distress and sometimes think Him cruel that He does not release us. He permits us to flutter and flutter on. Struggle seems to be His program sometimes.[47]

Perhaps that is why Lazarus had to come out of the tomb of his own volition—why Jesus called him out instead of sending Martha and Mary inside to get him. Resurrection often seems to require a willing response, even a struggle, on the part of the one being resurrected. Tombs can be comfortable, remember. And choosing to live can be hard.

—Lazarus Awakening

Read: 1 Corinthians 15:10

Reflect: According to this verse, what part does grace play in transformation, and how should we cooperate with that grace?

You are forgiving and good, O Lord, abounding in love to all who call to you. Psalm 86:5

April 13

We are not forgiven because we feel bad. We are not forgiven because deep down we're really good people and God knows that so He grants us pardon. We are not even forgiven because of God's amazing love. The only reason we're forgiven is because of what Jesus Christ did on the cross. Period.

But we must *appropriate* what He did. We must choose to *believe* that the work on the cross was enough to purchase freedom from sin for us.

That so many of us miss the great riches of righteousness available to us in Christ is the greatest tragedy of the church today. To settle for so little when Jesus has provided so much is like having a billion dollars sitting in a bank account under our name and at our disposal, yet never going to the bank to make a withdrawal.

What Christ has done for you and me through His death and resurrection is essentially to make a huge deposit in our account. His righteousness, according to Romans 4:11 (NKJV), has been "imputed" to us—that is, put under our name. We have been sanctified—set apart and made holy. Jesus's right standing before God and His power for right living are now ours.

For the asking.

For the taking.

But ask we must, and take we should.

Otherwise everything Christ has provided for us sits in the bank while we wander the streets of life, begging for bread, looking for meaning, trying to tell others about the goodness of God while we ourselves are starving, wretched, naked, and cold.

—Having a Mary Spirit

READ: Ephesians 1:3–8
REFLECT: Write down all the benefits of belonging to Jesus.

April 14

The LORD will perfect that which concerns me.... Do not forsake the works of Your hands. PSALM 138:8, NKJV

It takes a process to get a product. The car I drive didn't suddenly appear on the dealer's showroom floor. The house I live in took four months to build—and much longer if you take into account the growing season of the trees used to build it and the mining required to form the nails.

The same is true of our Christian walk. Becoming like Jesus requires a process.

Somewhere deep in my heart I had always harbored the hope that when I *really* gave my heart to Christ, I would pop out of a Holy Ghost phone booth completely clothed in blue and red with a big *S* plastered across my chest for "SUPER CHRISTIAN!" I'd be able to leap tall stumbling blocks in a single bound. I'd be faster than the fiery darts of the enemy. More powerful than all of hell's temptations.

Well, it didn't happen. In truth, I've resembled a mild-mannered, albeit female, Clark Kent more often than I've looked like any spiritual superhero. Some days it's all I can do to get out of bed. And try as I might, I've never gotten the outfit down.

You can imagine how relieved I felt when I finally got it through my head that Christianity is a process and not an event. It is a journey, not a destination.

"I thought it had been an easy thing to be a Christian," Samuel Rutherford wrote several centuries ago, "but oh, the windings, the turnings, the ups and the downs that he has led me through."[48] It is the twisting tests of life that produce character and faithfulness to God, Rutherford concludes.

And I've found that true as well.

—Having a Mary Heart

READ: Philippians 1:6

REFLECT: In the middle of your individual "process," in what can you have confidence?

The LORD disciplines those he loves.
PROVERBS 3:12

April 15

Some of life's greatest gifts come wrapped in disappointments. Listen to Charles Haddon Spurgeon's thoughts on Jesus's response to His disciples concerning Lazarus's death in John 11:15:

> If you want to ruin your son, never let him know a hardship. When he is a child carry him in your arms, when he becomes a youth still dandle him, and when he becomes a man still dry-nurse him, and you will succeed in producing an arrant fool. If you want to prevent his being made useful in the world, guard him from every kind of toil.... Do not suffer him to struggle. Wipe the sweat from his dainty brow and say, "Dear child, thou shalt never have another task so arduous." Pity him when he ought to be punished; supply all his wishes, avert all disappointments, prevent all troubles, and you will surely tutor him to be a reprobate and to break your heart. But put him where he must work, expose him to difficulties, purposely throw him into peril, and in this way you shall make him a man, and when he comes to do man's work and to bear man's trial, he shall be fit for either. My Master does not daintily cradle His children when they ought to run alone; and when they begin to run He is not always putting out His finger for them to lean upon, but He lets them tumble down to the cutting of their knees, because then they will walk more carefully by-and-by, and learn to stand upright by the strength which faith confers upon them....
>
> Jesus Christ was glad—glad that His disciples were blessed by trouble. Will you think of this, you who are so troubled this morning, Jesus Christ does sympathize with you, but still He does it wisely, and He says, "I am glad for your sakes that I was not there."[49]

—*Lazarus Awakening*

READ: Hebrews 12:7–11
REFLECT: How should we face hardship, and why?

April 16

Because you humbled yourself before me...I have heard you, declares the LORD. 2 CHRONICLES 34:27

In *The Voyage of the Dawn Treader,* C. S. Lewis tracks the adventures of an obnoxious boy named Eustace Grubb. While the ship is docked at an unknown island, the rebellious boy stumbles across a great pile of treasure in an abandoned dragon's lair. Eustace stuffs his pockets with jewels and gold, then falls asleep with dark dragonish thoughts filling his heart. When he awakes, Eustace finds he's become a dragon himself.

Dismayed, Eustace wants to be different. He tries to be different. But at the end of every day, he remains the same—a boy trapped inside a dragon's body.

One night Eustace meets the great lion Aslan, who leads him to a clear pool and tells him to "undress" before he goes in. Three times Eustace scratches at his scales and sheds his dragonish skin. But each time, he finds yet another layer underneath.

"You have to let me undress you," the Lion tells him. Here's how Eustace describes the process:

> The very first tear he made was so deep that I thought it had gone right into my heart. And when he began pulling the skin off, it hurt worse than anything I've ever felt. The only thing that made me able to bear it was just the pleasure of feeling the stuff peel off.... Well, he peeled the beastly stuff right off—just as I thought I'd done it myself the other three times, only they hadn't hurt—and there it was lying in the grass: only ever so much thicker, and darker, and more knobbly looking than the others had been. [50]

Naked and trembling, Eustace bathes in the pool and is once again a boy. Aslan gives him a new set of clothes and transports him back to his new life. His transformed life....

—*Having a Mary Spirit*

READ: Ezekiel 36:25–27
REFLECT: What does God promise to do for us if we'll allow it?

As far as the east is from the west, so far has He removed our transgressions from us. PSALM 103:12, NKJV

April 17

…Oh how we all need de-dragoning, every one of us. Left to ourselves we can only scratch and claw, making small amounts of progress, but little semblance of change. Until we lay our lives before the great Lion of Judah, asking Him to do the work, our efforts at self-improvement will only yield one layer of dragon-ish sin after another.

Perhaps that's why Paul implores us, "in view of God's mercy, to offer [ourselves] as living sacrifices, holy and pleasing to God" (Romans 12:1).

Climb up on the operating table, Paul advises. Put your entire self in the trustworthy hands of Christ. Let the divine Surgeon remove the fleshly encasement of sin that has bound you too long. Lie still under the razor-sharp scalpel of Christ's unfailing love and allow Him to release what you were created to be.

I love how C. S. Lewis concludes the story. "It would be nice, and fairly nearly true, to say that 'from that time forth Eustace was a different boy.' To be strictly accurate, he began to be a different boy. He had relapses.... But most of these I shall not notice. The cure had begun."[51]

And so has it begun for us as well.

Though I'm not yet what I ought to be, thank God, I'm not what I was.

And neither are you. For "he who began a good work in you will carry it on to completion until the day of Christ Jesus," Philippians 1:6 assures us. Though we may not see the finished product until heaven, you can be sure that what God has started, He will finish. And as long as we daily relinquish control of our lives to Jesus Christ, our transformation will continue.

And we will never be the same.

—Having a Mary Spirit

READ: Hebrews 7:25
REFLECT: What does the thought of Jesus interceding on your behalf mean to you?

April 18

No one who trusts in you will ever be disgraced. PSALM 25:3, NLT

"Lord, don't you care?" Like Martha, we have our questions. Like Martha, we have our doubts. I'm so glad God isn't threatened by our doubts and questions, our fears or even our frustration. He wants us to trust His love enough to tell Him what we are thinking and feeling. In Psalm 62:8, we're told, "Trust in him at all times, O people; pour out your hearts to him, for God is our refuge."

Our friend Martha was on the right track that day in Bethany. Instead of allowing her doubtful questions to fester, she took her worries and her fears and voiced them to Jesus. While her bristling, abrasive approach is hardly the best model, there are still several important lessons we can learn from her gutsy encounter with Christ.

First, *we can bring our needs to Jesus anytime and anywhere.* "Ask and it will be given to you," Jesus said in Matthew 7:7. In the Greek, the form of the word for "ask" implies "keep on asking." We can't wear our Savior out. He's never too busy to hear our hearts' cries.

Second, *Jesus really cares about what concerns us.* "Cast all your anxiety on him," 1 Peter 5:7 tells us, "because he cares for you." Jesus didn't laugh off Martha's concerns. He spoke to her with infinite gentleness and tenderness, recognizing the pain behind her whining words.

Finally, *Jesus loves us enough to confront us when our attitude is wrong.* "Those whom I love," says the Lord, "I rebuke and discipline" (Revelation 3:19). And that is what the Savior did with Martha. He intuitively understood Martha's pain, but that didn't stop Him from telling her what she needed to hear. And Martha, to her credit, listened.

—*Having a Mary Heart*

READ: Deuteronomy 31:8
REFLECT: In light of His promise to never leave or forsake you, thank God for the ways He meets you in the three areas mentioned above.

"Willingness to die is the price you must pay if you want to be raised from the dead to live and work and walk in the power of the third morning," Major Ian Thomas writes. "Once the willingness to die is there for us, there are no more issues to face, only instructions to obey."[52]

Walking in the power of the third morning. Practicing resurrection. More of Jesus and less of me. It all comes down to dying to self—of that, I am convinced. So was George Müller, whose work in England's orphanages made him famous in the last half of the nineteenth century:

> To one who asked him the secret of his service he said: "There was a day when I died, *utterly died*"; and, as he spoke, he bent lower and lower until he almost touched the floor—"died to George Müller, his opinions, preferences, tastes, and will—died to the world, its approval or censure—died to the approval or blame even of my brethren and friends—and since then I have studied only to show myself 'approved unto God.'"[53]

I don't know what that story does to you, but every time I read it, I feel compelled to hold yet another funeral in my own life…and then another. For while I wish I could tell you my resurrection required only one death and one burial, it wouldn't be true. Instead, my story has many obituaries.

For there is a daily dying that must take place if we want to really live.

—*Lazarus Awakening*

Read: Philippians 3:10–11
Reflect: Take a moment and write a short obituary, listing the things that you need to "die to" as George Müller did.

April 20

Then you will know the truth, and the truth will set you free. JOHN 8:32

While only Christ can make dead men live, only we can remove the obstacles that stand between us and our Savior.

All of us, you see, have blockages in our souls that we've allowed and perhaps even nurtured. False beliefs we've internalized as truth, to the point we believe them before we believe God. As a result, many of us have become, as Craig Groeschel puts it, Christian atheists—"believing in God but living as if He doesn't exist."[54]

I've identified three specific "boulders" that I believe many Christians struggle with. Three obstacles we must examine and relinquish so that God can do the work He longs to do. For while Lazarus was powerless to roll away the stone that sealed his tomb, we are not. Our choices and attitudes really do make a difference in our ability to accept Christ's offer of freedom.

So what stones must be rolled away?

The first is the stone of unworthiness—the lie that we are unloved and unlovable.

The second is the stone of unforgiveness—the lie that we must hold on to the hurts of the past.

And the third is the stone of unbelief—the lie that God can't or won't help us, so we must do everything ourselves.

Unworthiness, unforgiveness, unbelief—they're daunting, intimidating blockages that lock us in and cut us off. But not one of them is impossible to remove. Not when we put our shoulders to our boulders and cry out to God for help.

—*Lazarus Awakening*

READ: Isaiah 57:14

REFLECT: What obstacles are blocking access to your heart today?

For troubles without number surround me; my sins have overtaken me, and I cannot see. PSALM 40:12

April 21

Remember my friend Lisa, the vibrant Christian who confessed that she could tell everyone else Jesus loved them but couldn't convince herself she was accepted by God?

As she and I spent time together that day, we asked the Holy Spirit to reveal the boulder that was blocking her heart from truly receiving the good news of God's love.

With tears running down her cheeks, Lisa shared something that had haunted her for years. A secret she had told no one, not even her husband. "I had an abortion in high school. But not just one, Joanna. I had multiple abortions." Sobs shook my friend's body. "How could God ever forgive me?" she asked, finally voicing the fear-filled unworthiness that had entombed her for the majority of her life. "How could He ever love me after what I've done?"

I held my friend as she cried and poured out her grief—grief not only for her sin but also for the children she'd never known. "Don't you know, Lisa?" I whispered against her hair as a revelation suddenly hit my heart. "Don't you know that's why Jesus had to come? That's why He had to die."

We've all sinned. We've all fallen short of what is best and good and right. We've all taken shortcuts of convenience, choosing to ignore God's law and invoking the consequences. My goody-two-shoes past was and is just as dark and sin laced as Lisa's wild years.

"He doesn't forgive us because we deserve it," I told her as well as myself. "God forgives us because we so desperately need it."

And that is what makes the good news so very, very good. The price has been paid. Our part is to accept the gift Christ offers.

—*Lazarus Awakening*

READ: Psalm 130:3–4

REFLECT: What past sin still haunts you at times? What good news do you find in these verses?

April 22

He who conceals his sins does not prosper, but whoever confesses and renounces them finds mercy. PROVERBS 28:13

Your sin and mine have resulted in a type of death—death of hope, death of confidence, death of any future happiness.

But Jesus took it all on the cross. And in the process He broke the yardstick—the condemnation that has hung over our lives, declaring us unworthy.

As my friend Lisa discovered, His sacrifice has the power to roll away our shame if we will allow it. Because of Christ's death we have been accepted into the ranks of the righteous. Our track record has nothing to do with it—we need to settle that fact forever. The only thing that saves us is the cross and nothing but the cross. We can't add to it, nor can we diminish it. We simply have to embrace it. And when we do, the stone of unworthiness rolls away.

It has been thrilling to watch Lisa resurrect! Though she'd repented of her sin years before, it wasn't until she revealed her secret to someone else, as frightening as that must have been, that she experienced a breakthrough in her relationship with the Lord.

Perhaps that's why the Holy Spirit inspired James, a brother of Jesus, to write, "Confess your sins to each other and pray for each other so that you may be healed" (James 5:16). While it didn't happen overnight, Lisa's healing has come. Today she shares her story with junior-high and high-school students, urging them to commit to sexual purity but also reminding them that there is forgiveness and a fresh start in Jesus Christ.

What once brought Lisa great shame is now being used by God to bring Him great glory. It all started with a courageous decision to roll away her stone.

—Lazarus Awakening

READ: Psalm 32:5 and James 5:16
REFLECT: If you've struggled with the lie of unworthiness, use these two verses as a guide to confession and repentance.

Sometimes, the good news can seem just too good to receive. After all, the free grace that Jesus Christ offers to anyone who believes in Him can be quite scandalous.

Author Donald Miller describes this beautifully in his wry account of his own struggle with the message of grace. He tells about a time when "I used to get really ticked about preachers who talked too much about grace, because they tempted me to not be disciplined." Miller writes, "I believed if word got out about grace, the whole church was going to turn into a brothel." (He adds, pointedly, "I was a real jerk, I think.")

Miller had fallen into the Pharisee trap that tends to trip us all—as he puts it, "trying to discipline myself to 'behave' as if I loved light and not 'behave' as if I loved darkness."[55] But the only thing this macho, legalistic type of self-improvement brought him was failure and despair.

The Law outlined in the Old Testament serves an important purpose: It illuminates the sin in our lives. But that's all the Law can do. It can show us what's wrong with us, but it is absolutely powerless to make us right. By itself, it is incapable of bridging the chasm that sin made between *Abba* God and His children—the gaping crevasse in our souls that leaves us forever lonely, forever removed from the only love that can make us whole.

Bottom line, self-induced holiness is a miserable exercise in futility. For no matter how strictly we observe it, the Law will never make us righteous. It will never come close to making us changed, different, Christlike people.

Only grace—God's grace—has the power to make us new.

—Having a Mary Spirit

READ: Ephesians 2:8–9
REFLECT: Have you ever fallen into the "Pharisee trap" described above? What keeps you from receiving the good news of grace?

April 24

Though your sins are like scarlet, they shall be as white as snow. ISAIAH 1:18

Whitewashed tombs were common in Jesus's day. Especially during the Passover and other religious festivals, graves were painted bright white so no one would accidentally touch them at night, becoming ceremonially unclean and thus unfit to worship. Such tombs might look beautiful on the outside, Jesus reminded the crowd, but their insides were filled with dead, rotting things and "everything unclean" (Matthew 23:27).

Christ offers us a "personal whiteness"[56] so white that the human mind cannot comprehend, but only receive it. It doesn't come through our striving, our internal grubbing and external scrubbing. Only the mighty power of God working within us—the same power that raised Christ from the grave—can change us from the inside out.

You see, God doesn't want us whitewashing our tombs.

He wants to raise us from the dead.

I don't know how I missed this amazing and important reality. I was raised in a grace-filled home and a grace-filled church. But, as a young adult, I somehow fell for the lie that after I accepted Jesus as my Savior, the rest was up to me. As though, after an initial warm hug of welcome, God had tossed me into the sea of life, stepped back, and crossed His arms as if to say, "It's up to you now, sweetheart—sink or swim."

But no matter how fast I paddled, no matter how hard I tried to keep my head above water, my efforts were never enough. The only thing my inner Pharisee had given me was deep despair and hopeless frustration. But coming to the end of myself also turned me towards freedom.

—*Having a Mary Spirit*

READ: Psalm 22:4–5

REFLECT: Describe a time when coming to the end of yourself helped you turn to God.

Forgive as the Lord forgave you.
Colossians 3:13

April 25

For many of us, our tombstones and spiritual blockages result from what has been done to us—and our attitudes about it. We've been hurt. We've been falsely accused or misunderstood, misused or betrayed. And we can't seem to get past our anger, resentment, or bitterness.

We *want* to forgive—well, most of the time. Trouble is, we aren't sure we *can* forgive. The hurt has gone so deep that the tendrils of our pain seem to go on forever. How do you let go of something that has such a hold on you?

That was my dilemma several years ago. "I have to get alone with God," I told my husband, John. "I'm in a very bad place."

We'd walked through a trying time in ministry, and for the most part I'd handled it pretty well. A space of grace had opened up for me to walk through the difficulty without feeling the intense need to fix it or change the people involved. Opportunities for self-pity had floated through my mind before, but up to that point I hadn't indulged them. Instead, I'd been experiencing the also-miraculous phenomenon of a disciplined mind.

I'd learned that just because a painful recollection came to memory, I didn't have to embrace it—a revolutionary discovery, let me tell you. Instead of nursing and rehearsing the past, with the Holy Spirit's help, I was learning to disperse it, refusing the offense entrance to my heart and, more important, denying it occupancy in my mind.

But somewhere near the anniversary of the hurt, I began to nurse a grudge against someone in the situation. Pain-laced memories began to stick in my craw and bother me anew as the darkness of resentment cast its shadow over my heart.…

—*Lazarus Awakening*

Read: Proverbs 20:22

Reflect: What injustice or "wrong" do you need to release to the Lord?

April 26

A man's wisdom gives him patience;
it is to his glory to overlook an offense.
Proverbs 19:11

...After experiencing so much victory in my thinking, I grew a bit careless. A particularly painful memory slipped in through a side entrance of my mind. At first it was so tiny I hardly noticed it. But as I allowed my hurt a platform to state its woes, it began to grow, and a boulder of unforgiveness began to move across my soul.

Finally the chill of bitterness sank in so deep I couldn't even find the "want to" to forgive. That terrified me. With John's blessing, I holed up in a friend's cabin and poured out my heart before the Lord. It was slow going at first. My emotions were rock hard, but as I hammered out obedience to forgiveness, things began to change.

At the Spirit's prompting, I wrote a letter to the person who had hurt me. I didn't measure my words; I just spilled out my pain. I knew I had to get honest before God about what I was feeling in order for the infection to drain from my heart.

Other letters followed, but not one would be postmarked. I wasn't writing them for anyone but me. My friends may not have felt the stranglehold of my judgment, but I certainly had. Finally, I wrote a letter to God, relinquishing all rights to resentment and asking Him to bless the people involved.

I was absolutely exhausted when I penned the last note. But with the exhaustion came the beginning of a sweet sense of release.

For in the mind-over-emotion choice to forgive, my stone of unforgiveness started to move. And somewhere in the letting go of those who had hurt me, I walked out free.

—*Lazarus Awakening*

Read: Ephesians 4:32

Reflect: In order to "forgive one another as quickly and thoroughly as God in Christ forgave you" (msg), consider writing a letter(s) of release today.

Grant me a willing spirit, to sustain me. PSALM 51:12

April 27

Do you ever find yourself clinging to the pencil, refusing to let God write on the pages of your life? I've discovered that the Lord is infinitely kind and patient in His dealings with us. He will show us how to relinquish our rights for His best. If you're struggling in this area, maybe these steps will help you:

1. ***Ask God to make you willing.*** Sometimes this is the necessary first step. If you just can't muster up the willingness to surrender control to God, then pray first for a change of attitude, asking for a willingness to be willing.

2. ***Recognize you have an adversary.*** The last thing Satan wants is for you to totally surrender your life to God. Pray for the wisdom and strength not to listen to his lies. Then pick up "the sword of the Spirit, which is the word of God" (Ephesians 6:17) and battle those lies with truth.

3. ***Let go, one piece at a time.*** Sometimes we cling to control because we fear we'll be asked to make drastic changes we're not ready for. But God, in His kindness, takes us at a pace we can handle. If we will obey what He asks of us at the moment, He'll lead us to the next step when we need to take it.

—*Having a Mary Heart*

READ: Philippians 3:7–8

REFLECT: Is there something you need to surrender to God? Prayerfully walk through the steps outlined above, asking the Lord to give you specific directions as to how to let go.

April 28

May he turn our hearts to him, to walk in all his ways. 1 KINGS 8:58

Desperate to serve God with his whole heart, Brother Lawrence joined a monastery. But as hard as the poor monk tried to be holy and without sin, he constantly failed. Finally, as he describes in his timeless book *The Practice of the Presence of God,* he began to converse openly and honestly with the Lord. Looking to Christ rather than to his own character for strength, Brother Lawrence flung himself entirely upon God's mercy and grace.

When faced with an opportunity to practice a virtue, he prayed, "Lord, I cannot do this unless Thou enablest me."

And when he failed, he was quick to acknowledge, "I shall never do otherwise if You leave me to myself; it is You who must hinder my falling and mend what is amiss."

After doing that, his biographer writes, Brother Lawrence "gave himself no further uneasiness about it."[57]

Do those words minister to you as they do to me? To think we can have such an intimate relationship with the Almighty that we no longer have to whitewash our faults or deny our need of Him—well, that blesses me. For true relationship must be based on honesty. The only way we will ever experience lasting change is to be willing to stand naked and needy before our heavenly Father. Honest and bold in our request.

Yearning for His transforming touch, yet secure in His steadfast love.

—Having a Mary Spirit

READ: Romans 8:31–33

REFLECT: How does it comfort your heart to know God is for you?

May your unfailing love rest upon us,
O LORD, even as we put our hope in you.
PSALM 33:22

April 29

Nothing is more detrimental than allowing the stone of unbelief to wedge itself between us and the heart of God. I appreciate the honesty with which Ann Spangler writes of her struggle to truly believe in the love of God.

> I have never found it easy to believe in God's love for me, except perhaps in the first days and weeks of my conversion.... Nearly every prayer in those days was answered, sometimes wondrously. I remember thinking that the problem with many people was that they expected so little from a God who was prepared to give so much.
>
> But years passed and something happened. It wasn't one thing but many.... It was tests of faith [and...] sins accruing. It was disappointments and difficulties beyond comprehending. All these heaped together like a great black mound, casting a shadow over my sense that God still loved me, still cared for me as tenderly as when he had first... won my heart.[58]

In an attempt to recapture that sense of God's love, Ann went back to the promises of the Bible. Unfortunately, "like many people who tend to be self-critical," she writes, "I find it easier to absorb the harsher sounding passages in the Bible.... Somehow, the tender words seem to roll right off me, much like water that beads up and rolls off a well-waxed automobile."[59]

But Ann persisted. Over the next year, she immersed herself in the Word of God, allowing truth to wash over her until God's love stopped being a concept and started to feel like a reality.

"Act as though God loves you," a friend advised her. And that's what Ann did. She put the full force of her mind behind believing the truth, exercising her faith rather than depending on her feelings.

And the stone of unbelief began to roll away.

—Lazarus Awakening

READ & REFLECT: Using a concordance or Bible website, look up several verses on the love of God. Write them out, then choose one to memorize.

April 30

See to it, brothers, that none of you has a sinful, unbelieving heart that turns away from the living God. HEBREWS 3:12

I don't think any of us set out deliberately to block ourselves off with stones of unworthiness, unforgiveness, and/or unbelief. But boulders often roll across the doors of our hearts unnoticed. Perhaps it's time to get out the heavy equipment and, with the Holy Spirit's help, begin removing the blockage in your soul.

For Lisa, the lie of unworthiness required the blasting cap of confession. Before she could live free, she had to reveal the dark secret that had kept her spiritually gagged and emotionally bound for most of her adult life.

For me, a jackhammer of forgiveness was needed to break the rock of resentment lodged against my heart. I had to relinquish my right to be offended so that I might choose instead to forgive.

For Ann, the rock of unbelief required a large dose of the *dunamis*—or dynamite[60]—of God's Word. Once she chose to exalt His truth over her feelings, the lie that she was unloved could finally be removed.

"Take away the stone," Jesus commanded those standing around Lazarus's tomb on that long-ago day in Bethany (John 11:39). Though Martha was clearly uncomfortable with the idea, she chose to obey. Though she didn't fully understand why Jesus asked what He asked, she did what she could so that Jesus could do the rest.

And in a sense, that's all Christ asks of you and me.

Roll away the stone, beloved. Do what only you can do. Choose to receive My love…choose to forgive…choose to trust in Me no matter what. Then watch what I will do.

—*Lazarus Awakening*

READ: John 8:36 and Joshua 18:3

REFLECT: What is keeping you from taking possession of the freedom that is yours in Christ?

Hope deferred makes the heart sick.
PROVERBS 13:12

May 1

In John 11:5–6, we see this strange paradox: "Jesus *loved* Martha and her sister and Lazarus. *Yet* when he heard that Lazarus was sick, he *stayed* where he was two more days" (emphasis mine).

Jesus loved…yet He stayed where He was.

He loved…but He didn't show up when He was expected.

How can that be? our hearts cry. It just doesn't make sense.

And that is the core of our problem, isn't it? Because most of the love-doubt we feel can be traced back to troubling contradictions not unlike the one in the story of Lazarus. Doubts that eat away at the bedrock of our faith, leaving us floundering, gasping for air as we try to keep our spiritual heads above water.

I'm sure the sorrow Mary and Martha felt must have threatened to swamp all they knew and believed about Jesus. It certainly left them shaken.

John 11:20 tells us, "When Martha heard that Jesus was coming, she went out to meet him, but Mary stayed at home."

Two different responses from two very different sisters—and unexpected ones, at that. Strangely, it was the sister who had once questioned Jesus's love ("Lord, don't you care?" Luke 10:40), who now went running toward Him. While the sister who had sat at the Master's feet in sweet communion remained in the house, paralyzed by grief.

A condition all of us experience at one time or another.

—*Lazarus Awakening*

READ: Psalm 46:1–2
REFLECT: Where do you tend to run in times of trouble?

May 2

Trust in him at all times, O people; pour out your hearts to him, for God is our refuge. PSALM 62:8

I have no way of knowing for sure, but I believe Martha ran to Jesus because she had already gone through a testing of faith, while Mary was just entering that crucible process (as eventually all of us do).

As strange as it might sound, it may have been the Lord's denial of what Martha had wanted earlier in their relationship that allowed her to find what her heart needed most on that grief-filled day.

Rather than responding with practical help when she demanded more assistance in the kitchen, Jesus had simply replied, "Martha, Martha,...you are worried and upset about many things, but only one thing is needed" (Luke 10:41–42). With those words, He'd exposed Martha's biggest problem—and her deepest need.

She hadn't needed more help in the kitchen. She'd needed the "one thing"—Jesus Himself. Though His rebuke must have hurt, I believe Martha took His words to heart. As she humbled herself and embraced the Lord's correction, her heart was enabled to embrace His love. No wonder she was the sister who ran down the road to meet Jesus after her brother died.

Somewhere in that earlier time of testing, I believe Martha discovered three marvelous, indomitable truths we all need to know. Three rock-solid facts on which we too can rest our hearts:

1. God is *love*—therefore I am loved.
2. God is *good*—therefore I am safe.
3. God is *faithful*—therefore it's going to be okay. For God is incapable of doing anything less than marvelous things.[61]

—Lazarus Awakening

READ: Proverbs 3:5–6

REFLECT: In light of these verses, what three things should we do when our faith is tested, and what will God do on our behalf?

Martha chose to trust God's love and His faithful goodness. Because of that, when tough times came, she was able to trust His sovereignty as well—His right to do as He deems best, when and how He wants to do it.

That's why she could run to Jesus, fall at His feet, and pour out her heart with both pain and sweet abandon. "Lord," she cried, "if you had been here, my brother would not have died. But I know that even now God will give you whatever you ask" (John 11:21–22).

Here is the quill of my will, Lord, Martha was saying. *You write the end of the story. For You do all things well.*

Surrendering the quill of my will has always been a difficult process for me. You see, I have such good ideas about how my story, not to mention the stories of the people I love, should be written.

Unfortunately, none of my planning and plotting has ever drawn me closer to God. In fact, it usually does the opposite. For while I'm busy scheming, my Father is apt to move on, leaving me to work the angles on my own. *That wasn't My plan, Joanna,* He gently whispers when I finally call out to Him. *If you want to walk with Me, you have to surrender your itinerary and trust Mine.*

Surrender was the key to Martha's amazing transformation, and it is the key to ours as well.

—*Lazarus Awakening*

READ: Daniel 3:1–18

REFLECT: Are you facing pressure to bow to someone or something other than God? Take a moment and declare verses 16–18 aloud, paraphrasing them to fit your situation.

May 4

Sometimes a picture is worth a thousand words.

My thirty-something birthday had dawned bright and busy. Tucked into a pile of bills and credit-card applications I found a card sent from my friend Janet McHenry. The picture on the front illustrated everything I'd been feeling that dreary, getting-older day.

"That's me," I said to my husband, poking at the black-and-white glossy of a young woman with eight or nine Hula-Hoops swinging madly around her waist. "How does she do that?" I wanted to know.

It had been a frustrating day of too many responsibilities and not enough me to go around. One by one, I named the Hula-Hoops I had been trying to keep in motion: wife, mother, pastor's wife, friend, writer, piano instructor, cook, cleaning lady, and the big one—Little League mother.

I looked once more at the girl on the card. There were so many hoops, but she appeared calm. Her face captured me. Looking straight into the camera, she smiled peacefully as though she hadn't a care in the world.

Then it dawned on me—I saw her secret. "She found a rhythm," I whispered to myself. "She established her center, then let everything move around that."

That's exactly what I *wasn't* doing in my life. All the things I'd been trying to accomplish were important, but I had lost my center. Busy being busy, I'd forgotten to tend to my inner self, the spiritual me.

If there was an adequate pause, I'd spend some time with the Lord. But lately, more often than not, my busy days had slipped by without a quiet time. And my life was revealing what my spirit had missed.

"Teach me, Lord. Show me the rhythm of life," I found myself praying. "Be my center."

—Having a Mary Heart

 READ: 1 Chronicles 16:11

REFLECT: Use this verse as a template to pray over your day.

So we fix our eyes not on what is seen, but on what is unseen. 2 CORINTHIANS 4:18

May 5

As I read the note included in the birthday card I held in my hand, I couldn't help but marvel at the work God had done in the life of my friend who'd sent it.

A year earlier, a number of painful crises, including an unjust lawsuit, had slammed into her family's lives without warning. Melancholy in personality, yet driven to excel, Janet found herself swamped by despair. She couldn't fix her situation. She couldn't change it. But in the middle of it all, God was calling her to Himself.

Each morning before work, Janet donned her sweats and spent an hour walking around her small California town, praying for people and situations as they came to mind. "I can't believe the change getting alone with God is making in my life," she wrote in the birthday card. "I actually caught myself singing the other day!"[62]

Hudson Taylor once said, "We will all have trials. The question is not when the pressure will come, but where the pressure will lie. Will it come between us and the Lord? Or will it press us ever closer to His breast?"[63] Rather than let her circumstances drag her away from God, Janet chose to let them draw her closer.

My friend was experiencing the truth Selwyn Hughes writes about: "Life works better when we know how to glance at things but gaze at God. Seeing Him clearly will enable us to see all other things clearly."[64]

—Having a Mary Heart

READ: Hebrews 12:2–3
REFLECT: Why should we look to Jesus?

May 6

Words kill, words give life; they're either poison or fruit—you choose.
PROVERBS 18:21, MSG

How does your life sound? What if a hidden microphone were recording every exchange in your house? at your job? in your marriage? What if someone threatened to play those recordings back on the local nightly news? How much would you pay to have the tapes destroyed?

The thought of having to give account for our words is enough to make most women break out in a cold sweat! Yet that is exactly what the Bible says we will have to do one day: "But I tell you that men will have to give account on the day of judgment for every careless word they have spoken," Matthew 12:36–37 tells us. "For by your words you will be acquitted, and by your words you will be condemned."

Wow. Does that hit you like it hits me? Although I am saved by grace and I am bound for heaven, the Bible says I will nevertheless be held accountable for the way I speak and the things I say. Not only for those words meant to hurt and cut, but also those careless, off-the-cuff comments I blurt out without thinking. My thoughtless sarcasm. Pointless babbling. Those little zingers at others people's expense. The white lies and embroidered truths. They're all on the record.

Our words are that important. They aren't just bits of fluff and stuff floating around, harmless flotsam left over from frustration or the careless flapping of the jaw. They count. And we must take responsibility for our words if we ever hope to be changed for the better.

—Having a Mary Spirit

READ: Proverbs 13:3

REFLECT: Have your words ever caused you trouble? What could you do to better guard your lips?

If you want a happy, good life, keep control of your tongue. 1 PETER 3:10, TLB

May 7

Controlling my tongue has been one of the hardest exercises of my spiritual life. As Proverbs 10:19 says, "When words are many, sin is not absent, but he who holds his tongue is wise."

Fortunately, the Word of God is filled with instructions on taming our tongues:

- ***Take responsibility for your words and begin to exercise restraint*** (Psalm 39:1). Silence really can be golden, and the simple fact that I have an opinion doesn't mean I have to share it. When I let my mouth run unrestrained, I usually end up in trouble.

- ***Listen more and speak less*** (James 1:19). When we focus on listening to people rather than on coming up with an appropriate response, we show that we value them and lessen the likelihood that we will misspeak.

- ***Get rid of iffy language and inappropriate humor*** (Ephesians 5:3–4). Cursing and taking the Lord's name in vain—we know that is displeasing to the Lord. But so is any off-color remark, sexual innuendo, or dirty joke.

- ***Refuse to gossip*** (Leviticus 19:16, NLT). Gossip can be addictive. Knowing things no one else knows gives us a feeling of power and leverage. How do we stop it? As someone once said, "If you don't want garbage in your garbage can, put a lid on it." In other words, don't entertain the conversation. Stop it before it begins.

- ***Avoid arguments*** (2 Timothy 2:23). Whether it is arguing about politics or theological differences, the more heated the debate, the more some of us like it. Unfortunately, God isn't fond of arguing, for controversy rarely benefits relationships. It makes us love our opinions more than we love one another.

—*Having a Mary Spirit*

READ & REFLECT: Look up each of the verses listed above. Write out on a card the verse that speaks the most to you, and post it where you can see it each day.

May 8

They overcame him by the blood of the Lamb and by the word of their testimony.
REVELATION 12:11

I used to long for a powerful testimony. When you are saved at the age of four, there isn't a whole lot of "before" you can point to in order to validate your "after." Not a lot of transformation that people can ooh and aah about.

Over the years when preachers would say, "Think about the day you were saved and what you were before you met Jesus," I honestly wished I could. Dramatic testimonies seemed to be the ones God really used. Which bothered me a lot as a young Christian. What did I have to offer?

Sure, I loved Jesus. But had I been transformed?

I knew *something* had happened when Jesus came into my heart. After all, I didn't want to sin, and I hurt inside when I did. I felt a love in my heart for people and prayed diligently that my life would make a difference for God's kingdom. But I knew His kingdom needed to make a difference in me as well.

So began my lifelong prayer: *Lord, change me.*

And He has done just that. Though I still don't have a dramatic conversion story, every time I've allowed God to get His hands on me, He's given me a testimony—a real before-and-after story to share. Because every time I've given God access to yet another place in my heart, abdicating control and allowing Jesus to rule and reign, I've been changed in some important ways. While I'm not yet what I ought to be, I'm no longer what I was, thank God!

That's the kind of testimony the Lord wants to give to every one of us. A testimony of resurrection that's just too good not to share.

—*Lazarus Awakening*

READ: Acts 9:1–9 and 17–22

REFLECT: Saul, later known as Paul, was determined to wipe out Christianity, but what happened when he encountered Jesus?

"You don't just wake up a sweet old lady," my friend Rosemarie Kowalski reminded me not long ago. "It has to start now. My auntie is proof of that."

Disabled and bedridden by a stroke, Rosemarie's Aunt Amalia still radiates with the joy of the Lord. Though her once-active lifestyle is now behind her and there are plenty of reasons to murmur, Rosemarie's uncle says, "I've never once heard her complain."

Now that's a far cry from my prop-me-up-on-the-couch-and-listen-to-me-whine approach to suffering. If I have the sniffles or my back aches, everyone knows about it. I want Jell-O and tapioca pudding served on a tray just like Grandma used to bring when I was little and out of sorts. Stroke my hair and rub my back. And don't forget a glass of 7-Up for my upset tummy.

Suffer in silence? Not me. My misery loves company and a large audience as well.

Needless to say, my family is not looking forward to my old age. And neither am I. It's miserable being miserable.

"Keep me sweet, Lord!" has become my after-forty prayer. I don't want to be a contentious, demanding, fearful old woman. But that means I've got to stop being a contentious, demanding, fearful younger woman. Which means I must get serious about living according to what I *know* rather than what I *feel*.

—Having a Mary Spirit

READ: Proverbs 31:10–31

REFLECT: Which virtuous-woman qualities would you like to invite God to help you cultivate in your life?

May 10

It is better to live in the corner of an attic than with a crabby woman in a lovely home. PROVERBS 21:9, TLB

I love the following prayer I came across years ago. It's attributed to a seventeenth-century nun, which seems a little strange to me considering its contemporary tone. But it definitely echoes the cry of my heart.

> Lord, you know better than I know myself that I am growing older and will someday be old. Keep me from getting talkative, particularly from the fatal habit of thinking that I must say something on every subject and on every occasion.
>
> Release me from craving to straighten out everybody's affairs. Make me thoughtful, but not moody; helpful, but not bossy. With my vast store of wisdom it seems a pity not to use it all, but you know, Lord, that I want a few friends at the end. Keep my mind from the recital of endless details—give me wings to come to the point.
>
> I ask for grace enough to listen to the tales of others' pains. Seal my lips on my own aches and pains—they are increasing, and my love of rehearsing them is becoming sweeter as the years go by. Help me to endure them with patience.
>
> I dare not ask for improved memory, but for a growing humility and a lessening cocksureness when my memory seems to clash with the memories of others. Teach me the glorious lesson that occasionally it is possible that I may be mistaken.
>
> Keep me reasonably sweet. I do not want to be a saint—some of them are so hard to live with—but a sour old woman is one of the crowning works of the devil.
>
> Give me the ability to see good things in unexpected places, and talents in unexpected people. And give me, O Lord, the grace to tell them so.[65]

—Having a Mary Spirit

READ: Titus 2:3–5

REFLECT: What attitudes listed in the prayer above do you struggle with? What qualities from these verses would you like to better reflect?

And you, dear brothers and sisters,
are children of the promise.
GALATIANS 4:28, NLT

May 11

I think part of our attitude problem stems from the fact that we settle for the position of slave girls rather than taking our rightful place as daughters of the King. Listen to these encouraging words penned by David Seamands, a missionary to India:

> The servant is accepted and appreciated on the basis of what he does, the child on the basis of who he is. The servant starts the day anxious and worried, wondering if his work will really please his master. The child rests in the secure love of his family. The servant is accepted because of his productivity and performance. The child belongs because of his position as a person. At the end of the day, the servant has peace of mind only if he is sure he has proven his worth by his work. The next morning his anxiety begins again. The child can be secure all day, and know that tomorrow won't change his status. When a servant fails, his whole position is at stake; he might lose his job. When a child fails, he will be grieved because he has hurt his parents, and he will be corrected and disciplined. But he is not afraid of being thrown out. His basic confidence is in belonging and being loved, and his performance does not change the stability of his position.[66]

Jesus said, "I no longer call you servants, because a servant does not know his master's business. Instead, I have called you friends" (John 15:15).

This is the intimacy we've been invited to share. Friendship, not servanthood. But more than friendship, adoption into God's family. "How great is the love the Father has lavished on us, that we should be called children of God! And that is what we are!" (1 John 3:1).

—Outtake from *Lazarus Awakening*

READ: Galatians 4:31
REFLECT: How would your life be different if you accepted that you've been born again for freedom and not for slavery?

May 12

I will bind up the injured and strengthen the weak. Ezekiel 34:16

When baby Joshua joined our family fourteen years after his closest sibling, he brought more joy than I ever thought possible. But more than joy, Joshua brought a new understanding of God's love that I'd never considered before.

After Josh was born a month early, the doctors immediately knew something wasn't quite right. Diagnosed with low muscle tone, Joshua felt like a rag doll, loose and limp in my arms. He was slow to nurse, slow to roll over, slow to sit up, slow to do many things. At three-and-a-half years of age, he still has delays in motor skills as well as speech development.

But do you know what? It doesn't matter. I don't bother comparing Josh to other kids, because Josh isn't like other kids. I don't keep a list of things babies should do at one or two or three years of age. It's all immaterial. Josh will do it when Josh can. And we'll do—and are doing—everything possible to help him. After being an uptight mom the first time around, constantly comparing to see how my kids measured up to others their age, I can't tell you how freeing this has been.

In some ways, these four years with Josh have been the most enjoyable years of my life. Why? Because we celebrate everything! Every little advance is met with great joy and applause. And I've realized recently that loving Josh has taught me a wonderful lesson about how God loves me.

Not for what I do, but simply because I belong to Him.…

—Having a Mary Spirit

READ: Psalm 103:13–14

REFLECT: What kind of heavenly Father do we have, and what does He understand about us?

*For the Lord takes pleasure in his
people; he adorns the humble with
victory.* Psalm 149:4, RSV

May 13

…A deeper revelation of God's love came to me at an Oregon women's retreat. My sister, Linda, had come along to watch one-year-old Josh while I spoke.

After the evening session, she met me at the door. "You won't believe what Joshua did!" she said, dragging me to where he sat playing with some toys. "Watch this!" Linda cleared the space around him, placing his favorite plaything in front of him, just out of reach. With a little smile, Josh bent forward and stretched out nearly flat to grab the toy that rested beyond his toes. He'd never done that before. But there was more to come.

Grunting and groaning, with beads of perspiration breaking out on his forehead, he worked himself back into a sitting position, still grasping the toy. The whole process took at least thirty seconds, ten times the amount of time another child would have required. But rather than being disappointed, Linda and I whooped and hollered and cried.

It was a moment of pure joy. As I lay in bed that night still rejoicing over Joshua's accomplishment, I felt God whisper to my spirit, *That's how I feel, you know.*

"What do you mean, Lord?" I asked.

The joy you feel watching Joshua do something you know is difficult—that's how I feel when I see you stretch beyond what you've tried before. When you believe Me for something that seems impossible…trust Me in the midst of difficulties…do what I ask even though you don't feel able…that's how I feel.

That I could bring that much joy to the Lord had never occurred to me. Weeping, I whispered words of praise to the One who knew me so intimately and yet loved me so completely.

—*Having a Mary Spirit*

Read: Zephaniah 3:17

Reflect: Read this portion of Scripture aloud, replacing pronouns with your name. Let the words sink deep into your soul, then respond with a prayer of gratitude.

May 14

In all things God works for the good of those who love him. ROMANS 8:28

What God started on the day I surrendered my life to Him, He has promised to complete. For Jesus Christ is Lord of the Process, and the process is divine.

It is a mystery to me how God can take something as imperfect as my life and turn it into an agent for His glory. In her book *When God Shines Through,* Claire Cloninger writes about this imaginative God who takes the broken, scattered pieces of our lives and turns them into something beautiful:

> For me, one of the greatest frustrations of walking through the "daili-ness" of my life as a Christian is that I don't always get to see how the bits and pieces of who I am fit into the big picture of God's plan. It's tempting at times to see my life as a meal here, a meeting there, a carpool, a phone call, a sack of groceries—all disjointed fragments of mothering in particular.
>
> And yet I know I am called, as God's child, to believe by faith that they do add up. That in some way every single scrap of my life, every step and every struggle, is in the process of being fitted together into God's huge and perfect pattern for good.[67]

Claire concludes that it is those very scattered pieces that God uses to make a kaleidoscope. Instead of waiting for us to arrive, God shines the Light of Christ through the fragments we place in His hands, transforming "the disorder into beauty and symmetry," splashing the colors of our brokenness like fireworks across the sky.

—Having a Mary Heart

READ: Psalm 138:8
REFLECT: Turn this verse into a prayer as you commit the scattered pieces of your life to God's hand.

The Lord upholds all those who fall and lifts up all who are bowed down.
Psalm 145:14

May 15

I have a problem. You wouldn't notice it just looking at me—at least I hope not. I look pretty normal walking around. But as I've reviewed the surveillance footage of my life, I have to admit a disturbing truth:

I am a chronic tripper.

If there is a slight unevenness in the surface I'm walking on, my toe will invariably find the imperfection. Any little flooring flaw has the power to send me hurtling through space, arms windmilling wildly as I attempt to regain my balance. I'm especially susceptible to microphone cords, as I found out one Sunday in our early years of pastoring.

Eager to welcome a newcomer, I left my place on the worship team just before the call was given to greet each other. Two steps into my journey off the platform, I suddenly took flight. My shoe heel had caught on one of the cords. But thinking quickly, I managed to slip out of the snared pump as I sailed through the air.

The crowd, still seated, watched in amazement as I landed on my feet in the aisle, right next to the pew I had been aiming for.

"So glad you could join us," I said sheepishly as I shook the startled guest's hand. The crowd chuckled.

"It was nice of you to drop in," the man replied with some quick thinking of his own.

We all erupted in laughter. It was a moment I'll never forget but one I'm not eager to repeat. Because tripping is not only humiliating. It's dangerous.

Especially when it comes to our walk with God. Perhaps that's why the writers of Proverbs as well as Hebrews encourage us: "Make level paths for your feet" (Proverbs 4:26 and Hebrews 12:13).

—*Lazarus Awakening*

Read: 1 Corinthians 10:6–12
Reflect: According to verses 11–12, why does the Bible give us examples of people who failed?

May 16

Let us strip off anything that slows us down or holds us back.
HEBREWS 12:1, TLB

Though our spirits have been fully resurrected by Christ and we've been born again, remnants of our flesh still linger. Loose ends of our lower nature dangle around our lives, threatening to trip us up in our walk with God.

In a sense, the graveclothes that hindered Lazarus describe well the graveclothes that hinder us as Christians:

- His feet were bound, affecting his *walk* with God.
- His hands were bound, limiting his *work* for God.
- His face was covered, clouding his *watchfulness.*
- His mouth was covered, muffling his *witness.*[68]

Any of that sound familiar? I know it does to me. No wonder many of us feel ineffective in our walk with God. For we, too, struggle with a shroud.

Graveclothes in themselves are only pieces of flimsy cloth. Yet if they aren't systematically removed with the Lord's help, they turn into spiritual chains that restrain us. Blindfolds that keep us from seeing us the enemy's devices. Muzzles that smother our attempts to proclaim the good news.

Unfortunately, it is possible to grow so used to our graveclothes that we actually like them. They're comfortable. They're familiar. They're like an old pair of sweats broken in by years of wear and stretched out in just the right places to fit our natural bent toward waywardness.

Once we've gotten to that point, taking off our graveclothes and putting on something else seems a bit extreme. Why work at becoming new when old ways come so much easier?

Wrinkled, tattered, and torn though our graveclothes may be, wearing them feels more natural and comes more easily to our fallen natures than the time-consuming task of changing in order to become new.

—Lazarus Awakening

READ: Revelation 3:17–18

REFLECT: What does Jesus offer if we will only admit our need and come to Him?

Graveclothes are often revealed by repeated reactions and cyclical responses. For instance, if you find yourself offended by someone, only to be offended by someone else the very next day, that's a sign that other people might not be the problem.

Consider the following emotions and behaviors, and number the three that occur most often for you. (Note there is space for you to add others that come to mind.)

_____insecurity	_____need to control	_____urge to escape
_____negativity	_____depression	_____self-pity
_____touchiness	_____emotional "stuffing"	_____sharp tongue
_____self-hatred	_____fear	_____self-centeredness
_____quick temper	_____dishonesty	_____easily offended
_____procrastination	_____emotional bully	_____isolation
_____shame	_____defensiveness	_____judgmentalism
_____blame	_____self-medicating	_____envy
_____fantasizing	_____denial	_____people pleasing
_____self-justification	_____resentment	_____paranoia
_____other:	_____other:	_____other:

—*Lazarus Awakening*

READ: Psalm 26:2

REFLECT: Look again at the responses you noted above as overly familiar, then take them to God in a prayer of repentance, asking that He help remove anything that hinders your walk with Him.

May 18

But I tell you: Love your enemies and pray for those who persecute you.
MATTHEW 5:44

In a very real sense, when we live according to the Spirit we live life upside down. It doesn't make sense in the natural. Nor through the lens of the Old Testament, where vengeance and payback seemed to be a part of God's wrath and were considered a personal right when an individual was wronged. Eye for an eye, tooth for a tooth.

Apart from the New Covenant pattern Jesus instituted by His life and death, our offended natures tend to mirror King David's in Psalm 109:8–10. Praying against his enemies, he rages, "May his days be few.... May his children be fatherless and his wife a widow. May his children be wandering beggars; may they be driven from their ruined homes."

Payback. Retribution. Revenge. It makes perfect sense from a human point of view. But take a moment and consider: is that what Jesus would have us do?

Something amazing happened with the coming of the Holy Spirit. People changed. Really changed! In the face of certain death, Stephen prayed *for*—not against—the people who were about to stone him. It wasn't a "get 'em, God!" kind of prayer. It wasn't even a "let this cup pass from me" Gethsemane prayer.

When Stephen's annoying habit of lifting up Jesus and the miracles that accompanied his life prompted temple leaders to pick up rocks, Stephen didn't backpedal and deny his Savior. Instead he stepped forward, as it were, face turned heavenward, and willingly embraced their lethal stones.

What amazes me most about this story are Stephen's last words—his final prayer. Falling to his knees he cried out, "Lord, do not hold this sin against them" (Acts 7:60).

Oh that our response would be the same. No matter how large the injustice or small the slight, may forgiveness be our first thought rather than our last.

—Outtake from *Having a Mary Spirit*

READ: Luke 23:33–34
REFLECT: What was Jesus's response to injustice?

Allowing Scripture to prescribe personal life limits is not a popular idea today, even in the church. Somehow we've allowed the world's propaganda to infiltrate our thinking, to the point that we've labeled the very idea of having scruples—that is, strong moral or ethical beliefs that affect behavior—as intolerant or legalistic.

"Well, it might be wrong for you," we say, "but don't tell me it's wrong for me."

I'm the first to applaud the fact we're no longer bound by the legalistic rules that marked much of the last hundred years of evangelical Christianity. I'm thrilled with the newer emphasis on grace that sets us free. But I'm a bit concerned that we may carry this idea of personal freedom to such an extreme that it becomes something entirely different from what God intended.

The apostle Paul spoke directly to that concern when he wrote, in 1 Corinthians 6:12, " 'Everything is permissible for me'—but not everything is beneficial. 'Everything is permissible for me'—but I will not be mastered by anything."

In other words, even good things can enslave us if we're not careful, ruling over us like masters and usurping the place of God. And it is possible to distort our freedom in Christ to such a point that we do whatever we want—including flat-out sin—just to prove we can. That's the heresy Paul, the great defender of grace, encountered in the church at Galatia. "You, my brothers, were called to be free. But do not use your freedom to indulge the sinful nature" (Galatians 5:13).

For freedom is not freedom if it hurts the heart of God.

—*Having a Mary Spirit*

READ: Hebrews 10:26, 29

REFLECT: What warning is given concerning willful sin, and what does that communicate to God when we continue in it?

May 20

The LORD detests all the proud of heart. Be sure of this: They will not go unpunished. PROVERBS 16:5

When we choose the highway of haughtiness over the lowly road of humility, we find ourselves at odds with almighty God. King Nebuchadnezzar learned that lesson the hard way, reminding us in Daniel 4:37, "Those who walk in pride [God] is able to humble."

No matter how hard we try to justify our I-know-best actions and reactions, insisting it's our duty to set the world straight, the simple truth is this: God cannot and will not bless pride. In fact, He downright hates it (Proverbs 16:5).

Choosing humility, on the other hand, touches the heart of God like nothing else. It opens the resource room of heaven, making available all the strength, all the wisdom, all the Holy Spirit power we need to live overcoming lives. Filling us, puny as we are, with everything we need to face and conquer everything we meet. Anytime, anywhere.

How I want that. How I need that.

For I've learned that if I don't deal with my pride, the Lord will. Speaking to the proud and pious, Jesus warned in Matthew 21:44, "He who falls on this stone [speaking of Himself] will be broken to pieces, but he on whom it falls will be crushed."

Willingly submit to God, or continue on our own stubborn way? That is the decision you and I must make every day. One leads to life. The other to destruction.

But if we'll choose to fall upon the Rock and stay there, the Lord promises to adjust our hidden life so that our outer life lines up with His Word. It is always painful, but as each area pops into its rightful place, we find victory.

And that, after all, is why Jesus came.

—Outtake from *Having a Mary Heart*

 READ: Daniel 4:28–37

REFLECT: Write out the last sentence of verse 37, and place it somewhere you see it often.

But his delight is in the law of the LORD, and on his law he meditates day and night. PSALM 1:2

May 21

As a young adult, I knew that I was saved and that if I died, I'd go to heaven. But somewhere along the way, I had twisted God's love into something I had to earn. If I could just be good enough, then God had to love me. But of course I stumbled, again and again. Each time, it took me weeks to work up enough spiritual brownie points to feel like I was back on God's good side.

No wonder I worried. No wonder I was afraid. I was constantly sewing fig leaves, trying to cover up my inadequacy. I was anxious for the same reason the first man and woman became anxious: I was not secure in God's love. "Perfect love casteth out fear," 1 John 4:18 (KJV) tells us.

In pursuing freedom from fear, I began to meditate on God's Word day and night, as King David did (Psalm 1:2). The word for *meditate* in the psalm means "to chew," much as a cow chews its cud. Instead of gnawing on my problem, I trained my mind to chew on the promises of God. As the Holy Spirit and I brought the Word to remembrance, something exciting happened. Anxiety fled in the face of truth, and peace—the kind of peace that quieted the disciples' raging storm—came to take its place.

The kind of peace only Jesus can give. *Peace, be still.*

When Jesus said, "Martha, Martha…" so gently that frantic day in Bethany, He was speaking to you and me as well.

Come find love, Jesus invites us. *Come find a love so perfect that it covers all your faults and pronounces you "not guilty." Come find a love that chases fear out the door! Come find everything you've ever longed for. Come find peace for your soul.*

—*Having a Mary Heart*

READ: Isaiah 26:3

REFLECT: Memorize this verse and quote it whenever fear threatens to arise.

May 22

I call on the LORD in my distress, and he answers me. PSALM 120:1

I'll never forget coming home late after church one Sunday evening when the kids were little. The night was dark. No moon. No stars. I held John Michael's hand as we left the car and walked toward the house.

Suddenly the deep-pitched barking of a very large dog broke the stillness. It sounded as if it were right behind us. Startled, we both tensed and squeezed hands. I was about to reassure him that the dog was several houses away. But before I could, in a quivery little voice, my four-year-old son began to quote, "The Lord is my helper; I will not be afraid. What can man do to me?" (Hebrews 13:6).

I'm so glad that Colleen, John Michael's Space Cub teacher, didn't think three- and four-year-olds were too young to hide God's Word in their hearts. As a result of her dedication and the fact that we both practiced our memory verses as we drove in the car, my little boy knew fourteen scriptures by the time he was five. And it wasn't just head knowledge or rote memorization, because the Holy Spirit brought it to his heart when he needed it.

When it was dark and danger barked loudly behind him, John Michael didn't look to me. He knew to look to God.

—Having a Mary Spirit

READ: Deuteronomy 11:18–21
REFLECT: How can you better "fix" God's Word in your heart and mind?

Memorizing Scripture

Memorizing Scripture is a very basic and important way to grow in our spiritual walk. I used to believe I couldn't do it. But the following steps, adapted from the Navigators' 2:7 Discipleship Course,[69] have helped me overcome that mental roadblock and begin to make God's Word my own.

1. Choose a verse (or verses) you want to memorize. Write it on an index card so you can carry it around with you.

2. Read the verse out loud several times. Think about what it means; focus on the message.

3. Learn the reference and first phrase of the verse together as a unit.

4. After you've reviewed the reference and first phrase a few times, add the next phrase. Repeat the two phrases several times until you can say them smoothly. Gradually add phrases and repeat the reference once again at the end.

5. Always review the verse using the following pattern: REFERENCE, then VERSE, then REFERENCE again (for instance: "John 11:35, 'Jesus wept,' John 11:35"). Don't leave out the reference. If you don't know the location of the verse, what you say will have less authority.

6. Say the verse out loud whenever possible. This reinforces the passage in your mind.

7. Have a friend or family member help you review. Ask that person to signal mistakes but to only prompt you when you ask for it. Focus on saying the verse word for word. It is easier to retain a verse that you have learned perfectly.

The secret to memorizing Scripture is *review, review, review.* Even after you can quote the whole verse without making a mistake, keep on reviewing it. You'll find Scripture memorization not only gives you truth to share, but it feeds your soul as well, changing you from the inside out.

And isn't that what we all need?

—*Having a Mary Spirit*

My son, keep my words and store up my commands within you.

PROVERBS 7:1

147

May 23

Some trust in chariots and some in horses, but we trust in the name of the LORD our God. PSALM 20:7

One of my favorite verses is found in Isaiah 30. It is a verse the Lord often uses to center me when my heart wants to chase after fear. "In repentance and rest is your salvation," God said to the people of Israel through the prophet. "In quietness and trust is your strength" (verse 15).

Return to Me, the Lord said, offering sweet shelter. But Israel refused, choosing instead, to run—to "flee away" (verse 17)—from their enemies.

And so, very often, do we.

I believe that women are especially prone to run away in response to fear— or at least we'd like to. When we're weary and overwhelmed, our first thought is escape. We look desperately for ways to be anywhere but where we are.

Not that we actually "flee on horses" the way Isaiah's people did. But we run away by avoiding conflict, losing ourselves in books or movies, the Internet or shopping, overmedicating or eating to anesthetize our pain. We may even attempt to distract ourselves with good, important work. And while many of those things are fine in moderation, escapism can become a nasty habit. When we choose to run away rather than turn to God, we experience the same fate God promised the people of Israel when Isaiah warned them, "Your pursuers will be swift!" (verse 16).

You see, fear avoidance doesn't work, because when we run, our fears pursue us. They hunt us down and devour us, for that is the nature of anxiety. Fleeing only makes things worse. For just when we think we've succeeded in outrunning fear, we run straight into its arms.

—Having a Mary Spirit

READ: Isaiah 30:15–18

REFLECT: What happens when, instead of fleeing, we choose to wait on the Lord?

I have learned to be content whatever the circumstances. PHILIPPIANS 4:11

May 24

Not all running is fleeing *away* when it comes to fear. Sometimes we're the pursuers. For fear makes us doubt God's love and His ability to provide for us. So we decide to take care of ourselves, running for all we're worth to chase down our wants and our desires.

If I could only be there, if I could only have that, we think, *then I would be happy.* Satan dangles our "if onlys" in front of our faces like a carrot in front of an old, worn-out nag. And we respond, galloping after our dreams day and night, only to find, when we get there, that "there" has moved—and happiness and fulfillment remain out of reach.

God's kingdom is not like that. He doesn't tempt and tease or ruthlessly hunt us down. Instead, He simply asks us to trust Him, and He provides. "The LORD longs to be gracious to you; he rises to show you compassion," Isaiah 30:18 promises. "Blessed are all who wait for him!"

What a difference. Running from our fears and chasing our dreams bring us nothing but anxiety and frustrated hopes. But waiting on the Lord not only renews our strength (Isaiah 40:31, NKJV); it also brings us everything we need.

It may not happen according to our timetable, but God will come through. In fact, Deuteronomy 28:2 says, "All these blessings shall come upon you and overtake you, because you obey the voice of the LORD your God" (NKJV).

Did you catch that? Instead of your pursuing blessings—blessings will pursue you! Now, that's an amazing promise. For as you choose faith over fear, you'll experience a holy makeover that not only removes your worry lines but refreshes your heart and meets your needs.

An inner beauty treatment that goes far beyond skin-deep.

—*Having a Mary Spirit*

READ: Psalm 34:4–10

REFLECT: List the blessings that result from looking to God for what you need.

May 25

This is the one I esteem: he who is humble and contrite in spirit, and trembles at my word. ISAIAH 66:2

"You do not delight in sacrifice," David writes in Psalm 51:16, "or I would bring it; you do not take pleasure in burnt offerings." So what does God desire? David tells us in verse 17: "The sacrifices of God are a broken spirit; a broken and contrite heart, O God, you will not despise."

As counterintuitive as it seems to our human nature, there is a beauty in brokenness. For in brokenness we are emptied so that we might be filled. In brokenness we lay down our schemes so that we might dream God's dreams. And perhaps most important, in brokenness we relinquish the pieces of our lives so that Christ can make us whole.

Unfortunately, none of us enjoy the feeling of being undone. We work incredibly hard to hold ourselves together. Yet my most intimate moments with Christ have come during times I felt as though my life were coming apart at the seams.

Why is it, then, we so resent the humility of brokenness? Why do we reach for paint and spackle to patch our flaws rather than peeling back any and all facades so God can heal us? If it is in the deconstruction of our lives that we are made new, shouldn't we embrace the crumbling that leads to restoration?

When Mary willingly broke open her treasured alabaster box, the fragrance of her sacrifice filled the room and still lingers today. When Martha bowed her heart rather than raising her fist at Christ's rebuke, the fragrance of humility was released and her life was changed.

And when Jesus, in humble obedience, allowed Himself to be broken upon the cross, His sacrificial death made it possible for you and me to really live.

So bring on the breaking, Lord! Whatever it takes to make me Yours.

—Outtake from *Having a Mary Heart*

READ: 2 Corinthians 2:14–15

REFLECT: What fragrance are we to wear? How would humility beautify that fragrance?

Put a knife to your throat if you are given to gluttony. PROVERBS 23:2

May 26

I'm on a diet. Just the word makes me hungry. But the grace of God which brings salvation has appeared to me, and it is teaching me to say no to ungodliness and Sausage & Egg McMuffins with cheese. Yea, even though I am surrounded by a case of Frappuccinos bought on sale at Costco and several boxes of Girl Scout cookies, I will fear no evil. For Thou art with me. Thy rod and Thy staff, they comfort me.

I am so glad God doesn't leave me to myself when it comes to transformation. He really is a very present help in times of trouble, temptation, and triple-fudge brownies. But I have to cooperate with grace—adding my "try" to the "umph!" of the Spirit. For without a little discipline on my part and a whole lot of help from God, I will remain the same. Frustrated and depressed. Way behind schedule on my holy makeover.

All because I choose a life of ease rather than a life that pleases God.

Discipline is such a four-letter word. Not only does it have negative connotations; it requires W-O-R-K! My idea of discipline tends to be more like that of Phyllis Diller, who once defined exercise as "a good brisk sit."[70] But as my derrière will attest, sitting only makes the problem grow. The sad truth is, if we want to be what Christ has called us to be, we will have to stop being spiritual couch potatoes and get into the gym of the Holy Spirit. For that is the only way to "work out" what God has so generously "work[ed] in" (Philippians 2:12–13).

—*Having a Mary Spirit*

READ: Hebrews 5:13–14
REFLECT: When it comes to our spiritual fitness, why is our spiritual diet as important as our physical diet?

May 27

Continue to work out your salvation with fear and trembling. PHILIPPIANS 2:12

I think most of us suffer from the "Fairy-Godmother Syndrome" when it comes to cooperating with transformation. We don't want to be challenged; we just want to be changed. Don't tell us to work out our salvation, God. Just wave Your wand, sprinkle pixie dust, and voilà! We'll be what we've always wanted to be—Cinderella Christians complete with a new gown, glass slippers, and a glistening coach to ride in to the ball.

Unfortunately, if we haven't experienced a true holy makeover, the heat of trials and the harsh reality of life will strip us down to our rags and leave us to find our way home barefoot and weeping. Wondering if all we experienced when we came to Christ was just a dream.

Our heavenly Father is not a fairy godmother. He is much too wise to give us the easy way. The instant fix. For He knows we need to learn discipline if we are to grow into the beautiful women He wants us to be.

Perhaps that's why 1 Timothy 4:7 tells us to "exercise" ourselves "towards godliness" (NKJV). Because something happens—both physically and spiritually—when we say no to our flesh.

Mark Twain once suggested that the way to build character is to "do something every day that you don't want to do."[71] I think he was on to something. Because sometimes we really have to push ourselves in order to pay the price of change. Yielding to God by refusing our flesh is not an easy process. But it is more important than we know.

—Having a Mary Spirit

READ: 1 Corinthians 9:25–27
REFLECT: What are the benefits of "strict training," spiritually speaking?
Think of a practical way you could apply Mark Twain's advice to help build character. Now do it!

While Scripture is the main way God speaks to me, it's not the only way. In fact, as I've grown in my walk with the Lord, I've been amazed at His creativity and the variety of experiences He uses to communicate with me. I'm learning to watch as well as listen for the following methods the Spirit seems to often use:

- *Repeated themes.* Like every wise parent, God repeats Himself when we don't listen the first time![72] So I've learned to be on the lookout for similar messages on similar topics coming from different sources. If the same topic keeps coming up, God is usually trying to tell me something. (Around the same time the Spirit revealed my problem with anger, I encountered two sermons, several articles, and a conversation among friends on the very same topic!)

- *Impressions.* This wisdom from the Spirit usually involves an inner urge or prodding to do something or go a certain direction. Sometimes it's very specific—*Call your mother* or *Stop at that store.* To be honest, it's often tricky to tell whether the impulse is God's idea or my own. After I obey the nudge, however, I can look back and see it really was from God....

—Lazarus Awakening

Read: Luke 8:18a
Reflect: Describe a time God used repeated themes or impressions
to speak to you.

May 29

Your ears will hear a voice behind you, saying, "This is the way; walk in it."
ISAIAH 30:21

...In my quest to hear God's voice, I'm also learning to look for the following:

- **Confirmations.** This clarification from the Holy Spirit is especially important when I'm uncertain whether I'm hearing God correctly—whether the impression I've felt or the theme I've sensed is really for me at that particular time. Sometimes corroboration comes through Scripture or from other people, but it can also come from a sense of settled peace.

- **Checks.** Sometimes instead of confirmation, I may feel a check regarding certain decisions or actions. I can't always explain it, but something doesn't feel right in my spirit. There may be nothing obviously wrong with the action I'm contemplating, nothing that bothers my conscience, but I don't have peace about it. In those moments, I remember my mother's words: "When in doubt, don't." Later, I may (or may not) come to understand what the Spirit was warning against, but that isn't as important as the fact I've obeyed.

Regardless of which of these methods God uses to speak to us, it's important to remember that He will never go against His Word. Therefore, I check any communication I believe I've received from Him against the principles of Scripture. If it fails to measure up with the Bible, I must set it aside, no matter how genuinely I believe I've heard from God.

That is why it is so important that we know the Word—and not just with our heads. "The law of his God is in his heart," the psalmist writes. "His feet do not slip" (Psalm 37:31).

—*Lazarus Awakening*

READ: Psalm 119:105

REFLECT: Describe a time God used confirmations or checks to speak to you. Why is it so important that we consider everything in light of God's Word?

My eyes are ever on the LORD, for only he will release my feet from the snare.
PSALM 25:15

May 30

One of the most powerful promises in the Bible is 1 Corinthians 10:13: "No temptation has seized you except what is common to man. And God is faithful; he will not let you be tempted beyond what you can bear. But when you are tempted, he will also provide a way out so that you can stand up under it."

No matter what temptation I currently face, it isn't something new. For Satan isn't very inventive. He tends to use the same things over and over, generation after generation. Doubt, discouragement, pride, prejudice, frustration, fear, lust, hatred, envy—they've all been felt before, and they will be felt by those who follow us. But what we do with these temptations is crucial if we want to become more like Jesus.

My friend Cheryl has a wonderful testimony. It's not a poof-magic-wand conversion. She didn't meet Jesus on Tuesday and become different on Wednesday. Hers was a more gradual transformation. In fact, she'll admit she spent many Sunday mornings up in our church balcony nursing a hangover. She wanted a different life, but she didn't know how to get one.

Still, God kept wooing Cheryl, and she kept responding as best she could. Even when Flesh Woman seemed to be having the upper hand.

"I had a problem with alcohol, and I knew it," Cheryl says. "I kept begging God to take it away. But I worked in a restaurant that had a bar, and every Friday night I'd find myself having drinks with friends. Then I would beat myself up with guilt and despair"—which of course, didn't help....

—*Having a Mary Spirit*

READ: Hebrews 2:18
REFLECT: What difference does it make for you to know that Jesus understands temptation and is willing to help you?

155

May 31

Let us not become weary in doing good. Galatians 6:9

...In the midst of the battle with her flesh over its desire for alcohol, Cheryl memorized 1 Corinthians 10:13 and began asking God, "Show me the way of escape. You promise You will provide a way out, Lord. Help me see it."

One Friday as Cheryl was getting ready to go pick up her paycheck at the restaurant, her middle son, Matthew, asked to go along.

"He'd been asking for weeks," Cheryl said, "and I always put him off because I knew I'd probably end up drinking. But that night when he asked, I suddenly realized—here's my way out! It had been in front of me all along."

From then on, Matthew was Cheryl's Friday-night buddy. And wouldn't you know it—the cycle of that particular sin in her life began to be broken. Cheryl couldn't sit around and drink with her little boy watching, and she certainly wasn't going to drive drunk with him in the car. With that pattern of sin no longer an option, the power of alcohol began to lose its grip on her.[73]

What "way out" is God providing for you in your current situation? Ask the Holy Spirit for eyes to see it. God is faithful to His Word—you will find it. And when you do, don't wait to act. Take full advantage of the escape route the Lord has so graciously provided.

As you do, you may find freedom waiting for you in other areas of your life as well.

—Having a Mary Spirit

Read: Psalm 124:6–8
Reflect: Claim these verses over your situation, and keep an eye out for your way of escape.

I love teetertotters. My sister and I used to play for hours on an old wood plank clamped to a metal bar at the church camp we attended every summer. Being older, I was the heaviest, so I had to scoot up several inches while she sat on the very edge. Then we were ready to go. Back and forth, up and down, through sun-speckled July afternoons we'd teetertotter amid the pine trees of Glacier Bible Camp. But we especially enjoyed finding that perfect spot of synchronicity—scooting around until both of our ends were suspended in midair. Pure, exquisite balance.

I wonder if God had teetertotters in mind when He placed Luke's story of Mary and Martha between two famous passages: the story of the Good Samaritan (Luke 10:30–37) and Christ's teaching on the Lord's Prayer (11:1–4). One deals with our relationship with people. The other deals with our relationship with God. One teaches us how to serve. The other teaches us how to pray. One breaks down the wall that divides cultures. The other breaks down the wall that divides God and humanity.

Perhaps that is why this tiny section of Scripture is so important. In Luke's story of two women and one Savior we find the fulcrum, the pivot point of our spiritual teetertotters—the secret of balancing the practical with the spiritual, and duties with devotion. Without a fulcrum, these stories are two separate wooden planks. Both are important. Both are true. But when we place the fundamental truths of service and prayer on the pivot point of practicality—when we get down to the company's-here-and-what-do-I-do? application, the fun really begins.

—Having a Mary Heart

READ: Luke 10:30–37 and 11:1–4

REFLECT: How do the truths in these two portions of Scripture help you find balance in your life?

June 2

Whoever loves God must also love his brother. 1 John 4:21

Jesus gave us a picture of what our teetertotter of work and worship should look like in Luke 10:25–28, a familiar portion of the *Torah* quoted in an exchange between Jesus and a religious expert.

"What must I do to inherit eternal life?" an expert in the law asked.

"What is written in the Law?" Jesus asked. "How do you read it?"

I can almost hear the lawyer's voice deepen as he gathered his robes around him and assumed the proper posture for quoting Scripture. " 'Love the Lord your God with all your heart and with all your soul and with all your strength and with all your mind'; and, 'Love your neighbor as yourself' " (Luke 10:27).

I can almost see Jesus smile and nod as He said, "You have answered correctly.… Do this and you will live."

You see, loving the Lord your God and your neighbor as yourself was and is the very thing God has always wanted us to do—it's a perfect picture of the perfectly balanced life. These two verses sum up all of the Old Testament and the New Testament combined (Matthew 22:40).

God wants us to love Him. Really love Him.

And He wants us to love each other. Really love each other. That's how we can know we belong to Him—if we have love one for another (John 13:35).

Love for God. Love for others. Worship and service. These are the two ends of our teetertotter. Though love for God comes first, the two can't be separated. One flows from the other—and back again. That's what it means to live a balanced life, a Christlike life.

—*Having a Mary Heart*

 Read: Mark 12:33

Reflect: Imagine your teetertotter. Which way does it currently tilt—toward worship or service?

For you, Lord, have never forsaken those who seek you. Psalm 9:10

June 3

When it comes to choosing the Better Part, Jesus is our supreme example. He was never in a hurry. He knew who He was and where He was going. He wasn't held hostage to the world's demands or even its desperate needs. "I only do what the Father tells me to do," Jesus told His disciples (John 8:28–29).

Someone has said that Jesus went from place of prayer to place of prayer and did miracles in between. How incredible to be so in tune with God that not one action is wasted, not one word falls to the ground!

Luke tells us that "Martha was distracted by all the preparations that had to be made" (10:40). Key word: *had.* In Martha's mind, nothing less than the very best would do. She *had* to go all out for Jesus.

We can get caught in the same performance trap, feeling as though we must prove our love for God by doing great things for Him. So we rush past the intimacy of the Living Room to get busy for Him in the Kitchen—implementing great ministries and wonderful projects, all in an effort to spread the good news. We do all our works in His name. We call Him "Lord, Lord." But in the end, will He know us? Will we know Him?

The kingdom of God, you see, is a paradox. While the world applauds achievement, God desires companionship. The world clamors, "Do more! Be all that you can be!" But our Father whispers, "Be still, and know that I am God."

—Having a Mary Heart

Read: Luke 5:15–16

Reflect: What was Jesus's habit even in the midst of a thriving ministry?

June 4

For we know, brothers loved by God, that he has chosen you. 1 Thessalonians 1:4

You would think after accepting Christ at a young age and being raised in a loving Christian home with a loving, gracious father, I would have been convinced from the beginning that my heavenly Father loved me.

Yet for some reason, I'd come to see God as distant and somewhat removed. Rather than transposing upon God the model of my earthly father's balanced love—both unconditional yet corrective—I saw my heavenly Father as a stern teacher with a yardstick in His hand, pacing up and down the classroom of my life as He looked for any and all infractions. Measuring me against what sometimes felt like impossible standards and occasionally slapping me when I failed to make the grade.

Yes, He loved me, I supposed. But I didn't always feel God's love. Most of the time I lived in fear of the yardstick. Who knew when His judgment would snap down its disapproval, leaving a nasty mark on my heart as well as my soul?

As a result, I lived the first three decades of my life like an insecure adolescent, forever picking daisies and tearing them apart, never stopping to enjoy their beauty. *He loves me...He loves me not.*

Powerful church services and sweet altar times. Ah, I felt secure in His love. Real life and less-than-sweet responses? I felt lost and all alone. My overzealous self-analysis never brought the peace I longed for.

Because the peace you and I were created for doesn't come from picking daisies. It only comes from a living relationship with a loving God.

—*Lazarus Awakening*

Read: Psalm 86:15

Reflect: Pray this verse back to God. Then write it out on a card and start memorizing it.

As the deer pants for streams of water, so my soul pants for you, O God. PSALM 42:1

June 5

Because we were created for balance, we feel the difference in our souls when our lives tilt too far in one direction or another. The imbalance will show in our attitudes, in our energy level, and in the way we interact with people. Any of the following could be an indication that you need more time in the Living Room with Jesus:

- ***Irritability and frustration.*** You find yourself snapping at people, wound so tight you're about to "snap" yourself, and especially short-tempered with those you perceive as lazy or uncooperative.
- ***Uncomfortable with quiet.*** Silence makes you nervous, so you're quick to turn on the TV or the radio.
- ***Low joy threshold.*** It's been a long time since you've sensed that undercurrent of joy and abundance running through your heart.
- ***A sense of isolation.*** You feel all alone—as if no one is there for you and no one understands.
- ***Increased drivenness.*** You're haunted by a sense that you must do more and more. You keep volunteering for more projects and more committees, even though you know your plate is full.
- ***Sense of dryness and emptiness.*** No wonder! You have many outlets and demands, but no inlets or source of strength.

If you're struggling with any of these symptoms, may I encourage you to get alone with Jesus? He has everything you need. Wisdom. Joy. Strength. Peace. All this and more is poured into your life as you daily sit His feet.

—Having a Mary Heart

READ: Psalm 16:11

REFLECT: Which, if any, of the signs listed above describe your current condition? Are there other symptoms not mentioned that point to your need for time alone with God?

June 6

God…will not forget your work and the love you have shown him as you have helped his people. HEBREWS 6:10

While time alone with God is important, we are filled to be spilled. We are meant to be outlets for His love and grace to those around us. When we don't give out what we've received, we become stagnant pools rather than streams of Living Water. Are you experiencing any of the following symptoms that may indicate you need to spend more time in Kitchen Service?

- *Slight depression.* You feel a vague unhappiness, a sense of being down.
- *Resentment of intrusion.* Rather than welcoming people into your life, you find yourself wishing they'd go away.
- *Frustration over direction of life.* You feel a sense of purpose-lessness and sometimes wonder, "Is this all there is?"
- *Increased self-indulgence.* You feel an itch to treat yourself with favorite foods or shopping.
- *Apathetic attitude.* You find that very little moves you. You know your compassion level is low, but part of you just doesn't care.
- *Low energy level.* Like the Dead Sea, you may have many inlets, but no outlets—and therefore you're growing stagnant.

If you've felt any of these warning signs, may I suggest you look for ways to step outside your comfort zone and begin to give your life away in service to other people? As the old song says, "Jesus and Others and You—what a wonderful way to spell joy!"[74]

—*Having a Mary Heart*

READ: Colossians 1:10

REFLECT: Which, if any, of the signs above describe your current condition? Are there other indications that point to a need for more service?

All my fountains are in you. Psalm 87:7

June 7

It was the last and greatest day of the Feast of Tabernacles. Jerusalem was filled with worshipers celebrating the harvest and giving thanks to God for His goodness. Each day of the preceding week, a priest had taken a golden pitcher, drawn water from the Pool of Siloam, then marched back to the temple through the Water Gate while the people recited Isaiah 12:3: "With joy you will draw water from the wells of salvation."

It may have been in this setting at the Water Gate, at the very moment the priest lifted up the pitcher to pour it out upon the altar, that Jesus stood and said in a loud voice the words we read in John 7:37–38: "If anyone is thirsty, let him come to me and drink. Whoever believes in me, as the Scripture has said, streams of living water will flow from within him."[75]

Can you hear how revolutionary Jesus's words must have sounded? A mere man offering what priests could only hint at? With open arms, He invited thirsty, weary people to drink so deeply of Himself that they would never thirst again.

Jesus makes the same offer to you and me today. *If you're thirsty, if you can't seem to satisfy that longing in your soul…come to Me and drink. If you've tried the well of religion, if you've looked to relationships for meaning but need something more…come to Me and drink.*

But Jesus offers more than water to satisfy our thirst. He desires to create in us a wellspring of Himself—a bubbling surge of life that satisfies our needs as well as the needs of others.

For we weren't created to be mud puddles for Jesus. We were meant to be rushing rivers, pouring out His love and mercy to everyone around us.

—*Having a Mary Spirit*

Read: John 4:13–14
Reflect: What makes the water Jesus offers so different?

June 8

Serve one another in love. GALATIANS 5:13

Author Beth Moore tells of a time she noticed an old man sitting in a wheelchair at a crowded airport. He was a strange sight, with long stringy gray hair, and she tried not to stare. But the more she tried to concentrate on the Bible lying in her lap, the more she felt drawn to the old man.

Though she tried to resist the prompting, it only grew stronger. God said clearly, *I want you to brush his hair.*

Finally Beth gave up arguing. She walked over to the man and asked for permission. He looked confused at first, but then he said, "If you really want to."

With a hairbrush she found in his bag, Beth began gently brushing the old man's hair. "A miraculous thing happened to me as I started brushing…," she remembers. "Everybody else in the room disappeared.… I know this sounds so strange but I've never felt that kind of love for another soul in my entire life. I believe with all my heart, I—for that few minutes—felt a portion of the very love of God. That He had overtaken my heart…like someone renting a room and making Himself at home for a short while."

The emotions were still strong when Beth finished. She knelt in front of his chair. "Sir, do you know Jesus?"

"Yes, I do," he said. "[My wife] wouldn't marry me until I got to know the Savior." He paused a moment, then explained that illness had kept them apart for months. "I was sitting here thinking to myself, *What a mess I must be for my bride.*"[76]

—Lazarus Awakening

READ: Romans 12:10

REFLECT: What practical way could you show Christ's love to someone today?

What an amazing privilege it is to be the very hands of God in someone else's life.

I wonder how many opportunities I've missed to love as Jesus loved. How many wounded strangers I've passed by because I was too busy to stop. How many piles of burial garments I've avoided, not knowing that a resurrected sister or brother lay inside struggling to get out. Or how many butterfly metamorphoses I've interrupted because my human compassion assumed that I knew the person's needs better than God did.

I want to participate in the miraculous. I want to be a little bit of God's kingdom come to earth—Christ's hand extended, reaching out in love. But that means I have to slow down and listen. I must tune my heart to the prompting of the Holy Spirit so that when He beckons, "Loose him; let him go," I step forward rather than pull back. So that when He prompts, "Wait and pray," I'm willing to intercede rather than interfere. So that whatever I do, I do it with His wisdom and love.

"Who's my neighbor?" the expert asked Jesus.

As Warren Wiersbe puts it, the answer has less to do with geography and more to do with opportunity.[77] Because the best way to love the Lord with all my heart, soul, mind, and strength is to love the person who happens to be standing next to me.

—Lazarus Awakening

READ: Romans 13:8–10

REFLECT: What debt do we owe one another, and how is it related to fulfilling the Law?

June 10

Let love and faithfulness never leave you;
bind them around your neck, write them
on the tablet of your heart. PROVERBS 3:3

Unfortunately, as the world well knows, it's easy for Christians to forget what we're here for. It's easy to fall into the hypocrisy of talking one way and living another way—or to get so involved with our religious activities that we simply neglect to reach out to those around us.

Mahatma Gandhi once said, "If Christians lived according to their faith, there would be no more Hindus left in India."[78] This great leader was fascinated at the thought of knowing Christ. But when he met Christians, he felt let down. The world is filled with people who feel the same. They are intrigued by the claims of Christ, but they shrink back because of disappointment with His offspring.

"Don't look at people," we might protest. "Look at Jesus." But whether we like it or not, we're the only Jesus some will ever see. Dwight L. Moody put it this way: "Of one hundred men, one will read the Bible; the ninety-nine will read the Christian."[79]

The apostle Paul understood the responsibility of representing Christ to others. More than nine times in the New Testament, Paul writes something to the effect of "Follow me as I follow Christ."

There were no Gideon Bibles in the New Testament church. There were no Bibles at all, except for the Hebrew Scriptures. The only evidence of this new and living way came in the form of the walking, breathing, living epistles that filled the young church's meeting rooms and spilled out into the street.

"You are a letter from Christ," Paul reminded the Christians at Corinth (2 Corinthians 3:3). You are a letter that is known and read by everyone.

I wonder… What message will they read in you and me?

—Having a Mary Heart

READ: 1 Thessalonians 1:6–8
REFLECT: What did the Thessalonians do with the message Paul preached, and what was the result?

Jesus must have been exhausted that long-ago evening sketched in Matthew 14. All day long, the crowds had pressed in with their needs. I have a feeling Jesus didn't mind that. It was the very thing He had come to do—"to heal the brokenhearted, to proclaim liberty to the captives" (Isaiah 61:1, NKJV).

But who would heal Jesus's broken heart? His cousin John had been executed just days before, and Jesus grieved.

Now, as the evening came on, Jesus wanted to be alone. He needed to be alone. Only the Father could comfort this overwhelming sadness and soothe this bone-weary exhaustion.

"There He is!" Voices echoed across the water as a long stream of people made their way around the lake. The disciples groaned. "Let's send them away," one suggested.

But instead of sending the people away, Jesus "had compassion on them and healed their sick" (Matthew 14:14). He moved past His own neediness and loved them. He did what He could to help them. And then He provided dinner for the hungry crowd. Fish and chips for five thousand.

The Greek word Matthew uses for "compassion" in this passage is *splagchnizomai.* It means that Jesus didn't respond to the people out of duty; He ministered to them because He literally felt their distress in His gut.

And that is the essence of ministry that goes out of its way. It puts self aside and reaches out in true compassion.

"True love hurts," Mother Teresa once said. "It always has to hurt." And elsewhere she has written pointedly, "If you really love one another, you will not be able to avoid making sacrifices."[80]

—Having a Mary Heart

READ & REFLECT: Using a concordance or Bible website, look up *compassion,* and note the instances it is used in reference to Jesus. What do you learn about your Savior?

June 12

I have come to do your will, O God.
HEBREWS 10:7

Have you ever wondered how other people have learned to discern God's will? George Müller, a nineteenth-century English pastor known for his life of prayer and his close walk with God, once shared this simple method for determining God's will through prayer and the Word:

1. "I seek at the beginning to get my heart into such a state that it has no will of its own in regard to a given matter....
2. "Having done this, I do not leave the result to feeling or simple impression. If so, I make myself liable to great delusions.
3. "I seek the Will of the Spirit of God through, or in connection with, the Word of God.... If the Holy Ghost guides us at all, He will do it according to the Scriptures and never contrary to them.
4. "Next I take into account providential circumstances. These often plainly indicate God's Will in connection with His Word and Spirit.
5. "I ask God in prayer to reveal His Will to me aright.
6. "Thus, (1) through prayer to God, (2) the study of the Word, and (3) reflection, I come to a deliberate judgment according to the best of my ability and knowledge, and if my mind is thus at peace, and continues so after two or three more petitions, I proceed accordingly."[81]

—Having a Mary Heart

READ: James 1:5
REFLECT: Write this verse on a card, and place it where you can see it. Consider memorizing it.

Let the little children come to me, and do not hinder them, for the kingdom of God belongs to such as these. LUKE 18:16

As a child, my favorite time of the day was when Dad relaxed in the living room after dinner, reading the newspaper in our blue velvet rocker. My sister and I loved to disturb his reading. We'd make funny noises, hit his paper, and run. It wasn't long before Daddy would drop the paper and grab his girls, pulling us into his arms or down on the carpet floor for another bout of All-Star wrestling.

We'd giggle and wiggle, and he'd growl and blow zerberts on our bare little tummies. It was our favorite time of day. We had Daddy's full attention.

I wonder if sometimes God doesn't long to take us in His arms and have a little fun. While I love the sacred reverence of hallowed halls of worship, I wonder if God doesn't delight when we just get real and even a bit giddy around Him?

When Jesus called God His Father, it infuriated the religious elite. How could this mere man call the Unseen One "Father"? They rarely referred to the Almighty as such; their prophets used the term just a few times in the Old Testament. Most often, they referred to Abraham as their father. And when identifying God, they referenced their ancestors' relationship with Him—He was the God of Abraham, Isaac, and Jacob. An individual one-on-One relationship with Yahweh apparently wasn't considered.

Yet here was this riffraff from Nazareth saying that He not only knew God, but He knew Him on the most intimate terms. *"Abba,"* Jesus called the Holy One. Daddy God.

And He was inviting people—common, ordinary people—to do the same (Romans 8:15).

—Outtake from *Having a Mary Heart*

 READ: Luke 18:16–17

REFLECT: Jesus welcomed little children and made childlike faith a prerequisite to enter His kingdom. What do you think makes that quality so important?

June 14

Our Father in heaven, hallowed be your name. MATTHEW 6:9

When the disciples asked Jesus to teach them to pray in Luke 11:1–2 (NKJV), Jesus said, "When you pray, say: 'Our Father...'"

Father. It was a word not normally connected with the Eternal One. Yet Matthew records Jesus referring to God as "Father" 42 times. John records 107 times. In the repetition, it seems that Jesus was emphasizing an important message and offering a relationship with God that humanity had never known before.

Our Father so longed to have fellowship with us that He was willing to die to make us His own.

Radical love. That was, and still is, the offer. Desiring a radical relationship that surpasses religion and formal acquaintance, Jesus came so that you and I could be adopted into the family of God and experience the full benefits of being *Abba*'s sons and daughters. Doing life together. Hanging out in the Living Room. Even getting down on the floor with a Daddy willing to interact and play with us, correct and encourage us. And maybe, just maybe, now and then blow zerberts on our tummies.

Sounds sacrilegious, doesn't it? That's how it struck the Sadducees and Pharisees as well. The familiarity Jesus spoke about was unthinkable. Such freedom in the presence of God could invite abuse, and yes, I guess I have to agree, it certainly could.

But unfortunately, rather than reveling in the sweet relationship God offers, it seems to me we've spent much of the last two thousand years either missing it or avoiding it. Because the same doubts that assailed the religious back in Jesus's day assail us as well.

How could God want to know me?

It boggles the mind, I know, but He really does.

—Outtake from *Having a Mary Heart*

READ: Romans 8:15–17

REFLECT: Describe in your own words the kind of relationship we are meant to have with God.

Every good and perfect gift is from above, coming down from the Father of the heavenly lights, who does not change like shifting shadows. JAMES 1:17

June 15

So much of our understanding of God's love is shaped by what we've experienced in life. Which of the following types of earthly fathers has had a negative impact on your ability to accept God as your heavenly Father?

Abusive Father: You never know what you are going to get with this kind of father. His love is determined by his moods. You avoid him as much as possible.

But your true Father is "gracious and compassionate, slow to anger and rich in love" (Psalm 145:8).

Neglectful Father: This dad is far too busy (or just too selfish) to be concerned with you. He has more important business to attend to than your insignificant needs. You have to take care of yourself.

But your true Father says, "Look at the birds of the air; they do not sow or reap or store away in barns, and yet your heavenly Father feeds them. Are you not much more valuable than they?" (Matthew 6:26)

Biased Father: You know this father loves you—or at least you think he does. But he seems to shower affection and gifts on all the other kids. Bottom line: he has favorites, and you're not one of them.

But your true Father "does not show favoritism" (Romans 2:11).

Demanding Father: Perfect in nearly every way, this father demands that you be perfect as well. No matter how hard you try, it's never enough. While there are moments when he seems proud of you, they are few and far between.

But your true Father "has compassion on his children...for he knows how we are formed, he remembers that we are dust" (Psalm 103:13–14).

—Lazarus Awakening

READ & REFLECT: What kind of father image do you struggle with? Consider the corresponding verse(s) describing your true Father. Allow the truth you find there to sink deep in your soul.

171

June 16

I and the Father are one. JOHN 10:30

The Israelites caught a glimpse of God's glory in the wilderness, and they weren't particularly eager for a close encounter of the personal kind. "You go talk to Him," they told Moses. "We're afraid." Frankly, this God who had chosen them to be His people terrified them (Exodus 20:18–19).

Appearing as a pillar of cloud by day and a pillar of fire by night, He'd led them out of Egypt after bringing the strongest empire in the world to its knees. Through His mighty works they'd seen rivers turned to blood; they'd watched as toads tormented and gnats nettled. They'd heard the shrieks and wailing as an entire nation mourned the deaths of their firstborn sons.

Now this God wanted to speak to them? "I don't think so," they said. "You go, Moses. Then come back and tell us what He said."

It's always easier to let someone else negotiate when you're uncertain where you stand. Jesus came to break the cycle of fear and guilt that had kept humanity from coming to God. His death brokered a peace treaty that reconciled sinful man to a holy God. No longer required to stand afar off, because of Christ we are invited to come near.

"Jesus made possible an intimacy with God that had never before existed," Philip Yancey writes. "Jesus offered a long, slow look at the face of God."[82]

The "Word became flesh and dwelt among us," John 1:14 tells us, "and we beheld His glory" (NKJV). No longer distant, God came with "skin on"—so that we could know Him, touch Him, hear Him, and feel His presence.

Emmanuel. God with us.

No need to fear. Love had come.

—Outtake from *Having a Mary Heart*

READ: Micah 7:18–19

REFLECT: Describe the kind of God that Jesus came to reveal.

For much of my young-adult life, I had let my thoughts come and go without realizing that if Satan controls my thought life, he controls me. I'd carelessly let my emotions lead me down the treacherous paths of self-reliance. I'd allowed my worry to lead me by the poisoned waters of doubt. My fears had made me lie down in green pastures of self-pity.

But no longer. The Word leapt to life for me the day I read the old British *Revised Version* translation of Isaiah 26:3: "Thou wilt keep him in perfect peace whose *imagination* is stayed on Thee."[83]

It was the diagnosis I'd needed to hear. My imagination had controlled my life for so long that it had grown into a giant sheepdog, loping unrestrained across the meadows of my mind. My emotions trailed behind my imagination like frolicking puppies, never certain where they were being led, but quite happy to go along for the ride.

"Here, Imagination! Here, boy." Sometimes I said it out loud. So strong was the pull to fear that it took a living word picture to pull me back to center. Back to faith. I'd point to the ground beside me and instruct both my imagination and any stray emotions to "Stay."

Crazy? Yes, maybe. But it worked for me. Nothing could be crazier than the anxious way I had lived before.

I began to search the Scriptures for verses on fear and worry and the mind. When I found a verse that fit, I memorized it. Then, when the temptation to fear came, I could answer it with the Word of God: "For God hath not given us the spirit of fear; but of power, and of love, and of a sound mind" (2 Timothy 1:7, KJV).

And as I did, things began to change.

—Having a Mary Heart

READ: John 14:27
REFLECT: In your experience, how does God's peace differ from the world's peace?

Praying God's Word

In her powerful book *Praying God's Word*, Beth Moore recounts the freedom found in linking the spiritual weapons of God's Word and prayer (Ephesians 6:17–18). She gives the following steps to help you start:

1. Ask God to guide you (Psalm 25:4–5) and to open your eyes to His Word (Psalm 119:18). You may not find a detailed description of your stronghold in Scripture, but you will find verses that apply.[84]

2. Using a Bible concordance or topical Bible resource, search for scriptures pertaining to any issue that is preoccupying you and robbing you of abundant life.[85]

3. Once you've found a list of pertinent scriptures, paraphrase and rewrite them into personal prayers using personal pronouns like *I, my, me,* etc.[86] For instance:

   > *My Father,* You are the Lord my God, I desire to love You, listen to Your voice, and hold fast to You, for You, Lord, are my life. (Deuteronomy 30:20)

4. Daily pray the scriptures relating to your struggle until you experience freedom. Continue to use verses God has used most powerfully in your life to maintain that freedom.[87]

5. Ask God to reveal any coinciding areas to your stronghold that may need prayer. For instance, pride often masquerades behind anger.[88]

6. Pray scripture as a preventive measure as well as a protective measure.[89]

7. Pray pertinent scripture as intercession for someone else who is struggling.[90]

To get started, write out the following scriptures as prayers:

Unbelief—Mark 9:24   Rejection—Isaiah 49:15–16
Pride—Ephesians 4:2   Despair—Jeremiah 29:11

—Outtake from *Lazarus Awakening*

June 18

For everyone who has ever struggled to hold their tongue and failed, for everyone who has had great intentions derailed by clumsy words and actions—Peter is our patron saint. Making bold statements of faith in one breath and denying the Lord the next. Seeing Jesus transfigured, talking to Moses and Elijah—standing on truly holy ground—only to destroy the moment by offering to pick up plywood at Home Depot so he could build the three of them shelters (Luke 9:28–33).

Shelters? As if the natural could ever hope to hold, let alone protect, such a manifestation of God's glory! I love the parenthetical explanation of Peter's suggestion that Luke 9:33 offers: "He did not know what he was saying."

I wonder how many times grace has had to add that particular footnote to the story of my life? "She meant well, but she had no idea what she was doing."

Mark 9:6 adds a little more information concerning Peter's statement: "He did not know what to say, they were so *frightened*" (emphasis mine).

I think that addition is crucial. Perhaps you've never thought of fear as a factor that makes people shallow and insecure, loud and obnoxious, pushy and anxious. I know I didn't. But Peter also mentions fear in 1 Peter 3:5–6 when he addresses the need for a quiet and gentle spirit:

> For this is the way the holy women of the past who put their hope in God used to make themselves beautiful. They were submissive to their own husbands, like Sarah, who obeyed Abraham and called him her master. You are her daughters if you do what is right and *do not give way to fear* (emphasis mine).

—Having a Mary Spirit

READ: 1 Peter 3:14–15a
REFLECT: Instead of giving way to fear, what are we to do?

June 19

Do what is right and do not give way to fear. 1 PETER 3:6

Fear makes us do slightly crazy, often inappropriate things. Fear blurts out thoughtless, sometimes hurtful words. Fear babbles. It freaks out. It searches frantically for explanations and solutions. Fear sews together fig leaves to cover our inadequacies and paints bright smiles to hide our tears. It builds makeshift shelters and puts on far too much makeup. It forces us to hide behind facades simply because we don't know what else to do.

Perhaps that's why Peter instructs us to spend less time on outward adornment—the building of ornate shelters to house our fragile egos—and to spend more time making our inner lives lovely (1 Peter 3:3–4). To become so secure in who we are in Christ that we have no trouble calling Him "Master" or trusting Him as Lord.

When Bill Gothard mentioned 1 Peter 3:3–6 in a seminar years ago, my ears perked up. What would he say? I had prayed for a quiet and gentle spirit for years.

"A quiet and gentle spirit," Gothard said, connecting verses 4 and 6, "is a heart free from fear."[91]

Well, I couldn't help it! I had to shout "Hallelujah!" right there in the middle of the silent crowd. Everyone looked at me strangely, but I didn't care. God had done exactly that over the previous year—He had delivered me from fear. It had never occurred to me that the quiet and gentle spirit I had been praying for was really a heart at rest. A mind free from anxiety. But when it finally came together and I saw what God had done—well, when the Holy Spirit changes you in such a deep, elemental way, you've just got to shout about it!

—*Having a Mary Spirit*

READ: Psalm 131
REFLECT: Which of these verses, if applied, could help you overcome anxiety in your life?

When I prayed for a quiet and gentle spirit, I thought that would mean that the Holy Spirit would change my personality. That I would become one of those sweet, subdued women I admire so much. Women who know how to respond appropriately to situations. Women who don't shout "Hallelujah!" and disrupt otherwise quiet and gentle proceedings. Women who never lose their tempers or say things they later regret. Women who always look put together and never drop meatballs on their dresses at church potlucks. Angels, really—secret agents born straight from heaven.

No wonder my friends doubted the likelihood of my prayer being answered. "God made you the way you are," they tried to reassure me as I mopped up the ranch dressing I'd dribbled on my shirt. "He's not going to make you stop being you."

And they were right. God is infinitely more creative than that. He is a God of diversity and not monotony. He's much more interested in taking our personalities, tempering and taming them by His Holy Spirit, and recruiting them for work in His kingdom than He is in churning out church-lady clones. Like Martha of Bethany, I'd spent most of my life "worried and upset about many things" (Luke 10:41). And like Martha, I'd asked for what I thought I lacked—more help in the kitchen. Tools to live more effectively in this life. Something to make me...well, less like me.

But God in His wisdom had given me what I needed and what Martha needed as well—freedom from fear.

He hadn't changed my personality. He'd changed me.

He hadn't made me quiet. He'd quieted my soul.

—Having a Mary Spirit

READ: Isaiah 32:17–18

REFLECT: Read these verses out loud prayerfully. What do you need most today?

June 21

I sought the LORD, and he answered me; he delivered me from all my fears.
PSALM 34:4

In order to overcome anxiety, I've compiled a list, à la David Letterman, called the Top Ten Ways to Tame Your Worry Habit.

10. ***Separate toxic worry from genuine concern.*** Determine if you can do anything about your situation. If so, sketch a plan to handle it (Proverbs 16:3).

9. ***Don't worry alone.*** Share your concerns with a friend or a counselor. Talking about your fears often reveals solutions (Proverbs 27:9).

8. ***Take care of your physical body.*** Regular exercise and adequate rest can defuse a lot of worry. Healthy bodies handle stress better and react more appropriately (1 Corinthians 6:19–20).

7. ***Do what is right.*** A guilty conscience causes great anxiety. Do your best to live above reproach. Confess quickly and seek forgiveness (Acts 24:16).

6. ***Look on the bright side.*** Consciously focus on what is good around you. Don't speak negatively, even about yourself (Ephesians 4:29).

5. ***Control your imagination.*** Be realistic about problems, but try to live in the "here and now" not in the "what might be" (Isaiah 35:3–4).

4. ***Prepare for the unexpected.*** Put aside a cash reserve and take sensible measures so you'll be ready if difficulties arise (Proverbs 21:20).

3. ***Trust God.*** Keep reminding yourself to put God in your equation. When fear knocks send faith to answer the door (Psalm 112:7).

2. ***Meditate on God's promises.*** Scripture has the power to transform our minds. Look for scriptures that will help you answer life's difficulties with God's Word (2 Peter 1:4).

1. And the number one way to tame a worry habit? ***Pray!*** Joseph M. Scriven's hymn says it all: "O what peace we often forfeit...all because we do not carry everything to God in prayer"[92] (Colossians 4:2).

—*Having a Mary Heart*

READ & REFLECT: Look up the corresponding verses for two of the Top Ten ways that speak most to you. Consider memorizing one.

He will bring to light what is hidden in darkness and will expose the motives of men's hearts. 1 CORINTHIANS 4:5

June 22

Life has a way of bringing to the surface who we really are, the deep hidden motivations of our heart. "For out of the overflow of the heart the mouth speaks," Jesus said in Matthew 12:34–35. "The good man brings good things out of the good stored up in him, and the evil man brings evil things out of the evil stored up in him."

It certainly happened in Judas. But it happened in Mary as well. For you see, no matter how "good" we are, each of us has an underbelly of weakness that floats to the surface now and again. Especially when life is difficult and times are hard.

From all appearances, Mary seems to have been contemplative by nature. But while spiritual intuitiveness made her a wonderful worshiper, it also made her susceptible to despair. Especially after Lazarus died. Rather than running down the road to meet Jesus as Martha did when the Savior finally arrived, John 11:20 tells us, "Mary stayed at home." Downcast and alone amid the crowds of friends, she had sunk deeper and deeper into her grief, and even the news of Jesus's coming had not been able to lift her sorrow.

But—thank God!—Jesus meets us where we are. He comes into those dark, hidden corners of our lives and, if we're willing, He shines the sweet spotlight of heaven, His precious Holy Spirit. If we allow him, He offers to clean out our personalities, tempering them through the Holy Spirit so we won't fall to the strong sides of our weaknesses and the weak sides of our strengths.

—Having a Mary Heart

READ: Psalm 51:1–2
REFLECT: Turn these verses into a prayer asking God to heal the weak places in you.

June 23

I tell you the truth, one of you is going to betray me. JOHN 13:21

Even though Mary sensed, with her keen intuitiveness, the graveness of her Lord's situation during His last visit to Bethany, this time she did not collapse. Instead of just sitting passively and listening to the Savior, instead of being overwhelmed by grief as she was at the time of Lazarus's death, this time Mary responded. She gave herself in worship to the One who had given so much to her and her family.

Not so with Judas, apparently. Though Jesus knew the disciple's weaknesses, He had given Judas chance after chance in the three years they had traveled together. According to John 13:29, Jesus had even made the man treasurer of the group.

"Sometimes," William Barclay writes in *The Gospel of John,* "the best way to reclaim someone who is on the wrong path is to treat him not with suspicion but with trust; not as if we expected the worst, but as if we expected the best."[93] That's exactly what Jesus had done with Judas. But Judas had remained unchanged.

Imagine spending three years of your life with the Messiah, yet walking away more or less the same—or even worse than when you started. Judas did just that. It can happen to any of us if we don't settle, once and for all, the question of Christ's lordship in our lives.

Until we determine whom we will serve, we run the risk of developing a Judas heart instead of a heart of sacrificial love. For whenever *our* interests conflict with *His* interests, we'll be tempted to sell Christ off as a slave to the highest bidder, rather than spend our all to anoint His feet.

—Having a Mary Heart

READ: John 12:4–6 and Matthew 26:14–16

REFLECT: What seems to be the impetus for Judas's betrayal? Has self-interest ever tempted you to compromise your allegiance to Jesus?

I tell you the truth, wherever the gospel is preached…, what she has done will also be told. MARK 14:9

June 24

Instead of being shamed by Mary's extravagance when she spilled all she had on Jesus, Judas became critical of what she gave. His greed warped his perception. "If we find ourselves becoming critical of other people," William Barclay says, "we should stop examining them, and start examining ourselves."[94]

Consider the following differences between the hearts of Mary and Judas. Which kind of heart do you have?

- Mary had a heart of gratitude; Judas had a heart of greed.
- Mary came with abandon; Judas came with an agenda.
- Mary heard what Jesus was saying—and she responded; Judas heard but did not understand.
- Mary held nothing back; Judas gave nothing up.

Extravagant love for the Lord is still rarely understood. "Don't you think you're going a little overboard with this 'God stuff'?" a friend may ask. "Why spend so much time in prayer? After all, God knows your heart," another may reason.

But true love always costs the giver something. Otherwise the giving remains only a philanthropic contribution. At best, kind. At worst, self-serving. In the light of Mary's total abandonment, and the sacrifice Christ made for us, halfway love is truly the "least" we can do.

Do we love Jesus with extravagance? Or only when it's convenient?

—*Having a Mary Heart*

READ: Luke 12:13–21
REFLECT: What is the result of a greedy heart?

June 25

You do not have in mind the things of God, but the things of men. MARK 8:33

Though we may be eager to do things for God, it's important to realize that ministry, like any kind of power or position, can be fancy food for the flesh. Our carnal nature can grow up around our call (and even our careers) like a wild vine, choking out the sweetness of Jesus, leaving behind the foul stench of selfish ambition and vain conceit.

And all the while, Jesus is whispering, *"You do not know what manner of spirit you are of"* (Luke 9:55, NKJV, emphasis mine).

If we don't pause and listen to Christ's correction, God often allows us to run into a continuous string of mishaps and misunderstandings at church, at home, and on the job. We speak the truth in love only to have people misinterpret our words as judgmental. Or mislabel our gift of administration as controlling. Or misconstrue our desire to help as meddling. Our families may even accuse us (unfairly, of course) of loving everyone else except them.

As we continue our wrong-spirited, carnal-minded efforts, we'll inevitably find that people neglect—or refuse outright!—to follow the scripts we've so carefully prepared for them. They won't do what we want. They won't say what we need to hear. And we're left with hurt feelings and rejection.

In fact, life may come to feel as though it's made up of one self-fulfilling prophecy after another: *I knew they would leave me out. I knew they'd give that position to someone else. No one appreciates how hard I work.* And with each hurt we experience, Satan just stands back and chuckles, watching as we add yet another brick to the wall we're building around our hearts.

Continuing to wonder why people don't treat us right.

Never realizing that the problem may lie within us.

—Having a Mary Spirit

READ: Numbers 20:2–12

REFLECT: Though Moses was experiencing unfair opposition, what did God diagnose as his true problem? (Hint: Look closely at verse 12.)

All our righteous acts are like filthy rags. Isaiah 64:6

June 26

The beggar could hardly believe his luck!

Just that morning he'd been prowling the streets looking for food, scrounging in Dumpsters, and begging at back doors of restaurants. But tonight he would be dining with a king.

"Your presence has been requested" was the only explanation given by the driver of the long, black limo.

When they arrived at the palace, a butler brought a set of new clothes for the man to wear. The beggar changed into the garments but carefully rolled up the rags he'd been wearing and tucked them under his arm. After all, he never knew when he might need them.

That night the beggar sat by the king himself. Rich paintings and expensive chandeliers hung all around him. Bowls and platters of the finest food lined the expansive table. But most beautiful of all was the kind attention the king gave the nervous man—asking him questions, drawing out details about the beggar's life he had never shared with anyone.

"I hope you will stay," the king said as the meal was about to end. "I would like you to consider this your home."

So the beggar remained. Every night he dined at the king's table—not as a guest, but as a friend. Yet he insisted on carrying his bundle of rags everywhere he went. For he never knew when he might need them.

Many years later, when the man died, they buried him with his bundle of rags. For the torn, tattered, rolled-up clothes had become his identity. The "ragman," they called him. And everyone mourned, including the king.

For his friend, the beggar, could have been so much more if he'd only been able to let go of what he once was.[95]

—*Having a Mary Spirit*

Read: Isaiah 64:6 and Zechariah 3:3–4

Reflect: What does God want to give you in exchange for your rags?

June 27

Forgetting what is behind and straining toward what is ahead, I press on toward the goal. PHILIPPIANS 3:13–14

When it comes to getting rid of the graveclothes that trip me up, I've always wanted God to deal with me quickly, the way a chef slices an onion. But God knows what I need, and in His wisdom and mercy, He takes me at a pace I can handle. Here's the shroud-shedding process I've found helpful as I have tried to cooperate with God's work in my life.

1. Ask God to reveal the graveclothes you need to remove (Psalm 139:23–24). They may include the reactions or cyclical patterns you instinctively return to.

2. Choose new responses *before* you find yourself in "trigger" situations. In many cases, this involves determining to do the opposite of what comes naturally—for instance, being quiet rather than reacting with lots of words (Romans 12:2).

3. Don't get discouraged when the process takes time. Some graveclothes have more layers than others. The fact that a certain issue reappears doesn't negate or diminish what God has done in you. It may not be the same layer but a deeper one (2 Corinthians 3:18).

4. Multiple layers of graveclothes may indicate an area of vulnerability that you will always struggle with. Guard yourself and your responses accordingly (2 Corinthians 12:9).

5. Keep pressing on toward Jesus. Graveclothes are shed best as we pursue our friendship with Him. For as we fix our eyes on Jesus, we become less like us and more like Him (Psalm 34:5).

—Lazarus Awakening

READ & REFLECT: Read the verses in the list above. Prayerfully walk through the steps outlined concerning areas that keep tripping you up.

I will not leave you as orphans; I will come to you. JOHN 14:18

June 28

Aren't you glad Jesus isn't threatened by our tombs? In fact, He seems to go out of His way to find them and destroy their power.

The story of the tomb-dwelling man in Luke 8 smashes the myth that our tombs—the strongholds the enemy uses to keep us bound—offer anything remotely like true identity.

When Jesus asked the tormented man, "What is your name?" (verse 30), the demons were the first to speak up, identifying themselves rather than allowing the man to speak. It was as though the poor guy didn't exist.

Isn't that what happens with our strongholds? Somewhere in our bondage we cease being us and become only our problems. Defined solely by our hurts, hang-ups, and habits,[96] we wear a grave marker like a nametag.

Adulterer! it shouts. *Glutton!* it gloats. *Abused and misused, betrayed and abandoned,* it declares.

But over the cacophony of condemning and demeaning voices, please hear what our heavenly Father says about you and about me. "Fear not, for I have redeemed you," says the Lord in Isaiah 43:1. "I have summoned you by *name; you are mine*" (emphasis mine).

In other words, don't listen to labels. Listen to your God. You are His child. He knows your name by heart: "I will not forget you! See, I have engraved you on the palms of my hands" (Isaiah 49:15–16).

It is not your sin, but His love, that marks and defines you in His eyes.

—*Lazarus Awakening*

READ: Luke 8:26–39

REFLECT: What phrases in this story stand out to you, and why?

June 29

It had been a difficult day. Overwhelmed by responsibilities and tired from the busyness of life, I was tempted to give up. No matter how much I did, it wasn't enough. The day was going downhill fast. But then I checked the mail, and there it was—my message from heaven. A little note of encouragement, written by a friend. As I read and then reread the note, each love-laced word seemed to come from God's heart to mine.

See, Joanna? I haven't forgotten. You matter to Me.

I still have that little card with the bouquet of flowers on the front. It still refreshes my heart. And it also reminds me how much power resides in a few well-chosen words.

"A word aptly spoken is like apples of gold in settings of silver," Proverbs 25:11 tells us. Giving just the right word at just the right time is not only an art—it is a ministry.

I don't know if my friend Cindy realized how deeply her note would affect me. After all, she'd written it several days before, and I wasn't going through a low time then. But God knew what I would need and when I would need it, and so, with a gentle nudge of His Spirit, He brought me to Cindy's mind. And Cindy, in response, took action.

The Greek word for "encourage" is *parakaleo,* which means "to call near, invite." Not coincidentally, the word is very close to the Greek name for the Holy Spirit: *paraklete,* "the one who comes alongside." When we exhort one another, when we encourage and cheer one another on, we are doing the work of the Holy Spirit.

And important work it is. For we all need someone who believes we are more than we appear to be.

—Having a Mary Spirit

READ: 2 Thessalonians 2:16–17

REFLECT: Considering the encouragement God has given you, think of a practical way to encourage someone else today.

He was a good man, full of the Holy Spirit and faith. Acts 11:24

June 30

His real name is nearly forgotten. But the legacy of Joseph, a Levite from Cyprus, lives on.

We call him Barnabas, which means "Son of Encouragement." He specialized in seeing the potential in people and then doing what he could to turn that potential into reality.

When the disciples were frightened to meet with Saul, the famous persecutor of the church, it was Barnabas who brought them all together in Acts 9:26–28 and confirmed the new convert's testimony. And Saul (later renamed Paul), who would author much of the New Testament, was welcomed into the family of God.

When Gentiles began coming to Christ in Antioch, it was Barnabas whom the apostles in Jerusalem sent to encourage the baby church there. Then Barnabas tracked down Paul at Tarsus and brought him to Antioch, where together they discipled and taught the people who would first wear the name of *Christian.*

When Paul didn't want to take a chance on Barnabas's young cousin, John Mark, who had "deserted them in Pamphylia" (Acts 15:36–39), the two friends parted ways, launching two missionary journeys instead of one.

Barnabas's faith must have been well placed, for even Paul changed his mind about John Mark, calling him "a fellow worker" and "a comfort" in Colossians 4:10–11. Later, Mark authored the gospel that bears his name.

Because of one man's gift of encouragement, two men who might have been left behind, Paul and John Mark, were given the gift of a second chance. We are called to do the same. To believe the best about people rather than the worst. Despite their reputations, despite their questionable past performances. To look at people through the eyes of God and see what He sees.

Assets, not liabilities.

Beloved children in need of grace.

—Having a Mary Spirit

READ: 1 Thessalonians 5:11–15

REFLECT: List the ways we can encourage those around us.

187

July 1

They will see the glory of the LORD, the splendor of our God. ISAIAH 35:2

Joanie Burnside glows. I had the privilege of watching this talented actress perform a monologue one Palm Sunday at the Mount Hermon Christian Writers Conference.

I inevitably leave the pre-Easter service shaken at the immensity of Christ's work on the cross. But Joanie's presentation that year reminded me of not only what Jesus did, but what He longs to do in you and me.

Imagine with me an old woman, center stage, clothed in a dark coat and carrying a dingy laundry-type bag over her shoulder. She clings tightly to an out-of-date purse. Dirty rags cover her feet. Stooped and bent over a cane, the old woman's face is twisted with suspicion, her voice sharp and brittle.

"I've come to tell you the story of a butterfly," the woman begins. Her only props are the clothes that she wears and a simple wooden cross that stands behind her. "She started out as all others, a lowly caterpillar, one who would have grown but never changed. Her life would have become old, ugly, and embittered had it not been for the grace of the Creator.

"*This* is what she would have become," the old woman says, pointing at her twisted, decrepit form. "Though she willed herself to change...she could not. Submitting to His power was her only chance.

"Here was her scarf, which covered her head, her precious brain, her above-average intelligence, which she used to shrink others down to her size.

"Her hair was merely a reflection of the anxieties that riddled her life, for she was prematurely gray. She worried about everything—her future, her past, her mistakes, her dreams."...[97]

—*Having a Mary Heart*

READ: Matthew 6:27
REFLECT: What does Jesus say about worry?

Do not be stiff-necked…submit to the
LORD. 2 CHRONICLES 30:8

July 2

…The old woman on stage continues her monologue. "Her teeth"—she bites down for emphasis—"the guardians of her mouth, one of her most vicious weapons, were ever ready to bite, to cut others to the quick with sarcasm and barb. For out of the overflow of the heart speaks the tongue.

"Her purse was her security, for it housed her beloved checkbook. She was born into affluence, and as long as there was money in the bank to protect her, she was safe. She walled herself about with material goods—none of them evil in and of themselves, but all of them evil when worshiped and adored instead of God.

"Her cane she used like a finger, to point accusingly at the sins she saw in others. It became a wonderful crutch, this overdeveloped superego, for whenever she felt bad about herself, she could easily find bad in the lives of others around her.

"Her shoes covered one of her saddest features, her feet. Those poor beaten stubs. She had spent a lifetime wandering aimlessly. She had no purpose, no one to follow, nowhere to go."

The woman shifts a large sack she carries on her shoulder, then points at it. "Here was her burden, the sin she bore that weighed her down, every year getting heavier and heavier, disfiguring the beauty she was meant to be.

"Lastly was her heart, a shriveled shadow of what the Creator had given her."

Pantomiming the movement, the woman takes a small, stony heart out of her chest and holds it between two fingers. "It was hard and unrelenting, not letting any love in…not letting any love out…protected from intruders by her head, her mouth, her purse, and her cane."…[98]

—Having a Mary Heart

 READ: Zechariah 7:11–14
REFLECT: What happened to the people who hardened their hearts and refused to listen to God?

*It's in Christ that we find out who
we are and what we are living for.*
EPHESIANS 1:11, MSG

...Stretching out her hand as though holding a stony heart, the sadness on Joanie's face shifts to joy as she tells what happened next.

"Then one day this woman met some friends who offered her the Living Water, and when she could bear the thirst no longer, she took a taste...just a taste, mind you. But that taste was so sweet and it made her thirst beyond compare. She took, and drank, and that Living Water filled her and satisfied her from her crown to her toes."

The face of the woman onstage now glows as piece by piece she begins to remove the unnecessary articles of clothing that once bound her.

"The scarf was removed and her knowledge used for His glory. Her thoughts became His thoughts as she surrendered to His Spirit." The woman unties the scarf and drops it to the floor.

"The hair, once gray with concern, was made new again." The woman ruffles her hair with glee.

"The mouth that had cut down others now began to build them up, to seek ways to soothe hurts rather than cause them.

"The purse became a tool. Her moneys were used to advance His kingdom rather than to protect her own," the woman says as she lifts the purse for all to see.

"The cane was no longer needed as her urge to judge faded in the light of His grace.

"And her feet..." The woman pauses. "At first they began to walk, then run, skip, leap, and dance with joy, for finally she had a reason to live. A Master to follow. A path that He prepared specifically for her....[99]

—Having a Mary Heart

READ: Isaiah 49:8–10

REFLECT: What does the prophet say Jesus will do? Are any of these phrases significant to you? Why?

Nothing between us and God, our faces shining with the brightness of his face. And so we are transfigured.
2 Corinthians 3:18, msg

July 4

…"The burden of her sins He took," the woman on stage says, her voice becoming stronger and sounding younger. Her posture straightens as she drapes her things over the cross on the platform behind her.

"Her heart of stone was transformed into a new, vital, living heart." With trembling hands she lifts the small, imaginary heart heavenward, receiving a large, beating one in exchange. With her face uplifted, her eyes filled with wonder, the woman pantomimes the act of placing the new heart inside her chest.

"Create in me a clean heart, O God," she whispers, "and renew a right spirit within me" (Psalm 51:10, kjv).

The words are soft, pleading, and thankful as they drift across the quiet auditorium. The moment is holy as David's prayer echoes through each one of us.

"Thank you for hearing my tale," the woman says finally. Her voice is low and tender as she unbuttons her coat. "For as you see…I am the butterfly."

She sheds the cloak, revealing a splendid purple leotard with flowing multicolored wings. Sparkling and shimmering in the morning light, the costume is beautiful. Exquisite.

With arms extended, the woman exits reborn. Floating, dancing, skipping. Leaving all of her earthly garments behind. Inviting each one of us to do the same.[100]

New lives for old. That's what Jesus offers. Warm hearts for cold. And all for the price of being teachable.

As I've surrendered my life to Jesus's teaching, even His rebukes, I've learned the value of God's tender discipline. So don't be afraid to shed the familiarity of old patterns and old clothes.

Jesus, remember, came to make all things new. So hear Him and obey. Receive His discipline.

And then…get ready to fly.

—*Having a Mary Heart*

Read: 2 Corinthians 3:16–18

Reflect: Describe the freedom and transformation available through the New Covenant.

191

July 5

Woman, you are set free. LUKE 13:12

After being bound in darkness for so long, the light was nearly blinding. But as the Man pulled her to her feet, gently smoothing her wild hair, she could feel His love. The demons had not been kind. Many years of torment had left her only a shell.

The demons had taken. This Man gave. His words, His acceptance, the smile in His eyes welcomed her back to life. For the first time in years, she felt a stirring of hope. As if the person she used to be and the person His eyes told her she could now be were about to meet.

As she stood to her feet and looked Him in the face, she realized the fear was gone. So was the seething self-hatred. Only hope remained. And, to her surprise, a small bubble of joy slipped out in breathless laughter.

He laughed as well. For they both knew something marvelous had happened.

She'd been set free.

When Mary Magdalene met Jesus, she experienced an extreme makeover. A makeover no television show, no plastic surgeon or Hollywood dentist could ever hope to match. For this was not a makeover on the outside. This was a transformation that went to the deepest places of the heart. A healing that mended every fragmented part of her personality. A deliverance that shattered every stronghold of darkness, setting her free from seven demons (Luke 8:2). A love that melted every stony wall that circled her heart.

For God is thorough. He heals to the uttermost. He knows what we need and how to provide it. And God longs for us to let Him do exactly that in our lives.

—Having a Mary Spirit

READ: Jeremiah 33:6–9

REFLECT: What kind of healing does God want to bring to your life?

He sent forth his word and healed them; he rescued them from the grave.
PSALM 107:20

July 6

While most of us have never experienced the bondage of demon possession like Mary Magdalene, many of us are just as bound. Bound by bitterness and doubt. Pride and fear and unbelief. Even now, we stand with one foot in our prison cell while Jesus beckons us to walk out in freedom. But we can't seem to figure out how to leave one life to enjoy the other.

We simply don't understand how to live free.

Sadly, it is possible for Christians to walk in and out of church Sunday after Sunday yet still live bound to the past by regret and shame. Tormented by fear and worry about the future. Shackled by frustration and discontentment.

We go through the motions of worship, sitting when we're supposed to sit and standing when we're supposed to stand. Even singing when we're supposed to sing. But the song on our lips never quite reaches our heart. And because we secretly fear there is no other option, we settle for what we can get. Religion. Ritual. A form of godliness without any power at all. Borderland.

Trapped between the no-longer and the someday. Lost in the not-yet.

Never even dreaming what it would be like to live our lives in complete abandonment to God.

Yet what Christ wants for every one of us is a holy makeover. The same kind of transformation that made Mary Magdalene into a whole new person and launched her on an adventure she'd never regret.

—Having a Mary Spirit

READ: Luke 8:1–3

REFLECT: Along with other women, Mary Magdalene traveled with Jesus as He ministered. Try to imagine what that must have been like after her years of lonely torment. Write a journal entry as if you were her.

July 7

"Come, follow me," Jesus said.
MATTHEW 4:19

For some mysterious yet marvelous reason, God willingly links His hopes and dreams to fickle, failing humans like you and me. And in that divine insanity, I see three amazing implications:

- God must really love us.
- He must be up to something bigger and more wonderful than we know.
- He must want us to join Him in the adventure.

Oh how the angels must tremble to realize these truths. How they must lean over the portals of heaven, waiting to see, listening to hear. Dumbfounded to think that the whole future of Christianity hangs, again and again, on your answer and mine—on our willingness to say yes to what God asks. To rearrange our lives in order to accomplish His plans.

Gladys Aylward was born in London in 1904. She dedicated her life to Jesus Christ as a young woman and became convinced she was called to preach in China. When she heard of an elderly missionary looking for someone to carry on her work, Gladys wrote and received word that if she could get to China, she would have a place to serve the Lord.

In October of 1930, with only her passport, her Bible, and two pounds, nine pence to her name, Gladys Aylward left England and made her way to China by the Trans-Siberian Railway. And so began a ministry that would make her one of the most famous missionaries of the twentieth century. All because she was willing. All because she said yes to God.[101]

It's amazing what God can do with a heart surrendered to Him. A heart that says yes in spite of the cost.

—Having a Mary Spirit

READ: Luke 9:57–62

REFLECT: What "responsibilities" or other not-so-well-disguised excuses are keeping you from following Jesus wherever He might lead?

O women, hear the word of the LORD; open your ears to the words of his mouth. JEREMIAH 9:20

July 8

Have you ever wished God would speak a little louder? Or, better yet, that He would sit next to you with skin on so you could really hear what He said? Could you listen better then?

Don't be so sure!

In the Old Testament, God spoke so loudly at times that His voice made mountains shake and people tremble. But instead of drawing the children of Israel closer, His audible voice made them step back a bit. "Speak to us yourself and we will listen," they told Moses in Exodus 20:19. "But do not have God speak to us or we will die."

Though Moses did his best to translate God's heart to the people, familiarity does tend to breed contempt. While they heard the voice of God and feared it, Philip Yancey writes, they also "soon learned to ignore it."[102] So completely, it seems, they hardly noticed when that Voice fell silent for more than four hundred years.

In the New Testament, God's voice sounded once again—first in a baby's cry, and later through an altogether approachable man named Jesus Christ. His voice sounded like our own, but He spoke with an authority and wisdom never heard before. His voice could be tender and soft with children and adulterous women, demanding and hard with hypocrites and the spiritually proud. Yet the very proximity that wooed us allowed us to crucify Him as well.

You see, history proves it isn't a louder voice we need. Nor is it a voice physically embodied and sitting beside us. What we need most is to learn how to listen. Perhaps that's why Jesus said over and over again—fourteen times in the New Testament:

"He who has ears, let him hear" (Matthew 11:15, for example).

—*Lazarus Awakening*

READ: Jeremiah 33:3

REFLECT: What amazing promise are we given in this verse?

July 9

Then Jesus said, "He who has ears to hear, let him hear." MARK 4:9

How does hearing God work? you may wonder. If God isn't going to speak audibly, and if He's not physically present as a human who speaks our language, how are we supposed to understand what He's saying? How do we *get* those ears to hear?

The disciples must have wondered the same thing when Jesus told them He was leaving to return to His Father. But the Lord reassured them that He wouldn't leave them alone or stop communicating with them. "The Counselor, the Holy Spirit, whom the Father will send in my name, will teach you all things and will remind you of everything I have said to you" (John 14:26).

And that's exactly what happened ten days after Jesus ascended to heaven. The Spirit came, the fire fell, and the trembling, fearful people who had felt so lost after Jesus died were now suddenly filled with power (Acts 1–2). More important, they were filled with Christ Himself.

For Emmanuel—"God *with* us"—had sent the Holy Spirit to be "God *in* us." And nothing would ever be the same. Not for them. Not for you and me.

The Spirit of God now dwells in the heart of every believer. Filling us, if we'll allow Him, with everything we need for this life and the one to come. Leading and guiding us into all truth (John 16:13). Confirming that we are, indeed, children of God and deeply loved (Romans 8:15–16).

And yes, speaking to us—though not always in the ways we might expect.

"Listen to your heart," Henri Nouwen writes. "It's there that Jesus speaks most intimately to you.… He doesn't shout. He doesn't thrust himself upon you. His voice is an unassuming voice, very nearly a whisper, the voice of a gentle love."[103]

—*Lazarus Awakening*

READ: 1 Kings 19:11–13

REFLECT: In what form did God's voice come to Elijah? How does this compare with your experience?

It's harder to win back the friendship of an offended brother than capture a fortified city. His anger shuts you out like iron bars. PROVERBS 18:19, TLB

July 10

My mind was in turmoil as I took the kids to school one cold winter morning several years ago. Yesterday's slush had hardened into large, icy ruts that caused my van to lurch from side to side. I had to struggle to keep hold of the steering wheel. But the real struggle that morning was inside me.

A misunderstanding had erupted between a dear friend and me, and it was never far from my mind. Jessica's sweet voice drifted from the backseat as she sang along with a popular Christian song on the radio. "Has Jesus ever crossed your heart?"

The words were strangely familiar. They echoed the words I'd used the day before to pronounce judgment on my friend. "Well, I guess you find out what people are really like when you cross them," I'd told my husband in a moment of anger. But now I sensed the Holy Spirit turning my own words like a spotlight on the darkness of my soul.

What about you, Joanna? I felt the Lord prompt softly. *What has this "crossing" of your heart brought out in you?*

What He showed me wasn't pretty. There were things in my life I'd left unsettled, core issues I'd refused to contemplate. But it was time to face them, and I knew it.

I've found that Jesus goes out of His way to prepare my heart to listen and learn from His gentle rebuke. If you haven't experienced this sweet aspect of our Savior's discipline, may I suggest you spend a little more time in the Living Room? Because when you're busy in the Kitchen, the rebuke sounds harsh and demanding, just one more duty to fulfill. But when you listen from the Living Room, you hear the love in God's voice and it sounds like life for your soul.

—*Having a Mary Heart*

READ: 1 Peter 3:8–9

REFLECT: When we are insulted or sinned against, what are we to do?

July 11

Let all my words sink deep into your own heart first. Listen to them carefully for yourself. Ezekiel 3:10, NLT

Am I teachable? When it comes right down to it, this may be the most important question we ask ourselves. For unless we are willing to receive the rebuke of the Lord as well as the correction that comes from other sources, we will never change. As a result, we will never become more like Jesus. And isn't that what we want—and really need?

Consider the following statements to give you an idea of your teachability quotient. Answer (U) for Usually; (S) for Sometimes; and (R) for Rarely.

____ I feel comfortable asking for advice.
____ I easily admit when I'm wrong.
____ I enjoy reading for information rather than escape.
____ I'm able to receive criticism without being hurt.
____ I enjoy listening to other peoples' thoughts and opinions without feeling the need to express my own.
____ When I read something in the Bible, I automatically think of ways to apply it.
____ I enjoy church and Bible classes and usually take notes.
____ I'm able to disagree with someone without feeling like I have to debate the issue.
____ I'm willing to look at all sides of a situation before I form an opinion.
____ I'd rather be righteous than always have to be "right."

Give yourself 3 points for each "U" answer, 2 points for each "S," and 0 points for every "R." Then, add up the numbers. If you scored 24–30 points, you are well on your way to a teachable heart. If you scored 15–23, keep at it! You are definitely trainable. If you scored 0–14, you may need to make your teachability quotient a matter of prayer, because you'll find a teachable heart is one of life's greatest treasures.

—Having a Mary Heart

READ: Proverbs 27:5–6
REFLECT: How could you better respond to the rebuke of your Savior? Or of those around you?

The cords of the grave coiled around me; the snares of death confronted me.
2 Samuel 22:6

July 12

According to scholars it wasn't unusual for tombs around Israel to be inhabited by the poor or the insane. Graveyards were sometimes the only places outcasts could find shelter.[104]

Dug into hillsides or straight into the ground, most tombs in Jesus's day were made up of two chambers. The first room, sometimes called a vestibule, held a simple stone seat, while the inner chamber featured a carved-out niche (or niches) where the body was laid.

I'm assuming the outcasts must have made their home in the vestibule. It served as a kind of middle ground—protected from the outside elements yet not quite in the place of death.

Unfortunately, metaphorically speaking, this "midchamber" describes the place where many of us live. Suspended halfway between death and life, we've accepted the Lord as our Savior, but we have yet to step out into the fullness of life Christ came to give. We're holed up in the dark, held captive by our hurts, our hang-ups, and our habits. The painful memories we just can't shake. The attitudes that keep us bound. The coping mechanisms we continually return to, though they lead us everywhere but to the heart of God.

"Strongholds," the Bible calls them (2 Corinthians 10:4). And it's a good name, for they truly have a strong hold on us.

If we are ever to experience abundant life in Jesus, we must give God access to anything that holds us back, including the skeletons in our closets and the dark corners of our minds. For He wants to help us "demolish strongholds… and every pretension that sets itself up against the knowledge of God" (2 Corinthians 10:4–5).

—Lazarus Awakening

Read: Ezekiel 37:13–14
Reflect: What does God promise to do in these verses?

July 13

*From the depths of the grave I called
for help, and you listened to my cry.*
JONAH 2:2

It may seem a little strange to think that believers could still be tomb dwellers. But I think we've all felt the intense struggle of shedding our "old self" so that we might experience the "new self" Paul writes about in Ephesians 4:22–24. Strongholds are simply those places in us where sin and the "old self" have established such an immense power base that we feel helpless to escape their control. We love Jesus, but we remain stuck in our midchambers, unable to live free.

So where do you feel stuck in your Christian walk?

What hurt keeps you emotionally bound, frozen at a point of past failure or pain?

What hang-up keeps tripping you up, ensnaring you time and time again?

What habit or behavior controls you, making you feel perpetually defeated and continually undone?

I find it interesting that in the Greek, the root of the word for "tombs" means "to recall or remember."[105] For isn't it true that the majority of our strongholds have their origins in our pasts?

In a sense, many of us live in graveyards, wandering through life in perpetual mourning over the things we have done and the things that have been done to us. We do our best to outrun the mistakes and regret, the hurts and disappointment, but apart from God, we find it difficult to escape the cycle of shame and self-hatred that keeps our "sin...ever before" us (Psalm 51:3, KJV).

That's why Paul prayed that we might be sanctified and made holy "through and through" (1 Thessalonians 5:23). For although Christ has been enthroned in our spirits, there are kingdoms in our souls that have yet to receive the good news.

—Lazarus Awakening

READ: Jonah 2:2–10
REFLECT: What happened when Jonah called out from his "grave"? What parts of his prayer are significant to you and your situation?

These who have turned the world upside down have come here too. Acts 17:6, NKJV

July 14

If we only realized the difference the Holy Spirit can make in our lives—just as He has done throughout the centuries.

For He's the same quickening power that turned Peter from shifting sand into a solid rock upon which Christ could build His church.

He's the transforming power that turned Saul, a murdering persecutor of the body of Christ, into Paul, a church-planting father of the faith.

He's the revolutionary power that took a handful of believers in a Jerusalem upper room and used them, in the words of their detractors, to turn "the world upside down" (Acts 17:6, NKJV).

It wasn't until after the Spirit came, in fact, that Jesus's disciples made any kind of impact on their world. Though they had lived and walked with Jesus for three years, being in His presence hadn't changed them all that much.

Here's the bottom line: We can *know* what we ought to do. We can even have God physically present beside us, a flesh-and-blood example of what life should be—yet still be powerless to live as we ought to live.

In order to truly change—to stop our self-sabotage, oust Flesh Woman, and open our lives to transformation—we need a Helper. A Strengthener. An internal Source of power.

Praise God, that's exactly what Jesus sent the Holy Spirit to be for us. Fifty days after the resurrected Christ appeared to His disciples, after He breathed on them saying, "Receive the Holy Spirit," the Spirit came at Pentecost (Acts 2).

And nothing has ever been the same.

—*Having a Mary Spirit*

Read: 1 Corinthians 2:4–5
Reflect: What did Paul depend on when it came to ministry, and why?

July 15

Now to Him who is able to do exceedingly abundantly above all that we ask or think. EPHESIANS 3:20, NKJV

When Martha met Jesus on the road after her brother died, a powerful exchange of truth occurred between the two of them. After pouring out her pain and confusion, Martha gave Jesus permission to do what He thought best, saying, "But I know that even now God will give you whatever you ask" (John 11:22).

In response, Jesus made one of His seven great "I Am" declarations, all recorded in the gospel of John. "I am the resurrection and the life," He told Martha. "Do you believe this?" (verses 25–26).

"Yes, Lord,…I believe you are the Christ," she replied (verse 27). And Martha did believe! Unlike some of her fellow Jews, she had faith in an end-time resurrection. She knew her brother would live again. In that faith-filled moment, Martha may have even believed Jesus could speak resurrection life into her brother that very day.

But later, as Martha stood before Lazarus's tomb, her faith faltered. Face to face with grief-filled reality, she found it difficult to believe that anyone—even Jesus—could bring life out of such obvious death and decay.

It can be just as hard for us to imagine such a transformation in our lives today.

Yes, Lord, we know that one day we'll be made truly alive when we see You face to face. But to think we might experience resurrection right here in the middle of our messy, mixed-up existence? *It just doesn't seem possible,* we decide, settling for the midchamber and just hanging on until Jesus comes.

Yet all the while, the Resurrection and the Life stands outside our tombs, calling our names.

"Lazarus… Joanna…" Put your name on His lips.

Then listen as Jesus commands, "Come forth!"

—*Lazarus Awakening*

READ: Mark 9:21–24

REFLECT: In what area of your life do you need God's help to overcome unbelief?

When I missed my book deadline six months into a contract, I had the bare tracings of three chapters—a far cry from the ten I'd promised to deliver.

"I feel like I'm holding a pregnancy test stick, and it says I'm expecting a book," I told my publisher, "but I have absolutely no symptoms. No movement, not even a tummy bump to tell me it will be born."

The only assurance I felt was that this book was God's idea and not my own. More important, I could hear God challenging me to believe, no matter what the situation looked like.

So it appears impossible? I felt the Holy Spirit whisper to my spirit. *So it looks like you'll never finish this project?*

"Did I not tell you that if you believed, you would see the glory of God?" Jesus asked Martha at the door of her brother's tomb (John 11:40). Standing at the threshold of my impossibility, I heard that same question daily for twenty-four months.

Four days is a long time to wait for a resurrection. Two years feels like an eternity to write a book.

But if you'll believe, Joanna, you will see.

"Lean not on your own understanding," Proverbs 3:5–6 reminds us. "In all your ways acknowledge Him, and He shall direct your paths" (NKJV).

Don't look at how far you have to go, God seemed to whisper each day as I sat down to write. *Instead, look for Me on the journey. Acknowledge My presence even in the middle of this emptiness. Don't try to work up faith for the outcome. Just believe in Me. Then you will see.*

—*Lazarus Awakening*

READ: Luke 1:45

REFLECT: What doubt is holding you back? Write this verse on a card, and repeat it whenever you are tempted to give way to fear.

July 17

Catch for us the foxes, the little foxes that ruin the vineyards. SONG OF SONGS 2:15

My mother is a master gardener. I wish you could sip iced tea with us as we look over her backyard. Every corner is filled with a beautiful tapestry of color that spills over her carefully edged flower beds. The scents are intoxicating, and the fruits of her labor luscious as we eat raspberries just picked from the vine.

None of this beauty happened by accident. It has been carefully planned and tended, with a lot of backbreaking work. As we walk through the garden, my mother points out each of the plants by name.

"This rosebush didn't bloom much last year, so I had to cut it back," she says, cradling a lovely blossom in her hand. "This peony had to be moved to get more sun, and I had to pull out a lot of irises to make more room for corn."

Her eyes glow warmly as she talks about her tasks, but what she describes is a series of seemingly brutal acts. Leafy branches chopped off. Healthy bushes pulled up by their roots. Blooming plants dug up and taken away. Each act is a certain kind of death. But all of it is done with love in the interest of summer bounty.

As I stroll with my mother through her garden, I'm reminded of the times I've questioned the One who tends the garden of my life.

Especially when, in the interest of growth, God takes away in order to add.

—Lazarus Awakening

READ: Hebrews 6:7–12

REFLECT: What is required to make sure our lives produce a harvest?

I chose you and appointed you to go and bear fruit—fruit that will last.
JOHN 15:16

July 18

"I never knew suicide was so slow or so painful," I told my husband one night after falling into bed exhausted from an especially difficult period of battling my lower nature. But it wasn't just the "suicide" I was struggling with. It wasn't just my choosing to die to self. God seemed to be working me over as well.

It was the confusing period I wrote about earlier, when God allowed a painful misunderstanding with friends to strip me of everything I assumed I needed for life. Their love, their friendship, their kind understanding and support—all of that was gone. The removal of their approval hurt me so deeply I thought I was going to die.

Which was the point, of course. But this wasn't the kind of death I had signed up for. I guess I'd expected to just close my eyes like Sleeping Beauty, then awaken refreshed and resurrected at the kiss of my handsome Savior Prince.

Instead, the Lord showed up in blue jeans and a canvas hat, with a water bottle and a sack lunch protruding from a backpack. And in His glove-covered hands—what were those?

A pair of heavy-duty shears.

For the "death" I was experiencing was really a season of pruning—lots and lots of pruning. It felt as though the Gardener was cutting off parts of me, pulling me up by the roots, taking away everything that gave testimony to life. The leafy branches that had once bloomed with color and dripped heavy with fruit had been stripped away, leaving me brown and bare, clinging to the trellis where I'd been tied.

Then came the long winter. And it too felt like death.

—*Lazarus Awakening*

READ: John 15:1–8

REFLECT: Describe the process needed to bear fruit. Why is it important that you cooperate?

July 19

Have nothing to do with the fruitless deeds of darkness. EPHESIANS 5:11

Throughout the Word of God, the analogy of fruit is used. All four Gospels include Christ's picture of the Vine and the branches. Out of the twenty-seven books in the New Testament, fifteen mention the kinds of fruit we are to have in our lives, including:

The fruit of our lips: "Let us continually offer to God a sacrifice of praise—the fruit of lips that confess his name" (Hebrews 13:15).

The fruit of our deeds: "That you may live a life worthy of the Lord and may please him in every way: bearing fruit in every good work, growing in the knowledge of God" (Colossians 1:10).

The fruit of our attitudes: "But the fruit of the Spirit is love, joy, peace, patience, kindness, goodness, faithfulness, gentleness and self-control" (Galatians 5:22–23).

So how can I make sure my life is producing this kind of fruit?

It's not really that difficult. You see, fruit isn't something you can sit down and manufacture in your life. Fruit *happens.* You get connected to the Vine and pretty soon you've got zucchini—tons and tons of zucchini.

So much zucchini you just have to share!

As we "abide" in intimate relationship with Christ, something incredible happens. We begin loving as we never loved before. Our lives change, and we become examples worth imitating.

We begin producing fruit. Juicy, lusciously lovely, lip-smacking-delicious fruit. Fruit in our lives that tells the world unmistakably who we are and what our God is like. Fruit that makes them hungry for a relationship with the One who gives true life.

The One who truly satisfies.

—*Having a Mary Heart*

READ: Psalm 1:1–3

REFLECT: If you want to be fruitful, what must you do?

You are no longer a slave, but a son.
GALATIANS 4:7

July 20

I didn't realize how much I longed for God until that dark night I cried out to hear the good news. Although I had served Him since I was a child, there was a devastating emptiness about my relationship with my heavenly Father. I had worked and worked to please Him, yet I couldn't feel His love.

The Galatians knew that same kind of emptiness. They had accepted Christ as Savior and thrived under Paul's teaching and care. But when Paul left Galatia, the Judaizers moved in, telling them they still had a long way to go before they could enjoy true closeness to God. These were Jewish Christians who believed that the ceremonial practices of the Old Testament—including circumcision—were still binding upon the New Testament church.

Paul sent a wake-up letter to his beloved church in Galatia. He called the Judaizers' gospel slavery, and he added, "You foolish Galatians! Who has bewitched you?… After beginning with the Spirit, are you now trying to attain your goal by human effort?" (Galatians 3:1, 3).

If we aren't careful, we can fall prey to the same kind of lies the Galatians fell for—lies that tell us that we must perform in order to earn God's love. We can add so many requirements to our faith that the "one thing" is swallowed by the "many," and the "best" is obliterated by the "good."

The thing we must understand is that God did not choose us to "use" us. We are not spiritual Oompa-Loompas in some cosmic chocolate factory, working night and day to churn out a smoother, better-tasting Christianity.

No, the Bible makes it clear that God created us because He longs to have fellowship with us.

What does God desire? He wants you. All of you.

—Having a Mary Heart

READ: Galatians 3:23–26
REFLECT: What were you before faith? What are you now through faith in Christ Jesus?

Creative Quiet Times

If you've found yourself yawning during devotions—or just eager for a change—you may want to consider the following suggestions for creative intimacy with God.

1. **Take God out for coffee.** Find a quiet corner in a café and meet with God. With your Bible and a notebook in hand, you're set for a heart-to-heart with your very Best Friend.

2. **Add a spiritual classic to your devotional diet.** While nothing should replace the Word of God, Christian books provide delicious and enriching side dishes!

3. **Put feet to your faith.** Take a walk with God! Praise Him for His handiwork. Listen to the Bible on your iPod. Pray. Your body and spirit will appreciate the workout.

4. **Journal your journey.** Keep a spiritual diary. Record thoughts as you meditate on Scripture. List prayer requests and answers.

5. **Come before Him with singing.** Add music to your devotions. Use a praise CD or sing a cappella. Read a hymn out loud. Praise ushers us into the presence of God.

6. **Let faith come by hearing.** Download sermons from favorite speakers. Anointed preaching builds both knowledge and faith.

7. **Dig a little deeper.** A good Bible study will take you beyond just reading the Word. It will help you rightly divide the Word of Truth and apply it to your life.

8. **All the King's versions.** Find a Bible translation you understand for your regular devotions. Read from other versions to add a fresh perspective.

9. **Hide the Word.** Memorizing Scripture plants the Word of God deep in your heart. Write verses on index cards and carry them with you to practice.

10. **Spend a half-day in prayer.** It may seem impossible, but as you set aside a large portion of time to spend with the Lord, He will meet you in extraordinary ways.

—Having a Mary Heart

In one of my all-time favorite books, *The Indwelling Life of Christ,* Major Ian Thomas explores the mystery and the power of living resurrected:

> The true Christian life can be explained only in terms of Jesus Christ, and if your life as a Christian can still be explained in terms of you— your personality, your willpower, your gifts, your talents, your money, your courage, your scholarship, your dedication, your sacrifice, or your anything—then although you may have the Christian life, you are not yet living it.
>
> If your life as a Christian can be explained in terms of you, what have you to offer to your neighbor next door? The way he lives his life can already be explained in terms of him, and as far as he is concerned, the only difference between him and you is that you happen to be "religious" while he is not. "Christianity" may be your hobby, but not his, and there is nothing about the way you practice it which strikes him as at all remarkable. There is nothing about you which leaves him guessing, and nothing commendable of which he does not feel himself equally capable without the inconvenience of becoming a Christian.
>
> Only when your quality of life baffles your neighbors are you likely to get their attention. It must become patently obvious to them that the kind of life you are living is not only commendable, but beyond all human explanation.[106]

Oh how I want to live an inexplicable life that points to Jesus, and Jesus alone. Don't you?

—*Lazarus Awakening*

READ: Acts 4:13

REFLECT: What would you like people to note about your life?

July 22

There remains, then, a Sabbath-rest for the people of God. Hebrews 4:9

The story is told of a migrant South American tribe that regularly went on long marches. Day after day they would tramp the roads. But then, all of a sudden, they would stop walking and make camp for a couple days. When asked why they stopped, the tribe explained that they needed the time of rest so that their souls could catch up with them.

Isn't that great concept? Letting your soul catch up. When I read this little story, it resonated deep within me. I can get to running so fast that I leave everything important behind. Not just God. Not just people. I can lose my own soul as well.

I think that's why God instructed us to observe a regular period of extended rest in the middle of our busy lives. That's why He gave us a Sabbath.

In Hebrew the word *Sabbath* literally means "a ceasing of labor." It refers specifically to a day of the week set aside for rest and for worship.

The Jews have always observed the Sabbath from sundown on Fridays until sundown on Saturdays. We Christians set aside Sunday, the day of Jesus's resurrection, for our Sabbath. But the chosen day is not as important as the chosen purpose—to bring balance and perspective to our work-weary lives on a weekly basis.

"If you call the Sabbath a delight and the Lord's holy day honorable," says the prophet Isaiah, "and if you honor it by not going your own way...then you will find your joy in the Lord" (58:13–14).

—*Having a Mary Heart*

Read: Exodus 20:8–11

Reflect: How could you better practice rest on this day God has given you?

For where two or three come together
in my name, there am I with them.
MATTHEW 18:20

July 23

The redwoods of California have stood tall for centuries, weathering the violent storms that come rushing in off the Pacific Ocean. I was surprised to learn that the root systems of these massive trees, some towering above three hundred feet, are relatively shallow. How have they stood so long and so strong?

The answer to that question has a spiritual parallel for Christians: as they grow, redwood trees interlock their roots with other redwoods until, in a sense, they become a single tree, standing stronger together than they would alone, able to face any storms that come.

Maybe that's why the author of Hebrews writes, "Let us not give up meeting together, as some are in the habit of doing, but let us encourage one another—and all the more as you see the Day approaching" (10:25).

We need one another. Part of the Sabbath God ordained involves meeting together in corporate worship. Whether or not you realize it, you need the church, the body of Christ. And the church needs you! It's just not the same when "u" are not in it.

Here's the bottom line: we need fellowship. I need to lock roots with your roots and you need to lock roots with mine. So that together, we can better withstand the storms of life. Growing stronger and higher than we ever could alone.

—Outtake from *Having a Mary Heart*

READ: Hebrews 10:24–25

REFLECT: We are meant to do life together. According to these verses, what does that involve?

July 24

Every single one of us will be hurt. It's a fact of life. Live around people long enough, and you will be disappointed. You will be ignored and forgotten. Your needs will be disregarded and your feelings trampled upon. You will be slandered and betrayed—sometimes innocently, sometimes on purpose. And not because you are overly deserving of pain, but simply because you are a human living with other humans in a fallen world. Because ever since the Fall, these three things have been true:

- Life is unfair.
- People will hurt us and let us down.
- We won't always understand why.

Taken together, those three realities are a recipe for pain. Worse, they can lead to destruction. Because hurt and disappointment left to fester will eventually become resentment. Resentment unchecked will harden into bitterness. And bitterness destroys. As someone once put it, "Bitterness is like drinking poison and waiting for the other person to die."

Perhaps that is why Jesus placed such a high premium on forgiveness. For He knew from personal experience that people do indeed let you down. They say one thing and do another. They kiss you on the cheek and stab you in the heart…or promise undying allegiance at the seashore but deny you at the fire. They bow down and hail you "King!" one day— and cry "Crucify!" the next.

Injustice will happen—that much is sure. Though the saying is trite, it is nonetheless true. We have a choice: will we be bitter or will we be better?

The answer is determined by how we respond.

—Having a Mary Spirit

READ: Romans 12:19–21
REFLECT: When we are mistreated, what are we to do?

Do not be overcome by evil, but overcome evil with good. ROMANS 12:21

July 25

Like you and me, Jesus was hurt by His fellow human beings. The Bible assures us He was "tempted in every way" (Hebrews 4:15)—which surely means He was tempted to hurl back insults. Tempted to plot revenge. Tempted to withdraw in order to avoid being hurt.

No wonder Christ made such a point of teaching forgiveness. For although He completely understood our natural response to pain, He also knew what unforgiveness does—that it not only destroys human relationships but also separates us from God (Matthew 6:14–15). So while unforgiveness may have tempted Christ, He resisted. He forgave even those who put Him to death. By doing so, He emphasized God's mercy to the world. Rather than giving His enemies what they deserved, Jesus put aside His right to vengeance and gave up His life instead.

And we are called to do the same.

Unfortunately, forgiveness is completely foreign to our human nature. It feels wrong, unjust, unfair. "What about them?" we ask, pointing our fingers. "What about what they've done?"

As I study God's Word, I'm amazed at how very personal its instruction is. Almost always, it's about my response. Focusing on what *I'm* supposed to do, regardless of what the other person may be doing. When someone slaps me on the cheek—whether they're right or wrong—I'm to offer the other side of my face for more punishment (Luke 6:29). Rather than overcoming evil by getting even, I'm told to overcome evil by doing good (Romans 12:21). And when someone hurts me or lets me down in any way, I'm called to give up my right to be avenged or even justified.

Christianity is a radical lifestyle! And nowhere is it more radical than in this sweeping command to forgive unconditionally.

—Having a Mary Spirit

READ: Luke 6:27–31

REFLECT: Instead of returning evil for evil, what are we supposed to do?

July 26

Bless and do not curse. ROMANS 12:14

As my friends and I have looked back at the painful conflict that arose between us, we've been able to point to lessons God taught us on the path to healing.

For me, one of the most important was practicing the art of blessing. When we're hurt, the last thing we want to do is bless the one who hurt us. Yet the Bible tells us over and over that this is part of our calling as Christians.

"Do not repay evil with evil or insult with insult," 1 Peter 3:9 says, "but with blessing...that you may inherit a blessing."

For me, the practical application of this truth was a daily necessity. Usually somewhere in the course of my day, I had to drive past the home of one of the friends I felt had wronged me. At first I couldn't even look in the direction of her house. The hurt was so deep it startled me. I'd never experienced such a tangible unwillingness to forgive.

I want you to bless her, don't curse her, I sensed the Lord saying.

"But, God," I argued, "I haven't cursed her."

No, not with your mouth. But your unwillingness to bless is just as much a curse.

All right. I couldn't argue with that. So I began the practice of consciously blessing my friend. Gradually I felt the knot in my heart slowly unravel. Before long, I was able to sense the depth of her pain and intercede for her.

"How I know I have forgiven someone," author and speaker Karyl Huntley says, "is that he or she has harmless passage in my mind."[107]

No accusing arrows. No passive attempts at revenge. The person's name is safe on my tongue—and I'm kept safe from the poison of my own resentment.

—*Having a Mary Spirit*

READ: Luke 6:32–36
REFLECT: Why are we called to such radical mercy?

"It all begins at the water line." That's how Jeanne Mayo describes the key to balancing work and worship. Then she shares this story.

In the autumn of 1992, a man named Michael Plant commenced a solo crossing of the North Atlantic. An expert yachtsman, Plant had made the trip several times before. His brand-new sailboat, the *Coyote,* was so technologically advanced there were few like it in the world.

Plant set off alone, leaving his support team to monitor his trip by satellite and radio. Everything was going well. Even when a storm disrupted communications, no one worried much. After all, this guy was one of the best sailors and navigators to be found. His boat was equipped with state-of-the-art navigational and emergency equipment. Plant would resume radio contact when everything settled down.

But Michael Plant was never heard from again. After numerous attempts to reach him by radio, the Coast Guard sent helicopters out to look for him. They found the *Coyote* floating upside down. Its captain and sole passenger was never found.

Why? How could this happen? the experts wondered. Everyone knows that sailboats are very hard to turn over. Their deep keels and massive rudders right themselves. But as the ship was examined, the cause of the tragedy became clear. For all its technological advances and beauty, the *Coyote* didn't have enough weight beneath the water line. There wasn't enough ballast below to outweigh the fancy gadgetry above. And so it flipped over as it lost its ability to balance in the water.

"Our lives will capsize as well," Jeanne Mayo concludes, "if what lies below the spiritual water line of our lives doesn't outweigh what lies above."[108]

—Having a Mary Heart

READ: Proverbs 7:1–2 and Psalm 119:11

REFLECT: What do you need to "store up" in your heart, and what is the benefit?

July 28

But exhort one another daily…lest any of you be hardened through the deceitfulness of sin. HEBREWS 3:13, NKJV

Sin always matters. Please don't forget that bedrock truth in the glorious light of God's grace. Because Christ is so quick to forgive us when we confess our sins, we can mistakenly believe that what we do doesn't make any difference. So confident of God's forgiveness and willingness to give us a new beginning, we continue to sin. We don't realize that if we're always returning to the starting block, we never arrive where we were meant to be—the finish line.

"When a person first sins," Chip Ingram writes in *Holy Transformation*, "there may be a short-lived thrill, but there also enters into the heart remorse and regret. But if the person continues in sin, there comes a time when he loses all sensation and can do the most shameful things without any feeling at all. His conscience has become petrified."[109]

After excusing one sin, in other words, we find it that much easier to commit others. For sin's nature is to reproduce itself in every area of our lives, causing us to do things we previously would have found unimaginable.

I once had lunch with a friend who had recently left her husband and children to move in with another man. Rather than being embarrassed by the situation, she bubbled with excitement over her newfound love.

"Oh, Joanna!" she effused. "You don't understand. We *pray* together before we make love!"

This woman sincerely felt she had God's blessing on her sin—though the Bible is abundantly clear about adultery. Any mention of such principles was quickly met with dismissals of why those particular scriptures didn't apply to her.

While I'm grateful to report that my friend eventually repented and her marriage was restored, the cost of the sin was high. It always is. For sin matters.

—*Having a Mary Spirit*

READ: Galatians 6:7–8

REFLECT: What warning is given to those who believe they will escape sin's consequences?

He who sows righteousness reaps a sure reward. PROVERBS 11:18

July 29

While you can't go back and undo the past or avoid sin's consequences, you can make choices today that improve your future. Even when you are living out consequences not entirely of your own making.

When my friend Lauraine[110] went through a terrible divorce, she spent a long time feeling as though she was being punished for her husband's unfaithfulness. Bitterness and hurt wrapped around her heart, threatening to choke out any hope of a happy future. She found herself becoming an angry, hard woman.

"I hate what this is doing to me," she told me one day. "But all I can think about is what he stole from me."

"You're definitely reaping the consequences of his actions," I agreed. My heart broke as I listened to all the things my friend had to face—her children's pain, the struggle with her finances, an uncertain future. It seemed so unfair, and I found myself growing angry along with her. But then God interrupted my sympathy with a profound thought.

"What are you planting today, Lauraine?" I asked my friend. "Because what you plant today determines what you harvest tomorrow."

We both began to cry as we allowed God to heal our perspective. For it really isn't what has been done to us or even what we have done that matters. It is what we let those events do to our hearts. And so we both prayed, "Lord, change me."

Because sin—both the act and our response to the act—really does matter.

—Having a Mary Spirit

READ: Hosea 10:12
REFLECT: What part do you play in determining the harvest you will reap?

July 30

We do not want you to become lazy, but to imitate those who through faith and patience inherit what has been promised.
HEBREWS 6:12

Though the race we're called to run is far from easy, the writer of Hebrews reminds us that you and I are surrounded by encouragement as we run it. We not only have a Savior waiting for us at the finish line; we also have His Holy Spirit bearing us up, infusing us with strength as we run. Our Helper lives within us. He is our Comforter, Teacher, and Friend.

Hebrews 12:1 tells us there are also people lining the grandstands of heaven cheering us on. Among them are spiritual giants who accomplished great things for God.

But may I remind you? Those forerunners of faith struggled to shed some of the same graveclothes you and I struggle to leave behind. Though each of these men and women fell a time or two in their race, they all got up from their failures and kept pursuing God.

Some, like Abraham and Sarah, received their promises. Others, however, "were still living by faith when they died," Hebrews 11:13 says. "They did not receive the things promised."

I don't know about you, but I'd struggle with the inequity of that. Yet these heroes of faith didn't let disillusionment trip them up. Instead, they refused to get wrapped up in this life, for "they were longing for a better country—a heavenly one" (Hebrews 11:16). Though imperfect and flawed, they pursued a higher goal.

"Therefore God is not ashamed to be called their God," verse 16 tells us, and, oh, how that resonates in my soul.

For while none of them walked entirely free of graveclothes before they died, they didn't let that stop their pursuit of heaven. Their eyes were fixed on the unchanging One.

And in return, the unchanging One changed them.

—*Lazarus Awakening*

READ: Hebrews 11:32–12:1
REFLECT: Describe the kinds of people that make up the "great cloud of witnesses."

We want each of you to show this same diligence to the very end, in order to make your hope sure. HEBREWS 6:11

July 31

Is it just me, or have we lost the anticipation of another world awaiting us as Christians? Have we become so attached to this world and its comforts that we've forgotten we are only pilgrims? Aliens as it were—created for another place. This life is just a spaceship meant to carry us through this world to our one true home.

I love the way Elisabeth Elliot describes it:

Heaven is not *here,* it's *There.* If we were given all we wanted here, our hearts would settle for this world rather than the next. God is forever luring us up and away from this one, wooing us to Himself and His still invisible Kingdom, where we will certainly find what we so keenly long for.[111]

Someone once asked, "Why do we tend to live like eternity lasts eighty years, but this life lasts forever?"

It's an important question, I think. As a young Christian, I realized that if I were to draw a time line of eternity, then attempt to place my lifetime on that continuum, it wouldn't even show up. In reality, these eighty-plus years we're given are only a blip on the screen, a "vapor" as James 4:14 (NKJV) describes it. A mist that quickly fades away.

But how we live this life is of utmost importance. For in a sense, we are training for eternity.

—Lazarus Awakening

READ: Matthew 25:1–13

REFLECT: What are we to do while we wait for the Bridegroom's return?

August 1

The Lord *spoke to me with his strong hand upon me.* Isaiah 8:11

When I was going through that black, difficult time with my friends, the word that most often came to mind to describe what was happening was the word *confound.* That in itself was strange because *confound* is not a word I normally use. Still, I couldn't shake the sense that God was using my circumstances to confound me. So I went to the dictionary and the Bible to find what it might mean.

The word *confound* means "to confuse or perplex" as well as "to contradict or refute." An archaic meaning is "to defeat or overthrow."

Unfortunately, the Bible seemed to concur with that last definition. Because the only people God confounded in Scripture were His enemies.

Thankfully, I knew that wasn't the case. God had constantly reminded me of His love and favor throughout this difficult time, reassuring me that this wasn't punishment, but a necessary pruning. But why this confounding? this pain? this frustrating confusion?

During the same period, God kept bringing my heart back to the quiet and gentle beauty 1 Peter 3:4 talks about. And the corresponding term *meekness* seemed to be popping up everywhere I went. As I shared with my friend Patty what God was teaching me, she asked what *meekness* means.

"Well, the most popular definition is 'strength under control,'" I told her. "You know, like a wild stallion that has been tamed."

Suddenly, like a lightning bolt in my mind, the two concepts that had been stirring in my soul seemed to transpose over each other. And suddenly I saw what God was up to....

—Having a Mary Spirit

 Read & Reflect: Using a concordance or Bible website, look up verses connected to *meekness* (kjv) and its corresponding term *gentleness* (niv). What did you learn?

Humble yourselves, therefore, under God's mighty hand, that he may lift you up in due time. 1 PETER 5:6

August 2

...*Confound* and *meekness.* The two terms fused into a revelation around the idea of a horse being tamed.

"That's what it is!" I told Patty as I stared at her in wonder. "That's why God has been confounding me."

Then I tried to explain what I was only beginning to understand. How do you break a wild horse? You confound it. It wants to go right; you pull on the reins and make it go left. It wants to run; you pull it to a stop. It wants to stand; you make it run. You confuse and contradict and, in a sense, defeat it—by refusing to give the horse its way. You confound the horse because it needs to obey. For until it does the animal will be useless to its master.

Patty caught the analogy and took it further, her brown eyes sparkling with excitement. "My friend told me she purchased a new horse and said it has the softest mouth. It responds to her every move without being forced. She only has to suggest a turn with the rein or press with her knee, and the horse immediately goes where she wants it to go."

By then we were both overwhelmed by the thought of being loved so much by God that He would break us so we might be useful to Him. What an amazing privilege!

This awesome truth stayed with me through the day and into the night. "Give me a soft mouth like that, Lord," I prayed as I lay in the dark. "I want to be so in tune with what You want that I obey before You even ask. Do whatever it takes to break my stubborn will and awful pride.

"Confound me for as long as it takes to make me entirely Yours."

—*Having a Mary Spirit*

READ: Psalm 32:8–10

REFLECT: What does God offer if we will only respond to Him?

August 3

A rebuke impresses a man of discernment more than a hundred lashes a fool.
PROVERBS 17:10

I wish I could say I've been broken once and for all and have lived ever since in useful, graceful humility.

Sadly, I can't say it. Even more sadly, I'm in good company. The entire history of the Old Testament is, in fact, the story of a loving God and a nation who repeatedly refused to humble themselves and be broken. They chose instead to break God's heart.

"In his love and mercy he redeemed them; he lifted them up and carried them all the days of old," Isaiah 63:9–10 says. "Yet they rebelled and grieved his Holy Spirit. So he turned and became their enemy and he himself fought against them."

Sounds harsh, doesn't it? But this was the same God, remember, who had lovingly pursued Israel for centuries. Forgiving His people when they repented. Restoring them when they turned back to Him. Receiving them every time they returned. The Old Testament saga spans nearly four thousand years, a miraculous story of a tenacious God who kept reaching out to a humanity who repeatedly spurned His advances.

No wonder God called them "stiff-necked." The Hebrew word, which crops up again and again from Exodus through Jeremiah, means "stubborn, unyielding, arrogant, and proud."[112] Little has changed today, I'm afraid.

One day during my devotions, I asked the Lord, "Why do we Christians have so much 'head' knowledge and so little 'heart' knowledge?" Immediately that word *stiff-necked* came to mind. In my spirit, I sensed the Lord saying, *It's because My people are unwilling to be broken. It is only as they allow Me to break their stiff-necked pride that the truth can filter down into their hearts.*

"Then break me, Lord," I prayed once again. "I want to know You—truly know You. Not by head, but by heart."

—Having a Mary Spirit

READ: Psalm 78
REFLECT: Note key phrases in this psalm that depict God's relentless love.

Because you have seen me, you have believed; blessed are those who have not seen and yet have believed. JOHN 20:29

The story is told of a woman who dreamed she saw three people praying. She watched Jesus draw near and approach the first figure, leaning over and speaking to her tenderly. Then He proceeded to the next figure, placing a gentle hand on her head and nodding with "loving approval." But what happened next perplexed the dreaming woman:

> The third woman He passed almost abruptly without stopping for a word or glance. The woman in her dream said to herself, "How greatly He must love the first one, to the second He gave His approval,...and the third must have grieved Him deeply, for He gave her no word at all and not even a passing look."...
>
> As she tried to account for the action of her Lord, He Himself stood by her and said: "O woman! how wrongly hast thou interpreted Me. The first kneeling woman needs all the weight of My tenderness and care to keep her feet in My narrow way. She needs My love, thought, and help every moment of the day. Without it she would fail and fall.
>
> "The second has stronger faith and deeper love, and I can trust her to trust Me however things may go and whatever people do.
>
> "The third, whom I seemed not to notice, and even to neglect, has faith and love of the finest quality, and her I am training by quick and drastic processes for the highest and holiest service.
>
> "She knows Me so intimately, and trusts Me so utterly, that she is independent of words or looks or any outward intimation of my approval...because she knows that I am working in her for eternity, and that what I do, though she knows not the explanation now, she will understand hereafter."[113]

—*Lazarus Awakening*

READ: 1 Peter 1:8–9

REFLECT: What is the importance of believing God is with us, even when we don't necessarily feel Him at our side?

August 5

Why are you silent? HABAKKUK 1:13

Dear friend, don't be afraid of the times when Christ seems "silent in his love" (Zephaniah 3:17, DRA), when He answers "not a word" (Matthew 15:23, KJV). Because God is up to something more in your life and mine than just giving us the comfort of His voice.

He is working in us for eternity. He wants to be able to say of us, "She knows Me so well...I can trust her with My silence."

As Lettie B. Cowman puts it, "The silences of Jesus are as eloquent as His speech and may be a sign, not of His disapproval, but of His approval and of a deep purpose of blessing for you."[114]

So in those times when God is quiet, trust Him and wait. For when the right time comes, you'll hear from Him again.

The very act of waiting, in fact, may help us tune in to His voice better than any other spiritual discipline. For I've found that God often speaks in the middle of the night. When I'm quiet. When my heart's focused and my ears are ready to hear.

Driving across the dark highways of Montana late at night, I can pick up radio stations from all around the country. Spanish stations from Texas. Financial talk shows from New York. Obscure religious stations from who knows where.

So many voices. So many choices. But if I'll take the time to dial in through all the noise, I'll find the one I seek.

Spiritually, that's true as well. For as I consistently tune my heart to the real thing, the counterfeits fade. Until all I hear is the Voice I need.

Love. Calling my name. And your name as well.

—*Lazarus Awakening*

READ: Proverbs 4:20–22

REFLECT: What choices can you make to better incline your ear to hear God speak?

Devote yourselves to prayer, being watchful and thankful. COLOSSIANS 4:2

August 6

"Teach us how to pray," the disciples asked Jesus one day as He came back from yet another time of prayer. They'd watched their Teacher carefully and a pattern had developed. Luke 5:16 tells us, "Jesus often withdrew to lonely places and prayed." Whether it was early in the morning (Mark 1:35) or toward evening (Matthew 14:23), Jesus found a place of holy solitude.

The disciples recognized that something powerful happened when Jesus prayed. They saw the miracles, and it was enough to make them want what Jesus had.

The fellowship Christ enjoyed with His Father empowered His ministry to the world. For prayer always affects more than just us. At least, that's how it should be. This is not an exclusive relationship we enjoy with the Lord; it is an inclusive one. A corporate fellowship—not just me, myself, and God.

Perhaps that's why Jesus taught His disciples to pray "*our* Father" instead of "*my* Father." To pray for "*Thy* kingdom" instead of "*my* kingdom." So that when we present our needs, "give *me*" gives way to "give *us*." Jesus knew that prayer can easily turn egocentric, as most of us suffer with some kind of "I-disease"—I want this; I need that.

In the Lord's Prayer, Jesus gave us a design for intercession that expands our vision beyond ourselves, exalting God's will as our highest priority. When we begin to pray from a heavenly point of view, our "I-disease" gives way to a fresh vision of God—as our hearts focus on establishing *His* kingdom rather than insisting He build our own.

—Outtake from *Having a Mary Heart*

READ: Matthew 6:9–13

REFLECT: Pray through the Lord's Prayer slowly line by line, expounding on each one with your own personal prayer.

August 7

Commit to the LORD whatever you do, and your plans will succeed. PROVERBS 16:3

The one thing that Jesus said was needed in Martha's life was fellowship with Him—and that's true for us, too. But the principle of "one thing" also has smaller, practical implications that can help when life feels overwhelming. Here are some ways to practice one-thing thinking each and every day.

1. ***Invite Jesus to rule and reign.*** Each morning before you get out of bed, invite the Lord to come take the throne of your life, to be your "one thing." Present your day to Him and ask Him for wisdom and guidance.

2. ***Ask God to reveal the next step.*** As you go through your day, keep asking the Lord, "What is the one thing I need to do next?" Don't let the big picture overwhelm you. Just take the next step as He reveals it—wash one dish, make one phone call, put on your jogging clothes. Then take the next step...and the next.

3. ***Have faith that what needs to get done will get done.*** Since you have dedicated your day to the Lord, trust that He'll show you the one thing or many things that must be done. Do what you can do in the time allotted. Then trust that what wasn't accomplished was either unnecessary or is being taken care of by God.

4. ***Be open to the Spirit's leading.*** You may find your day interrupted by divine appointments. Instead of resisting the interruptions, flow with the one thing as God brings it across your path. You'll be amazed at the joy and freedom that comes from surrendering your agenda and cooperating with His.

—Having a Mary Heart

READ: Psalm 37:23–24
REFLECT: Walk through the steps given above as you prayerfully commit your day to the Lord.

Let the wise listen and add to their learning, and let the discerning get guidance. PROVERBS 1:5

August 8

Sometimes I think I struggle to discern God's will because I'm surrounded by obvious needs. When our church scheduled a missions banquet, someone— *obviously*—needed to head it up, so I cheerfully volunteered, certain I was doing God a favor. "Oh Lord," I told Him, "You are going to love what I have planned for You!" Then I set off, certain He was walking beside me.

Unfortunately, everything about the event was a struggle. There were interpersonal rumblings and my own amount of grumbling. But after it was through, I felt quite satisfied. The banquet was beautiful, and money was raised for crucial needs.

I remember sighing with pride, "Wasn't that wonderful, God?" But I heard no reply in my spirit.

Over here, Joanna, He said, patiently waiting on the path where I'd first told Him of my glorious plan.

"I thought You were in this, Lord," I said as I walked back to where He was.

He gently took my hand. *It was good. Perhaps it was even important. But it wasn't My plan for you.*

I realized then that, while there are many things that need to be done, things I'm capable of doing and want to do, I am not always the one to do them.

How I wish I would have learned earlier in ministry to wait upon the Lord. I still tend to rush in, presuming to know His will rather than waiting to hear what He desires. It is a costly mistake, for often, when the Holy Spirit does ask something of me, I'm either knee-deep in another project or too exhausted from my latest exercise in futility to do what God wants of me.

—*Having a Mary Heart*

READ: Isaiah 48:17–18

REFLECT: Have you ever run ahead of God? What are the blessings related to only doing what He asks of us?

August 9

He tends his flock like a shepherd: He gathers the lambs in his arms and carries them close to his heart. ISAIAH 40:11

One extra-busy day, I came across this poem in Mother Teresa's book *Life in the Spirit*. This retelling of the Twenty-third Psalm from Japan ministered to my weary heart, reminding me that I have a Gentle Shepherd. One who knows better than I both the things I need as well as the pace I should go. But best of all, it reminded me that I never walk alone. And neither do you, dear friend.

> The Lord is my pace setter…I shall not rush
> He makes me stop for quiet intervals
> He provides me with images of stillness which restore my serenity
> He leads me in the way of efficiency through calmness of mind and
>   his guidance is peace
> Even though I have a great many things to accomplish each day, I will
>   not fret, for his presence is here
> His timelessness, his all importance will keep me in balance
> He prepares refreshment and renewal in the midst of my activity by
>   anointing my mind with his oils of tranquility
> My cup of joyous energy overflows
> Truly harmony and effectiveness shall be the fruits of my hours for I shall
>   walk in the Pace of my Lord and dwell in his house for ever.[115]

—Having a Mary Heart

READ: Psalm 23
REFLECT: What part of this psalm do you need most today?

May the Just One set me straight,
may the Kind One correct me.
PSALM 141:5, MSG

August 10

Jesus often revealed sin in the New Testament. When He pointed out flaws in people He met, He wasn't trying to humiliate them; He wanted to alert them to danger and point the way toward their healing.

To the Pharisees intent on appearing religious, Jesus pointed out the fault line of hypocrisy.

To the rich young ruler requesting the way to heaven, Jesus exposed the dangerous tendency of loving money more than God.

And that day in Bethany when Martha came whining to Jesus demanding assistance, it wasn't insensitivity that caused Jesus to rebuke her (Luke 10:38–42). He knew the last thing Martha needed at that moment was more help in the kitchen. What she really needed was to recognize the fault line in her soul.

"Martha, Martha," He told her gently. "You are worried and upset about many things" (verse 41). With those words, Jesus pointed to the weak spot of her psyche—her anxiety, her need to succeed, and the fear of failure which fed a demanding spirit.

Whether it is resentful anger like Cain's, a Pharisee's need to appear successful, a young ruler's passion for possessions, or a Martha-like pursuit of perfection—we all have fault lines, core issues that fuel our desires and shape our actions. And when we give in to our natural impulses and go against God's way, we may get what we want but lose what we need most.

An awareness of God's presence.

And His blessing on our lives.

—Having a Mary Spirit

READ: Proverbs 13:18
REFLECT: How should we respond to the rebuke of the Lord?

August 11

If I had cherished sin in my heart,
the Lord would not have listened.
PSALM 66:18

Unlike King David, my core issues and fault-line weaknesses haven't led to adultery and hiring hit men, but my fatal flaws have certainly caused enough trouble on their own. And so I find myself praying another of David's prayers:

> Search me, O God, and know my heart;
>   test me and know my anxious thoughts.
> See if there is any offensive way in me,
>   and lead me in the way everlasting. (Psalm 139:23–24)

God loves to answer prayers like that.

When we hide our sins, God cannot help us (Psalm 66:18). But when we volunteer for a spiritual polygraph, as David did, we bring joy to our Father and potential freedom to our souls. When we willingly invite God to search the hidden corners of our hearts and scrub them clean, we can declare, "You forgave me! All my guilt is gone" (Psalm 32:5, NLT).

David's prayer in Psalm 139 is not a one-time prayer. We need to forever be aware of the weak places in our souls. I'm not talking about an unhealthy obsession or living under constant condemnation, but about the holy awareness Romans 12:3 encourages us to cultivate. "Do not think of yourself more highly than you ought," Paul warns, "but rather think of yourself with sober judgment." Post sentries at vulnerable spots in your wall, he advises. Fault-lines, left unattended, give Satan direct access to our souls.

But the soul-patrol isn't left entirely up to us. While we are to "guard the good deposit" God has given us, 2 Timothy 1:14 also tells us we "guard it with the help of the Holy Spirit who lives in us."

And aren't you glad for that? Such an important task is far too big to attempt on our own.

—Outtake from *Having a Mary Spirit*

READ: Psalm 19:12–13
REFLECT: Use these verses as a template for prayer, asking God to both reveal and forgive any hidden faults.

Make level paths for your feet…
HEBREWS 12:13

August 12

In order to guard vulnerable places in my soul, I've found it helpful to do a motivation check before I step out on potentially rocky ground. So, on a regular basis, I ask myself why I do the things I do: *Am I doing this for the Lord or so people will like me?* I might ask about a particular activity. *What insecurity in my life is causing me to need affirmation or to be the center of attention?*

Your specific struggle and weak spot may require different kinds of questions:

- *Why do I feel the need to own this particular item?* Do I genuinely need what I yearn for, or am I really yearning for prestige or acceptance?
- *Why did I assume it was the other person's fault?* What makes it hard for me to take responsibility for my part in the situation?
- *Why was I less than honest in that last conversation?* Is it because I'm afraid people might reject me or because I really don't know who I am?
- *Why am I avoiding this phone call or difficult conversation?* Does this habit indicate passive-aggressive rebellion or a type of fear?

You may have to wrestle with these issues a little—asking the Holy Spirit to help you overcome denial, self-deception, and rationalization. Journaling your thoughts and prayers about these issues may also help—it has certainly helped me. But keep in mind that the point isn't so much to find "right answers," as it is to get honest before the Lord. Because until we recognize our weaknesses and ask for God's help with them, we will continually stumble. As long as we live on earth, we'll need God's help and protection for the vulnerable spots in our souls.

—Having a Mary Spirit

READ: Proverbs 16:2

REFLECT: When it comes to discerning your motives, whose help do you need?

231

August 13

Direct my footsteps according to your word; let no sin rule over me.
PSALM 119:133

Have you ever felt as though you've taken one step forward with the Lord only to fall two steps back? I certainly have. Why does it keep happening, we wonder, especially when we are so eager to please the Lord? James gives some insight into our dilemma when he writes, "But each one is tempted when, *by his own evil desire,* he is dragged away and enticed" (1:14, emphasis mine).

In other words, it is our own moral weak spots that often get in our way.

When it comes right down to it, what keeps tripping us up is *us.*

Strangely, it is often legitimate needs that cause the most trouble. Our hunger to be loved. Our need to be significant. Our longing to feel secure. Unless these needs are ultimately met by the Lord, they are easily distorted into "abnormal desires," which is how the *New American Commentary* translates "evil desires" in James 1:14.[116]

Satan loves to turn legitimate needs and emotional vulnerabilities into unholy obsessions, twisting what we long for into lures fashioned for our destruction.

Like a fisherman who baits a hook and dangles it in front of a waiting fish, Satan uses counterfeit love, false security, and tin-plated success to lure our hearts away from God. Because the hook is usually hidden and we're slow to feel its pain, we can fool ourselves into thinking the temptation is harmless. That we can get away with sniffing without touching. Touching without tasting. Tasting without chewing. Chewing without swallowing.

Yet in the end, nothing could be further from the truth.

—Lazarus Awakening

READ: Isaiah 44:18–20
REFLECT: What is the danger of making idols out of abnormal desires, according to verse 20?

Do not deceive yourselves.
1 Corinthians 3:18

August 14

The Bible is clear. "Do not be deceived," Galatians 6:7 tells us, "God is not mocked; for whatever a man sows, this he will also reap" (NASB).

In other words, don't be deceived. That e-mail relationship you've rekindled with an old flame is eventually going to burn you.

Don't be deceived. That tendency to blurt out confidential information to get attention will ultimately come back to bite you in the end.

Don't be deceived. That compromise you think is crucial to climbing the ladder of success will eventually cause you to fall further than you ever dreamed.

The simple truth is this: God loves us enough to let us trip on our grave-clothes. For until we stop pursuing abnormal desires and "chasing after the wind," as Ecclesiastes 1:14 puts it, God has no choice but to give us over to our "stubborn hearts to follow [our] own devices" (Psalm 81:12).

Unfortunately, by then, we've usually swallowed the devil's bait—hook, line, and sinker. Caught in a full-blown affair, shunned by friends, entangled in a web of deceit, frantically trying to recover a life we so carelessly threw away. Or living with less obvious but just as deadly consequences. For even when it seems we've gotten away with rebellion, its fruit will manifest itself somewhere. Especially when it comes to our spiritual progress and growth in the Lord.

For it is impossible to move forward with Jesus when we're sucking on Satan's lure.

Just ask the Israelites. When they insisted on doing things their own way, Psalm 106:15 tells us, God "gave them their request, but sent leanness into their soul" (NKJV).

A dangerous and less-than-satisfying exchange, if you ask me.

—*Lazarus Awakening*

READ: Proverbs 1:29–33

REFLECT: What is the danger of ignoring God's advice? What is the blessing of listening?

August 15

As obedient children, do not conform to the evil desires you had when you lived in ignorance. 1 PETER 1:14

Of all the abnormal desires the enemy likes to exploit within us, I'm convinced that nothing is as deadly as the unconscious patterns we tend to develop in our lives. Though we've been born again in our spirits, our soulish natures—consisting of our minds, wills, and emotions—tend to run in ruts created by repetition. Self-defeating grooves formed by less-than-holy reactions arising from our flesh.

One of my early patterns had to do with self-pity, as I've noted before. It was tied to an abnormal desire to be loved and accepted.

How did I know this was a pattern? Simple—I kept repeating it. No matter the situation or conflict, I always seemed to end up huddled in an emotional corner, singing a sad medley of songs. "Nobody loves me. Everybody hates me.… Poor, poor, pitiful me." Convinced that others were to blame while dismissing my own responsibility.

At first self-pity wrapped itself tenderly around me like a warm shawl, confirming my victim status, but it quickly turned into a straitjacket. The graveclothes that initially comforted me eventually tightened around me, choking out my joy. My hope. My breath. My life.

I don't know what cyclical responses you keep returning to, but may I suggest it would be wise to find out. Begin by asking yourself, "What pattern keeps popping up time and time again?" Then consider this: "What abnormal desire might lie behind that reaction?"

Is it pride that lurks behind the rage that erupts when certain buttons are pushed?

Is it insecurity that causes overwhelming paranoia when you overhear someone talking but can't quite hear what they say?

Is it love-hunger that makes feelings of rejection surge within you when recognition is given to another or your value is ignored?

—*Lazarus Awakening*

READ: Jude 1:16–19

REFLECT: Though these verses were written against godless men who used grace as a license to sin (verse 4), does any of their behavior bring to mind patterns you need to renounce?

Therefore each of you must put off falsehood and speak truthfully to his neighbor, for we are all members of one body. EPHESIANS 4:25

August 16

What would happen if we Christians loved one another enough to get involved in each others' lives? I don't mean a spiritualized voyeurism so many people call "concern." I'm speaking of the godly friend who humbly asks, "Have you considered this? Have you looked at that?"

I'm thankful that someone took time to correct me when I was a young pastor's wife. My core need of approval was leading me down some dangerous paths. She cared enough to take me by the shoulders and speak some sense into me. "Joanna, I know you don't mean to," my friend said, "but you're a flirt. You like to laugh and tease with the guys. It's wrong, and you need to stop."

I was mortified. Though I wanted to plead my innocence, her words revealed a great gaping hole in my soul I had been unaware of until that moment. Despite being married and very much in love, the awkward teenager inside me still craved attention and admiration from the opposite sex.

I cried, and we prayed. God heard and He forgave. I walked away from that encounter a different woman—praise the Lord!

Oh, there are times when Flesh Woman still tries to exert her need to sparkle and shine, but there is a deep abhorrence and holy fear in my heart that I would ever again betray my husband—or my Lord!

Had someone not cared enough to speak the truth, though she knew it would hurt, I shudder to think what could have happened because of that vulnerable, weak place in me.

"Faithful are the wounds of a friend," says Proverbs 27:6 (NKJV). "Friendly" wounds that heal rather than scar—life-giving words that speak the truth in love.

—Having a Mary Spirit

READ: Ephesians 4:15–16
REFLECT: How might speaking the truth in love help us grow up as the body of Christ?

August 17

If one falls down, his friend can help him up. But pity the man who falls and has no one to help him up! Ecclesiastes 4:10

If we want to be the people God designed us to be, we must be willing to engage in godly confrontation—or as my father puts it, "care-frontation." But to do that, we may need to check our attitudes at the door, admit our biases, drop our agendas, and do some serious praying.

How do we know that our hearts are right enough to try to "right" someone else? I think the key is found in Galatians 5:26, which provides a simple checklist for examining our attitude toward a person needing correction: "Let us not become conceited, provoking and envying each other." Clearly, before we open our mouths to say something to an erring brother or sister, we'd do well to examine *why* we feel compelled to speak:

- *"Let us not become conceited..."* Do I feel I am "better" than this person and incapable of this sin?
- *"provoking...each other..."* Is my main motivation for confrontation to prove the other person is wrong and I am right? Do I hope the person will argue so I can convince him or her of the sin?
- *"envying...each other."* Do I secretly want to see the other person humiliated? Is my truth telling motivated in any way by jealousy, a desire to get even, or a need to see the other person exposed?

It's the motivation of our hearts, you see, that makes all the difference.

—Having a Mary Spirit

Read: Matthew 7:3–5
Reflect: What are you to do before you try to help restore a brother or sister?

By this all men will know that you are
my disciples, if you love one another.
JOHN 13:35

August 18

The year was 1998. Dr. Don Argue had been invited to meet with the president of the People's Republic of China, Jiang Zemin, to discuss China's stance on religious freedom. Tens of thousands of Christians were being persecuted for their faith, with thousands more in prison or already executed. Dr. Argue had earlier presented the logic of allowing Christians to practice their faith.

"They will be your best workers," Argue had told the president. "They are honest and trustworthy." But the conversation had moved on from there, swallowed up in political posturing and diplomatic niceties.

"I know who you are," President Jiang said in a low voice as he bent toward Dr. Argue. With the help of an interpreter he shared this story: "When I was a youth, I was very sick and in a hospital. One of your people, a Christian nurse, cared for me. Even at the end of a long and busy day, she would not leave until all of our needs were met."

President Jiang smiled and nodded.

"I know who you are."[117]

Of all the identifying marks of a Christian, Jesus said love would be the thing that gives us away. "By this all men will know that you are my disciples," He said, "if you love one another" (John 13:35). *Agape* is to be our signature—the unconditional, never-ending love of God flowing through and out of our lives. We need a love that loves "in spite of" and "because of." In spite of rejection, hardship, or persecution, we love. Because of the great compassion God lavished upon us, we share it with our world—both in words and in sacrificial service.

We've been filled with great treasure for one purpose: to be spilled.

—*Having a Mary Heart*

READ: 1 Timothy 6:18–19
REFLECT: Underline the phrases in this passage that speak most to you, and respond to them in prayer.

August 19

I have set you an example that you should do as I have done for you.
JOHN 13:15

Christ illustrated *agape* love to His disciples by washing their feet. "As I have loved you, so you must love one another," Jesus told the group of men in John 13:34, their freshly laundered toes a gentle witness to His words.

What Jesus did must have shocked the disciples. The *Midrash* taught that no Hebrew, even a slave, could be commanded to wash feet. The streets and roads of Palestine were rugged back then, unsurfaced and unclean. William Barclay says, "In dry weather they were inches deep in dust and in wet they were liquid mud."[118] Add the fact that most people wore sandals, a simple flap of leather fastened to the foot by a few straps, and foot washing was a dirty job, to say the least.

Though disciples, by tradition, attended to their favorite rabbi's many needs, they never considered such a filthy task. Nor was it expected. It simply wasn't done.

So when Jesus bent His knee to serve His followers, it was a graphic display of humility. Their Teacher became the lowest of the low. Then He invited—no, commanded—them to do the same. "It is noteworthy that only once did Jesus say that he was leaving his disciples an example, and that was when he washed their feet," says J. Oswald Sanders.[119]

Kitchen Service, you see, isn't optional for Christians. We're supposed to spend a good part of our time following our Lord's example. We're supposed to serve others and show love to them—and, in the process, to represent Jesus to the world around us.

—Having a Mary Heart

READ: Mark 10:42–45

REFLECT: If we want to be like Jesus, what are we called to do?

Always be eager to practice hospitality.
ROMANS 12:13, NLT

August 20

Genetically, I should be predisposed to hospitality. While I was growing up, my mother made hospitality look easy.

But it isn't easy—at least not always. It's something I struggle with personally, mostly because I'm just so busy. It's a challenge to make space in my life to bring people in. So many times I've felt like the Benedictine monk whom Kathleen Norris tells about in her book *Amazing Grace: A Vocabulary of Faith.*

Benedictine monks are experts at hospitality. Their founder, St. Benedict, made caring for strangers one of the fundamental rules of the order. "Receive visitors as you would receive Christ," he instructed. No one is to be turned away. It's been that way with the Benedictines for centuries. And yet one busy monk, when approached by a visitor with questions concerning the abbey, replied brusquely, "I don't have time for this; we're trying to run a monastery here!"[120]

Ouch! How easy it is to get so caught up in our busy lives that we forget the reason Jesus came and the purpose for which we were called.

When we lived in the church parsonage, transients would come several times a week from the nearby railroad tracks searching for food or shelter. I would always be busy, and they would be scruffy or even smelly. I'm ashamed to admit that there were times I'd whisper inside, *Go away! We're trying to run a church here!*

But then they'd say something like, "The guys at the gas station told me to come here. They said this church helped anybody."

Ouch again! As Christians—as a church—we are called to be a hospital, the very root of *hospitality.* Our lives should be a refuge for the hurting, not a country club for the comfortable.

—Having a Mary Heart

READ: James 2:14–17
REFLECT: According to James, the brother of Jesus, what is our responsibility as Christians?

August 21

I no longer live, but Christ lives in me.
GALATIANS 2:20

I love the story I once heard about a young boy who approached an evangelist after a revival tent meeting. "Excuse me, sir?" the little boy said politely. "You said everyone should ask Jesus into their hearts, right?"

"That's right, son." The evangelist squatted down so he could look the boy in the eye. "Did you ask Him in?"

"Well, I'd like to," the boy said, shuffling dirt with the toe of his shoe before returning his gaze to the evangelist. "But I got to figurin'…I'm so little and Jesus is so big—He's just gonna stick out all over!"

"That's the point, son," the evangelist said with a smile. "That's the point."

I don't know about you, but I want Jesus to be so evident in my life that people don't just consider me a nice moral person, full of good works. I want my relationship with God to be so real and vital, so like that of the apostles Peter and John, that people can't help but sit up and take notice.

Wouldn't it be wonderful to have words said of us like those Acts 4:13 records? "When they saw the courage of Peter and John and realized that they were unschooled, ordinary men, they were astonished and they took note that these men had been with Jesus."

—*Having a Mary Heart*

READ: 2 Corinthians 5:18–20

REFLECT: How can we be better "ambassadors" of Christ? What qualities of Jesus would you like to develop in your life?

I was blessed with a wonderful childhood. My grandma Nora lived with us, so there was always someone to come home to after school. But once in a while, the house would be empty when I got home. Really empty. An unusual occurrence that always struck fear in my heart that the Rapture had taken place and I'd been left behind.

Now, some might think that a terrible burden for a child to bear and blame it on too much hell-fire preaching, but nothing could be further from the truth. It didn't terrorize me as much as make me want to be certain all was right between the Lord and me. I wasn't fearful of losing my salvation as much as disregarding it.

But one thing could set my heart at peace during those lonely, tad-bit-frightening afternoons. I'd call my aunt Gert's number. Her heart for God and sweet spirit made me certain that she'd be the first one to go in the Rapture. If she didn't answer the phone, I was really in trouble.

As I write this I have to smile at the memory. Films like *Thief in the Night* probably fed my young-girl fears, but I'm grateful for the awareness that one day the trumpet will sound and the "dead in Christ will rise first" and we will all be caught up together "to meet the Lord in the air"(1 Thessalonians 4:16–17, NKJV). It isn't a matter of "if"; it is a matter of "when." And while I don't think we should be in fear of that day, I do think it would do the body of Christ a lot of good if we started living in anticipation of the return of the Lord Jesus Christ.

Because, whether we realize it or not, this life isn't all there is. Not by a long shot.

—Outtake from *Lazarus Awakening*

READ: Matthew 24:36–46

REFLECT: What should we do in anticipation of the Lord's return, and what is the warning for those who don't?

August 23

For to me, to live is Christ and to die is gain. PHILIPPIANS 1:21

Death was not a part of God's original plan. You and I were made for life—life eternal. An eternity lived in the company of our Maker and each other.

Unfortunately, our great-great-not-so-great-grandparents Adam and Eve decided they wanted more than what God offered. So they bit at the serpent's bait and attempted to seize control.

Consequently, the Father had to limit their freedom. He banished them from the garden and blocked access to the tree of life (Genesis 3:22–23). As a result, death was given access to beings who had been created to live forever.

Does that sound harsh? Though God's actions might seem extreme, we must understand the punishment was birthed out of great mercy.

Just think. Without death, the evicted Adam and Eve—not to mention you and I—would be assigned to an eternity of lonely wandering. A 24/7 life of hopeless toil and meaningless monotony. An empty existence bereft of the constant sense of God's presence Adam and Eve had once enjoyed.

God's mercy and grace marked our lives here on earth with a finish line. And with sweet irony, our loving Father took the very thing we'd feared the most—the threat of death—and turned it on its head. Transforming tombs into doorways and our endings into new beginnings. Turning hearses into glistening carriages to carry us to a glorious mansion being prepared as we speak—the eternal home for which we were made (2 Corinthians 5:1).

"Where, O death, is your victory?" Paul writes in 1 Corinthians 15:55 as he considers our final destination and the vehicle that will get us there. "Where, O death, is your sting?"

Through Jesus Christ, "death has been swallowed up in victory" (verse 54).

—*Lazarus Awakening*

READ: 1 Corinthians 15:51–55
REFLECT: How does God's promise of heaven renew your hope?

Your life is now hidden with Christ in God. COLOSSIANS 3:3

August 24

As a young man, Martin Luther was a tortured soul. He wanted to please God. Desperately. So he joined a monastery and dedicated his entire life to becoming holy, no matter the cost. Fastidious about sin, he was constantly going to his confessor to repent of his wrongdoing. The kind prelate tried to direct him to God's love, but Luther's failings haunted him continually.

It wasn't until God showed Luther the meaning of the words in Romans 1:17 that he finally found peace. "For in the gospel a righteousness from God is revealed," the verse says, "a righteousness that is by faith from first to last, just as it is written: 'The righteous will live by faith.'"

Suddenly Luther realized that God was not demanding that he be holy on his own. Instead, God offered the very thing this tired monk had spent so many years striving for—not just right living, but the righteousness of God Himself. "At this I felt myself straightway born afresh and to have entered through the open gates into paradise itself," Luther writes.[121]

I love how the movie *Luther* portrays this moment.

"Look to Christ," his father confessor tells the young monk as he presses a crucifix into Luther's hand. "Bind yourself to Christ. Say to him, 'I am Yours. Save me.'"

Sitting on the cold stone floor of his cell, Luther stares at the cross, then wraps his hand around it. "I am Yours," he whispers to Jesus. "Save me." And at the moment he decides to trust, he is finally set free. No longer in torment, Luther is a man at peace.[122]

As are we…when we give up striving and choose rather to draw from the rich storehouse of grace Christ purchased for us on the cross.

—Having a Mary Spirit

READ: Romans 8:1–2
REFLECT: To what source besides Jesus have you been looking to save you? Repeat Luther's words and let go of your striving.

August 25

So those who have faith are blessed along with Abraham, the man of faith.
GALATIANS 3:9

During a video session of Beth Moore's *Believing God* study, God took me on a spiritual side trip. He reminded me of how I've lived with a set of scales in my heart—scales that measured my worth by my performance. I was always trying to make the good outweigh the bad. But no matter how hard I tried, the smallest of failures easily displaced any success.

Using the accounting metaphor from Romans 4, Beth quoted verse 8: "Blessed is the man whose sin the Lord will never count against him."[123]

Suddenly that truth converged with the reality of Isaiah 64:6: "All our righteous acts are like filthy rags"—absolutely worthless, weighing nothing in our favor. Placed beside my sin upon the scale analogy in my mind, I realized, they don't count. Neither do the bad things I do. If I've put my faith in Jesus, they just don't count!

I don't think I can fully explain what this did in my spirit. Truth, like a scroll unfolding, began to fill my heart. *If my sins don't count and my good deeds don't count, then what does?*

Faith. That's the only thing that counts in God's mathematics.

Abraham believed God, and his belief was credited to him as righteousness (Genesis 15:6). Because he chose to trust God in the face of impossibilities, a deposit of holiness was made in his spiritual bank account: *"Ka-ching!"*

But the kind of faith that pleases God, that tilts the reckoning in our favor, is not passive. Far from it. True faith requires obedience. It requires being willing to stake everything on God's love and faithfulness—and then doing what He asks.

Even when we don't understand.

Even when He demands that we give up the things we love the most.

—Having a Mary Spirit

READ: Romans 4:18–25
REFLECT: What phrase(s) in this passage speaks to your heart today? What is God asking you to believe He has the power to do?

Consider the kind of faith Abraham showed when he packed up his son and a load of firewood and headed for Mount Moriah (Genesis 22). If you'd been there listening, I think you might have heard, *"Ka-ching!"* Righteousness deposited on the patriarch's behalf.

And had you been there when Abraham raised his knife and blessed his God, fully intending to obey while fully believing God would still fulfill His promise (Hebrews 11:19), I believe you would have heard something besides a voice from heaven telling him to stop and the rustling of a sacrificial ram caught in the thicket. I can almost hear it now: *"Ka-ching!"*

For though God had promised Abraham that "through Isaac...your offspring will be reckoned" (Genesis 21:12), the greatest act of Abraham's faith was leaving the reckoning up to God. And it is the same for us.

When we stop trying to manhandle our circumstances and start giving them to God, something incredible happens. God takes everything we give Him and begins to work on our behalf. Because we've chosen to believe and trust rather than doubt and fear, He makes all of it—the good and the bad—count *for* us rather than against us. And that's when we start laying up serious treasure in heaven. And treasure on earth.

"Ka-ching!" Faith is credited to us as righteousness—and that righteousness comes in the form of Christlikeness. For when I believe that Jesus is not only able to save me but also to make me holy, I make deposits in my righteousness bank. *"Ka-ching, ka-ching, ka-ching!"*

And every time I do, by any reckoning, I end up looking more like Jesus and less like me.

—Having a Mary Spirit

READ: James 2:21–23

REFLECT: What action did Abraham add to his faith? What obedience is God asking of you today?

August 27

Did God really say...? Genesis 3:1

I remember being offended years ago when people talked about hearing the voice of God. "God told me this…" they'd say, or "God told me that…"

After all, I was a twenty-eight-year-old pastor's wife. I'd been raised in the church and loved Jesus since I was a little girl. But I'd never actually heard God's voice—or so I thought.

I've come to realize, however, that although I still have yet to hear God speak audibly, it would be untrue to say I haven't heard His voice. In fact, I believe that the Lord is speaking to me more often than I know.

Priscilla Shirer describes this problem in her excellent book *Discerning the Voice of God.*

> If God wants us to hear His voice, the Father of Lies is going to do everything he can to make us think that we *aren't* hearing it. When we hear from God, we call it intuition, coincidence, or even luck.… We're so used to dismissing His voice that we've convinced ourselves that He no longer speaks to His children. But the Bible says over and over that God *does* speak to us. We *are* hearing from Him. We just may not know it's Him.[124]

Some people think that claiming to "hear God's voice" is not only presumptuous but dangerous. I can understand their concerns. After all, such claims have been the excuse for a lot of insanity and evil over the centuries. But to conclude from such instances of misuse and abuse that God *doesn't* speak today would be to miss a precious part of our walk with Him and a necessary key to our freedom.

For if we don't hear God speak, we won't be able to obey.

And if we don't obey, we'll never be free.

—Lazarus Awakening

READ: John 10:2–5

REFLECT: How do sheep come to know their shepherd's voice in the natural realm? How do you and I come to know our Shepherd's voice in the spiritual?

This is my Son, whom I love; with him I am well pleased. Listen to him!
MATTHEW 17:5

August 28

I wish I could outline "Ten Easy Steps to Hear God Speak—Guaranteed!" That would appeal to the craving we all have for formulas. But God's communication is far more individual and intimate than anything a self-help bestseller could teach.

Our heavenly Father knows the best kind of communication flows out of relationship. Anything less is just an exchange of information. Since intimacy with us has always been God's goal, it makes sense that hearing His voice would be linked to that very thing. Perhaps that's one reason God keeps the voice of His Spirit quiet and subtle—so we'll lean in and listen carefully. And perhaps that's why He doesn't continually converse with us every moment of every day—so we'll treasure the times when He does.

I'm no expert on hearing God speak. In many ways, I'm still a learner. However, I truly believe God wants to draw close to me and speak truth individually tailored to my specific needs. But in order to have ears to hear, I must open my heart to His voice. And that happens best when I

- prayerfully invite Him into my everyday life,
- fill my heart and mind with His Word,
- remain alert to different ways He may speak to me,
- respond with obedience.

—*Lazarus Awakening*

READ: 1 Corinthians 2:9–12
REFLECT: How is the Holy Spirit involved in helping you better hear God's voice?

August 29

If anyone would come after me, he must deny himself. LUKE 9:23

One of the mantras of weight-loss gurus is "You must do it for yourself."

Well, I must beg to differ. "Doing it for myself" is what got me in trouble in the first place. It all started with the stretch pants of the nineties. And an overly developed case of self-love.

"Oh, just a little piece won't hurt," I used to tell myself eyeing the cheese-cake selection. "After all, I deserve it." I had been a good girl that day. I'd had salad rather than onion rings. Or I had exercised that morning. Or I had helped an old lady cross the street. The specific reason really didn't matter—somehow, some way I always deserved it. And so I partook and partook. And never forsook.

Nearly fifty pounds later, all that self-love started to accumulate, expanding my waist while decreasing my wardrobe. Because pampering Flesh Woman only increases her appetite for more.

The Bible warns of this lust of the flesh in 1 John 2:15–16. "Do not love the world or the things in the world," the apostle John writes. "...For all that is in the world—the lust of the flesh, the lust of the eyes, and the pride of life—is not of the Father but is of the world" (NKJV).

That Greek word for "lust" is *epithumia,* which translates as "a longing—especially for that which is forbidden." But I like how Oswald Chambers further illuminates the term: "Lust means—I must have it at once."[125] It doesn't matter what you want, if you must have it right away—if you are unwilling to wait or work for it or, harder still, tell yourself no—you are lusting after it. And that is not of the Father. It is of the world.

—Outtake from *Having a Mary Spirit*

READ: Luke 16:13

REFLECT: Personalize the verse above by filling in the following blank with the area you tend to give in to more than you should: "I cannot serve both God and _____." Now take that area to the Lord in prayer.

The world and its desires pass away, but the man who does the will of God lives forever. 1 JOHN 2:17

August 30

"I don't want to be like those women who are slaves to their bodies," I used to say when asked if I belonged to a gym. Of course, the fact that I could barely bend over to tie my shoes and had trouble scratching my own back should have clued me in to the fact I was a slave in more ways than one.

Unhealthy self-love—lust that refuses to say no to the flesh—will always lead to bondage. It will keep us ineffective in every way. For many of us, excess weight is the least of our problems. In fact, we've gone to the other extreme and exercise night and day, counting calories until our friends want to scream. We love our bodies so much we nearly worship them.

Others of us have secret cravings that rule our thoughts and shape our days. We can't go twenty-four hours without giving in to Flesh Woman's demands. We make promises lying in bed at night, only to break them in the light of day. We beat ourselves up with self-hatred only to give in once again to self-love—perpetuating a never-ending cycle of self-gratification and self-flagellation. A pattern that, I must tell you, brings Satan unending delight. For it keeps us from the riches of grace—the true food our souls need.

Those who look to God for sustenance will "feast on the abundance of your house; you give them drink from your river of delights" (Psalm 36:8).

Lay aside the penny candy and let the Lord set before you a table that will satisfy every desire you've ever had. For He wants to give you Himself. The Bread of Life. Everything you've ever craved and more.

—Outtake from *Having a Mary Spirit*

READ: John 6:24–27, 35
REFLECT: What did the people want from Jesus, and what did He tell them they should desire instead?

August 31

For you know the grace of our Lord Jesus Christ... 2 Corinthians 8:9

Often, in our pursuit of holiness, we experience moments so filled with power that we are enabled to do what we could not do before. We find ourselves in holy places where "heaven touches earth and we happen to be standing there," as my friend Michael Snider puts it.

If you've ever experienced an extra ability to overcome sin or a sudden lack of desire for a once-cherished indulgence—that was a space of grace. To maintain it:

- ***Don't ignore it.*** This space of grace is a gift from God. Give Him praise and thanks. Then walk carefully in His provision (Romans 1:21).
- ***Don't misinterpret it.*** We often attribute God's gift of freedom to willpower we worked up on our own. Pride grows, and as a result, we are often one step away from a fall (Isaiah 2:11).
- ***Don't abuse it.*** When we misuse grace by willfully returning to our sin after being set free, we grieve the Spirit, and the grace to easily overcome is often removed (Hebrews 10:26–29).
- ***Don't give up.*** If you've abused God's mercy or have yet to find that gracious place, repent and keep seeking God. He *wants* to set you free! (Joel 2:13).

I love how Paul reflects on the power of God that so transformed his life, saying, "By the grace of God I am what I am, and his grace to me was not without effect" (1 Corinthians 15:10).

Will you and I allow God's power to change us—to measurably "effect" us in the way we live and love? Or will we, like the prodigal son, squander the riches of grace our Father so lovingly provides?

—Having a Mary Spirit

 Read & Reflect: Look up and read the four passages noted above, then respond to the Lord in prayer.

Our offenses and sins weigh us down....
How then can we live? EZEKIEL 33:10

September 1

One of my favorite reality television programs is *The Biggest Loser.* I love the transformation that occurs as contestants daily work at shedding the pounds that have imprisoned them for so long.

At some point in the process, they are asked to run a course—an easy task, considering how far they've come and how hard they've trained. But there is a twist. As they run, they must wear a backpack filled with weight that is equivalent to the amount they have lost.

"I never knew how hard it was to move, let alone live, with all this weight," someone invariably says in an interview following the race.

If we could only see the freedom that awaits us if we'd get rid of the things that hinder us. The abundant life that could be ours if we'd abandon our secret affection for the things that weigh us down and trip us up.

When runners prepare for a race, they know they must run light and lean if they hope to win. Anything that slows them down or hinders movement must be removed, and anything with the potential to trip them up must be dealt with, or they risk losing the race, no matter how hard they run.

The writer of Hebrews applies this same light-and-lean strategy to our lives in Christ: "Let us throw off everything that hinders and the sin that so easily entangles, and let us run with perseverance the race marked out for us" (12:1).

—*Lazarus Awakening*

READ: Ezekiel 18:31
REFLECT: What are you to get rid of, and what will you receive in return?

September 2

I run in the path of your commands, for you have set my heart free. PSALM 119:32

This spiritual contest we are in is serious business. It requires careful preparation. The term "throw off" in Hebrews 12:1 doesn't denote a casual activity, like shrugging off excess clothing. Instead, the Greek word describes a much more deliberate and energetic action. Greek scholar Rick Renner says *apotithimi* means to "lay something down and to push it far away and beyond reach." It implies "a deliberate decision to make a permanent change of attitude and behavior"[126]—exactly what is needed to shed graveclothes.

Hebrews defines two things we must remove if we want to run free:

1. "everything that hinders"
2. "and the sin that so easily entangles"

While sin's removal seems obvious, it is the more generic "everything" of point one that often gets us into trouble, especially if we're seasoned Christians.

The King James Version word for "everything that hinders" is *weight*. It can refer to the heavy things of life like overdue bills, marital strife, job layoffs, rebellious kids. But weights can also consist of the "riches and pleasures" mentioned in Luke 8:14. As Ray Ortlund puts it,

> Your danger and mine is not that we become criminals, but rather, that
> we become respectable, decent, commonplace, mediocre Christians.…
> The twenty-first-century temptations that really sap our spiritual power
> are the television, banana cream pie, the easy chair, and the credit card.
> Christian, you will win or lose in those seemingly innocent little
> moments of decision.[127]

Because, you see, one aspect of "weight" has do with the importance we assign things—the value we give them in our lives.

—Lazarus Awakening

READ: Romans 13:12–14
REFLECT: What are we to discard, and what are we to put on?

Whoever claims to live in him must walk as Jesus did. 1 JOHN 2:6

September 3

Too often, we determine the worth of things according to the wrong set of scales, using the "differing weights and differing measures" of the world, which Proverbs 20:10 tells us "the Lord detests."

Whenever we give in to our culture's topsy-turvy tendency to call "evil good and good evil," whenever we exchange "darkness for light and light for darkness" (Isaiah 5:20), whenever we rationalize something as acceptable when God says it isn't, we've got it all wrong. Such fraudulent scales must be abandoned if we are to ever run free.

So how do we do that? It's not as difficult as we often make it. Instead of trying to shed hindrances on your own, take both the things that weigh you down and the false weights that throw you off, and bring them to Jesus. Allow Him to give you a new set of standards by which to live. Trade in the dishonest scales of the world so that you will be able to discern heaven's true measure— "that good and acceptable and perfect will of God" (Romans 12:2, NKJV).

At the end of the obstacle course, all the *Biggest Loser* contestants are given a chance to throw away the backpacks that hold the weight that used to define them. You don't see them hugging those backpacks or wistfully kissing them good-bye. They don't reminisce fondly about the number that used to appear on the scale. Instead, they take those packs and they fling them as far as they can possibly throw such a large amount of weight.

And as they do, nearly all of them say, "Never again. Never again."

—*Lazarus Awakening*

READ: Deuteronomy 25:13–16
REFLECT: Why do you think accurate weights and measures are so important to God, both spiritually and practically speaking?

253

September 4

The sinful mind is hostile to God.
ROMANS 8:7

"For most of my life," Joyce Meyer writes in her book *Battlefield of the Mind,* "I didn't think about what I was thinking about. I simply thought whatever fell into my head. I had no revelation that Satan could inject thoughts into my mind. Much of what was in my head was either lies that Satan was telling me or just plain nonsense, things that really were not worth spending my time thinking about. The devil was controlling my life because he was controlling my thoughts."[128]

God has recently been convicting me of such careless thinking. Of allowing thoughts to come and go much like cars crossing the Oklahoma-Arkansas border. No roadblocks. No checkpoints. No sin-sniffing dogs. No discipline of the will.

Careless thinking is a dangerous habit. For as our thoughts go, so go our emotions. And as our emotions go, so often goes our faith. If the enemy can get me confused, he can get me discouraged. If he can get me discouraged, he can cause me to doubt. If he can make me doubt, he can distract my mind—and that's just a step away from dividing my heart.

No wonder God says our transformation must involve what Romans 12:2 calls "the renewing of your mind." We need a mental makeover that heals our faulty assumptions and twisted thinking, our knee-jerk and often inappropriate emotional responses, our skewed and selfish decision making, and even the way we talk to ourselves.

—Having a Mary Spirit

 READ: James 1:22–25
REFLECT: Describe how cooperating with the Word of God can transform our hearts and minds.

May the words of my mouth and the meditation of my heart be pleasing in your sight, O LORD, my Rock and my Redeemer. PSALM 19:14

Studies have shown that when we speak normally, we speak at the rate of about 120 words a minute. But psychologists tell us that when we self-talk—that is, carry on a conversation with ourselves inside our heads—we talk at a rate of about thirteen hundred words a minute![129]

Imagine the impact of this constant self-talk. Thirteen hundred words a minute comes to 1,248,000 words a day (not including the eight hours we sleep). And the bad news, according to author Tim Hansel, "is that 70 percent or so of our self-talk normally is negative. That means that you and I spend quite a bit of time saying such things as *Oh no, I shouldn't have done that,* or *Oh, what a jerk I am,* and other similar, self-defeating phrases."[130]

The impact of such self-talk is really destructive. For if Tim Hansel is right, we listen to nearly a million pieces of degrading, God-forgetting self-talk per day.

And to make matters worse, it may not always be me who is talking to me.

"Satan is just as capable of using the personal pronouns *I, you,* and *me* as we are," explains Anabel Gillham.[131] In her book *The Confident Woman* she writes:

> These thoughts will correlate perfectly with your unique version of the flesh (your old ways, your old habit patterns) and will be disguised as the way you have always thought, the way your [mental] computer has been programmed. His success comes when you, because the thoughts are so familiar, so "like you," accept these thoughts. Then he has you, and you wind up doing the very thing you don't want to do.[132]

—*Having a Mary Spirit*

READ: 1 Peter 5:8–9
REFLECT: How should you resist the devil?

September 6

Why are you troubled, and why do doubts rise in your minds? LUKE 24:38

Negative self-talk often slips into my mind before I even have time to think. Satan disguises lies as personal assessment, and he plays and replays the demeaning statements inside my head like a never-ending song:

- "There's no use starting this project—I'll never finish it."
- "I can't believe I forgot to do that! I'm such a flake."
- "I'm a domestic nightmare—even the dog won't eat my cooking."

Your self-talk tapes may be different from mine, of course. They are shaped by your own experiences and misconceptions about life (with a little help from the enemy of your soul). As a result, they're beautifully adapted to your specific core issues. That's why they're so hard to see—and so hard to change.

But change *is* possible. That's the whole point of renewing the mind. With the help of the Holy Spirit, we can learn to recognize the lies. We can learn to push *stop* on the constant playback of these mind tapes, to eject the "if only" videos that replay our failures, and erase the "what if" software that exploits our fears.

Next time you and I are tempted to verbally assault ourselves, let's choose "the law of kindness" instead (Proverbs 31:26, NKJV). Encouraging ourselves with edifying words that build up rather than negative words that tear down. Choosing to offer ourselves the same grace we'd give to a stranger.

—Having a Mary Spirit

READ: 2 Corinthians 10:5
REFLECT: What are you to do with thoughts and self-talk that exalt themselves in your mind?

When God tells us in the Bible not to worry, it isn't a suggestion. It's a command. Worry and/or anxiety is specifically mentioned twenty-five times in the New Testament alone as something we should avoid.

The words used most often for "worry" and "anxiety" in the New Testament come from the same Greek word, *meridzoe,* which means "to be divided, to be pulled in opposite directions, to choke."

In the parable of the sower, Jesus tells us that the seed of God's Word can be "choked by life's worries," leaving us unable to "mature" (Luke 8:14). Gasping for spiritual breath, worry-bound, thorny-ground Christians may survive, but they never truly thrive.

Why is the Bible so adamant about our avoiding fear and worry? Because God knows worry short-circuits our relationship with Him. It fixes our eyes on our situation rather than on our Savior.

It works a little like a thick London fog—the kind of fog that is legendary. "Thick as pea soup," Londoners describe it. "Can't see your hand in front of your face," they say.

However, while physical fog may seem dense and almost solid, scientists tell us that a fog bank a hundred feet deep and covering seven city blocks is composed of less than one glass of water. Divided into billions of droplets, it hasn't much substance. Yet it has the power to bring an entire city to a standstill.[133]

So it is with anxiety. Our minds disperse the problem into billions of fear-droplets, obscuring God's face. Taking our anxiety to the Lord is often the last thing we think of when we are spiritually fogged in. And yet only the "Son" has the power to disperse it. Without Him, one fear leads to another, and our lives slow to a painful crawl.

—Having a Mary Heart

READ: Mark 4:15–20

REFLECT: Describe how worries, wealth's deceit, and desires for things have sometimes choked the Word in your life, making it less than fruitful. Ask God to show you how to cultivate good soil.

September 8

Don't fret or worry…. Let petitions and praises shape your worries into prayers, letting God know your concerns.

PHILIPPIANS 4:6, MSG

What is the difference between healthy concern and toxic worry? Here are a few things I've discovered in my own battle against fear:

CONCERN	WORRY
• Involves a legitimate threat	• Is often unfounded
• Is specific (one thing)	• Is generalized (spreads to many things)
• Addresses the problem	• Obsesses about the problem
• Solves problems	• Creates more problems
• Looks to God for answers	• Looks to self or other people for answers

Pastor and teacher Gary E. Gilley sums up the difference like this: "Worry is allowing problems and distress to come between us and the heart of God. It is the view that God has somehow lost control of the situation and we cannot trust Him. A legitimate concern presses us closer to the heart of God and causes us to lean and trust on Him all the more."[134]

Concern draws us to God. Worry pulls us from Him. I think this distinction is especially helpful for those of us who tend to spiritualize worry, convincing ourselves that it's our duty to fret about such things as the state of the world, our finances, or our futures.

We face legitimate concerns every day of our lives. But instead of fretting, instead of worrying, we need to focus on discerning what *we* can do (with God's help) and what should be left entirely up to God.

Even more important, we need to keep our focus on who God is and what God can do.

—*Having a Mary Heart*

READ: Philippians 4:6–7
REFLECT: What worry do you need to leave in God's hands today?

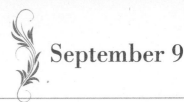

I will refresh the weary and satisfy the faint. JEREMIAH 31:25

September 9

Keeping the Sabbath meant a lot of work for the women of Jesus's day. Though the Sabbath was mandated as a day of rest for women as well as men, the day *before* the Sabbath was filled with frantic preparation. There were three kosher meals to prepare, lamps to be filled with olive oil, and jugs to be filled to the brim with water for ceremonial washing. The house had to be cleaned, and the whole family needed freshly laundered tunics to wear the next day.[135]

And that was for an "ordinary" Sabbath. Feast days and special events required extra preparations.

The day Jesus visited Martha and Mary was probably busier than usual. The Feast of the Tabernacles was near. The pilgrimage feast was held early in the fall and was one of three feasts every adult male Jew within a fifteen-mile radius was required to come to Jerusalem to celebrate. In order to make room for worshipers, the boundaries of Jerusalem were usually extended to include Bethany.

So when Martha invited Jesus and His disciples to stay at her home on their way to Jerusalem, they accepted her kind hospitality. Martha continued with her expected tasks—making everything comfortable so everyone else could worship.

The thought of joining Jesus never occurred to her because it simply wasn't allowed. But she loved Jesus. I think she knew she was entertaining the Messiah. And so Martha showed her devotion by giving the gift she knew best. The gift of service.

But even welcome wagons can grow heavy, as Martha quickly discovered. Especially when they're laden with the extra weight of our human agendas and expectations.

—Having a Mary Heart

READ: Isaiah 40:29–31

REFLECT: What does God offer us if we will "wait" on Him (NKJV)?

September 10

Praise be to the Lord, to God our Savior, who daily bears our burdens.
PSALM 68:19

The Jews, eager to please God, were big on rules and regulations. God had given the Law, and because they loved Him, they were determined to live it out to the fullest. If a little law was good, then surely more law was even better.

In their desire to be a perfect nation, the Pharisees created the *Mishnah,* a collection of over six hundred rules and regulations designed to help Jews live out the Law to the last jot and tittle. The mandates ranged from the sublime to the ridiculous. Especially those surrounding the Sabbath.

God's Law required this weekly day of rest, a ceasing from labor and a laying down of burdens. From the appearance of the first evening star on Friday night until the setting sun on Saturday, Jews were required to cease from all work—and the rules about what constituted work were quite exacting. The Pharisees interpreted this to mean that a man who carried a needle in his cloak on the Sabbath was sewing. If he dragged a chair across a sandy floor, he was plowing. If he carried his mattress, he was bearing a burden. If he plucked corn and rubbed it in his hands, he was reaping. In all of these things, he was considered to be breaking the Law.[136]

The Pharisees even argued that it was wrong to eat an egg laid on a Sabbath because the *hen* had been working. The "official" Sabbath burden that one could legally carry was the weight of one dried fig.[137]

But instead of drawing the nation of Israel closer to God, the Pharisaic law became a stumbling block. It was impossible to keep every petty particular of what Jesus called "heavy loads" (Matthew 23:2–4).

When Jesus died on the cross, He took the burden of our striving and opened the way for us to experience a true Sabbath. Reconciling our hearts to God and giving us genuine rest for our souls (Hebrews 4:9–10).

—Having a Mary Heart

READ: Romans 5:10–11
REFLECT: How has our relationship with God changed because of Jesus?

September 11

When Jesus breathed on the disciples in John 20:22 and said, "Receive the Holy Spirit," He was, in essence, both answering David's prayer in Psalm 51:10–11 to "renew a right spirit within me" (KJV) and fulfilling Ezekiel's prophecy that God would "give you a new heart and put a new spirit in you" (Ezekiel 36:26–27). The word for "spirit" in the Greek is *pneuma*. In the Old Testament Hebrew it's *ruwach*. Both can be translated "breath."[138]

Jesus came to breathe His breath—His sweetness, His completeness, His very being—into you and me so that He is the operating system to which we default. So that in Him "we live and move and have our being" (Acts 17:28).

Trying to live apart from the Holy Spirit is like a goldfish trying to survive outside water. We may look alive. We may flop around a lot and move our mouths, making strange gasping noises now and then, but we will never know what it means to really live. To glide free, breathe, and live effortlessly in the liquid life of grace.

Too often, I fear, we Christians have settled for this fish-out-of-water kind of existence. "Well, I'm a just a sinner saved by grace," we gasp, as though that somehow excuses and explains away our spastic, flip-floppy behavior—almost holy one moment, completely unholy the next.

As though Christ's coming and dying did nothing more than secure a place for us in heaven.

As though spiritual mediocrity is the best we can hope for here on earth.

As though God created us to be captives even though everything in the Bible says we've already been set free.

—*Having a Mary Spirit*

READ: 2 Peter 1:3–4

REFLECT: When it comes to living a victorious life, what has God made available to help you?

September 12

But the fruit of the Spirit is love…
GALATIANS 5:22

The Holy Spirit came to do more than enable us to live victoriously. He came to help us do the one thing Jesus said would cause the world to stand up and take notice that we were God's children: "By this all men will know that you are my disciples, if you *love* one another" (John 13:35, emphasis mine).

And that is exactly what happened! The baptism of love the New Testament church experienced after the Spirit's coming was unlike anything the world had ever seen. People set aside time daily just to be together. When someone was in need, others sold their possessions so the needy person could be helped. Slave or free, Jew or Gentile, or even a complete stranger—everyone had a place in God's family. When pagan observers were asked to describe the early church, their oft-quoted comment was "Behold, how they love each other!"

But this was no ordinary human love. Human love wears thin with time and lack of gratitude. Human love is willing to help, but only so much. (It fears unhealthy dependence, not to mention long-term commitment.) Human love may strive to be pure and giving, but selfishness inevitably creeps into the mix somewhere.

But this love…*this* love! There had been nothing quite like it in the history of the world. And it is this same selfless love we are called to live out every day.

—*Having a Mary Spirit*

READ: Philippians 2:1–4
REFLECT: What should be the evidence in your life of being united with Christ?

My command is this: Love each other as I have loved you. JOHN 15:12

September 13

Transformation has always been the stuff of fairy tales—Cinderella's rags turned into a glistening gown and Beauty's love unlocking the Beast's curse. However, no fairy tale compares to the life-changing love story Jesus longs to live out with us. Strangely, while we are part of that story, we are also called to help write it. Wes Seeliger puts it so well, using a familiar tale to describe the important "unwrapping" work Christ-followers are called to share:

> Ever feel like a frog? Frogs feel slow, low, ugly, puffy, drooped, pooped. I know. One told me. The frog feeling comes when you want to be bright but feel dumb, when you want to share but are selfish, when you want to be thankful but feel resentment, when you want to be great but are small, when you want to care but are indifferent.
>
> Yes, at one time or another each of us has found himself on a lily pad floating down the great river of life. Frightened and disgusted, we're too froggish to budge. Once upon a time there was a frog. But he really wasn't a frog. He was a prince who looked and felt like a frog. A wicked witch had cast a spell on him. Only the kiss of a beautiful maiden could save him. But since when do cute chicks kiss frogs? So there he sat, unkissed prince in frog form. But miracles happen. One day a beautiful maiden grabbed him up and gave him a big smack. Crash! Boom! Zap! There he was, a handsome prince. And you know the rest. They lived happily ever after. So what's the task of the [Christian]? To kiss frogs, of course.[139]

—Lazarus Awakening

READ: 1 John 4:7–12

REFLECT: Why are we called to love one another?

September 14

For we are God's workmanship, created in Christ Jesus to do good works.
EPHESIANS 2:10

I'm afraid that instead of mobilizing the body of Christ, the movement toward discovering our spiritual as well as natural gifts may have provided many of us with a handy excuse. Now when churches call for workers, we have a spiritual reason why we can't help.

"It just isn't my gift," we can say piously, pointing to the twelfth chapters of Romans and 1 Corinthians.

Despite our excuses, a question still remains: What exactly *do* we do?

I don't want to minimize the importance of understanding our strengths and our weaknesses. There is much to be learned about the ministry gifts God gives to the church and our part in the body of Christ. Certainly a need is not necessarily a call—and no one is called to do *everything.* That is why we always must spend time waiting before the Lord and asking Him what He'd have us do.

But as far as I can tell, the biblical description of gifts were never intended as excuses to pick the kind of service that feels comfortable and convenient, then ignore all the others!

After all, the same chapter of Romans that lists spiritual gifts also makes it clear that we are *all* called to serve regardless of our specific gifts. We may or may not have the *gift* of servant hospitality (Romans 12:7), but we are *all* called to "practice hospitality" (verse 13). We may or may not have the *gift* of giving (verse 8), but we are *all* called to "share with God's people who are in need" (verse 13).

"Rather than picking and choosing ministry opportunities based solely on our talents and interests," Jack Hoey writes in *Discipleship Journal,* "we are directed, 'Always give yourselves fully to the work of the Lord.' "[140]

—Having a Mary Heart

READ: 1 Corinthians 15:58
REFLECT: What work of the Lord will you give yourself fully to today?

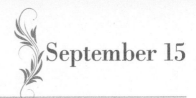

September 15

I can't imagine what it must have been like to see Lazarus shuffle out of the darkness of the tomb, wrapped in thin strips of linen according to the custom of the day. His arms and legs were probably wrapped individually, which allowed some movement. But to say the man was restricted would be an understatement.

The stench of death surely lingered around him. Depending on the original sickness, bloody patches may have marked the burial garment here and there, interspersed with yellow-crusted infection. Though a welcome sight to those who loved him, the resurrected Lazarus might also have been a bit frightening to behold.

I wonder what Mary and Martha thought when Jesus said, "Loose him, and let him go" (John 11:44, NKJV). As happy as I'd be to see my brother alive, I wouldn't want to touch the strips of linen that had clung to his rotting flesh. After all, who knew what lay beneath the bandages? Just how resurrected was he?

Unwinding graveclothes. It's a dirty job. But someone has to do it.

Someone has to do it. And that's one of the factors of Lazarus's story that shocks me most. For while Jesus Christ did what only He could do—bring a dead man back to life—He invited those who stood around watching to help with the process.

"Loose him, and let him go." It's the same command Christ gives the church today.

—*Lazarus Awakening*

READ: Isaiah 58:6–9a
REFLECT: Describe the kind of "fast" God has chosen and the blessing that accompanies it.

*Administer true justice; show mercy
and compassion to one another.*
ZECHARIAH 7:9

Concerning Lazarus's resurrection, author Jerry Goebel writes, "The work of Jesus is to bring life; the work of the congregation is to unbind people from the trappings of death. The words that Christ speaks are so full; he literally tells the 'congregation'; 'Destroy what holds him down. Send him forth free.'"[141]

Unfortunately, most of us would rather observe a resurrection than actually participate in one. Like the priest and Levite who passed by the wounded man in the story of the Good Samaritan, we shy away from actually getting involved in the work of loving someone back to life. Some of us may even prefer the role of cynic, refusing to believe that God has really changed a person or that the change can last.

"All too often, we never unbind those who Christ has resurrected," Goebel says. "We are more excited for them to fail than to change…[saying of their experience], 'Oh yea, well. I know that feeling and it will only last a month.'"[142]

An attitude like that breaks God's heart. Goebel continues:

> We bind people through our attitudes toward them. We bind them when we hold onto their faults instead of lifting up and encouraging their attempts to change. We bind people when we don't forgive them.…
>
> We free them when we are determined to see new life in them.… We free them when we forgive them.… We free them the most when we seek them in their tombs and, "snorting at death," we command them in the name of Christ to come into new life.[143]

That is the work we are called to as brothers and sisters in the Lord—unbinding, through acceptance and love, those whom Jesus has resurrected.

—*Lazarus Awakening*

READ: Isaiah 58:9b–12
REFLECT: What are we to "do away with" and spend ourselves upon? What will be the result?

Put on the new self, created to be like
God in true righteousness and holiness.
EPHESIANS 4:24

September 17

Do you want to wear the latest fashion? Do you want to turn heads and set trends? Put on Christ. There is nothing more beautiful than His nature draped around ours.

Yes, it feels a little strange at times. It takes some getting used to.

In fact, C. S. Lewis wryly calls the whole process of "dressing up as Christ" an "outrageous piece of cheek." After all, he writes in *Mere Christianity,* "you are not a being like The Son of God, whose will and interests are at one with those of the Father: you are a bundle of self-centered fears, hopes, greed, jealousies, and self-conceit all doomed to death.... But the odd thing is, that He has ordered us to do it."[144]

Lewis explains that our dressing up like Christ is a lot like children playing games—frivolous at times, but an important part of growing up. Playing with dolls helps little kids become good parents. Pretending to run a shop or teach a class prepares little people for future occupations. And choosing to act like Christ, to take on His qualities even when we may not feel like it—well, that is an important part of becoming like Him.

"Very often the only way to get a quality in reality is to start behaving as if you had it already," Lewis concludes. "When you are not feeling particularly friendly, but know you ought to be, the best thing you can do very often is to put on a friendly manner and behave as if you were a nicer person than you actually are. And in a few minutes, as we have all noted, you will be really feeling friendlier than you were."[145]

—Having a Mary Spirit

READ: Colossians 3:12–14

REFLECT: With the Lord's help, which of these qualities do you want to put on today? What all-important accessory ties them all together (verse 14)?

September 18

Live as children of light. EPHESIANS 5:8

You couldn't help but notice Jason. A medium-height, stocky young black man, he had a face that glowed with joy. I saw him from across the crowded room while 147 of us waited to see what would become of our flight back from Paris to the United States. He wore a white sports jersey. Maybe that's why he glowed. But I was fairly certain it was something more.

In a crowd of frustrated, weary travelers—myself included—Jason exuded a peace and a joy that almost seemed inappropriate. After all, we'd just spent eight hours waiting for a flight that was finally canceled. Now we were waiting for word on what our fate would be.

I watched as the young man helped people with their carry-on luggage. He stepped aside to allow those more aggressive to get farther in line. But it wasn't until we ended up seated next to each other on the bus that would take us to a hotel for the night that I confirmed what I had suspected.

Jason was a Christian. And, not only that, he was clothed with Christ.

"I've been in Italy for six weeks studying the culture," he told me. "But not knowing the language or any of the other students, I ended up spending most of my time with the Lord. It was incredible!" He laughed. Then he told me about the sweet times he'd spent with his Master…the songs he'd written…the new passion and vision he was taking home to the youth ministry he'd established in Mississippi.

Jason had spent six weeks with Jesus. And, oh, you could tell!…

—*Having a Mary Spirit*

READ: Ephesians 5:1–2
REFLECT: How do we live a "life of love," and whom should we imitate?

...While I had been praying that the Lord would redeem the time in the airport and use me for His glory, my new friend had been a living example of Jesus. While I had rushed to get my place in line, Jason had stepped back and served. While I had run over people's toes with my rolling luggage, Jason had no carry-ons to wrestle with. No bundle of rags. He traveled light.

And, as a result, he *was* Light. Clothed in white. Jesus Christ Himself, loving and helping people right there in the middle of Charles de Gaulle Airport.

Humbled, I went to my hotel room that night. I was embarrassed at how easily I forget that I have been called to be Jesus to my world. That, when I willingly take off self and put on Christ, something wonderful happens: I am transformed.

I'm a beggar girl, made a princess, still walking and living among other beggars. Free to love and accept them because I have found the love and acceptance of the King. Clothed in compassion, kindness, humility, gentleness, and patience. Able to bear with others, to forgive them as I have been forgiven, to love them with an all-embracing love.

Looking just like Jesus. Wearing Him. *Becoming* Him.

All dressed up. Without the pretend.

—Having a Mary Spirit

READ: Matthew 5:14–16

REFLECT: Prayerfully consider the different arenas of your life (home, work, church). Ask God to show you how His light could be seen more clearly through you.

September 20

Let him who walks in the dark, who has no light, trust in the name of the LORD and rely on his God. ISAIAH 50:10

For nearly all of my twenties, I awoke every morning with a sense of impending doom. As though something terrible was about to happen. And with that sense had come an urgent need to run faster, to work harder, to somehow stay ahead of the darkness that stalked my soul. It was as though a dark cloud hovered over my life, squelching any glimmer of hope or ray of happiness.

Oh, I laughed. I lived. I went through the motions and even experienced the emotions of a victorious Christian. But at night, though it was quiet, my heart still clamored with anxiety. I finally admitted to my husband, "I can't remember having a moment of pure joy." Every event or celebration seemed tainted by fear of the future, regret from the past, or frustration with the present.

Some would diagnose my condition as depression, and perhaps it was. But I believe my problem went deeper than that—all the way down to a flaw in my spiritual foundation. The same old false belief that my Christianity was up to me. That God was up there somewhere with a holy fly swatter just waiting for me to fail.

However, somewhere around my twenty-eighth birthday, all that began to change. And it started with a rebuke.

You don't trust Me, God whispered to my heart one day during my quiet time.

"Of course, I trust You," I argued. "I love You."

But you don't trust Me, God countered....

—*Having a Mary Spirit*

READ: Psalm 9:9–10

REFLECT: Write this passage on a card, and place it where you see it often. Consider memorizing it.

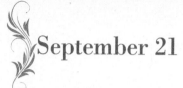

For this is the way the holy women of the past who put their hope in God used to make themselves beautiful. They were submissive to their own husbands. 1 PETER 3:5

September 21

…As I stilled my heart long enough to listen, God began showing me all the little ways I looked to myself rather than to Him, all the times I got tired of praying and waiting and decided to act on my own. The Holy Spirit especially put His finger on the area of my marriage and my difficulty in submitting to my husband.

I was having a tough time right about then. John and I were both overwhelmed in our ministry positions, and Flesh Woman was flexing her muscles. My core issue of approval and need for success meant I couldn't bear the thought of failure. And my self-deception painted it all as my husband's fault.

If John would just do this… If John would just do that… From my lofty position as all-knowing wife, I could see exactly what he needed to do. We'd both do much better if only he would listen to his helpmate, his gift from God, his very own personal Holy Spirit living right there next to him in the flesh.

Well, I was in the flesh all right. And that was the problem.

Anxiety had distorted my thinking and twisted any help I might have offered my hard-working husband. While I may have been right in some of my judgments, I was far from righteous. I had let frustration and perfectionism eat away at the fabric of our marriage until it was in tatters, shredded by the never-ending blast of my opinions and the cold wind of my disrespect.

"But, God…," I sputtered as He pointed all this out to me. "If John would just…"

Joanna, the problem isn't with John—the problem is with you. You don't trust John because you don't trust Me.…

—*Having a Mary Spirit*

READ: Proverbs 31:11–12
REFLECT: How could a lack of trust and respect do harm to a husband?

September 22

Submit to one another out of reverence for Christ. EPHESIANS 5:21

...As I wrestled with the desire to show John the error of his ways, the Lord reminded me of the last part of Ephesians 5:22—"Wives, submit to your husbands as to the Lord." (The same command is implied in 1 Peter 3:5.)

Ouch. Suddenly I could see what God was getting at. In my eagerness to *do* everything right so everything could *be* all right, I had usurped both John's role—and God's. When I attempted to manipulate my husband rather than submitting to his God-given role as head of our home, I was essentially telling God He had set things up all wrong.

"But what if my husband isn't doing what he ought to do?" I asked.

Unfortunately, God wasn't in the mood for my arguments. He wasn't impressed by my list of spiritual achievements or by the details of my husband's spiritual faults. When I looked closely at Ephesians 5:22, I saw that it didn't read as I had previously supposed.

It didn't say, "Wives, submit to your husbands *if* they are really wise and practically perfect."

It didn't say, "Wives, submit to your husbands *if* they are really godly, spend three hours a day in the Word, and have regular family devotions."

It didn't even say, "Wives, submit to your husbands *if* they are Christians."

It only said, "Wives, submit to your husbands" and then referred me back to God: "as unto the Lord."

The choice was simple, if not easy.

—Having a Mary Spirit

READ: 1 Peter 3:1–6

REFLECT: Underline key phrases in this passage, then ask God for a heart that does what is right and doesn't give way to fear.

Bible Study Helps

If you're like me, you know you need to do more than just read the Word of God; you need to "study to shew thyself approved unto God,...rightly dividing the word of truth" (2 Timothy 2:15, KJV). Here are some approaches to Bible study that I've found helpful.

Bible Study Methods

- *Topical Study.* Using a concordance or topical index, look up your topic using various forms and synonyms (for example, *anger, angry, wrath, rage,* etc.).
- *Book of the Bible Study.* Immerse yourself in one book of the Bible, verse by verse. Consider the author, audience, and themes explored. Use the Bible study tools listed below to help you go deeper in your study.
- *Character Study.* Focus on a single Bible character, which may lead to a certain book, such as Esther. Check to see where the character is referred to elsewhere. List qualities, both good and bad, any growth or digression, and lessons you can apply from that person's life.
- *Verse Study.* Explore a particular word or verse that captures your attention. Look up the meanings in the Greek and Hebrew, as well as other times the word is used in the Bible. Read the verse in various translations.
- *Theme Study.* Choose a specific theme (such as love, grace, faith, etc.) to trace throughout the Old and New Testament. Or look at passages that have to do with the same thing: the "I am" sayings of Jesus, His miracles or parables, the prayers of Paul, etc.

Bible Study Tools

- *Study Bible.* A good study Bible includes additional material at the bottom of each page to illuminate the scriptures above.
- *Other Translations.* Reading other Bible versions gives a well-rounded view of the scripture being studied.

- **Cross References.** Located in a center column or at the bottom of the page, additional verses are given that give deeper insight into parts of the verse you are studying. They are noted by a small letter in the text.
- **Commentaries.** Myriads of commentaries are available on individual books of the Bible. Ask your pastor for recommendations. Check out commentaries online.
- **Exhaustive Concordance.** This resource lists every instance a word is used as well as definitions of the original Hebrew and Greek words.
- **Topical Index.** Great for researching a word or particular subject.
- **Bible Dictionary.** Provides deeper insight into the culture, customs, and people of biblical times.
- **Lexicons.** Dedicated to the deeper study of the original and often varied meanings of Greek and Hebrew words.
- **Maps and Charts.** Gives understanding as to the geography and time-lines of Bible events.
- **Bible Software.** Available for download or to use online, Bible software can bring all of the tools mentioned together in one place.

Online Bible Study Helps

You can find many study helps online with search engines that help you explore: multiple Bible translations, concordances, commentaries, Bible dictionaries and encyclopedias, topical indexes, Greek and Hebrew lexicons, charts and maps, Bible reading guides, even devotionals. Many have mobile apps available. Here are a few sites you might find helpful:
- BibleGateway.com
- BibleStudyTools.com
- BlueLetterBible.org
- Net.Bible.org

Now the Bereans…received the message with
great eagerness and examined the Scriptures every
day to see if what Paul said was true.

ACTS 17:11

Blessed is the man who perseveres under trial. JAMES 1:12

September 23

One of the most disconcerting things I discovered early on as a Christian was that I still struggled with sin. I had expected that somehow victory over sin would just come with the territory—a fringe benefit of being God's child. I didn't expect to have to work for the victory, and I certainly didn't expect I'd have to sweat for it.

It's strange how we tend to gloss over the tough parts of the Gospel. We pick and choose the pieces we like and discard the parts we don't. "I'll take a megasized meal of blessing and prosperity," we tell the Holy Spirit. When He puts trouble and affliction on our plate, we push it away and go back to heaven's customer service counter to complain.

But for every promise of blessing in the Bible, there seems to be a promise of difficulty. And strangely enough, it is often through difficulty that the blessing comes.

"Consider it pure joy, my brothers, whenever you face trials of many kinds," James 1:2–4 tells us, "because you know that the testing of your faith develops perseverance. Perseverance must finish its work so that you may be mature and complete, not lacking anything."

Though we don't fully understand how something painful could be beneficial, this paradox is found throughout nature. Consider: it is a contrary wind that lifts a bird's wing and a crushing weight that makes a fine diamond. Why, then, are we so surprised that God would choose to harness the difficulties of our lives and use them for His glory?

For the strain we face creates the strength we need.

—Outtake from *Lazarus Awakening*

READ: Isaiah 30:20

REFLECT: What blessings can come out of adversity and affliction?

September 24

Be joyful in hope, patient in affliction, faithful in prayer. ROMANS 12:12

We all want a *test*imony, but we'd rather skip the *test* that gives us one. We all want a product. But we'd rather skip the process. As Charles Swindoll writes,

> I fear our generation has come dangerously near the "I'm-getting-tired-so-let's-just-quit" mentality. And not just in the spiritual realm. Dieting is a discipline, so we stay fat. Finishing school is a hassle, so we bail out. Cultivating a close relationship is painful, so we back off. Getting a book written is demanding, so we stop short. Working through conflicts in a marriage is a tiring struggle, so we walk away. Sticking with an occupation is tough, so we start looking elsewhere....
>
> And about the time we are ready to give it up, along comes the Master, who leans over and whispers: "Now keep going; don't quit. Keep on."[146]

When it comes to our spiritual lives, a lot of us are all-or-nothing people. If we aren't automatically perfect, we just give up. When Christlike virtues like patience and kindness seem hard to come by, we abandon our character development and decide holiness is for those better equipped. But when we give up, we're giving up on our part of the partnership. Perseverance is one of our responsibilities in this process of our being changed.

—*Having a Mary Heart*

READ: 2 Peter 1:5–8
REFLECT: What are you to add to your faith, and what is the blessing that will result?

I once heard a story about a missionary who was teaching a group of women 1 Corinthians 13, the "Love Chapter"—how love is patient and kind and "keeps no record of wrongs" (verse 5). She wasn't sure her students really understood what she was trying to say. Until one of the women knocked on her door and handed her a large notebook.

With tears in her eyes, the woman explained that, for years, she had meticulously recorded every instance her husband had failed her or let her down. Every sin committed against her had gone into that book. Thumbing through the pages, the missionary saw it was almost completely full of scribbled accusations.

"No more record of wrongs," the woman said in broken English as she pressed the book into the missionary's arms and turned to go. "No more record of wrongs."

It seems unlikely that any of us have kept an actual written record of our hurts and disappointments. But, then, most women I know don't need to. We're perfectly capable of keeping it all on our mental hard drives.

Let our husbands fail to tell us they'll be late for dinner, and by the time they (finally) walk in the door, we have a six-page warrant for their arrest—complete with a detailed listing of prior offenses and parole violations, no matter how distant and unrelated they might be.

Love "keeps no record of wrongs." Paul's words sound just as revolutionary to our modern ears as they must have sounded to those village women. But if we want to be like Jesus, we must forgive, we must give to the Lord our right to be treated fairly. And more than that, we must surrender our mental (and written!) records of the times when we weren't.

—*Having a Mary Spirit*

Read: Proverbs 12:16 and 1 Peter 4:8
Reflect: Rather than keeping a record of the times we're wronged, what are we to do instead?

September 26

Love is not…rude. It does not demand its own way. It is not irritable, and it keeps no record of being wronged.

1 Corinthians 13:4–5, NLT

I have a friend whom I love dearly. An amazing woman in so many ways, and yet she's just a shell of what she could be. Granted, her life has been rather hard. Though she's had her share of good things happen, any shining moment tends to be lost in the shadow of all the disappointments.

Under a thin layer of resignation resides a deep reserve of anger. Anger at people. Anger at God. Anger at herself for being so angry.

We've talked about it and prayed about it. She wants to be different. She knows she needs to be different. But the tomb has become comfortable. It's familiar and safe. To leave its cold depths would involve something she can't begin to consider: it would involve forgiving a person who hurt her a long time ago, and that feels impossible.

At least, not until that person apologizes, she says. Unless they acknowledge what they've done and beg pardon, she will stay where she is—harboring resentment, coddling a cold heart and a tormented mind, locked up halfway between death and life.

Isn't it amazing how we hold on to things, even things that lead to our own destruction? Though on the outside we may go on with our lives, ever present on the coffee tables of our minds lay photo albums to remind us of the past, effective illustrations to use when rehearsing our hurts to those who'll listen.

Unfortunately, we continually add pages to the albums, for that is the nature of offense. Satan (and life itself) will make sure we encounter plenty of careless people and unfair situations to populate the never-ending scrapbooks of our pain.

—Outtake from *Lazarus Awakening*

READ: Hebrews 12:15

REFLECT: Have you noticed that when you refuse to forgive, the "bitter root" affects other relationships as well? What is available to help us forgive?

One of the first things we must do on any journey of forgiveness is to get rid of the scripts we've written in our minds—the screenplays where those who have hurt us finally come to their senses and beg for forgiveness. In the first place, it probably won't happen. But, more important, forgiveness with the expectation of return is nothing like the unconditional forgiveness we've been called to as children of God.

In a sense, the best kind of forgiveness is done in private—initially processed between us and God. As humans—and especially as women!—we tend to want closure with people. We want to kiss and make up and get on with the happily-ever-after. But often what we want more is to have everyone agree that they were wrong and we were right.

Total forgiveness relinquishes the right to such childish behavior. Forgiving isn't about being proven right. It's about being made righteous. And that requires absolute relinquishment of a self-gratifying conclusion to our dilemma. In his book *Total Forgiveness,* R. T. Kendall says we must forgive in such a way that we "let them utterly off the hook," resigning ourselves to this knowledge:

- They won't get caught or found out.
- Nobody will ever know what they did.
- They will prosper and be blessed as if they had done no wrong.[147]

This may seem like a lot to swallow. But when we pray the Lord's Prayer, asking God to forgive "our trespasses as we forgive those who trespass against us," this is basically what we are praying. We are asking God to forgive others the way we want Him to forgive us—covering our sin, prospering and blessing us as if we'd done nothing wrong. We ask for His mercy toward those who have wronged us because we so desperately need His mercy ourselves.

—*Having a Mary Spirit*

Read: Matthew 18:21–35

Reflect: What kind of forgiveness does Jesus require?

September 28

Shall we accept good from God, and not trouble? JOB 2:10

Have you ever stopped to think that some of your lingering resentment may actually stem from anger toward God? Author R. T. Kendall thinks that's the root of much of our bitterness: "Deep in our hearts we believe that He is the one who allowed bad things to happen in our lives. Since He is all-powerful and all-knowing, couldn't He have prevented tragedies and offenses from happening?"[148]

This attitude of unforgiveness against God is perhaps the most damaging of all—primarily because most of us don't see it, and if we do, most of us are afraid to admit it. *Who am I to be mad at God?* we tell ourselves. We hesitate to admit our anger and resentment toward others as well because we're sure that He won't approve.

And so we continue to stand at a distance, an arm's length from the love our hearts so desperately need.

Please know there is nothing you can't tell your heavenly Father that He doesn't already know. Bringing your anger out in the open between the two of you won't destroy your relationship. In fact, it might just heal it. For when you hand Him your diary of wrongs done against you, that honesty opens the door to true relationship.

"Pour out your hearts to him," Psalm 62:8 encourages us, "for God is our refuge."

Our heavenly Father can handle our feelings even when we can't. And while He may not explain Himself or satisfy our curiosity as to why hurtful situations happen, I can assure you of this: His arms are open wide, and He is waiting for you to come back home to Him. His Holy Spirit stands ready to comfort you and show you the way to reconciliation and restoration…with God and with others.

—Having a Mary Spirit

READ: Job 2:10 and 42:1–6

REFLECT: After such a long period of suffering, Job asked questions that were never answered. What did he receive instead (42:5)?

The fruit of righteousness will be peace; the effect of righteousness will be quietness and confidence forever.
Isaiah 32:17

September 29

"Blessed is the man who trusts in the Lord, whose confidence is in him," God promises in Jeremiah 17:7–8. "He will be like a tree planted by the water that sends out its roots by the stream. It does not fear when heat comes; its leaves are always green. It has no worries in a year of drought and never fails to bear fruit."

I want to be like that—so rooted in the Lord that even in times of burning stress and lonely drought, I have no worries. I want my response to be faith, not fear. Instead of griping and groaning, I want to produce peace and joy.

Hudson Taylor, the famous nineteenth-century missionary to China, lived like that. A friend wrote these words after his death:

> He was an object lesson in quietness. He drew from the Bank of Heaven every farthing of his daily income—"My peace I give unto you." Whatever did not agitate the Saviour, or ruffle His spirit was not to agitate him. The serenity of the Lord Jesus concerning any matter and at its most critical moment, this was his ideal and practical possession. He knew nothing of rush or hurry, of quivering nerves or vexation of spirit. He knew there was a peace passing all understanding, and that he could not do without it.[149]

The longer I live, the more I realize how deeply I need that peace. And I'm learning, as Hudson Taylor clearly did, that such peace is available if I'll only trust God.

Under His protection, I have nothing to fear.

In His loving arms, I find quietness and rest.

And the gentle beauty "which is of great worth in God's sight" (1 Peter 3:4).

—*Having a Mary Spirit*

Read: 1 John 4:16–18
Reflect: What can you rely on and have confidence in?

September 30

Once you were alienated from God and were enemies in your minds.
COLOSSIANS 1:21

Throughout the Gospels, we read that Jesus often spoke of His impending death. In Matthew 16:21 the Bible tells us that "Jesus began to explain to his disciples that he must go to Jerusalem and suffer many things at the hands of the elders, chief priests and teachers of the law, and that he must be killed and on the third day be raised to life."

But Peter wouldn't hear of it. He took his Master aside and began to rebuke Him. "Never, Lord!" he said in verse 22. "This shall never happen to you!"

Peter probably thought he was being valiant, protecting and correcting the Lord. He must have felt pretty good about himself...until Jesus rebuked Peter's rebuke.

"Get behind me, Satan!" Jesus told Peter in verse 23. "You are a stumbling block to me; you do not have in mind the things of God, but the things of men."

Ouch. It's not every day the Son of God calls you "Satan," and when He does, it has to hurt. But if you are continually questioning God's plans for your life and the lives of others, if you are constantly working the angles in an effort to get God to see things your way, if you are trying to put a comma where God intends a period, don't be surprised when Jesus pops your pretty bubbles. Because when you attempt to breathe life into something God intends to die, you become a stumbling block to Christ.

—Having a Mary Heart

READ: Philippians 3:18–4:1

REFLECT: How do the enemies of the cross live? How are we to live as citizens of the light?

Brothers, stop thinking like children.
1 CORINTHIANS 14:20

October 1

From the moment we're born, we tend to associate love with what others do (or do not do) for us and the speed with which they do it. We learn to feel loved when we get our needs met—quickly.

And that's appropriate…for babies. Unfortunately, a lot of us never outgrow that view of love. When we cry (or whine creatively, as I like to call it), we expect an immediate response.

Sadly, many of us carry the same childish, demanding spirit into our relationship with God. But our heavenly Father knows that if He indulged our insatiable desire to have instantaneous help at every juncture, we would never grow up. Not really. Instead we'd be crippled emotionally and unable to stand, let alone walk, on our own.

Growing to maturity means learning to accept delayed gratification. Children and adults alike must learn to

- adapt to less-than-perfect situations,
- wait for the fulfillment of our needs,
- accept not only delays, but also denials of what we want.

For anything less results in demanding divas and toddler terrorists.

"When I was a child," Paul writes in 1 Corinthians 13:11, "I talked like a child, I thought like a child, I reasoned like a child. When I became a man, I put childish ways behind me." Part of putting childish ways behind us, spiritually speaking, involves subduing the whiny, demanding part of our flesh that insists that, if God loves us, He must act according to our specifications, our scripts, and especially our time lines.

So that "we will in all things *grow up* into him who is the Head, that is, Christ" (Ephesians 4:15, emphasis mine).

—*Lazarus Awakening*

READ: 1 Corinthians 3:1–3
REFLECT: What marks an immature life? What marks a mature one?

October 2

In me (that is, in my flesh) nothing good dwells. ROMANS 7:18, NKJV

One afternoon, as I pondered how to explain Flesh Woman and the role she plays in our lives, it suddenly came to me in high-definition color. A big-budget blockbuster film titled *Flesh Woman Crucified.*

A 683-pound sumo-wrestler chick makes her way through a crowd on the way to her cross. Squeezed into a purple-sequined evening gown, she pauses now and then to wave to all her fans lining the path.

"Wish you didn't have to go!" Gluttony calls from the crowd. Laziness and Procrastination agree. "Yeah, it hasn't been the same since you left the throne. (Sob!) We're having a tough time getting a break."

Flesh Woman throws final kisses to her dearest friends. But when she sees the crossbeam lying at my feet and the hammer I hold in my hand, she asks, "Is all this necessary?"

"I'm afraid so," I reply firmly.

She tries to talk me out of it, but I know I will never have any peace until I obey. "Those who belong to Christ Jesus have crucified the sinful nature with its passions and desires," Paul says in Galatians 5:24. He makes it sound so easy. I wonder if Paul had to brawl with a sparkling eggplant in his fight against sin.

I grit my teeth and begin to hum, "Have thine own way, Lord. Have thine own way…"[150] And suddenly He is there.

"Here, Lord," I say, stepping back and handing Him the hammer. "I guess it's more than I can do on my own."

Flesh Woman glares at Jesus. Then, subdued but not yet conquered, she turns to look at me. Her eyes narrow and cold, she asks, "Don't you know? When you kill me, you die, too."

"Yeah, I know." I smile. "In fact, that's the whole point."

—Having a Mary Spirit

READ: Romans 7:5–6

REFLECT: What is the result of being controlled by our lower nature? What must we do to escape its control?

Until we come to Christ, Flesh Woman sits upon the throne of both body and soul. (*Flesh,* remember, doesn't just mean our physical bodies, but our natural selves unchanged by God; our lower nature, tainted by sin.)

Even after salvation, Flesh Woman tends to call the shots. Because, although we've given Christ complete dominion over our spirits, He must be welcomed into the other areas of our lives. The dark corners of our hearts still need to be evangelized. Kingdoms in our souls have yet to hear the good news. And that multilevel transformation doesn't happen all at once.

Though our spirits are brought to life when we meet Christ, the other, more outward parts of us remain largely unchanged at first. We may feel the effects of the good news—we are happier; there is a peace and a lightness we've never experienced before. Yet Flesh Woman still rules in these areas—and she's not at all happy over our conversion.

After all, she has enjoyed unchallenged power in our lives since the day we were born. She will not give up such deep-rooted dominion without a fight. And fight she does—in any area of our lives where she's challenged.

When we accept the gift of salvation, the Spirit of God penetrates our spirits with the life of Jesus. But, as Ray Stedman writes, "The soul is still under the control of the flesh and remains so until the Spirit successively invades each area or relationship and establishes the Lordship of Jesus within. This is important to understand: *There is a throne in every area of the human soul!*"[151]

—Having a Mary Spirit

READ: 1 Thessalonians 5:23–24

REFLECT: Look up the word *sanctify* in a dictionary. What would being sanctified "through and through" look like in your life?

October 4

But in your hearts set apart Christ as Lord. 1 PETER 3:15

The question of Jesus's lordship must be fought anew in each area of our physical, mental, and emotional lives. This means we can be living by the Spirit in one area (say, daily devotions) and still be totally controlled by the flesh in another area (for instance, our choice of entertainment or patterns of escape). The process of unseating Flesh Woman in all these areas and making Jesus Lord of our bodies, souls, and spirits can literally take a lifetime.

In his powerful book *The Pursuit of God,* A. W. Tozer describes the process another way:

> There is within the human heart a tough, fibrous root of fallen life whose nature is to possess, always to possess…. The ancient curse will not go out painlessly; the tough old miser within us…must be torn out of our heart like a plant from the soil; he must be extracted in agony and blood like a tooth from the jaw. He must be expelled from our soul by violence, as Christ expelled the money changers from the temple. And we shall need to steel ourselves against his piteous begging, and to recognize it as springing out of self-pity, one of the most reprehensible sins of the human heart.[152]

This work that Tozer describes—the process of dethroning Flesh Woman and giving the Spirit of God the right to rule our whole lives—is traditionally called *sanctification* ("being made holy"). But *sanctification* is a fairly tame word for what is really an ongoing battle to overthrow the flesh and enthrone Christ in every corner of our lives.

As we engage in the battle, the Holy Spirit comes to our aid. Disarming our fallen nature and exposing the enemy's lies.

—Having a Mary Spirit

READ: Hebrews 12:3–6

REFLECT: To what point should we be willing to go in our struggle against sin, and how should we view the Lord's discipline when it comes?

*He who vindicates me is near. Who
then will bring charges against me?*
ISAIAH 50:8

October 5

Before salvation, Satan tells us we're just fine. We don't need a savior.

But after we're saved, the accuser points his bony finger at us and tells us we're no good. We don't deserve a savior.

He's lying, of course. Jesus says so in John 8:44. Satan is "the father of lies." In fact, lying is what he does best—it's "his native language." The word for "lie" in the Greek is *pseudos,* which means "falsehood" or "an attempt to deceive." We attach the prefix *pseudo* in the English language to convey the thought of a counterfeit, a false look-alike.

And that's exactly what we get when we listen to Satan's lies and settle for less than God's best: pseudo-Christianity, pseudo-grace. Satan usually doesn't try to make us swallow a blatant lie—he's too smart for that. Instead, he just doctors the truth for his own purpose, which is to keep us as far away from God as possible.

Look at what you've done, he whispers. *How could God ever forgive you?* He twists the truth of sin into a bludgeon of guilt and shame and beats us with it. *You're no good, you're no good, you're no good…baby, you're no good.*

If we let him, he's gonna sing it again. Because every time we listen to his lying lyrics, we take another step backward, away from the Living Room. Away from the closeness our hearts yearn for.

—*Having a Mary Heart*

READ: Isaiah 54:17
REFLECT: What happens to the weapons forged against us, as servants of the Lord?

October 6

For as high as the heavens are above the earth, so great is his love for those who fear him. PSALM 103:11

I believe that everything we were made for and everything we've ever wanted is found in Paul's prayer in Ephesians 3:17–19: "And I pray that you, being rooted and established in love, may have power, together with all the saints, to grasp how wide and long and high and deep is the love of Christ, and to know this love that surpasses knowledge—that you may be filled to the measure of all the fullness of God."

But in order to appropriate the all-encompassing love of God, we must grasp the important key that Paul's prayer reveals: "that you...may have power...to *know* this love that surpasses knowledge" (emphasis mine).

The marvelous incongruity of that statement hit me several years ago. "Wait, Lord! How can I know something that surpasses knowledge?" I asked.

His answer came sweet and low to my spirit. *You have to stop trying to understand it and start accepting it, Joanna. Just let Me love you.*

For the reality is, no matter how hard we try, we will never be able to explain or deserve such amazing grace and incredible love. Nor can we escape it.

It's just too *wide,* Ephesians 3:18 tells us. We can't get around it.

It's just too *high.* We can't get over it.

It's so *long* we'll never be able to outrun it.

And it's so *deep* we'll never be able to exhaust it.

Bottom line: You can't get away from God's love no matter how hard you try. For He's pursuing you, my friend. Maybe it's time to stop running away from love and start running toward it.

Even if, at times, it just seems too good to be true.

—Lazarus Awakening

READ: Psalm 103:1–12
REFLECT: Read this passage out loud, and let the words sink into your soul. This is what God has done for you. Receive it.

My grace is sufficient for you, for my power is made perfect in weakness.
2 CORINTHIANS 12:9

October 7

I wish I could tell you that after walking with the Lord some forty years, I'm now sanctified fully and so much like Jesus that a halo occasionally appears over my head. Sadly, that wouldn't be true.

While I can point to areas in which I've experienced immense victory, I still have weak spots that I've struggled with for years. A temper that flares when I'm provoked or tired. A habitual tendency to grumble and complain when things prove more difficult than I expected. Troubling inconsistencies that arise when I compare the person I want to be with the person I actually am.

But I've come to realize that while I am not what I should be, I am no longer what I was. I don't entirely understand why remnants of graveclothes still cling to the periphery of my heart, causing me to default to certain patterns when a particular button is pushed. But that doesn't negate God's deep work within me. It simply means there are layers still to be unwound.

Will you give that to Me? the Holy Spirit whispers, His hand outstretched, waiting to exchange my graveclothes for Christ's righteousness. *Will you give Me access to that?* He requests, pointing to a sin-infected place in my heart. *I want to set you free. But you must cooperate.*

The more I listen and obey, the more strength and endurance I find for my race. And the more I am able to "press on to take hold of that for which Christ Jesus took hold of me" (Philippians 3:12).

—Lazarus Awakening

READ: Philippians 3:12–14

REFLECT: Underline key phrases in this passage, then say it aloud, emphasizing the parts that mean the most to you.

October 8

Search me, O God, and know my heart;…see if there is any wicked way in me, and lead me in the way everlasting. PSALM 139:23–24, NKJV

The first rule of warfare is to know your enemy. E. E. Shelhamer's "Traits of the Carnal Mind" can help you identify the Flesh Woman inside so you can begin to put an end to her evil designs. Here are the first five telltale signs:

1. *A prideful spirit.* Do you have an exalted feeling because of success or position, good training or appearance, or natural gifts and abilities? Do you show an important, independent spirit? Do you tend to be married to your own opinion?

2. *A love of praise.* Do you have a secret fondness to be noticed? Do you draw attention to yourself in conversation? Does your ego swell when you have the opportunity to speak or pray before others?

3. *A touchy temper.* Do you cover up irritability or impatience by calling it nervousness or holy indignation? Do you have a touchy spirit, a tendency to resent and retaliate when reproved or contradicted? Do you throw sharp words at others?

4. *A willful attitude.* Do you show a stubborn, unteachable spirit? Do you like to argue? Are you harsh, sarcastic, driving, or demanding? Do you come across as unyielding or headstrong? Do you tend to criticize and pick flaws when you are ignored or decisions don't go your way? Do you love to be coaxed and humored?

5. *A fearful heart.* Does fear of what others think cause you to shrink from duty or compromise your principles? Are you afraid your commitment to righteousness will cause some prominent person to think less of you?[153]

—*Having a Mary Spirit*

READ: Isaiah 44:22

REFLECT: If you suffer from any of the traits above, confess them before the Lord, asking Him to remove them from you.

Each one should test his own actions.
GALATIANS 6:4

October 9

The Bible tells us to "examine yourselves to see whether you are in the faith" (2 Corinthians 13:5). Picking up from yesterday, let's consider Shelhamer's next six "Traits of the Carnal Mind."

6. ***A jealous mind.*** Do you hide a spirit of envy in your heart? Do you harbor an unpleasant sensation in view of the prosperity and success of another? When someone is more talented or appreciated than you, are you tempted to speak of his faults rather than his virtues?

7. ***A dishonest disposition.*** Do you evade or cover the truth? Do you hide or minimize your real faults and attempt to leave a better impression of yourself than is strictly true? Do you show false humility or exaggerate, straining the truth? Do you show one face to one person and the opposite to another?

8. ***A lack of faith.*** Are you easily discouraged in times of pressure and opposition? Do you lack quiet confidence and settled trust in God? Do you worry and complain in the midst of pain, poverty, or trials that God allows? Are you overly anxious about whether situations will turn out all right?

9. ***A wandering eye.*** Do you entertain lustful stirrings, showing undue affection and familiarity to those of the opposite sex? Do you act out sexually and dwell on romantic fantasies?

10. ***A spiritual deadness.*** Are you complacent about the lost? Is your relationship with God characterized by dryness and indifference? Does your life lack spiritual power? Do you regularly meet God?

11. ***A love of self.*** Do you cater to your appetites and hanker repeatedly for short-lived pleasure? Do your joys and sorrows fluctuate around your personal interests? Do you yearn for money and earthly possessions?[154]

—Having a Mary Spirit

READ: Psalm 19:14

REFLECT: Consider the traits above. Ask God to reveal and help you change any worldly thinking.

October 10

Humble yourselves before the Lord.
JAMES 4:10

Have you noticed how rare true humility is? I'm not talking about *false* humility, the kind that parades itself before others in a series of selfless acts, but secretly calls the newspaper so the generosity can be recorded.

I'm not talking about *self-effacing* humility—the "I'm-a-worthless-maggot-scum" kind of humility. God dealt with me severely early in my adulthood concerning that particular train of thought. After bemoaning my lack of self-esteem for the thousandth time, God finally let me know my problem was pride, not poor self-image. "How can that be?" I asked. "I don't even like myself."

Over the next few weeks, the Lord began to show me. *An inferiority complex is just as dangerous as a superiority complex—both involve preoccupation with self.* In essence, that is the definition of pride.

The center letter of *pride* is *I,* and that is where I'd gotten stuck. "I'm not this" and "I'm not that." Or "I should be this" and "I should be that." No one needed to criticize me; I was perfectly capable of ripping myself to shreds. But unbeknownst to me, my low self-worth had exalted itself against God. My eyes had turned inward rather than upward, and inferiority's dark fruit had become a reverse form of pride.

Which brings us back to humility, the opposite of pride. True humility is not to think poorly of oneself, but to think rightly, truthfully of oneself (Romans 12:3).

Considering both the good and bad, we bring it all to Jesus. Trusting Him alone to make us what we need to be.

—Outtake from *Having a Mary Heart*

READ: 1 Corinthians 4:2–5
REFLECT: Whom should we leave judgment to—even the judging of ourselves?

My son, give me your heart and let your eyes keep to my ways. PROVERBS 23:26

October 11

In old Italy it was difficult to find flawless marble. So after carving a statue, sculptors would secretly fill any imperfections with wax, smoothing it over with an iron until the wax melded into the rest of the marble. Flawless to the naked eye, the pieces would be sold to unsuspecting patrons excited to own such fine art. Delight turned to dismay when statues displayed in a garden were exposed to the full heat of the sun. Then the artist's deceit would be uncovered and the art's imperfections revealed.

Wary patrons began to demand a guarantee of authenticity. And so, on the pieces made of the best marble a mark was placed: *sine cera.* The word from which we get our term *sincere.* Without wax; unmixed; unalloyed.[155]

It is this same sincerity Paul advocates in Philippians 1:10: "…that ye may be sincere and without offence till the day of Christ" (KJV). But such flawlessness cannot be accomplished on our own. That's why I've come to welcome the spotlight of heaven and the heat of trials.

God only reveals so He can heal. He doesn't fill my flaws with wax or hide my sin; He removes my transgressions, and as I allow Him, He makes me new. Faultless. Blameless. Waxless.

Sine cera—through and through. A piece of marble He can sculpt into the image of His Son. Which means my part is fairly simple, and yet incredibly difficult. To lie still, be quiet, submitting to the hammer and the chisel—as well as to the sometimes accompanying pain of letting God have His way.

—Outtake from *Having a Mary Spirit*

READ: Jude 1:24–25

REFLECT: Write these verses on a card, and place it where you can see it often. Consider memorizing them.

October 12

*Did I not tell you that if you believed,
you would see the glory of God?*
JOHN 11:40

One of the most powerful testimonies I've ever heard came from David Ring, an evangelist born with cerebral palsy.

"Why, Mama?" David used to ask his mother when school kids teased him. "Why did I have to be born this way?" Although exceptionally bright, he was caught in a body that wouldn't do his bidding and was constantly tripped up by a stuttering tongue.

God gave that sweet mother incredible wisdom as she taught her son that perhaps *why* wasn't the best question after all.

"Asking why is like going to a well with a bucket and coming up empty every time," she told him. Instead, she said, the question should be, "What can I become?"[156]

What a powerful, life-changing concept for all of us, especially when we're trapped and tripped up by the whys of life. Because when it comes right down to it, life is full of questions that don't have adequate answers.

Such questions haunted my young friend Tom.[157] Though he loved Jesus, he struggled with the whys of his difficult life.

But one day he showed me his Bible and a verse he'd underlined. "Now I know why my life is the way it is," Tom said. Pointing to the story of the man who had been born blind, Tom read John 9:3 aloud: "This happened so that the work of God might be displayed in his life."

Oh that we all might have a vision to see beyond the misery of what is to the miracle of what we can become.

—Lazarus Awakening

READ: John 9:1–33
REFLECT: How was God glorified through the man born blind? What "why?" in your life might God want to use as well?

It had been a busy day. I'd dragged my kids through a morning of errands and grocery shopping, and now it was an hour past lunchtime. We were all hungry and a little bit grumpy, but the day brightened as I pulled the car into our favorite pizza place.

"Pizza, pizza, pizza!" my four-year-old son, Michael, chanted as he bounced up and down in the backseat. Jessica, two, clapped her hands at the thought of the merry-go-round in the kiddie playland. But our joy was cut short when I opened my checkbook and discovered I didn't have enough money in my checking account.

"It just isn't fair!" Michael informed me defiantly from the backseat as we drove toward home and plain old peanut-butter-and-jelly sandwiches. "You promised we could have pizza."

He was right. The pizza bribe had bought good behavior all morning. All my explanations fell on deaf ears. Michael sat scrunched against the car door, arms folded tightly across his chest, a scowl so fierce his eyebrows and angry pout nearly met.

Then from the other side of the backseat, little Jessica piped up, "Life's hard, Miko!"

Life is hard and rarely fair. While Martha may have been the first person to ask Jesus the question "Lord, don't you care?" she definitely wasn't the last. We've all felt the loneliness, the frustration, the left-out-ness and resentment she experienced in the kitchen that Bethany afternoon—doing all that work for others when no one seems to notice and no one seems to care.

We've all echoed my son's complaint. "It just isn't fair!"

—*Having a Mary Heart*

READ: Matthew 20:1–16

REFLECT: Describe a time you considered God unfair. What new perspective can you gain from verses 13–16?

October 14

But Martha was distracted by all the preparations that had to be made.
LUKE 10:40

Luke gives us a clear picture of Martha's struggles.

Surprise visitors appear on her doorstep. If the beginning of chapter 10 is any indication, it could have been as many as seventy people descending upon this quiet home. And Martha responds with open arms and a wide smile. But somewhere between the kitchen and the living room, a seed of resentment starts growing. Before long, it sprouts into a question that echoes in women's hearts today: "Lord, don't you care?"

The problem is obvious. Martha is doing all the work while Mary basks in all the glory. It just isn't right. At least Martha doesn't think so, and I know how she feels. A part of me wishes Jesus had said, "So sorry, Martha—terribly insensitive of us. Come on, Mary! Come on, guys, let's all pitch in and give Martha a hand."

After all, that's what Martha wanted. That's what I want when I'm feeling overwhelmed: soft, soothing words and plenty of helpful action. I want everyone to carry his own weight. But most of all, I want life to be fair.

Since childhood, we've all had an invisible set of scales that weighs what happens to us against what others experience. Fair or not fair. Equal or unequal. Just or unjust. We weigh it all. And if we're not careful, our view of the world can become distorted. Every little word can take on a hidden meaning. Each action can turn into a personal attack.

"I do all the work," we mutter to ourselves. "Why do they get all the glory?"

"How dare they treat me like that!"

When we look for injustice, we usually find it. And when we expect life to always be fair, we inevitably set ourselves up for a big disappointment.

—*Having a Mary Heart*

READ: Micah 6:8

REFLECT: How could pursuing the three things God "requires" positively affect our relationships with others? our relationship with God?

Count yourselves dead to sin but alive to God in Christ Jesus. ROMANS 6:11

October 15

Though there are many reasons to crucify our sinful natures, I think these may be the best: you can't tempt a dead person—or make one afraid.

Go ahead and try. Prop him up in a corner and parade beautiful women past him, and he won't even steal a glance. Set her on a throne and shower her with jewelry and fine clothes; she won't ask for a mirror. Threaten either one with a knife or a lawsuit, and you won't get a blink. Of all the millions of temptations and anxieties surrounding us today, not one can affect a dead man or woman.

That's why Paul, though faced with persecution and prison, beatings and even the threat of death, could say, "But none of these things move me" (Acts 20:24, NKJV).

How in the world was that possible?

I believe Paul remained unshaken and unmoved because he was already a dead man. He no longer belonged to himself. He no longer relied on *past* accomplishments or the *present* approval of men. Paul was motivated by a *future* hope that centered in Christ and being "found in Him" (Philippians 3:9).

That's why Paul could say with such confidence, "None of these things move me," then go on to say, "nor do I count my life dear to myself" (Acts 20:24, NKJV).

How dear is my life to me, I wonder. Too dear, I'm afraid. I tend to cling so tightly to my little life and its treasures that when the Lord tries to take away one of my precious toys, I fight to hold on.

Jesus didn't fight death. He climbed onto the cross willingly. "No one can take my life from me," He said in John 10:18. "I sacrifice it voluntarily" (NLT). Oh that I would do the same.

—*Lazarus Awakening*

READ: Romans 6:1–4

REFLECT: How can identifying with Christ's death and resurrection change the way we live?

October 16

For in my inner being I delight in God's law; but I see another law at work… waging war against the law of my mind.

Romans 7:22–23

Whether we realize it or not, there's a war going on. And Flesh Woman—well, she's a double agent.

"Satan's only real hope to control my life is *me*," author Mark Rutland writes in his book *Holiness*. "We often labor under the misguided notion that Satan wants us to do *his* will. Satan has no will in our lives. He only wants us to do *our* will. We have met the enemy, and he is us."[158]

Or, to be more precise, the enemy is Flesh Woman. And while Flesh Woman *is* us to a certain extent, she's also not the real us. No matter what she claims and no matter how enthusiastically Satan backs her up, she's not who God created us to be.

That is why Scripture holds little sympathy for our lower nature. For God knows Flesh Woman lives in direct opposition to Him. There really is no middle ground. We are told to "make no provision for the flesh" (Romans 13:14, NKJV) and that "those who are in the flesh cannot please God" (8:8, NKJV). So while it's important to remove Flesh Woman from the throne of our hearts, our holy makeover won't be complete until she's actually been put to death.

And this is where it all gets a bit complicated. Because the Bible says this work has already been done.

Because of the cross, I am no longer a slave to sin. No longer controlled by the spirit of this world. No longer held captive by the fault lines in my soul. And no longer under the dominion and sway of Flesh Woman, seductive and relentless though she may still appear to be.

—*Having a Mary Spirit*

Read: Romans 6:5–7

Reflect: What happened to our flesh at the cross, and what does that mean for us today?

*For though we live in the world, we
do not wage war as the world does.*
2 CORINTHIANS 10:3

October 17

After requesting permission to call down fire to destroy a Samaritan village that hadn't shown proper respect, James and John must have been stunned by Jesus's response.

"You do not know what manner of spirit you are of," Jesus said in a low, pained whisper. Gripping James and John gently by the shoulders, He declared, "The Son of Man did not come to destroy men's lives but to save them" (Luke 9:55–56, NKJV).

It is sobering to realize that, like the disciples, I can walk with Jesus, be taught by Jesus, yet still act and react out of human rationalization rather than the principles by which He told us to live. Even after serving the Lord for so long, I still tend to take matters in my own hands.

"Do you want me to take care of this, Lord?" I ask, flexing the strong arm of my flesh. "I'm really good at it, you know." And instantly Flesh Woman is strutting her stuff. Taking care of business. Setting everybody straight.

And when that happens, I need to ask, "Of what manner of spirit am I?"

Because, to be honest, the whole fire-breathing-dragon thing comes far too easily to me.

And that is my problem—our problem—in a nutshell. Left to ourselves, we will always default to the *carnal*, which is really just another word for *flesh*. Just as my computer defaults, or automatically goes, to one program though I desire access to another, so our life reactions tend to revert to fleshly thinking.

It's Flesh Woman all over again. And we might not even know she's there—because one of the hallmarks of carnal thinking is self-deception.

—*Having a Mary Spirit*

READ: 2 Chronicles 32:1–8

REFLECT: According to verse 8, the king of Assyria trusted in "the arm of flesh." In whom did King Hezekiah place his trust?

October 18

The LORD's searchlight penetrates the human spirit, exposing every hidden motive. PROVERBS 20:27, NLT

The wrong spirit infiltrates our hearts and minds far more easily than we realize. Here are five I consider very dangerous, especially for women:

- *A Competitive Spirit:* A woman with a competitive spirit needs to achieve, to be the best. She gloats over winning and pushes others to succeed so she looks good. Although she chases position and craves achievement, she can never get enough. Because no one can win all the time, she is often deeply frustrated (Ecclesiastes 2:22–23).
- *A Controlling Spirit:* A controller micromanages people and situations out of a desperate "need to know" all that's going on. She gives advice freely and expects compliance. Her belief that she must make things happen can lead to weary despair when no one cooperates (1 Peter 4:15, NKJV).
- *A Critical Spirit:* A woman with this attitude expects the worst rather than the best from people and situations. She cancels out positives with her constant negativity. Her secret self-criticism may cause depression or anger (Isaiah 58:9).
- *A Contentious Spirit:* This kind of woman loves to argue and debate, and she flies off the handle easily. She corrects others and creates drama by picking fights. She fiercely defends her children even when they're wrong—but she's hard on them too. Wound tight, she may suffer physical ailments (2 Timothy 2:23).
- *A Discontented Spirit:* Never at rest in her own skin, this type of woman is always on the go. She accumulates possessions and relationships in an attempt to fill her emptiness. Flitting from one thing to another in search for meaning, she starts projects but rarely finishes them. Disappointment with what isn't swallows the joy of what is (Philippians 4:12).

—Having a Mary Spirit

READ & REFLECT: Which of the wrong kinds of spirit do you struggle with? Look up the corresponding verse, and take the matter to God in prayer.

Return to me, and I will return to you.
MALACHI 3:7

October 19

I know of a woman who has never quite gotten around to accepting her husband's love. Because she grew up in a dysfunctional home, she's never felt worthy or very secure. Her husband does his best, yet nothing is ever enough.

"I just don't feel like he loves me," she whines, listing all the ways he's let her down, though the man works two or three jobs at a time to give her what she wants. She seems almost happy in her misery, because it's become her identity. As for her poor husband—well, he looks tired.

Her heavenly Father has received His share of her demanding diatribes. He's loved her long, and He's loved her well, but you wouldn't know it to talk to her. When one of His other children receives a blessing, she says, "Well, I guess God loves you better than me." When someone else's prayers are answered, she comments cynically, "I guess I better have you pray for me. He certainly doesn't listen to me."

She isn't always this cynical. Sometimes, especially when (in her view) God is behaving, she's fairly joyous. But when things don't go her way, she's quick to bad-mouth God.

I can't help but wonder how God feels when she slanders His name. Weary, I'm certain. Discouraged perhaps. For God knows He can't force her to let Him love her. It's a choice only she can make.

Unlike her husband, however, God doesn't put up with spoiled, demanding divas. He disciplines them even as He loves them. But they may never come to appreciate His love, let alone feel it, if they continue to insist, "He just doesn't love me the way I need to be loved."

—Lazarus Awakening

READ: 2 Timothy 3:1–5
REFLECT: What marks of the "last days" might interfere with our ability to truly receive God's love, and why?

October 20

*Don't murmur against God
and his dealings with you.*
1 CORINTHIANS 10:10, TLB

Isn't it strange how we humans tend to view God as our servant rather than our Master? Insisting that He do our bidding rather than standing ready to do His? It's no wonder we fail so often in the holy pursuit of being His friend.

"Here is a solemn thought for those who would be friends of God," Charles Haddon Spurgeon once wrote. "A man's friend must show himself friendly, and behave with tender care for his friend."[159]

Let me ask you two questions. Do you speak well of God? Is His name safe on your tongue?

More and more, I'm hearing Christians bad-mouth God. Rather than recalling what our heavenly Father has done for us in the past—His faithfulness and His goodness—we fixate on the unresolved problems of the present, accusing God of abandonment. Slandering His name rather than calling on it. Pushing away the love we so desperately need.

I understand how easy that is to do. Spiritual amnesia is a common condition among Christians. We tend to be slow to gratitude when things are good yet quick to complain when things are bad. But if we are ever to be a true friend of God, dear one, we need to start acting like one.

George Müller, one of the nineteenth-century's greatest missionaries, opened hundreds of orphanages, taking in the indigent children of England. It wasn't an easy job. And yet he wrote at the end of his life, "In the greatest difficulties…in the deepest poverty and necessities, [God] has never failed me; but because I was enabled by His grace to trust in Him, He has always appeared for my help. I delight in speaking well of His Name."[160]

Oh how I want that to be true of my life!

—*Lazarus Awakening*

READ: James 4:4–10
REFLECT: In order to be a friend of God, what changes do you need to make?

"Whom shall I send? And who will go for us?" Isaiah heard God ask. He answered, "Here am I. Send me!" (Isaiah 6:8).

Samuel, though only a little boy, heard the voice of the Lord calling his name and he said, "Speak, for your servant is listening" (1 Samuel 3:10).

Both encounters left these men forever changed.

Do you realize that God would like to speak to you as well? Did you know that He is actively looking for people who are willing to be part of His magnificent plan of redemption?

I think part of the reason we don't hear from God is because we are listening with the wrong set of ears. We are so conditioned to only pick up the practical, the tangible, and the proven that we struggle with the somewhat mystical ways God interacts with us.

But sometimes the opposite is just as true: we can be so conditioned to expect only the mystical, ethereal, and otherworldly manifestations of God that we miss the somewhat ordinary, everyday ways the Holy Spirit speaks to our hearts. His gentle nudge. The unexpected confirmation from an unexpected source.

To be honest, I am a little jealous of those who've heard God's voice. Though it isn't a daily occurrence for them, I personally know people who have heard the Lord speak audibly in their lives. Others I know seem to be especially perceptive of the Spirit's moving. They experience dreams and visions; the gifts of spiritual knowledge and discernment are active in their lives.

But such spiritual sensitivity doesn't come overnight. We must practice listening as well as obeying what we feel the Lord saying. Otherwise we risk losing the ability to hear at all.

—Outtake from *Having a Mary Spirit*

READ: John 16:13 and Acts 15:28
REFLECT: Describe a time the Holy Spirit directed your heart with an "it-seemed-good-to-the-Holy-Spirit-and-to-us" impression.

October 22

*Then everyone who has eyes will be
able to see the truth, and everyone
who has ears will be able to hear it.*
Isaiah 32:3, NLT

While we know God speaks clearly to us through the Bible, many of us are uncertain how to hear God's voice in our spirit. "How does God speak to you?" someone asked author and speaker Carole Mayhall. I have found her answer immensely practical and helpful:

> For me, He speaks by a distinct impression in my heart. He's never spoken to me aloud, but sometimes the thought that He puts in my soul is so vivid that He might as well have! Many times it is just a thought or an idea that flashes into my mind and I know it is from Him....
>
> Sometimes a thought pops into my mind—a thought so different from what I was thinking, or so creative I never would have thought of it, or opposite to what I wanted God to say to me. When that happens—and it lines up with God's Word—I know I've heard His voice in a distinctive way....
>
> I pray frequently that I'll hear His voice more often and more clearly. When I don't, I know He hasn't stopped speaking; rather, I have stopped listening.[161]

Acknowledging the fact that God wants to speak to us can be the best place to start in our quest to better hear Him. But we also must do what He asks us to do. For that is the only way to tune our hearts to His voice.

—Having a Mary Heart

Read: John 14:26
Reflect: How does the Holy Spirit help us discern God's voice? Listen for ways the Lord may be speaking this week.

Why spend money on what is not bread,
and your labor on what does not satisfy?
Isaiah 55:2

October 23

Teri Myers was, and still is, a dear friend and a spiritual mentor, a true picture of a Mary heart in a Martha world. She tells the story of having company over for dinner one night. She'd worked hard all day on a beautiful meal—four courses and a fancy dessert. It was going to be wonderful. But somewhere around the middle of the afternoon, Teri realized she was hungry.

"I'd been so busy cooking and cleaning," she says, "I had completely missed lunch." But it was only four o'clock and the guests weren't due until six. So she grabbed a couple of Snickers bars from her hidden candy stash.

"It did the trick! My stomach wasn't growling anymore. I was able to take my shower, do my hair, and get dressed with plenty of time to spare."

It wasn't until Teri sat down to dinner that she discovered her appetite was gone. With the edge off her hunger, she ended up picking at her plate as everyone else enjoyed their meal.

"The Lord spoke to me at that moment," Teri says. "He showed me that we often fill our lives with spiritual Snickers bars—things like friends, books, and shopping. They may be good things, completely innocent things—but not when they take the edge off our hunger for God."

We were designed for intimacy. Just as our bodies hunger and thirst for food and drink, our spirits hunger and thirst for God's presence. But just as it's possible to bloat our bodies with empty calories, we can find ways to pacify our spiritual cravings without really getting the nourishment we need. We can fill up with spiritual Snickers bars while all the time our spirits are withering for want of real food.

—*Having a Mary Heart*

Read: Psalm 106:13–15
Reflect: What happens when we forget to look to God and instead fill up with other things?

Half-Day of Prayer

"God's acquaintance is not made hurriedly," says E. M. Bounds. "He does not bestow His gifts on the casual or hasty comer and goer. To be much alone with God is the secret of knowing Him and of influence with Him."

Something powerful happens when we set apart a block of time to seek God's face intensively. Here are a few guidelines I've adapted from the Navigator's 2:7 course for a half-day of prayer:

1. ***Find a place free from distractions.*** I've found it helpful to go "away" for extended prayer times. A friend's vacant house, a church or Christian conference center, or even a motel room will do.

2. ***Take along your Bible, a notebook, a pen or pencil.*** You may also want a devotional, hymnal, a prayer list, memory verses, and your weekly schedule. Wear comfortable clothes and bring a sack lunch.

3. ***Stay awake and alert.*** Get adequate rest the night before. Change positions frequently. Sit awhile, walk around—vary your position to keep from growing dull or sleepy.

4. ***Try a variety of approaches.*** Read the Scriptures awhile, pray awhile, plan or organize awhile, and so on. You might divide the time into three parts: (a) wait on the Lord, (b) pray for others, and (c) pray for yourself.

5. ***Pray aloud*** in a whisper or soft voice. Sometimes thinking aloud also helps.

6. ***Make a worry list.*** Things often come to mind during prayer. Instead of trying to ignore them, write them down. Prayerfully prioritize them into a "to do" list. Ask God to show you how to accomplish what needs to be done.[162]

—*Having a Mary Heart*

> *But when you pray, go into your room, close the door and*
> *pray to your Father, who is unseen. Then your Father,*
> *who sees what is done in secret, will reward you.*
>
> Matthew 6:6

Blessed are those who hunger and thirst for righteousness, for they will be filled.
MATTHEW 5:6

October 24

If you're having a little trouble feeling close to God—or even wanting to draw close—you might want to consider what activities you are using to fill the empty places of your life. What's taking the edge off of your hunger for Him?

Then again, it could be that you just need to start "eating" the good things of the Lord to find out how spiritually hungry you really are. You see, spiritual hunger and thirst don't work the same way as our physical needs. When our physical body feels hunger pains, we eat and our hunger is satisfied. But spiritually speaking, it isn't until we "eat" that we realize how famished we are.[163] As we feast at God's table, something strange happens. We get hungrier. Thirstier. We want more! We have to have more.

"Our souls are elastic," Kent Hughes writes in his book *Liberating Ministry from the Success Syndrome.* "There are no limits to possible capacity. We can always open ourselves to hold more and more of his fullness. The walls can always stretch further; the roof can always rise higher; the floor can always hold more. The more we receive of his fullness, the more we can receive!"[164]

Once you've tasted the Living Room Intimacy Jesus offers, you'll find nothing else will satisfy. For even Snickers bars taste flat in comparison to the sweetness of the Lord's presence. When you've sampled the best of the best, you'll be willing to skip the junk food this world offers in order to have a real sit-down meal with the Savior.

"Taste," as the psalmist says, "and see that the LORD is good" (Psalm 34:8).

—Having a Mary Heart

READ: Philippians 1:9–11
REFLECT: What does Paul pray we'll abound in and be filled with?

October 25

Love the Lord your God with all your heart.... Love your neighbor as yourself.
MATTHEW 22:37, 39

By the end of his life, John, formerly known as a "Son of Thunder," became known as the apostle of love.

As you read John's later epistles, it's apparent that his fiery, sharp-edged manner had been tempered by the Spirit of Christ dwelling in him. In its place was a winsome Christianity that drew people instead of repelling them. Though John clearly rebuked heresy and false doctrine in his writings throughout his life, his final message embraced one theme. The historian Jerome recorded John's words: "Little children, love one another...this is the Lord's command, and enough is done when this is done."[165]

Because the same Spirit who lived in John dwells in us as well, we too can be changed. As we surrender our nature to Christ, He replaces it with His own.

Honing our gifts and talents so they can be used effectively by God.

Purifying our motives and intents so we're not undone when He chooses to use someone else.

Mending and healing our past so it no longer affects our future.

Tempering our personalities and spirits so they are not only fit for the Master's use, but easily received by others as well.

All of this describes the manner of Spirit who desires to live and move in you if you will allow Him access. For God's Holy Spirit can create in you a clean heart and a right spirit. Restoring to you joy in your salvation, and compassion in your heart.

For heaven's fiery love will fill your soul.

—Having a Mary Spirit

READ: Mark 10:35–37 and 1 John 2:15–17
REFLECT: How did John's attitude change from the start of his walk with Jesus to the end?

His heart is secure, he will have no fear; in the end he will look in triumph on his foes. PSALM 112:8

October 26

When Jesus came late to Bethany, His lateness was an act of love. A gift of perspective. A foreshadowing meant as a mercy—not only for Mary, Martha, and Lazarus, but for His disciples, and for you and me.

Jesus knew we would struggle with the concept of His death and resurrection. He knew we would have doubts when His tomb turned up empty. He knew there would be conspiracy theories and chat rooms jammed with people wanting to debate the likelihood of the dead coming back to life. So the Author of our faith, our great storytelling God, prefaced His Son's death with an act that would foreshadow the resurrection to come. When Jesus raised Lazarus from the dead, He put to death forever Satan's lie that the end is the end.

The truth of Lazarus and the secret of the resurrection is this: if Jesus Christ can turn death into life, sorrow into gladness, suffering into triumph—then nothing truly bad can ever touch our lives again. Not really. Unfortunate things may happen. Difficulties may come. But it all becomes fodder for a greater work, a more glorious glory.

Philip Yancey points to the cross and the empty tomb as turning points in the scriptural view of suffering: "When New Testament writers speak of hard times, they express none of the indignation that characterized Job, the prophets, and many of the psalmists. They offer no real explanation for suffering, but keep pointing to two events—the death and resurrection of Jesus."

As a result of Christ's work on the cross, Yancey says, "The three-day pattern—tragedy, darkness, triumph—became for New Testament writers a template that can be applied to all our times of testing."[166]

—*Having a Mary Heart*

READ: 1 Peter 5:10–11

REFLECT: What qualities does God promise to work in your life in the midst of your difficulties?

October 27

We live by faith, not by sight.
2 Corinthians 5:7

Have you noticed that when Jesus comes on the scene, what seems to be the end is rarely the end? In fact, it's nearly always a new beginning.

But Mary and Martha didn't know that at the time of Lazarus's death. And I'm prone to forget it as well.

Questions and disappointments, sorrow and fear tend to block out the bigger picture in situations like the one we see in Bethany. What do we do when God doesn't come through the way we hoped He would? What should we feel when what is dearest to our hearts is suddenly snatched away? How do we reconcile the love of God with the disappointments we face in life?

Such questions don't have easy answers. However, in this story of Jesus's three friends, I believe we can find clues to help us navigate the unknown and the tragic when we encounter them in our own lives. Tips to help us live in the *mean*time—that cruel in-between time when we are waiting for God to act— as well as insights to help us trust Him when He doesn't seem to be doing anything at all.

But most important, I believe the story of Lazarus reveals the scandalous availability of God's love if we will only reach out and accept it. Even when we don't deserve it. Even when life is hard and we don't understand.

For God's ways are higher than our ways, and His thoughts are higher than our thoughts, Isaiah 55:9 tells us.

He knows what He's doing. We can trust Him with our lives.

—*Lazarus Awakening*

Read: Isaiah 55:8–9

Reflect: Rewrite these verses in your own words, thanking God that when you don't understand, He does.

"Where have you laid him?" Jesus asked Martha and Mary through His tears (John 11:34).

"Come and see, Lord," they replied. Then together they went to Lazarus's tomb.

Oh how I wish we could grasp the immensity and emotion of this tender exchange and what it means for us today.

Where have you laid your pain? Jesus asks us tenderly. *Where do you keep all your shattered hopes and dreams? Where have you laid the part of you that died when you failed or were abandoned, forgotten, betrayed? Where are you entombed and enslaved, hemmed in, shut down, and closed off?*

Come and see, Lord.

That's the only response we need to give. Come and see.

For with the invitation, Jesus steps down into our pain and gathers us in His arms. He doesn't chastise us for what we've gone through or insist that we explain the death we now mourn. He holds us close and weeps over what sin and death have done to us, His beloved.

He doesn't look down on our wild-eyed nakedness, because Jesus understands. He has walked where we've walked, and He has felt what we've felt.

"For we do not have a high priest who is unable to sympathize with our weaknesses," Hebrews 4:15 tells us. We have a tender Savior with a heart big enough to handle our sorrow and gentle hands able to carry our pain.

—*Lazarus Awakening*

READ: Romans 8:34–37

REFLECT: Which parts of these verses mean the most to you in your current situation, and why?

October 29

This is how God showed his love among us: He sent his one and only Son. 1 JOHN 4:9

"Lord, don't you care?" Like Martha, we often wonder.

Of course He cares. That's why Jesus came.

If I were God, wanting to touch base with man, I'd drop by for a visit. Maybe a week or two with plenty of advance advertising, hitting the major cities before returning to my comfy celestial throne. Just long enough to get people's attention and straighten things out, then, "Beam me up, Scotty!" I'd be out of there.

Who in their right mind would leave heaven to actually live on earth? Why, that would be like a farmer selling his cozy farmhouse so he could live in his pigsty. Like Bill Gates giving up Microsoft's billions so he could run a hot-dog stand for minimum wage. Unthinkable. But that is exactly what Jesus did.

God became one of us so that when we ask, "Lord, don't you care?" we can know without a doubt that He does. Instead of paying a house call or a flashy extraterrestrial visit, He took up residence among us. Through Jesus Christ incarnate, God entered the world through the same doorway we do. Then He stuck around as long as we'd let Him, until we sent Him, dying, out the same painful exit we will go.

Does He care? You'd better believe it!

You'd *better* believe it. Because until you settle that question once and for all, you will never get past doubt to true belief. You'll forever be faced with a shiny apple and the hiss of temptation to take matters into your own hands.

—Having a Mary Heart

READ: John 20:30–31

REFLECT: What are we given to help us believe, and why is it important that we do?

On that day a fountain will be opened…
to cleanse them from sin and impurity.
Zechariah 13:1

October 30

A hand-hewn cross sits on the right side of our church stage. About nine feet tall, it is a constant reminder of all Christ has done for us. But one night during our annual week of prayer, it became a living object lesson of the ongoing power of Christ's shed blood in my life.

I was struggling once again with my continued inadequacies. "Will I ever change?" I asked God. "Will I ever be what You want me to be?"

There was no audible answer, but as I confessed my sins, a word picture came to my mind. Not a vision, but a visual thought. As though I could see a shower head attached to the top of the cross and, in the middle, a handle marked with the word *Repentance*.

How often do you shower, Joanna? the God-thought came softly to my heart.

Every day, my heart answered back. *Or at least every other day.*

Why is it, then, that you only find it necessary to come to the cross once in a while?

Wow. That stopped me in my tracks. Did I really think that moment I gave my heart to Christ as a four-year-old was the only time I would need the cleansing power of His precious blood?

After all, I sensed the Spirit reason, *in the natural you shower every day because your body produces toxins and life involves contact with things that make you dirty.*

The same is true in the spiritual realm. Don't wait till sin builds up to a spiritual crisis, I sensed the Lord saying. *Deal with it daily. Come clean so I can make you clean. The cross made you My child, and it is the cross that will also make you holy.*

—*Having a Mary Spirit*

Read: Hebrews 9:14
Reflect: What does the blood of Jesus do for us?

October 31

Look, the Lamb of God, who takes away the sin of the world! JOHN 1:29

Lately, the Lord has been giving me a larger view of my transgressions, a kind of third-person perspective that allows me to back up and see what He sees and call it what He calls it.

Falling short. Missing the mark. Sin.

Instead of fighting against the revelation or grieving myself into paralysis over its implications, I'm learning to simply confess my faults, my weaknesses, and even my willful sin, accept God's forgiveness, and move on with my life.

Somehow in the past, I had confused repentance with penance. "Bad me, bad me," I'd cry in my heart as I beat myself bloody for my failures. "How could I have done this? How can God still love me?" You see, I had picked up the false belief that I had to feel really bad for a certain amount of time before I could be forgiven; that I had to add something to the cross and the shed blood of Christ.

But the problem with that twisted way of thinking was that by the time I had "felt" bad enough for my sins to receive forgiveness, I had usually sinned again. Which, of course, launched me into another round of guilt and shame, a downward spiral of condemnation. I never experienced any release from the heavy load of guilt. Only the weight of sin piled upon sin piled upon sin.

No wonder I couldn't remember the good news. Spiritual amnesia had wiped out the power of the cross and left me with only myself as a savior. And, try as I might, I could never deliver myself from this particular body of sin and death.

For there is only one Messiah.

Only one perfect Lamb.

One Lion of Judah who can break every chain.

—*Having a Mary Spirit*

READ: Titus 3:4–7

REFLECT: Underline key words in this passage, then pray it back to God, thanking Him for the gift of His Son.

One of the things I love most about Jesus is that He seeks us out wherever we may be. He never tires of going out of His way to find us, crossing stormy seas as well as eternity just to make us His own.

Luke 8:22 tells us that "one day Jesus said to his disciples, 'Let's go over to the other side of the lake.'" According to the parallel time line given in Matthew, He had just finished a busy couple of weeks. After preaching the Sermon on the Mount to thousands (Matthew 5–7), Jesus healed a leper, then traveled to Capernaum to heal a suffering paralytic and Peter's fevered mother-in-law (8:1–15). That same evening, according to Matthew, "many who were demon-possessed were brought to him, and he drove out the spirits with a word and healed all the sick" (8:16).

It was after this exhausting schedule that Jesus gave the order to cross to the other side of the lake. But what might appear at first glance to be a weary man's attempt to get away from a demanding crowd was actually nothing of the kind. Jesus wasn't suggesting an escape route. He was moving toward the next destination God had logged into the navigational guide of His ministry from the beginning of time.

Though a crowd of needy people remained on one side of the lake, Jesus left them all in order to meet the needs of an individual on the other side. One lonely, tormented soul living on the outskirts of civilization.

And this same God, this same Savior, still goes out of His way to find you and me.

—*Lazarus Awakening*

READ: Matthew 18:12–14
REFLECT: What does it mean to you to realize that Jesus would leave the many to find the one who is lost?

The God of peace will soon crush Satan under your feet. ROMANS 16:20

Mark 5:2–5 describes the scene when Jesus arrived at the other side of the lake: "When Jesus got out of the boat, a man with an evil spirit came from the tombs to meet him.... No one could bind him any more, not even with a chain.... Night and day among the tombs and in the hills he would cry out and cut himself with stones."

What a sad, eerie picture of a tormented life. When the man saw Jesus, he ran and fell at His feet. "What do you want with me, Jesus, Son of the Most High God?" he shouted. "Swear to God that you won't torture me!" (verse 7).

Isn't it amazing how the very thing we need is often the last thing we want? When the man encountered the one and only One who could deliver him, he didn't call out for help. Instead, self-preservation was his first response. "What do you want with me? Don't torture me!"

Now, I realize it was the demons in the man who spoke these words. Yet Satan often uses the same arguments to keep us from surrendering to the work of God in our lives. *It will be too painful,* he hisses. *Why doesn't He just leave you alone? There's no hope for you anyway.*

It's much easier to stay in bondage, he suggests. *Sure, you roam the graveyard of your past day and night trying to find answers. Sure, your mind is tormented by the pain. But that's a whole lot less painful than what God has in store for you,* the deceiver insinuates. *Who knows what God might make you do if you allowed Him to set you free?*

Does any of this sound familiar to you? I know it does to me. For many of us have spent more time among the tombs than we'd care to admit.

—*Lazarus Awakening*

READ: 2 Corinthians 2:11
REFLECT: Though this verse is connected to the danger of unforgiveness, what other schemes does the devil use to outwit you and keep you from God's love?

The weapons we fight with are not the weapons of the world. On the contrary, they have divine power to demolish strongholds. 2 CORINTHIANS 10:4

November 3

Many of us believe the lie that we are helpless when it comes to finding true freedom. Our bondage seems too strong and the lies too intense. Yet regularly employing these four powerful principles releases the Holy Spirit to release *us:*

- ***Reveal.*** Ask God to show the area (or areas) in which you are bound. What stronghold is holding you back from freedom? What lie has exalted itself above the knowledge of God? Don't try to figure this out on your own. Ask for the Spirit's help.
- ***Repent.*** Ask God to forgive the times you've turned to your stronghold rather than to Him. Ask the Holy Spirit to take your sin and the accompanying lies and remove them from you "as far as the east is from the west" (Psalms 103:12).
- ***Renounce.*** Before God, renounce any authority you may have given to Satan by embracing your stronghold rather than God. As you name each sin aloud, renounce your attachment to the lie or behavior, giving authority in that area back to Jesus Christ.
- ***Replace.*** Look for scriptures that pertain to your stronghold or the lie you've believed. Write them down and place them where you can read them several times a day. Memorize and quote these verses whenever you feel the lie trying to reassert its power.

Please note that I'm not outlining four easy steps for curing your hurts, hang-ups, and habits. Strongholds may have a physical or spiritual component, so the process of breaking free can be lengthy and complicated. Some (especially addictions) may require significant time to overcome, as well as outside help, such as professional counseling, support groups, intercessory prayer, and more.

—Lazarus Awakening

READ: Isaiah 55:11

REFLECT: If you need freedom in an area of your life, apply the principles above, and find a verse to stand on whenever you are tempted to give way in that area.

317

November 4

Pastor Ed Kreiner is small of stature, but a mighty man of God. One evening at our church, he spoke on the importance of yielding daily to Christ in both the big and little decisions that come our way. A powerful idea in and of itself— but it was the way he chose to illustrate the sermon that has stayed with me through the years since I first heard it.

How we respond to the Holy Spirit's leading determines whether we walk in freedom or bondage, Pastor Ed said. Because whenever we resist the conviction of the Holy Spirit, we are really saying no to God and yes to Satan. And each time we do that, hell clamps chains upon our souls.

As Pastor Ed recited different scenarios, he acted out what our descent into bondage looks like. Standing in the middle of the stage, he began talking about the way the Holy Spirit speaks to us:

God says, *I want you to share Christ with your coworker.* We respond with excuses and reasons why that wouldn't be wise. And suddenly our left arm is fastened behind us.

God says, *Give a few bucks to that man begging for change.* But we resist compassion, and unbeknownst to us, our right arm joins our left.

God says, *Forgive your child for her careless remark.* We refuse. Our feet are bound together.

Admit that you lied. We say we will but procrastinate to save our pride. And suddenly, we are on our back with our knees tied to our chest.…[167]

—Having a Mary Spirit

READ: Romans 6:16
REFLECT: What happens when we say no to God?

…In order to illustrate what happens when we continually resist God's leading, Ed Kreiner lay down on the stage as if he were bound. As he struggled to speak from his awkward position, he reminded us that just as one choice followed by another had brought us down into bondage, so one choice followed by another would bring us out.

Call your mom and ask forgiveness, God instructs us. Whew. That's a tough one, but we obey. Suddenly the band around our cramped soul is loosened, and we can breathe once again.

Drop off a meal to the neighbor who's threatening to sue. We prepare lasagna and knock on the door, only to find the family visited by tragedy and in need of some TLC. We stick around, they are blessed, and we find we're able to stand.

Pray for your husband instead of complaining when you pick up his dirty socks. We bend our knee and bow our hearts. Suddenly the handcuffed feeling leaves, and we're free to love him both inwardly as well as outwardly.[168]

When Pastor Ed finished, he was once again standing up straight on the stage. And everyone in the congregation was feeling just a little more determined to say yes to the Holy Spirit. Because while change is costly, the price of not changing is even higher. It is the difference between lying helplessly hogtied to our cherished sins and walking victoriously free from hindering habits.

Once again, holiness is all about choices. One choice after another. Saying yes to God and saying no to Satan.

—*Having a Mary Spirit*

READ: Romans 6:17–19
REFLECT: What happens when we say yes to God?

November 6

Do not fear; I will help you. Isaiah 41:13

It's been said that worry is like a rocking chair—it gives you something to do, but it doesn't get you anywhere. One interesting set of statistics indicates that there is nothing we can do about 70 percent of our worries:

* 40 percent are things that will never happen.
* 30 percent are about the past—which can't be changed.
* 12 percent are about criticism by others, mostly untrue.
* 10 percent are about health, which gets worse with stress.
* 8 percent are about real problems that can be solved.[169]

When it comes down to it, worry is really a waste of time. But worry is not only futile; it's actually bad for us.

The physical and emotional damage caused by chronic anxiety is well known and well documented. Years ago Dr. Charles H. Mayo of the Mayo Clinic pointed out that worry affects circulation, the glands, and the whole nervous system, and profoundly affects the heart. "I have never known a man who died from overwork," he said, "but many who died from doubt." In the years since then, researchers have established connections between chronic worry and a vast array of serious illnesses.[170]

No wonder Jesus warned Martha about her anxiety. No wonder the Bible tells us more than 350 times to "fear not."

—*Having a Mary Heart*

READ: Isaiah 41:10
REFLECT: What reason do we have not to fear?

The Lord is my helper; I will not be afraid. HEBREWS 13:6

November 7

Paul had all kinds of reasons to worry as he sat in a Roman prison awaiting a possible death sentence. But instead of writing the Philippians a sob story, Paul crafted an incredible epistle of joy. And that epistle includes a passage that has been enormously helpful to me as I've tried to learn not to worry.

"Do not be anxious about anything," Paul wrote in Philippians 4:6–7, "but in everything, by prayer and petition, with thanksgiving, present your requests to God. And the peace of God, which transcends all understanding, will guard your hearts and your minds in Christ Jesus."

In this short passage, we find three concise and practical steps to victory over worry.

1. Be *anxious* about *nothing.*
2. Be *prayerful* about *everything.*
3. Be *thankful* for *all things.*

When Paul wrote the words, "Do not be anxious about anything," he literally meant "not even one thing!" Nothing. Not our families nor our finances, not our future nor our past. Not even one thing. That's important for someone like me to hear, because worry is such a treacherous habit. Allow one little worry in, and another is sure to follow, then another. It's better to cut it all off at the source. To be anxious about nothing.

But of course, the only way to carry off that first order is to carry out the second—to "pray about everything." And Paul literally meant "every single thing!" There is nothing too big, nothing too small, that we cannot bring to the heart of our Father. Corrie ten Boom put it this way: "Any concern too small to be turned into a prayer is too small to be made into a burden."[171]

—Having a Mary Heart

READ: Psalm 55:22

REFLECT: Write a list of things you are currently worried about. Now put the words "Dear Jesus" at the top of the page, and take these things to the Lord in prayer.

November 8

Let the peace of Christ rule in your hearts.... And be thankful.
COLOSSIANS 3:15

Paul finishes his prescription for worry in Philippians 4 with one last piece of crucial advice: Be thankful for all things! (verse 6). Look at everything God has done. In the words of the old hymn, "Count your blessings, name them one by one!"[172] If we aren't grateful for what God has done in the past and in the present, we won't have the faith to believe God for things in the future.

Gratitude is important because it has the power to change our attitude. When we are willing to give thanks to God in *all* things, not just some things—to consciously thank Him even when we don't feel very grateful—something in us begins to shift. We begin to see life as Christ sees it—full of opportunities rather than obstacles. And when we view life through eyes of faith, fear just has to flee.

So much depends on our perspective. If my God isn't bigger than life, then my life is bigger than God—and that's when anxiety takes over.

"It's an interesting thing, the human mind," say authors Bill and Kathy Peel in their book *Discover Your Destiny*. "It can only focus on a couple of things at a time. When we're preoccupied with a problem and focus on our own inadequacy to handle it, there's really no room to add God to the picture. The ability to think rationally returns only when we refocus on God's adequacy."[173]

This is the choice we are offered today. Will we pray? Or will we worry? We really can't do both.

—Having a Mary Heart

READ: 1 Thessalonians 5:18
REFLECT: What is God's will for you?

I can do everything through him who gives me strength. PHILIPPIANS 4:13

November 9

"I can't do this, Lord! I'm so undisciplined," I complained to God not long ago as I shut my laptop and listed all the reasons He'd chosen the wrong person to write a book.

The Lord was patient at first, bringing scripture after scripture to my heart, reminding me that He would help me. But one day He finally got tired of my unending litany of reasons why I couldn't.

Let me get this straight, I felt God whisper to my heart. *Although I spoke the universe into existence and hung the stars in space…even though I promised to help you when you said yes to My call…and even though you've cleared your life and made time to write this book…you still keep saying you can't do it.*

Well, that hit home. I started to squirm, but I could tell He was just warming up.

What you're really telling Me, the Lord said, *is that you're the omnipotent one around here. Because no matter how much I help you, no matter how willing I am to give you the words and the ability to write…you just know you'll find some way to mess it all up!*

Well, yes. That was pretty much what I was saying. Only it sounded so ugly and prideful the way He put it. Not nearly as humble and desperately pious as I felt.

It's unbelief, Joanna, the Lord concluded. *It is blasphemy. And it breaks My heart.*

And with that rebuke there finally came a deep inner breaking. Rather than humbling myself, I had actually been exalting myself against God. Telling the Almighty what He could and could not do. Focusing on my inadequacies rather than on His all-sufficiency and power.

No wonder God was offended.

—*Having a Mary Spirit*

READ: Hebrews 11:6

REFLECT: Write this verse on a card and repeat it often, asking God to increase your faith.

November 10

If you do not stand firm in your faith, you will not stand at all. Isaiah 7:9

Jesus said, "If you have faith as small as a mustard seed, you can say to this mountain, 'Move'…and it will move. Nothing will be impossible for you" (Matthew 17:20). Imagine what that kind of faith could do when it comes to rolling away the stones that block the entrance to our heart! Not a faith in formulas or a faith in our faith, but a heart-focused trust in our God. I'm asking the Lord to help me overcome my unbelief and replace it with three powerful types of faith.

An *"even if"* kind of faith…
I want a Shadrach-Meschach-and-Abednego faith that refuses to bow to other gods or bend to the fear of other people's displeasure, even if refusing could result in death (Daniel 3:17–18).

An *"even though"* kind of faith…
I want a faith that isn't dependent on circumstances or rattled by hardship—the kind of faith that chooses to praise even in the midst of unrelenting difficulties (Habakkuk 3:17–18, NLT).

A *"nevertheless"* kind of faith…
I want the kind of faith Jesus displayed in the Garden of Gethsemane. A faith that says, "Here's what I'd like to happen…" but in the end wants what God wants most of all (Matthew 26:39, NKJV).

—*Lazarus Awakening*

READ & REFLECT: What kind of faith do you need today? Look up the accompanying verse(s) and make it your prayer.

Not that I have already obtained all this, or have already been made perfect, but I press on to take hold of that for which Christ Jesus took hold of me. PHILIPPIANS 3:12

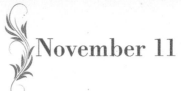

November 11

I appreciate the honesty with which so many Christian writers have shared their lives with us. It may seem like these folks were always holy, always passionate in their pursuit of Christ. But they, like us, faced difficult days.

One of my heroes in the faith is Amy Carmichael, a missionary who gave her life to the children of India. From a page in her journal, we get a peek into a heart that struggled just as we do:

> Sometimes when we read the words of those who have been more than conquerors, we feel almost despondent. I feel that I shall never be like that. But they won through step by step.
>
> > By little bits of wills
> > Little denials of self
> > Little inward victories
> > By faithfulness in very little things.
>
> They became what they are. No one sees these little hidden steps. They only see the accomplishment, but even so, those small steps were taken.
>
> > There is no sudden triumph
> > > no [sudden] spiritual maturity.
> > That is the work of the moment.[174]

Realizing that God is more interested in the process than the product has transformed my walk with Christ because it allows me to concentrate on obedience, not perfection. The goal of perfection only points out how far I have to go, but obedience marks how far I have already come.

I can't become everything I ought to be overnight. But I can proceed step by step if I'm obedient to what God asks of me today. That is the work of the moment.

—Having a Mary Spirit

READ: 2 Corinthians 4:16–18

REFLECT: Why should we not lose heart in the midst of our process?

November 12

I know whom I have believed, and am convinced that he is able to guard what I have entrusted to him for that day.
2 Timothy 1:12

When I received word that my mother had suffered a massive heart attack and was being rushed into emergency surgery, I immediately began driving the 150 miles south to be with her. That was fourteen years ago, before I had a cell phone, so I endured two hours without any updates, without any word of how the surgery was going. I wasn't even certain my mother was still alive.

As I prayed and drove and prayed and drove some more, I found myself giving my mother to the Lord. Entrusting her to His care. And with the surrender came a sweet peace like none I'd ever known before. I knew it was going to be okay.

But please understand, I still didn't know if *she* would be okay. The peace I felt wasn't a promise that my mother would survive the surgery. In fact, I found out later that she actually died on the table for a few minutes. The peace that enfolded me as I drove toward the unknown promised only this:

It would be okay. Whatever *it* turned out to be.

As I opened my hand and surrendered my mom to the God who loved her even more than I did, I felt a quiet joy fill my heart. A sweet underlying sense of okayness that surpassed happiness.

The settled peace I felt was a gift from the Lord, not something I could have worked up on my own. Lazarus must have felt that same peace when he walked out of the tomb and back into life—but magnified a hundredfold and tinged with amazing joy.

For he had traveled to the place we humans avoid most—death. And he found God waiting there.

—*Lazarus Awakening*

READ: Hebrews 2:14–15

REFLECT: Have you ever felt enslaved to the fear of death? Who came to set you free?

Now faith is being sure of what we hope for and certain of what we do not see.
Hebrews 11:1

It's hard to hope when hope is dead. It's hard to believe God's promises when your brother's body is lying in your living room. However, God's ways are not our ways.

According to one author, we often interpret God's delays as God's denials. But the story of Lazarus tells us that "a delay in answer is not a sign of God's indifference or his failure to hear. It is a sign of his love. The delay will help us. It will make us stronger."[175]

Jesus could have spoken the word and made Lazarus well. He did it with the Roman centurion's servant (Matthew 8:5–13). He did it for a Syrophoenician woman's daughter (Mark 7:24–30). Without physically being present, Jesus healed with just a word. He could have done that with Lazarus—as Mary and Martha well knew.

But God's ways are not our ways, and His timing rarely coincides with our own. While God is never late, I've found He's rarely early. That is why we must trust His schedule as well as His character.

CeCe Winans writes in her book *On a Positive Note:*

> Faith is about how you live your life in the meantime, how you make decisions when you don't know for sure what's next. What you do with yourself between the last time you heard from God and the next time you hear from God is the ongoing challenge of a life of faith.[176]

Waiting four days may have made Jesus late for a healing, but it made Him right on time for a resurrection. So never put a period where God puts a comma. Just when you think the sentence is over, the most important part may be yet to come.

—Having a Mary Heart

Read: Romans 11:33–36
Reflect: Read these verses aloud, acknowledging God's right to do things His way in your life.

327

November 14

O Lord, you took up my case; you redeemed my life. LAMENTATIONS 3:58

Of all the titles of Jesus, I've come to appreciate most that He is my Redeemer. After walking so many years with the Lord, through both good times and bad, I can declare along with Job, "I know that my Redeemer lives" (Job 19:25).

When God interrupted humanity's downward spiral by sending His own Son, Jesus came into a culture that expected the Messiah to set up a kingdom free from problems, sorrow, and pain. Even His own disciples expected He would topple Rome and set up a new regime complete with corner offices and special perks reserved just for them.

Those looking forward to the Promised One had always believed He would reinvent the world.

Instead, God chose to redeem it.

Which means sin is still present and Satan is still active. Murder and violent wars cover the earth. Sickness ravages bodies and minds and hearts. Too often, the innocent die young. Surely, we think, there has to be a better way.

After all, God could have pushed the reset button long ago, at the beginning of time. He could have taken one look at the mess we humans had made—our rebellion, our hatred, our immorality and idolatry—and decided to delete it all. With one push of a button, God could have rebooted and started over.

Instead, He became a man. On the cross He took the weight of our mistakes. All my failures, all your hurts, all our devastation. And with a final breath He redeemed it all.

—Lazarus Awakening

READ: Luke 1:68–75
REFLECT: Describe the redemption Jesus came to bring.

It was a beautiful summer afternoon. The sun sparkled against the water as the youth group floated down the wide, lazy river. Laughter and splashing mixed with sprays from water guns and squeals from teenage girls. It was a perfect day. But it was irrevocably interrupted by the sound of a large motorboat rounding the blind corner ahead.

Within moments the youth pastor's life was changed forever as the boat sliced over his inner tube and through his spine, leaving him paralyzed from the waist down.

A well-meaning saint of the church visited the young man later that week in the hospital. Wanting to comfort but struggling with what to say, he managed only a low murmur accompanied by an awkward pat. "These things sure have a way of coloring our lives, don't they?" the older man said.

"Yeah, they sure do," the youth pastor agreed. Then, with a slow smile, he added, "But I get to choose the color."

Terrible things happen in this life. Good people do mean things. Not-so-good people do even worse. Life is hard, and we don't get to choose what will and won't happen to us. But one thing we do get to do…we get to choose the color. Our response to life's difficulties and difficult people determines our path.

"I'm learning I don't have to be offended," my very-wise husband told me several years ago. "It's my choice. It's what I do with what happens to me."

—*Having a Mary Spirit*

READ: Acts 20:22–24

REFLECT: How did Paul view the trials awaiting him, according to verse 24?

November 16

At midnight the cry rang out: "Here's the bridegroom! Come out to meet him!"
MATTHEW 25:6

I learned an important truth early in ministry. There is only one Savior. And I am not He.

In fact, I do Christ a great disservice when I attempt to fill a role only He can fill. I also sabotage the process when I do things that the people being resurrected are meant to do.

Ministry can be heady stuff at times. It can be strangely satisfying to be the one a needy person turns to for help and answers. But it can also be dangerous…if we buy the lie that it's all up to us. That in some way we are meant to be another person's Messiah.

"If you become a necessity to a soul, you are out of God's order," Oswald Chambers writes.

> As a worker, your great responsibility is to be a friend of the Bridegroom.… Instead of putting out a hand to prevent the throes [in a person's life], pray that they grow ten times stronger until there is no power on earth or in hell that can hold that soul away from Jesus Christ. Over and over again, we become amateur providences, we come in and prevent God; and say—"This and that must not be." Instead of proving friends of the Bridegroom, we put our sympathy in the way, and the soul will one day say—"That one was a thief, he stole my affections from Jesus, and I lost my vision of Him."[177]

Friends of the Bridegroom—that's what we are called to be. Loyal to Christ and His work in the lives of those we minister to rather than loyal to our opinions of how that work should be done.

—*Lazarus Awakening*

READ: John 3:29–30
REFLECT: How did John the Baptist describe the job of the bridegroom's friend?

So I sought for a man among them who would…stand in the gap before Me.
EZEKIEL 22:30, NKJV

I'm coming to understand the best way to unwind other people's graveclothes is through intercession. But can I be honest? Prayer is often the last place I go. I'm ashamed to admit that I'm much quicker to get my hands on people than to get hold of heaven on people's behalf. No wonder I often end up doing too much or too little.

Reading Frank Peretti's book *Piercing the Darkness* has revolutionized how I view prayer. While it is a fictional account, it gives important insight into the spiritual battle that rages around every single one of us. And it shows the vital role intercession plays in the spiritual realm.

You may wonder, as I have, if prayer really makes a difference. I love the picture Peretti paints in his riveting story. Though a heavy spiritual darkness lay like a thick cloud over the small town, each time a prayer went up, a small hole appeared in the darkness. More prayers, more holes allowing the light of truth and illumination of the Spirit to reach the hearts and minds of those living there.[178]

If we only realized just how mighty our intercession can be, how it releases the power of God over people's lives and influences the spiritual battle being waged around them, we'd pray more.

In fact, I think we'd find ourselves investing in other people's freedom on a daily basis. Following through on our knees for as long as it takes for resurrection to happen and graveclothes to fall to the ground. Lifting people to the throne of grace until they're able to find their own way to the holy of holies. Covering them in the precious blood of Jesus until they learn how to walk and then how to run.

—*Lazarus Awakening*

READ: Numbers 14:11–20
REFLECT: According to verse 20, what happened when Moses interceded for his people?

November 18

Do not be surprised at the painful trial you are suffering, as though something strange were happening to you.
1 Peter 4:12

Why does God allow suffering?

Of all the questions we humans ask, perhaps no other trips us up like this one. If God is God, shouldn't He be able to keep bad things from happening? If God really cares, why doesn't He interrupt tragedy more often? He seems to intervene for some—why doesn't He do it for everyone? Especially for those who love Him so very much.

Why do Christ-followers seem to get the same amount of trouble—and at times, even more—than those who don't give Him a second thought? Shouldn't there be some special treatment reserved for those called by Jehovah's name—a get-out-of-cancer-free card or a lifetime guarantee your kids will never rebel?

But God doesn't work that way. And isn't that confusing and frustrating at times? Instead of being predictable, He chooses to be mysterious, yet unchanging—close, yet distant. A God who chooses to redeem our pain rather than providing handy escape routes.

My friend is struggling with God right now. In a big way. The actions of someone else have shattered her life. But the biggest casualty has been her faith. She can't make the God piece fit. Why didn't God stop the senseless act?

"I just need to know I matter," my friend says. "I need to know that God sees *my* pain and that He actually cares."

Isn't that what we all need at the end of the day? Perhaps that's why the shortest verse in the Bible may be the most power-packed phrase in all of the New Testament. Do you need to know you matter? Do you need to know He sees your pain?

Never forget: "Jesus wept" (John 11:35).

—Outtake from *Lazarus Awakening*

READ: 2 Corinthians 1:3–4
REFLECT: Describe a time when you were able to comfort someone with the comfort you've been given by God.

This High Priest of ours understands our weaknesses, for he faced all of the same testings we do, yet he did not sin.
HEBREWS 4:15, NLT

November 19

"Jesus wept" is famous as the shortest verse in the Bible, but the real power of that two-word passage from the story of Lazarus is the reassurance that Jesus understands what life is like for us, and He promises to be with us in all we have to go through. For example:

Jesus knew temptation: "He was in the desert forty days, being tempted by Satan" (Mark 1:13).

Jesus knew poverty: "Foxes have holes and birds of the air have nests, but the Son of Man has no place to lay his head" (Matthew 8:20).

Jesus knew frustration: "He scattered the coins of the money changers and overturned their tables.… 'Get these out of here! How dare you turn my Father's house into a market!'" (John 2:15–16).

Jesus knew weariness: "Jesus, tired as he was from the journey, sat down by the well" (John 4:6).

Jesus knew disappointment: "O Jerusalem, Jerusalem.., how often I have longed to gather your children together, as a hen gathers her chicks…, but you were not willing!" (Luke 13:34).

Jesus knew rejection: "From this time many of his disciples turned back and no longer followed him" (John 6:66).

Jesus knew sorrow: "My soul is overwhelmed with sorrow to the point of death" (Matthew 26:38).

Jesus knew ridicule: "Again and again they struck him…and spit on him. Falling on their knees, they paid [mocking] homage to him" (Mark 15:19).

Jesus knew loneliness: "My God, my God, why have you forsaken me?" (Matthew 27:46).

We do not travel life's pathway alone. The Holy Spirit is with us, leading and guiding us down roads Jesus has already walked.

—*Having a Mary Heart*

READ: 1 Peter 5:7
REFLECT: What difficulty are you struggling with today? Take your burden to Jesus. He cares for you.

November 20

Submit yourselves, then, to God. Resist the devil, and he will flee from you.
JAMES 4:7

Christ not only conquered death through His resurrection; He also demolished the works of Satan and thoroughly humiliated him in the process. The Message paraphrase describes the victorious event so beautifully: "[Christ] stripped all the spiritual tyrants in the universe of their sham authority at the Cross and marched them naked through the streets" (Colossians 2:15).

In other words, Satan has absolutely no power over you and me.

But don't be surprised when he tries to convince you otherwise.

Even though the devil's eventual destruction has been predetermined, he's still doing his best to stir up trouble. He still howls and prowls this earth, looking for ways to intimidate God's children (1 Peter 5:8).

Rick Renner describes it like this in his excellent devotional *Sparkling Gems from the Greek.*

> Because of Jesus' death on the Cross and His resurrection from the
> dead, the forces of hell are *already* defeated. However, even though they
> have been legally stripped of their authority and power, they continue to
> roam around this earth, carrying out evil deeds like criminals, bandits,
> hooligans, and thugs. And just like criminals who refuse to submit to
> the law, these evil spirits will continue to operate in this world until
> some believer uses his God-given authority to enforce their defeat![179]

I want to learn how to use that authority. I don't want to live enslaved to a tyrant who no longer has a right to demean and terrorize me, tormenting me with guilt and self-doubt. I'm tired of giving the devil more airtime in my mind than I give the Holy Spirit.

—Lazarus Awakening

READ: Ephesians 6:10–18
REFLECT: How could you better use the armor of God to defeat the enemy's attempts against you?

Let the word of Christ dwell in you richly. COLOSSIANS 3:16

November 21

Tim Hansel tells of a class he attended in which a brilliant Bible scholar asked what word was most important in the New Testament. "We all took stabs at it," Hansel writes. "Was it love? faith? hope? sanctification? grace?"

"No," the scholar answered. "It's the little word *let*. L-E-T."

Let. As in "let the word of Christ dwell in you richly in all wisdom" (Colossians 3:16, NKJV).

And "let this mind be in you which was also in Christ Jesus" (Philippians 2:5, NKJV).

And "let your light shine before men" (Matthew 5:16).

"*Let* is a word of transforming faith, with encyclopedias of meaning poured into it," Hansel writes. "*Let* assumes the total love and power of the Creator. It assumes that heaven is crammed with good gifts the Father wants to give his children. The profoundly simple word *let* is the gate that opens to that power. It gives God permission to work his might in us."[180]

Let. Allow. Choose.

Give Me permission, Christ promises, *and it is yours. My mind for yours* (1 Corinthians 2:16)—*a holy exchange.*

Perhaps it's silly, but I'm visual, so I've started taking this promise from God's Word and claiming it through a simple exercise. Sometimes in my mind, but sometimes (on especially difficult days) with an actual poke to my chest, I push an imaginary button. Then, by faith, I envision my mind dropping out of sight while the mind of Christ rises to take its place.

After all, there are situations and circumstances in my life when a sparkling, washed-by-the-Word mind is simply not enough. Times when I need my thoughts and feelings and will to be Christ's very own.

According to the Bible, I can have both. The natural made new, the supernatural made mine. My mind bound to His.

—*Having a Mary Spirit*

READ & REFLECT: Using a concordance or Bible website, find three New Testament verses that use the word *let* and meditate on them.

November 22

Praise the Lord, O my soul, and forget not all his benefits. Psalm 103:2

An attitude of gratitude is more important than we know. When we consider all of God's blessings, when we look back and see His hand upon our lives, our hearts are quieted. For we're reminded that God is our helper. We need not be afraid (Hebrews 13:6). But it is when we declare out loud our thankfulness that something truly transformative takes place.

"They overcame [Satan] by the blood of the Lamb and by the word of their testimony," John declares in Revelation 12:11.

Never underestimate the power of your story. Often we hesitate to share what Jesus has done for us because we're painfully aware of how far we have yet to go. But when we give God praise, when we actively and audibly express gratefulness to the power of His love and how far it has brought us, something amazing happens.

We see God more clearly and ourselves more accurately.

According to Romans 1:21, the greatest danger of not being grateful is spiritual blindness. "For although they knew God, they neither glorified him as God *nor gave thanks* to him, but their thinking became futile and their foolish hearts *were darkened*" (emphasis mine). It is a warning we must all take to heart. Even as believers.

"Although they claimed to be wise, they became fools and exchanged… the truth of God for a lie" (Romans 1:22, 25). We're in danger of doing the same thing if we refuse to cultivate an attitude of gratitude. Gradually, we end up worshiping the "created"—namely, us!—rather than the Creator. Blindly going down a path that always leads to destruction.

No wonder Paul instructs us to "give thanks in all circumstances."

Why? "For this is God's will for you in Christ Jesus" (1 Thessalonians 5:18).

—Outtake from *Having a Mary Heart*

Read: Luke 17:11–19

Reflect: What was Jesus's response to the only one who returned to give thanks?

Rabbi, who sinned, this man or his parents, that he was born blind?
JOHN 9:2

We humans are big on formulas. We need things to add up, so we're always coming up with rationales and reasons for the way the world works. And it's important that we do, for such curiosity helps make sense of things around us. But unfortunately, our insistence that life always adds up often results in faulty conclusions. Especially when we're attempting to reconcile the problem of pain and suffering with belief in a loving, caring God.

One of the most damaging misperceptions of many Christians is that if we are walking with God, nothing bad should ever happen to us. While we might not readily admit it or even see it, "Bless me, bless me" has been much of the church's cry and expectation these past few decades. If good things are happening to you, it is because you're doing something right. If you're walking through difficulty, then it is because you're doing something wrong.

Sounds logical to our human minds. And we see the same mind-set in the New Testament, for the scribes and Pharisees loved formulas as well. They had created an encyclopedia-sized index of rules and guidelines for gaining God's pleasure and, thus, His goodies.[181] If for some reason you fell ill, they reasoned only one thing could explain it: either you or your parents had sinned, and thus you deserved your current state.

It's no wonder that in Jesus's day the lame and the leper, the blind and the deaf were relegated to being outcasts and beggars. It was believed they deserved their fate. Which was a neat and tidy system...unless, of course, you happened to be one of those sick or maimed or afflicted.

—*Lazarus Awakening*

READ: Romans 14:10–13
REFLECT: If you've made judgmental assumptions about another person's situation, take a moment to repent.

November 24

This sickness will not end in death. No, it is for God's glory so that God's Son may be glorified through it. JOHN 11:4

When the writer of John 11:6 tells us Jesus stayed where He was for two days after learning Lazarus was sick, he uses the Greek word *meno.* "This term not only means that he stayed—or tarried—two days more," Jerry Goebel writes, "it also means he *endured* two more days. This adds great meaning to the verse. It tells us how difficult it was for Jesus to hold Himself back from rushing to Lazarus's side."[182]

Ah, the great restraint of God. We rarely think of how hard it must be for a Father who loves us so much to hold back from running constantly to our rescue. Yet in His merciful wisdom He does—because He knows there is a higher plan at work.

Jesus consistently resisted pleas to speed up His ministry, choosing instead to live by heaven's metronome. He refused to be pushed into a miracle by His mother (John 2:4), and He wouldn't be goaded by His brothers into going to Jerusalem before His time (John 7:6–10). Though our Lord eventually did both, He followed the timetable given by His Father, not popular opinion.

So when Jesus told the disciples, "Lazarus is dead, and for your sake I am glad I was not there, so that you may believe" (John 11:14–15), He was declaring His purpose as well as His love. It wasn't that He didn't care. He was simply pointing out that there was a whole lot more at stake than His friends knew. The stage was being set for Jesus to be crucified and God to be glorified. And all of it—the tragedy and the triumph, the sorrow and the joy—was part of what would become the foundation for your faith and mine.

—Lazarus Awakening

READ: John 12:9–11, 17–19

REFLECT: How did people respond after Lazarus's resurrection?

So do not throw away your confidence; it will be richly rewarded. HEBREWS 10:35

November 25

Scripture never shies away from the reality that bad things happen to good people. That God doesn't always come running to the rescue, at least not in the ways we expect. Love does tarry at times. And there are moments when Love seems to take a step back, allowing things to happen that we'd never dream of allowing ourselves.

Just ask Joseph as he scratches yet another day on the wall of his prison cell, counting down the long years since he'd dreamed God's dream and wondering how he'd apparently lost God's favor.

Just ask Daniel as he wraps his cloak around him and shivers in the pit, half from the cold and half from fear of the lion breathing hot upon his neck—all because Daniel wouldn't deny his God.

And just ask John, the disciple who told us the most about Lazarus. Years later he's an old man left to starve on the barren island of Patmos. He's heard about the brutal martyrdoms of his friends, disciples who had proven faithful, following Jesus all the way to their deaths. Would he be next?

In each seemingly hopeless case, however, Love's restraint accomplished God's purposes. Saving Egypt and the known world from starvation. Exalting God among a pagan nation as the one true God able to shut lions' mouths. And providing a glimpse of eternity (the book of Revelation) through the pen of a lonely old man.

The same tender-yet-tough-to-understand divine restraint may be required in your life and mine. But it will also accomplish God's purposes if we'll trust Him. Though we may never know the full story here on earth, nothing will be wasted by God.

Especially if we'll entrust all our confusion to His heart and our lives to His hands.

—Lazarus Awakening

READ: Romans 15:4

REFLECT: What is one reason God gave us the Scriptures?

November 26

My ears had heard of you but now my eyes have seen you. Job 42:5

Difficult times and dark nights of the soul tend to rattle our convictions and shake the foundations of our faith. Author Brian Jones writes about such a crisis in his book *Second Guessing God:*

> The year before I graduated from seminary, I lost my faith in God. That's not a smart thing to do, I'll admit. There's not a big job market out there for pastors who are atheists. But I couldn't help it. Life was becoming too painful. Truth had become too open to interpretation.… My doubts seemed to climb on top of one another, clamoring for attention. Before I knew what had happened, the new car smell of my faith had worn off, and I found myself fighting to hang on.

One night, frantic, he called a former professor who had been a mentor to him. "[Doubt] is washing away the sand underneath me," he told the older man. "If this keeps up, there won't be anything left to stand on."

Rather than reacting with a sermon on the necessity of faith, the wise professor acknowledged Brian's struggle, even sharing his own battle against disbelief. But then he added these final words: "Brian, listen to me when I say this. When the last grain of sand is finally gone, you're going to discover that you're standing on a rock."

"That one sentence saved me," Jones writes.[183] His doubts weren't obliterated overnight, but the professor's words provided Jones enough light to start heading back home. Back to the only place that's truly safe.

The heart of God.

—*Lazarus Awakening*

Read: Exodus 20:21 and Isaiah 45:3
Reflect: What significant things do you discover about "darkness" in these verses?

My soul finds rest in God alone; my salvation comes from him. PSALM 62:1

"Nobody likes me, everybody hates me, I'm gonna eat some worms. Fat ones, skinny ones, little itty-bitty ones! Nobody likes me, everybody hates me, I'm gonna eat some worms."

We used to sing this ditty in the sixth grade. It's a silly, nonsensical song, but I've found bits and pieces still echo through my life. When I'm feeling left out, I settle on the first line: "Nobody likes me." When I'm feeling hurt, I make the determination: "Everybody hates me." When I'm feeling sorry for myself, I swing to the extreme: "I'm gonna eat some worms."

But except for my friend's dad who invested heavily in red-worms-for-food farms in the late '70s, I've never heard of anyone who actually enjoys eating worms. They may go down fairly easy, but they leave a bad taste in your mouth. So do anger and paranoia, two slimy offspring of self-pity.

Anger compels us to defend ourselves, and paranoia tells us everyone is out to get us. We're all alone. No one cares, not even God.

Elijah tasted that bitter lie when Jezebel threatened his life and he fled for the desert. When he finally recovered from that journey, he traveled to Horeb, the mountain of God—always a good place to go when you're overwhelmed and weary, angry and slightly paranoid. But rather than greeting him with tender words, God cut to the heart of Elijah's matter and said, "What are you doing here?" (1 Kings 19:9, 13).

God knew Elijah didn't need commiseration; he needed truth. The same dose of reality we all need when we're tempted to feast on self-pity.

You are not alone, God reminded Elijah. And neither are we.

"The LORD is good, a refuge in times of trouble," a lesser-known prophet reminds us in Nahum 1:7. "He cares for those who trust in him."

—Outtake from *Having a Mary Heart*

READ: John 16:32

REFLECT: Though Jesus knew His followers would soon abandon Him, who did He say would be with Him?

November 28

I pour out my complaint before him;
before him I tell my trouble. PSALM 142:2

Hearing God's voice was enough to lance the boil of Elijah's self-pity. And out came the infectious sorrow, the years of rejection, as well as the exaggeration of the situation that tends to accompany a Martyr Complex.

Listen to Elijah's words in 1 Kings 19:10: "I have been very zealous for the LORD God Almighty. The Israelites have rejected your covenant, broken down your altars, and put your prophets to death with the sword. I am the only one left, and now they are trying to kill me too."

I love how God works. Rather than correcting or comforting Elijah, God simply reveals Himself. "Go out and stand on the mountain in the presence of the LORD," God tells him in verse 11, "for the LORD is about to pass by."

Elijah obeys and beholds a series of object lessons—a powerful wind, a shattering earthquake, a blazing fire, and finally, a gentle whisper. Then God repeats His initial question: "What are you doing here, Elijah?" (verse 13).

Have you noticed how we can get so mired in self-pity, we're oblivious to everything except our pain? Even after God meets him in a spectacular way, Elijah completely misses the point. He doesn't even acknowledge the majestic power he's just witnessed. Instead, word for word he echoes his original complaint, completely untouched, completely unchanged, by the presence of God.

That strikes fear in my heart. To think I could miss the manifestation of God because of a self-induced Martyr Complex. So enveloped by my anger and paranoia that I'm unable to see God's revelation, let alone allow it to comfort and change me.

Give me eyes to see what I need to see, Lord. And ears to hear. Whatever You do, don't leave me the same.

—Outtake from *Having a Mary Heart*

READ: Job 10:1 and Acts 8:23
REFLECT: What can be the danger of giving free rein to our bitter complaints instead of taking them to God?

November 29

I'm so glad we have a Savior who wants to do more than resurrect us. He wants to set us free. When you find yourself held down and held back by false weights, past lies, besetting sins, or reactive patterns, consider the advice Beth Moore gives in her book *Get Out of That Pit.* She suggests we follow three principles:

- **Cry out.** "Open your mouth, say, 'God, help me!' and mean it. Not as a figure of speech. Not with half a heart. With everything you've got, look up and cry out. Bring heaven to a standstill. Get some attention."
- **Confess.** Name every contribution you've made to your pit cycle as well as your self-destructive tendencies. "Get as specific as you can, and when you think you've thought of everything, ask God if there is anything you're overlooking."
- **Consent.** Agree with God concerning your situation and the instructions He gives. "God wants you out of that pit. He wants you in victory.... All you have to do is *consent* to what He already wants."[184]

I would also advise finding a trusted Christian you can talk to. There is something so powerful about confessing our "faults one to another" and praying so that we might be healed, as James 5:16 (KJV) suggests. We take the first step by being accountable. Choosing to live out our repentance not only before God, but also before a witness—going beyond just saying we're sorry, and actually proving that we've had a "change of mind, heart, and direction" by changing the way we live.[185]

—Lazarus Awakening

READ: Acts 3:19

REFLECT: What happens when we repent and turn to God?

November 30

God is within her, she will not fall.
PSALM 46:5

Years ago, God taught me a transformation tool that I call the "Yo-Yo Prayer."

Perhaps like me, you've tried for years to give a certain issue over to God. A habit, attitude, or addiction. Or an area of fear and doubt. "I'll be different, Lord," you've promised as you surrendered it to Him. And for a while you are.

But just when you think you've finally gained victory over that issue, there it is again—back in your hand. Somehow you've picked up the habit or situation once more, and you wonder if you were ever truly free. Which is exactly what Satan wants you to think.

You're such a hypocrite, he hisses to your heart. *See? I told you nothing would ever change. You'll never be free.*

But the real lies, of course, are Satan's—and you must take them to Jesus immediately. For if you listen to such blasphemy you will forever remain entangled in the old "yoke of slavery" (Galatians 5:1).

I've found that the quicker I return whatever I've somehow stolen from God's hand, the quicker I'll have peace in my heart. But in order to give it back, I have to ignore the lies of the enemy and keep agreeing with God. "All right, Lord. I don't know how I ended up with this, but it has no place in my life. I'm giving it back to You—now!"

As I've faithfully and diligently repented and turned issues over to God—no matter how many times I have to repeat the "Yo-Yo Prayer"—I've found that the power these issues once held over me is diminished and the string around my heart is loosened.

Until one day, when I give something to Him yet again, it doesn't return. No more yo-yo. And no more bondage.

—Having a Mary Spirit

READ: 1 Timothy 4:15–16

REFLECT: Why is it important to remain diligent when it comes to living a godly life?

Pride goes before destruction, a haughty spirit before a fall. PROVERBS 16:18

December 1

It was a perfect day. One of those "it doesn't get any better than this" kind of days. The sky was blue, the air so crisp it took my breath away as I schussed down the snow-covered slopes of Red Lodge, Montana. I was trying to catch up to my then-youth-pastor husband, John, and our guest speaker. Being total show-offs, they had raced halfway down the run and stood smugly leaning on their poles waiting—yawn!—for me.

I stopped and surveyed the run before me, adjusting my ski mask with a determination only scorned women can understand. Then, tucked into precise Olympic form, I carved my way over death-defying moguls, plunging this way and that, throwing caution to the wind. Okay, so maybe I snowplowed a couple of times. But I looked good—I mean, really good. Especially for an advanced beginner intermediate.

As I neared the spot where the guys stood watching me, their mouths gaping in awe, I concocted a brilliant plan. The moment of a lifetime lay within my grasp. Payback time. I would slide expertly to a stop, thereby spraying the two egomaniacs with a blanket of bone-chilling snow.

But then it happened. Some psychopath on skis came careening out of nowhere, right into my well-planned revenge. With razor-sharp reflexes, I missed the crazed skier. And then, dizzy with relief, ran head-on into my unsuspecting husband.

We have always been close, but at that moment we experienced the fulfillment of Scripture: "And the two shall become one flesh."

I remember lying there sprawled in the snow as the old television-sports slogan ran through my mind: "The thrill of victory, the agony of defeat…"

My feet felt fine. My ego, however…well, that's what brokenness is all about.[186]

—*Having a Mary Spirit*

READ: Proverbs 11:2

REFLECT: What is the result of pride? What is the result of humility?

December 2

Do not be arrogant, but be afraid.
Romans 11:20

"Pride cometh before a fall" isn't just a proverb. It's a law of nature. What goes up must come down, for pride will always fall victim to gravity. Jesus said it in Matthew 23:12: "For whoever exalts himself will be humbled."

Thinking too highly of ourselves is dangerous. So is thinking too lowly of ourselves—for this is pride as well. In fact, the whole haughty problem stems from a preoccupation with self, the habit of thinking entirely too much about us. Left unchecked, pride quickly grows into full-blown *I*-disease—a near-sightedness that leaves us unable to see other people and their needs because we can only see ourselves. "Me, me, me" becomes our unending vocal warmup to our self-centered repertoire.

"I am so beautiful…to me."

"Of all the me's I've loved before…"

You get the idea.

But pride is a liar. Rather than working for us, it works against us. Rather than looking out for our best interests, it pits us against a Father interested only in our greatest good. For inevitably, whenever we get too full of ourselves, we find ourselves in a boxing match, facing off against almighty God.

When James wrote, "God resists the proud, but gives grace to the humble" (4:6, NKJV), the word he used for *resist* implies taking an active fighting stance. God puts on boxing gloves and meets the arrogant in center ring. But to the humble, He multiplies grace upon grace, filling us with everything we need from His great riches in glory (Philippians 4:19, NKJV).

You see, there are only two ways to live: God's way or our own. Either we bend our knees or we thumb our noses.

—Having a Mary Spirit

READ: Luke 18:9–14
REFLECT: Which character in this parable most closely reflects your tendencies?

*You save the humble, but your eyes
are on the haughty to bring them low.*
2 Samuel 22:28

December 3

Is pride a problem in your life? The following comparison between self-centered and God-centered personalities may help you assess your own attitudes. Check which ones most often apply to you.

SELF-CENTERED

___ "I want it my way."

___ Is rigid and opinionated

___ Gets huffy and defensive if criticized

___ Hungers to be admired and praised; the center of attention

___ Makes sure others notice good works; demands credit

___ Indulges self; makes personal comfort a priority

___ Practices entitlement thinking: "I deserve this; I'm worth it."

___ Easily offended, nurtures resentment

___ Inflexible. Finds it hard to spring back from disappointments

___ Tends to excuse her own sin while condemning the sin of others

___ Obsesses about her obvious failures

___ Loves people who love her

GOD-CENTERED

___ "Your will be done."

___ Is flexible and open to others' ideas

___ Doesn't take criticism personally; listens and responds if appropriate

___ May enjoy praise but doesn't need it; lets others have the limelight

___ Performs good deeds without advertising them

___ Is willing to sacrifice personal comfort

___ Practices gratitude thinking: "I don't deserve this, but I'm thankful!"

___ Forgives quickly and completely; gives ongoing hurts to God

___ Resilient; able to rise above disappointments and use them creatively

___ Acknowledges sinful tendencies in self and others, but extends God's grace to both

___ Accepts God's forgiveness and moves on

___ Feels God's heart toward all humanity, is able to love the unlovable[187]

—Having a Mary Spirit

READ & REFLECT: Look up a verse on pride and turn it into a prayer.

December 4

He who listens to a life-giving rebuke will be at home among the wise.
PROVERBS 15:31

"Most of us fear being broken," Charles Stanley writes in *The Blessing of Brokenness*. "Because of our natural instinct for self-preservation, we fight hard to stay intact. Brokenness usually involves pain, and we will do almost anything to avoid that."[188]

But the very thing we resist most is the place where humility must begin: with receiving rebuke. With being willing to admit to God, "I am a sinner. I made a mistake." And to others, "You were right. I was wrong. Please forgive me."

You may need to look in the mirror and practice these lines. They come hard to most of us. But they are important confessions. For if we hope to be fit for the kingdom of God, we must accept correction—just as Martha of Bethany did when Jesus rebuked her in Luke 10:38–42.

It must have hurt Martha to be told that she was too uptight and that her unhelpful sister was doing the right thing. Part of her heart must have rebelled when she heard Jesus's words. After all, she was only asking for help in the kitchen. Did He really have to humiliate her in front of guests?

But correction is not rejection. While we might fight it, might even resent it at times, the Lord's rebuke is always a gift to our souls. For in every check to our nature is a promise of change—if we will receive it. If we will repent.

—*Having a Mary Spirit*

READ: Proverbs 3:11–12
REFLECT: What is the reason for rebuke, and how we should receive it?

When [the Spirit] comes, he will convict the world of guilt in regard to sin and righteousness and judgment. JOHN 16:8

December 5

Aren't you glad God doesn't let us get away with our sin? Part of the Holy Spirit's work is conviction—making us feel both the wrongness of our attitudes and the separation from God that sin causes. We need that inner sense of turmoil that will not let us rest, will not let us rationalize our actions or our attitudes, but keeps drawing us back to repentance. Back to our God.

I don't know how it works with you, but for me when the Spirit of God brings a check to my heart concerning a particular sin, there is a knowing—though perhaps, at the time, not a complete understanding. While I might not consciously admit it to myself or to the Lord, I know He is right. A light has been turned on in my mind. And if I'm willing to look, I'm enabled to see.

As I repent and turn from the heart attitude that led to the sin, the Holy Spirit helps me respond and react in new ways—in Christlike ways. That doesn't mean I never stumble or struggle with that specific area again. But gradually, as I continue to cooperate with the Spirit's work in my life, my patterns begin to change.

Humility. Brokenness. We fight them. We avoid them. Yet they are things our heavenly Father values immensely. "The sacrifices of God are a broken spirit," Psalm 51:17 tells us, "a broken and contrite heart, O God, you will not despise."

—Having a Mary Spirit

READ: Acts 24:24–26

REFLECT: Consider the story of Felix. What kind of excuses have you used in order to escape the conviction of the Holy Spirit?

December 6

Live a life of love, just as Christ loved us and gave himself up for us as a fragrant offering. EPHESIANS 5:2

It had been a hard day. Once again, my four-year-old son and I were in a tug of war of the wills. We pulled back and forth, neither of us willing to give in, to admit that perhaps—just perhaps—we might be out of line. I'd ask him to do something, and he wouldn't. He wanted to play, and I couldn't. Total frustration and nap deprivation on both our parts brought us to a nose-to-nose confrontation midafternoon.

"Your attitude stinks, John Michael!" I said sharply, one hand on my hip, the other shaking a finger in his little upturned face.

I'd summed up the problem in three little words. But while his defiance may have melted slightly, I could see hurt flooding in to take its place.

"Oh yeah?" he said in a small, trembling voice. A voice I needed to hear. "Well, your breath doesn't smell very good either."

From the mouth of babes…God continues to use this shrewd analysis to change my life. Because even when we're right, we can be wrong.

One of the most beautiful promises and prophecies concerning Christ's new covenant work is found in Ezekiel 36:26–27: "I will give you a new heart and put a new spirit in you.… I will put my Spirit in you and move you to follow my decrees and be careful to keep my laws."

What Jesus did on the cross not only saved us from our sins, but it can save us from ourselves—from our lousy attitudes, our faulty thinking, our stubborn self-deception. And the Lord does this not by pointing out where we should change or by calling us to wrestle Flesh Woman to the mat. He does this transforming work by filling us with Himself.

—Having a Mary Spirit

READ: Galatians 5:22–23
REFLECT: Which fruit of the Spirit do you need most today?

Jesus replied, "Are you not in error because you do not know the Scriptures or the power of God?" MARK 12:24

December 7

In his book *One Day at a Time,* Mike Quarles points out that filling our minds with "the crystal-clear Word of God" is the only effective way for us to have victory over Satan's lies and devices. "Merely trying to stop bad thoughts won't work," Quarles writes.

> Should we rebuke all those tempting, accusing and deceiving thoughts? No. If we attempted to win the war for our minds that way we would be doing nothing but rebuking thoughts every waking moment for the rest of our lives.
>
> It would be like telling a man in the middle of a lake to keep 12 corks submerged by hitting them with a small hammer. He would spend his entire life treading water and bopping down corks. What should he do? He should ignore the stupid corks and swim to shore. We are not called to dispel the darkness. We are called to turn on the light. We overcome the father of lies by choosing the truth![189]

As we fill our minds with the clarity of God's Word, Christ uses it to make us holy, "cleansing [us—His church] by the washing with water through the word" (Ephesians 5:26). And as our natural minds are being cleansed, something wonderful happens. New synaptic patterns are formed both in the natural and the supernatural realms, and we begin to think—and act—differently. As the New Living Translation of Romans 12:2 puts it, we "don't copy the behavior and customs of this world" because we've "let God transform [us] into a new person by changing the way [we] think."

Though it may take time, we are being changed—all because of the incredible mind-cleansing power of God's Word.

—Having a Mary Spirit

READ: Hebrews 4:12
REFLECT: Compared to other books, how have you found the Word of God to be living and active in your life?

Tips for Getting More from Your Bible Study

I've appreciated Kay Arthur's Precept Ministries and her emphasis on the deep study of God's Word. Here are her suggestions for in-depth study.

- *Begin with prayer.* Prayer is often the missing element in Bible study. No matter how effective the method of Bible study, apart from the work of the Holy Spirit, that's all it will be—a method.

- *Ask the "5 W's and an H."* As you study any passage of Scripture, constantly ask, Who? What? When? Where? Why? How? These questions hone observation skills, which are crucial for accurate interpretation.

- *Mark key words and phrases.* A key word is one that is essential to the text. Key words and phrases are repeated in order to convey the author's point or purpose for writing. For example, a form of the word *suffering* is used three times in 1 Peter 5.

- *Make lists.* Lists reveal truths and highlight important concepts and characteristics. First Peter 5:2–3, for example, contains a simple list regarding the role of the elder. Number the items in the text.

- *Watch for contrasts and comparisons.* Contrasts and comparisons use highly descriptive language to make it easier to remember what you've learned. First Peter 5:8 compares the devil to a roaring lion.

- *Note expressions of time.* The relationship of events in time often sheds light on the true meaning of the text. Marking them will help you see the sequence or timing of events and lead to more accurate interpretation.

- *Take note of geographic locations.* Often it's helpful to mark geographical locations, which tell you where an event takes place.

- *Mark terms of conclusion.* Words such as *therefore, thus,* and *for this reason* indicate that a conclusion or summary is being made. You may want to underline them.

- *Identify chapter themes.* The theme of a chapter will center on the main person, event, teaching, or subject of that section of Scripture. Review the key words and lists you developed. Try to express the theme as briefly as possible, using words found in the text.[190]

Emotions are a gift from God, but when what you feel threatens to block out what you know, it helps to go back to the truth of Scripture:

When I feel afraid...

"The LORD is my light and my salvation—whom shall I fear?" (Psalms 27:1).

When I feel overwhelmed...

"My grace is sufficient for you, for my power is made perfect in weakness" (2 Corinthians 12:9).

When I feel like running away...

"And he will stand, for the Lord is able to make him stand" (Romans 14:4).

When I feel threatened...

"O LORD my God, I take refuge in you; save and deliver me from all who pursue me" (Psalm 7:1).

When I feel betrayed...

"He will never leave you nor forsake you" (Deuteronomy 31:6).

When I feel confused...

"If any of you lacks wisdom, he should ask God...and it will be given to him" (James 1:5).

When I feel angry...

"Everyone should be...slow to become angry, for man's anger does not bring about the righteous life that God desires" (James 1:19–20).

When I feel depressed...

"He lifted me out of the pit of despair, out of the mud and the mire. He set my feet on solid ground" (Psalm 40:2, NLT).

When I feel unloved...

"I have loved you with an everlasting love.... I will build you up again and you will be rebuilt" (Jeremiah 31:3–4).

—*Having a Mary Spirit*

READ & REFLECT: Which of these reminders do you need most today? Write the correlating passage on a card, and carry it with you.

December 9

This then is...how we set our hearts at rest in his presence whenever our hearts condemn us. For God is greater than our hearts, and he knows everything. 1 JOHN 3:19–20

Crucifying Flesh Woman means I have to take a good honest look at myself—but only to a point. I've been known to self-examine myself sick. Prodding and poking at dead areas I hope are still dead, picking off scabs of things almost healed. Apart from the Holy Spirit's work, Hannah Whitall Smith says, self-examination can actually breathe life into the flesh we are trying to put to death.

> Self is always determined to secure attention and would rather be thought badly of than not to be thought of at all. And self-examination, with all its miseries, often gives a sort of morbid satisfaction to the self-life in us and even deludes self into thinking it is a very pious sort of self after all....
>
> We grow like what we look at, and if we spend our lives looking at our hateful selves, we shall become more and more hateful. Do we not find as a fact that self-examination, instead of making us better, always seems to make us worse?

The only healthy type of self-examination, according to Smith: "For one look at self, take ten looks at Christ."[191]

When I look to Jesus, the Holy Spirit brings into focus the things I need to see, so that in good, healthy, godly sorrow I respond in repentance and am set free.

Free from the tyranny of Flesh Woman who loves to masquerade as me.

—Having a Mary Spirit

READ: Colossians 3:1–4
REFLECT: Rather than looking at self, in what practical ways can we set our hearts and minds on things above?

I eagerly expect...that now as always
Christ will be exalted in my body,
whether by life or by death.
PHILIPPIANS 1:20

December 10

Lazarus knew that this earthly life isn't what we were made for. In the experience of dying and being resurrected, Lazarus must have discovered there was so much more to living than what he had known. To his reborn eyes, the life he'd been attached to, the one that had seemed so fraught with difficulty, must have looked like child's play.

From his brief glimpse of eternity, Lazarus could surely discern the counterfeit from the genuine. The cardboard facsimiles we work so hard to build. The papier-mâché dreams that occupy our hearts and minds. The silly games we play. The inconsequential things we inflate until they seem monumental.

What would it be like if you and I could finally shed the fear of death and the grasping, clinging obsession with this world that comes with it? What if, in coming to terms with death, we were enabled to fall back in love with the wonder of life itself?

I'm fairly certain we'd experience more joy and less fear. More faith and less doubt. More love and less selfishness. More life in this life!

If we focused on living in the light of eternity, understanding that there is a glorious lifetime in a perfect world to come, I think we'd learn to hold this one more loosely and the ones we love less possessively. God wouldn't always have to do what you and I think is best. We'd see eternal possibilities in everyday troubles. We'd more easily surrender ourselves and those we love to God's plan rather than our demands.

Most of all I think we'd learn to live with an open hand rather than a clenched fist.

—Lazarus Awakening

 READ: 2 Timothy 4:6–8
REFLECT: In what ways are you clinging to this life rather than looking ahead to the life that is to come?

December 11

My times are in your hands. PSALM 31:15

I remember how excited I was the morning of my twelfth Christmas. Of all the things I'd asked for, the one thing I really wanted was the one thing I actually needed (an advent of practicality I wouldn't experience again until my late thirties when my only Christmas wish was a really good office chair).

That year all I wanted was a metronome—a mechanical device my piano teacher promised would help my rhythm. Although I'd taken piano lessons for six years, I still struggled with one of the most important and fundamental principles of music. Keeping time.

The composition in front of me might call for *adagio,* which means "slowly." But I tended to play nearly everything *allegro*—"fast." No matter what the instructions, I *allegroed* everything. I just couldn't help it. I still tend to anticipate the beat today.

In my defense, I must say that long-ago Christmas gift wasn't a lot of help. Rather than performing the crisp *tick, tick, tick* its back-and-forth motion was designed to give, my new metronome had a little hitch in it, a hitch that was in direct opposition to the hitch in me. Rather than anticipating the count, it seemed to pause a bit before sounding the next beat.

I had my mother take the metronome back to the store. I even complained to my teacher. But both sources told us the device was fine. Yes, the pause was a little annoying, they agreed, but the beat itself was right on time. I needed to adjust to the metronome, they told me, rather than demand that it adjust to me.

That's a fundamental principle of life I'm still trying to learn—living according to God's timing and not my own.

—Lazarus Awakening

READ: Ecclesiastes 3:1–8
REFLECT: What season or "time" do you find yourself in today? How do Solomon's words encourage you?

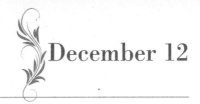

Four days is a long time to wait for a resurrection, especially when you feel that all hope is gone. Figuratively, you may be living in those dark 96 hours before dawn, wondering if the 5,760 minutes will ever end. Each of the 345,600 seconds that make up your waiting seems to hold its breath interminably, like a malfunctioning metronome, leaving you suspended between faith and doubt. Wondering if the dissonant chord hanging over your life will ever be resolved.

Four days is a long time to wait. I know. I've endured that incessant length myself.

But believe me, none of it is wasted time.

Although we may be "hard pressed on every side," Paul reminds us in 2 Corinthians 4:8–9, we are "not crushed." Though we may feel "perplexed," we are "not in despair." Though we are "persecuted," we are "not abandoned." Though "struck down," we are "not destroyed."

Instead, the apostle—beaten and stoned, shipwrecked three times—reminds us that we "carry around in our body the death of Jesus, so that the life of Jesus may also be revealed in our body" (verse 10).

Don't you love the creative irony of God! Paul is telling us that the very circumstances and events we believe will destroy us, the ones that generate so many of our whys, can actually serve as catalysts for the full manifestation of Christ in our lives—Jesus more accurately revealed in you and me.

In other words, don't get so caught up in what's happening that you miss what is really going on.[192] For nothing will be wasted.

Not the waiting. Not our questions. Not even our pain.

—*Lazarus Awakening*

READ: 1 Peter 4:12–14
REFLECT: How should we view suffering?

December 13

If you refuse to take up your cross and follow me, you are not worthy of being mine. MATTHEW 10:38, NLT

The Gospels clearly show that when Jesus walked the earth, it was difficult to be in His presence and not be changed. Individuals either walked away loving Him or hating Him, their lives better or worse. Staying indifferent to who He was and what He said was nearly impossible.

When Jesus came on the scene, occupations changed. Fishermen became fishers of men. Tax collectors became philanthropists, and one wrote a gospel. At His word, addresses changed. Demons became pig dwellers and lepers got to go home. At His arrival, reality was drastically altered. Dead children came back to life. The lame walked, the blind saw, the deaf heard. Water was turned into wine.

All because of the presence of Jesus. But the participants in nearly every encounter faced a choice: to heed and follow, or resist and walk away. The rich young ruler came seeking validation but went away downcast. Challenged, but unchanged. Though Judas had walked with Jesus for three years, his heart followed his own agenda. For it is possible to go through the motions of worship yet never give in to worship's demands.

We can claim Christianity, but until we allow Christ to claim us, we will never be transformed. For radical change requires a radical choice.

I love how Mark Buchanan describes the intensity of the invitation Jesus extended to His disciples and the response it still demands today. "Christ... looks big men in the eye and says, 'Follow me,' and then walks away, not waiting for a reply."[193]

For those who left all to follow Jesus, nothing would ever be the same. For those who refused to follow, nothing would ever change.

What will we do with the call of God?

—Outtake from *Having a Mary Spirit*

READ: Mark 10:17–22

REFLECT: What radical demand did Jesus make of the young man? How do we reconcile that demand with the fact Jesus loved him?

The word of the LORD holds true,
and we can trust everything he does.
PSALM 33:4, NLT

December 14

Why do we secretly believe that following Jesus should always be easy? I know we don't say it out loud. Instead, we talk about the price of obedience and the cost of discipleship. But when it gets right down to it and the going gets tough, haven't we all wondered if we somehow misunderstood God's instructions? If perhaps we missed God's will when, like Bugs Bunny, we took that left turn at Albuquerque? If we were really walking in obedience to God's plan, we reason, things shouldn't be so difficult.

Mary, the mother of Jesus, must have had all those thoughts and more when she heard what was going on with her oldest son in His ministry. She hadn't seen Jesus very often since He'd left home three years before. She missed Him so much that sometimes it took her breath away.

"Did you not know that I must be about My Father's business?" Jesus had told her and Joseph after a frantic search finally turned up their twelve-year-old teaching in the temple (Luke 2:49, NKJV). And it was His Father's business that kept Him away from her now.

Most of the time, Mary was okay with that. But as news of miracles and healings gave way to reports of Sanhedrin meetings and attempts to capture her son, Mary must have been grieved at the turn of events that seemed to be leading Him toward the cross rather than a crown. And so are we when all our grand plans to do something important for God go up in smoke and our high-flying hopes come crashing down.

At times like these, we need to remind ourselves that God knows what He's doing.

When we can't trace His hand, we must trust His heart.

—*Having a Mary Spirit*

READ: Psalm 62:5–6
REFLECT: How does having a strong foundation in God change your perspective during trials?

December 15

Perhaps you are in a wintry season right now. Perhaps you feel as though everything you've cared about has been taken away, and you've not found anything to take its place. Perhaps God has called you to lay aside a lifetime of striving so you can experience abiding. But to be honest, the stillness is getting on your nerves.

Winter always seems to take longer than we think it should.

Getting through such times, I've learned, is not for the faint of heart. It's not easy to endure the loss of what we once thought was vital. To shiver in the dark, feeling bereft and confused. To wonder when—or if—this season of dying will ever end in true resurrection.

I understand how you feel. And so does Jesus—more than either of us knows. The One who hung forgotten and forsaken, cut down in the prime of His life and buried deep in the tomb, is so intimately acquainted with our suffering that He alone can remind us what is at stake.

"I tell you the truth," Jesus told His disciples as they walked toward Jerusalem and His death, "unless a kernel of wheat falls to the ground and dies, it remains only a single seed. But if it dies, it produces many seeds" (John 12:24).

As strange as it sounds, it is in the dark nights of our souls—in those deathlike, midnight places where nothing seems to be happening—that God often does His best work. Preparing our lives—so barren at the moment—for an even greater outpouring of life.

For winter always precedes spring. And in the law of harvest, death always precedes life. But if we'll trust the Gardener, a harvest of fruit awaits—"much fruit," as John 15:5 calls it. Fruit formed out of the life of Christ released in us by our dying.

—*Lazarus Awakening*

READ: Psalm 27:13–14

REFLECT: What should characterize our attitude and behavior during difficult times?

I no longer call you servants.... I have called you friends. John 15:15

December 16

Surrounded by people who claim His name, Christ still longs for a genuine friend. A real, true-blue, when-the-chips-are-down kind of friend. A friend who cares about what He cares about. A friend who looks to bring joy and comfort to His heart, with no strings attached. No hidden agendas. No secret wish lists.

Interestingly, in the Greek language there are two distinct words for "friend"—*philos* and *hetairos.* It is unfortunate that the English translation for both terms is the same word, for the Greek terms could not be more different.

The first word, *philos,* is the term Jesus used when He called Lazarus "our friend" in John 11:11. It denotes someone "loved, dear, befriended." It is an intimate classification reserved for those close to the heart.

The second term used in the Greek, *hetairos,* can be translated "comrade or colleague," but it refers to a darker kind of relationship. According to Spiros Zodhiates, *hetairos* refers to followers who "were not necessarily companions for the sake of helping the chief, but for getting whatever advantage they could.... The verb *hetairé* basically means to keep company with or to establish…[a] pretentious, ostentatious, deceptive, and misleading friendship."[194]

Sounds a little like society today, doesn't it? Everywhere we are encouraged to network, schmooze, and work the angles. Do whatever it takes to succeed, we're told. Be friendly on the surface. Just make sure it furthers your agenda underneath.

"True friendship," on the other hand, as Zodhiates explains, "is expressed by the verb *phileo*…which means to appropriate another person's interests unselfishly."[195]

All of which leads us to a very important question: What kind of friend am I?

—Lazarus Awakening

READ: Exodus 33:11

REFLECT: What made Moses's friendship with God unique? What would it take to cultivate a more intimate relationship of your own with God?

December 17

He who loves a pure heart and whose speech is gracious will have the king for his friend. PROVERBS 22:11

Consider the following qualities of a good friend as they relate to your relationship with God. How do you rate? Mark each characteristic with a 5 (for "Always"), 4 ("Usually"), 3 ("Sometimes"), 2 ("Rarely"), or 1 ("Never").

____ *Good listener:* Interested in how the other person is doing. Asks good questions. Hears the other person out; doesn't interrupt. Cares about that person's feelings. Comfortable with silence.

____ *Low maintenance:* Isn't overly needy. Secure in self and friendship, not demanding. Doesn't need constant attention. Isn't threatened by time apart.

____ *Not easily offended:* Patient when needs aren't immediately met. Believes the best, not the worst. Doesn't jump to conclusions. Willing to talk things out.

____ *Available:* Always there when needed. Willing to set aside own plans in order to help a friend. Returns calls quickly and doesn't ignore e-mails.

____ *Not jealous:* Doesn't get mad when time is spent with other people or someone gets a nicer birthday gift. Doesn't give the cold shoulder or leave nasty notes when upset.

____ *Kind:* Quick with genuine words of affection and affirmation. Looks for practical ways to express love. Gentle sweetness creates a haven of safety.

____ *Trustworthy:* Can be trusted with delicate information and difficult situations. Doesn't participate in gossip. Will not betray a friend—loyal to the point of death.

—Lazarus Awakening

REFLECT: Count up your points. A score of 29–35 suggests you are well on your way to being a true friend of God; 22–28 means you still need some work; 14–21 means you probably didn't realize you were supposed to be God's friend; 7–13 means you just don't care. (Note: If you scored low, you may find your human relationships are suffering as well.)

December 18

Remember several years ago when the take-time-for-yourself experts were instructing all us overcommitted types to go to our mirrors and practice saying no?

I suppose having two toddlers gave me extra practice, but it wasn't long before that two-letter word just flowed off my lips. *No, I'm sorry, but I'm unavailable. No, I'm sorry, but that isn't convenient.* It was so effective, no one even bothered asking anymore.

No one except God, that is.

He wasn't impressed by my self-care or even my excuse of "family priorities." He knew my heart, and He was well aware that my no had become far too quick, a nearly thoughtless knee-jerk reaction. I was so busy protecting myself that I wasn't even stopping to consider that a request for my involvement might be part of God's call to me. And as I eventually discovered, you can't say no to God without suffering some major spiritual side effects.

Like the Israelites, I began to experience the spiritual consequence of prolonged self-interest: "They soon forgot His works; they did not wait for His counsel...[so] He gave them their request, but sent leanness into their soul" (Psalm 106:13–15, NKJV).

You see, we were created to say an enthusiastic yes to the call of God in our lives—both His call to devotion and His call to service.

At the same time, it's important to remember that saying yes to God doesn't mean saying yes to everything! When our lives are overbooked, it's easy for us to become spiritually dry and undernourished.

Learning to say no to overcommitment so that we can say yes to God is important. Not for the purpose of self-preservation, but so that we're able to obey when He asks us to give our lives away.

—Having a Mary Heart

READ: Philippians 2:14–16
REFLECT: What are we called to do and be?

December 19

The virgin will be with child and will give birth to a son, and will call him Immanuel. Isaiah 7:14

Have you ever considered how costly saying yes to God was for the virgin Mary?

Donna Otto writes:

Once Mary had said yes to the angel, as far as I can tell, she kept on saying yes to what God was doing in her life and her home. She said, "Yes, I'll go to Bethlehem with my husband, even though I'm very pregnant." She said, "Yes, I'll settle for a stable" and "Yes, I'll agree to let all those grungy shepherds in to see my newborn." Much later she said, "Yes, I'll let my Son leave home to be an itinerant preacher." And, "Yes, no matter what, I'll be there with Him—even at the foot of a cross."

The life of Mary shows that great things, important things, always begin with someone saying yes to God, and then they move along one yes at a time. When you keep in mind that your whole life is holy ground, you keep yourself open to the wonderful opportunities he has planned for you....

There will be sacrifices as well as surprises when you say yes to God—sacrifices of your time, of your plans, and sometimes of your dearly held dreams....

But...God's intention overall is to bless you—in your life as a woman, and in your life at home. He has already blessed you.... He has indeed favored you among women by giving you a vital part in the process of bringing about his kingdom on earth.

Once you say yes to the Lord, you won't know exactly where you will end up, but you can know you'll always find your way home.[196]

—Having a Mary Spirit

READ: Luke 1:26–38

REFLECT: List the reasons saying yes to God may have been inconvenient for Mary.

The angel said to her, "Rejoice, highly favored one, the Lord is with you; blessed are you among women!" LUKE 1:28, NKJV

December 20

We don't know when and where Mary received the message that her life was about to change. The Bible doesn't give many details. It only says that God sent the angel Gabriel to a young virgin in a village called Nazareth (Luke 1:26–27).

"Greetings, you who are highly favored!" the angel said (verse 28). "The Lord is with you."

And in that instant Mary's life changed forever.

God has always seemed to use the most unlikely people in the most unusual ways to perform His most perfect will. A risky practice, I think. After all, we humans have so many ways of messing things up. Procrastination. Pride. Not to mention our tendency to add a few things or skip a few steps in order to "enhance" God's plans.

So why, out of all the Jewish young women who'd ever lived, did God choose Mary?

Certainly, it might have been that she was in the right place at the right time. After all, she was a resident of Nazareth and pledged to be married to a descendent of David, a man who would soon return to Bethlehem for a census—all of which set the stage for the fulfillment of several prophecies. But to choose the woman who would bear His own Son? Surely there must have been something more on God's wish list than a pedigree, an address, and her availability for a road trip.

I believe there was. For Mary was no ordinary teenage girl. She was a woman willing to say yes to God—to lay down her own hopes and dreams so that His plans and purposes could come to pass.

Mary was the kind of woman God still looks for today.

—Having a Mary Spirit

READ: Luke 1:38

REFLECT: Write this verse on a card and consider memorizing Mary's response.

December 21

For the Mighty One has done great things for me—holy is his name.
LUKE 1:49

I must confess I have a hard time relating to Mary. She's everything I'm not—at least in the natural. Quiet. Submissive. Willing to trust God.

Had an angel appeared to me telling me I'd been chosen to carry the Son of God in my womb, I would have asked for a lot more details before I said, "May it be to me as you have said." And chances are, a praise song would not have been the first thing out of my mouth (Luke 1:46–55). Instead of pondering these things in my heart, as Mary did, I would probably have raced out the door to buy a maternity shirt with the word *MESSIAH* printed on the belly and *HIGHLY FAVORED OF GOD* on the back.

But oh how I want a willing spirit like the mother of Jesus had. I want to be able to say yes to the Lord without asking why and where and how. Unfortunately, I understand all too well what Richard Foster writes in his book *Prayer: Finding the Heart's True Home:* "To applaud the will of God, to do the will of God, even to fight for the will of God is not difficult…until it comes at cross-purposes with our will. Then the lines are drawn, the debate begins, and self-deception takes over."[197]

It is one thing to want God's will and quite another to do it. As we've seen, the human heart has a huge capacity for self-deception, and our flesh is contrary to His ways. So even when I'm nodding yes to Him, too often my actions are saying no.

I want to learn to say yes to God as Mary did. Nothing held back. Nothing reserved. Gladly allowing His will to be birthed in me. No matter how much it costs.

—Having a Mary Spirit

READ: Luke 1:39–55

REFLECT: Imagine what Elizabeth's words in verses 42–45 must have meant to Mary. Read aloud Mary's song, known as "The Magnificat," in verses 46–55, and make it your own song of praise.

How can this be, since I do not know a man? LUKE 1:34, NKJV

December 22

What is it about us women that creates such a desperate need to always "know," to always "understand"? We want an itinerary for our life, and when God doesn't immediately produce one, we set out to write our own.

"I need to know," we tell ourselves.

No, God answers softly, *you need to trust.*

But like the original first lady, we push aside His tender voice and head straight for the tree. Not the sacrificial tree of the cross, but the proud, towering beauty called Knowledge. Because, after all, knowledge is power. And power is what we secretly crave.

I believe Eve's eventual sin began with a tiny thought—a small, itching fear she was somehow missing something and that God didn't have her best interest at heart. What could be wrong with something so lovely, so desirable as the forbidden fruit? Perhaps a hidden resentment had worked down into her spirit. Adam got to name the animals while *she* got to pick papayas. Whatever the identity of the tiny irritation, it sent her looking for more.

And Satan was ready and waiting, willing to give her more than she'd ever bargained for. He filled her mind with questions. "Did God really say…?" Satan encouraged Eve to doubt God's word and God's goodness until the continual question marks finally obliterated her trust in God's love.

I'm learning it is wiser to give my doubts to a faithful God than to engage in prolonged conversation with a wily, wicked serpent.[198] For when I insist on having all my questions answered, I give Satan the opportunity to twist and distort the only truth I need.

I am loved. So are you. That's all we need to know.

—*Having a Mary Heart*

 READ: Luke 1:30, 37
REFLECT: Allow the angel's words to Mary to speak hope to any doubt or worry you might be carrying today.

December 23

She wrapped him in cloths and placed him in a manger, because there was no room for them in the inn. LUKE 2:7

From the beginning of time, God's love has been reaching.

A celestial science project didn't initiate creation; it was Love that started it all, and it was Love that sustained it. And that same Love pursues us today, though it has continually been rejected and scorned.

You know the story. It started in a garden. Sweet fellowship and tender laughter filled the days. Innocence and security guarded the nights. Yet, the love God offered wasn't enough. The desire for power and autonomy sent both Adam and Eve searching for something more. With one bite, the unhindered friendship they'd enjoyed with God was severed, and they were sent out into a dark, unfriendly world.

But before they went, Love provided the first sacrifice and covered their nakedness. Though they would be separated from Him for a time, God declared there would be an end to the exile. For one day the seed of the woman would bruise the serpent's head, and all would be made right. From the first bite into the apple, Max Lucado writes, "there appeared the shadow of a Cross on the horizon."[199]

After clothing His beloved children, Love watched as the exiles stepped out into the harsh environment of a fallen world. But it wasn't long before Love set about wooing man and woman back to Himself.

Unfortunately, the stubborn rebellion of humanity continued. They all chose to do what was right in their own eyes. Building monuments to themselves, emphasizing their desire to be as God. Congratulating one another on how wise and wonderful, capable and in control they were. All the while they ignored the Love that had watched over them for so long.

It is the same temptation we face today.

—Outtake from *Lazarus Awakening*

READ: Luke 2:1–20

REFLECT: Do you have room in your heart for Jesus, or is your heart crowded with other things?

Now dismiss your servant in peace.
For my eyes have seen your salvation.
Luke 2:29–30

December 24

In time, humanity's willful, sinful rebellion built to such a crescendo that the Father had to reclaim His creation from its self-destructive ways by destroying the ones He had made. And yet Love continued to reach out to them, saving a remnant through a man named Noah.

After floating upon God's wrath for so long, once upon dry ground, Noah built an altar and worshiped the One who had preserved him. But humanity once again rejected their Maker. In time, God found a man named Abraham through whom to build a nation. Because Love kept reaching.

Though beneficiaries of God's blessings and set apart for His purposes, Abraham's descendants turned away and served the evil deities of the nations surrounding them. They were given over to captivity in Egypt, but Love heard their cries and sent a deliverer. Though fickle love and stubborn unbelief kept Israel wandering in the desert for forty long years, Love travelled with them—feeding their children and providing for their needs.

Finally the Promised Land lay before them, and Love led them in. But in their prosperity, the chosen people forgot the Lord. In their ease, they looked to other gods and intermarried with other cultures. Love sent prophets to call them back, but they didn't listen. Instead, they demanded an earthly ruler, so God set up kings to lead them.

All the Father had ever wanted was a people to call His own. A place to lay His heart. A relationship with those He had made.

But while Love kept reaching, man kept rejecting. To the point God finally fell silent and let His beloved people go their own way.

Until one night, four hundred years later, Love broke the silence.

When from the womb of an ordinary woman came a tiny baby's cry.

—Outtake from *Lazarus Awakening*

Read: Luke 2:21–35
Reflect: As Simeon did, take a moment in your heart to behold your Salvation, the long-awaited Messiah who came for you.

December 25

Where is the one who has been born king of the Jews? We saw his star in the east and have come to worship him.
MATTHEW 2:2

For the four hundred silent years that span between the Old and New Testaments, God stepped back and gave Israel what they wanted. They lived life on their own terms. God no longer interfered by sending prophetic doomsday warnings. God no longer told them what to do. But the silence had to be deafening. "Where are You, God?" Israel must have cried. "Why have You forsaken us?"

Though He had stepped back, God hadn't left His children. Instead He waited for the perfect moment to launch a radical rescue mission that would not only redeem the children of Israel, but restore both you and me to the relationship He'd intended so long ago.

"At just the right time," Romans 5:6 tells us, God sent His only Son to redeem a world lost in sin. To a world that had rejected His advances and questioned His motives, God came. And He came in such a way that humanity could never again deny His love.

Frederick Buechner writes of this incredible grace in his book *The Hungering Dark.*

> The child [was] born in the night among beasts. The sweet breath and steaming dung of beasts. And nothing is ever the same again.
>
> Those who believe in God can never in a way be sure of him again. Once they have seen him in a stable, they can never be sure where he will appear or to what lengths he will go or to what ludicrous depths of self-humiliation he will descend in his wild pursuit of man.[200]

Love came to earth that long-ago night in Bethlehem. The tenacious, untiring love of God came wrapped in swaddling clothes. Lying in a manger. Behold your salvation, world. Emmanuel has come.

—Outtake from *Having a Mary Heart*

READ: Matthew 2:1–12

REFLECT: Take a moment and bow as the wise men did. Allow the love of God to apprehend your heart in a brand-new way this Christmas.

Did you not know that I must be about
My Father's business? LUKE 2:49, NKJV

December 26

Because of Jesus, perfect love has come. The power of fear in our lives has been destroyed. All we have to do is receive the gift. How do we do that? Well, this may sound kind of silly, but one way I do it is by falling backward onto my bed.

On those difficult, overwhelming days when I'm struggling with fear—when the heat waves of my failure obliterate my awareness of God's perfect love—I make a conscious choice to both repent and then believe I am forgiven in spite of what I feel. And not just forgiven, but cherished. Beloved. Protected. Held close with a love that far surpasses anything we could ever experience here on earth.

"And so we *know* and *rely* on the love God has for us," I say, repeating 1 John 4:16 with the italicized emphasis, throwing open my arms, and falling back on my bed. There I lie—safe and received, welcomed into the forgiving arms of my heavenly Daddy. When I get up, I purposely take with me that delicious sense of being loved and cared for. Fear loses its grip on my heart as my mind delights in God's grace.

"In this way, love is made complete among us," verse 17 says, "so that we will have *confidence* on the day of judgment" (emphasis mine). The only way to experience the perfect, dread-banishing love that casts out fear is to know and rely on what God tells us He's already given.

For when we trust His love—when we take the plunge and fall backward into joy—we no longer give way to anxiety. We are "made perfect in love" simply by resting in the One whose perfect love drives out fear (verse 18).

—Having a Mary Spirit

READ: John 3:16
REFLECT: Read this familiar portion aloud, replacing the words "the world" and "whoever" with your name.

December 27

I have fought the good fight, I have finished the race, I have kept the faith.
2 Timothy 4:7

In 1992, Derek Redmond of Great Britain was poised to fulfill a lifelong dream of winning a gold medal in the Barcelona Olympics' four-hundred-meter race. With the finish line in sight, he suddenly fell face down on the track with a torn hamstring.

The race seemed over, but before the medical team could reach him, Derek struggled to his feet. Though all the runners had already crossed the finish line, he began hopping forward with tears of pain and disappointment coursing down his cheeks.

Suddenly, his father was beside him. "You don't have to do this," Jim Redmond told his son.

"Yes, I do," Derek answered.

"Well, then," his father said, "we're going to finish the race together."

He wrapped his arm around Derek, and the two men limped and hopped together toward the finish line. The watching crowd rose to their feet and began to applaud, cheering and marveling at the son's determination and the father's support.[201]

Perhaps that's what the writer had in mind in Hebrews 12:1: "Let us run with perseverance the race marked out for us."

For you have a great cloud of witnesses who've already gone before, cheering you on from heaven's grandstand. You've got a strong Older Brother who has shown you how to run and waits at the finish line, arms open wide. And you have a *paraclete*—the Helper, the Holy Spirit—coming alongside, wrapping His arms under and around you, running in tandem as you keep step with Him.

You were made for the finish line, my friend. Not the sidelines.

So set your eyes on Jesus and run. For the best is yet to come.

—Outtake from *Lazarus Awakening*

 Read: James 1:2–4

Reflect: How should we consider difficulties, and what do we gain when we persevere?

For the Lamb at the center of the throne will be their shepherd.... And God will wipe away every tear from their eyes.

REVELATION 7:17

December 28

I'm starting to wonder if one reason God allows difficulties in our lives is to wean us from this world, to cure our addiction to temporal things that will never satisfy. Because it seems that the times we come face to face with pain and death are the times we're reminded best that this world is just a shadow. A crude drawing and a mere outline of the beauty that awaits us in a world outside this one.

In his marvelous book *Things Unseen*, Mark Buchanan tells the story of a couple who lost their barely born son to a rare and severe genetic disorder. Three months later, their two-year-old daughter died as well. In the wake of devastating loss, Marshall and Susan Shelley wrestled painfully with God. *Why, God?* they kept asking. *Why did You do that? What was all that about?*[202]

Marshall later shared his struggle to understand his son's death in an article he wrote for *Christianity Today*. "Why did God create a child to live two minutes?" he asked before answering:

> He didn't. [And] He didn't create Mandy to live two years. He did not create me to live 40 years (or whatever number he may choose to extend my days in this world).
>
> God created Toby for eternity. He created each of us for eternity, where we may be surprised to find our true calling, which always seemed just out of reach here on earth.[203]

What a powerful thought! We were not created for this earth alone but for an infinite future with God. A destiny beyond the realm of mere time and space. How would our lives change if we really woke up to that reality?

—*Lazarus Awakening*

READ: Revelation 21:1–4
REFLECT: Underline key words or phrases in this passage that mean the most to you.

December 29

I am coming soon. Hold on to what you have, so that no one will take your crown. REVELATION 3:11

In light of the fact that there is more to come, how then shall we live? If eternity, not this earth, is our true home, don't you think we should live differently than the world does? I'd like to suggest these principles:

- *Live fully.* Don't waste today regretting the past or fearing the future, for it may be your last day on earth. Make it count for God!
- *Hold things loosely.* Since we can't take our possessions with us, enjoy what you have, but don't cling so tightly to stuff or fall into the trap of always wanting more.
- *Value people highly.* People are the true treasures of life, worth nurturing and investing in, for they are the only thing on earth we can possibly take with us when we leave.
- *Travel lightly.* Don't carry baggage from past hurts, and don't pick up grudges as you go. Life's too short to be voluntarily miserable.
- *Love completely.* Let God reveal His love for people through you. Be tender-hearted, not hardheaded, patient and quick to forgive, merciful and slow to judge.
- *Give freely.* Don't hoard what you have. Instead, share it with a joyful heart, and you'll be given more. Generosity releases blessing as sowing seed leads to harvest.
- *Look expectantly.* Keep looking up even as you walk here on earth, always ready and waiting for the imminent return of Christ. Be heavenly minded so you can be of earthly good.

—Lazarus Awakening

READ: 2 Peter 3:13–14

REFLECT: Ask God to help you live in the light of eternity as you prayerfully walk through this list.

I recently traveled to speak at a women's conference in Georgia. In the office foyer of the host church hung a photograph of one of the most inspiring pieces of art I've ever seen.

It depicted a man with the bottom half of his body covered in bronze. But it was the top half that captured my attention.

With one arm thrust upward, the man gazed toward heaven. With his other hand he grasped the shell of bronze encasing his lower torso and peeled it away from his body, revealing something exquisite beneath—a pure, transparent, crystal human form. Yet it was so much more than that. A light seemed to emanate from within.

It was a breathtaking visual of what Paul describes in Colossians 1:27: "Christ *in* you, the hope of glory" (emphasis mine).

Part of our purpose on earth is to peel back the layers of our lower nature—to "put off [our] old self" as Ephesians 4:22 instructs—so that we might provide an accurate reflection of who God really is. I don't want the Light of the World to be hidden under a bushel, no. And I certainly don't want Him to get buried beneath my graveclothes.

The great Alpha and Omega, the Bright and Morning Star, was placed in us at salvation, and He's waiting to be revealed to a watching, wondering world. To let Him shine, we simply have to cooperate with grace and do what only we can do. Throwing off everything that might get in the way. Peeling off layer after layer of graveclothes that keep tripping us up and holding us back.

For when we do, something marvelous happens. Jesus is revealed in you and me.

All because we took His advice to loose Him and let Him go!

—Lazarus Awakening

READ: Ephesians 4:22–24

REFLECT: What are we to "put off," and how are we to be "made new"?

December 31

Pursue righteousness, godliness, faith, love, endurance and gentleness. Fight the good fight of the faith.
1 Timothy 6:11–12

Over the years, the apostle Paul has become one of my dearest friends. He not only identifies with my struggles; he puts into words the frustration and the exhilaration I've experienced in my own walk with God. Through the inspiration of the Holy Spirit, Paul points out what I'm not, but he's also quick to tell me what I can become—and how it can happen.

"Not that I have already obtained all this, or have already been made perfect," Paul writes in Philippians 3:12, "but I press on to take hold of that for which Christ Jesus took hold of me."

I press on. Those words echo in my heart, bringing me comfort and courage.

My deepest fear is waking up twenty years from now the same woman I am today. The same annoying habits and petty attitudes, with the same besetting sins and false beliefs. I can't imagine anything more terrible than getting to the end of my life only to discover that God had so much more in mind for me—more freedom, more joy, more peace, more true effectiveness. And I had missed it all, simply because I refused to change.

So I press on, and I hope you will too. If we will allow the spotlight of heaven to shine on the dark recesses of our souls, God will transform us by His Holy Spirit.

Until one day, to our surprise, we'll wake up and realize we look just like… Jesus!

I'm not saying it will be easy. Or fully accomplished here on earth. Even with God doing the real work, we'll have to cooperate. We will have to change, and change hurts.

But I can promise you this. It hurts good.

—Having a Mary Spirit

READ: Romans 12:1–2
REFLECT: Write these verses on a card. Say them out loud as a prayer of consecration. Consider memorizing them.

Bible Reading Plan

Nothing has changed my life like reading and studying God's Word!

In this devotional, I've emphasized reading through the Bible slowly to focus on meaning and personal application. But it is also important to get the broader view of Scripture that reading through the Bible in a year provides. After I regularly got stuck somewhere between Leviticus and Deuteronomy, a friend introduced me to a reading guide that made the Bible come alive for me. When I couldn't find the source, I decided to create the guide you find here.

Each day you will read approximately two chapters from the Old or New Testament as well as one more chapter from the books of Psalms to Isaiah. After finishing Genesis, for instance, you'll go to Matthew; then back to Exodus, then to Acts, back to Leviticus, and then to Mark, and so on. I've purposefully put room between the Gospels so that the reader can approach each one with a fresh eye. Scattered throughout are open days you can use for reflection or catching up.

And you don't have to start on January 1. Go to www.becominghis.com to choose the date you'd like to start and the book of Bible you'd like to begin with, then print off your own personal reading guide.

I know God will bless you as you spend time at His feet, dedicating your heart and your life to becoming His.

—Joanna

DATE	1st PORTION	2nd PORTION		DATE	1st PORTION	2nd PORTION
January						
☐ 1	Gen. 1–2	Ps. 1		☐ 11	Gen. 27–29	Ps. 10
☐ 2	Gen. 3–5	Ps. 2		☐ 12	Gen. 30–32	Ps. 11
☐ 3	Gen. 6–9	Ps. 3		☐ 13	Gen. 33–36	Ps. 12
☐ 4	Gen. 10–11	Ps. 4		☐ 14	*Catch Up & Reflect*	
☐ 5	Gen. 12–14	Ps. 5		☐ 15	Gen. 37–39	Ps. 13
☐ 6	Gen. 15–17	Ps. 6		☐ 16	Gen. 40–42	Ps. 14
☐ 7	*Catch Up & Reflect*			☐ 17	Gen. 43–46	Ps. 15
☐ 8	Gen. 18–20	Ps. 7		☐ 18	Gen. 47–50	Ps. 16
☐ 9	Gen. 21–23	Ps. 8		☐ 19	Matt. 1–4	Ps. 17
☐ 10	Gen. 24–26	Ps. 9		☐ 20	Matt. 5–7	Ps. 18:1–24

DATE	1st PORTION	2nd PORTION		DATE	1st PORTION	2nd PORTION
☐ 21	*Catch Up & Reflect*			☐ 27	Lev. 9–11	Prov. 17:1–14
☐ 22	Matt. 8–10	Ps. 18:25–50		☐ 28	Lev. 12–14	Prov. 17:15–28
☐ 23	Matt. 11–13	Ps. 19				
☐ 24	Matt. 14–16	Ps. 20		**March**		
☐ 25	Matt. 17–19	Ps. 21		☐ 1	Lev. 15–18	Ps. 24
☐ 26	Matt. 20–22	Ps. 22:1–11		☐ 2	Lev. 19–21	Ps. 25
☐ 27	Matt. 23–25	Ps. 22:12–31		☐ 3	Lev. 22–24	Ps. 26
☐ 28	Matt. 26–28	Ps. 23		☐ 4	Lev. 25–27	Ps. 27
☐ 29	*Catch Up & Reflect*			☐ 5	Mark 1–3	Ps. 28
☐ 30	*Catch Up & Reflect*			☐ 6	Mark 4–6	Ps. 29
☐ 31	*Catch Up & Reflect*			☐ 7	*Catch Up & Reflect*	
				☐ 8	Mark 7–9	Ps. 30
February				☐ 9	Mark 10–12	Ps. 31
☐ 1	Exod. 1–4	Prov. 1		☐ 10	Mark 13–16	Ps. 32
☐ 2	Exod. 5–8	Prov. 2		☐ 11	Num. 1–3	Ps. 33
☐ 3	Exod. 9–11	Prov. 3		☐ 12	Num. 4–7	Ps. 34
☐ 4	Exod. 12–14	Prov. 4		☐ 13	Num. 8–10	Ps. 35
☐ 5	Exod. 15–17	Prov. 5		☐ 14	*Catch Up & Reflect*	
☐ 6	Exod. 18–20	Prov. 6		☐ 15	Num. 11–14	Ps. 36
☐ 7	*Catch Up & Reflect*			☐ 16	Num. 15–17	Ps. 37:1–22
☐ 8	Exod. 21–24	Prov. 7		☐ 17	Num. 18–21	Ps. 37:23–40
☐ 9	Exod. 25–27	Prov. 8		☐ 18	Num. 22–24	Ps. 38
☐ 10	Exod. 28–31	Prov. 9		☐ 19	Num. 25–27	Ps. 39
☐ 11	Exod. 32–34	Prov. 10:1–16		☐ 20	Num. 28–30	Ps. 40
☐ 12	Exod. 35–37	Prov. 10:17–32		☐ 21	*Catch Up & Reflect*	
☐ 13	Exod. 38–40	Prov. 11:1–15		☐ 22	Num. 31–33	Ps. 41
☐ 14	*Catch Up & Reflect*			☐ 23	Num. 34–36	Ps. 42
☐ 15	Acts 1–3	Prov. 11:16–31		☐ 24	Rom. 1–3	Ps. 43
☐ 16	Acts 4–6	Prov. 12:1–14		☐ 25	Rom. 4–5	Ps. 44
☐ 17	Acts 7–9	Prov. 12:15–28		☐ 26	Rom. 6–8	Ps. 45
☐ 18	Acts 10–12	Prov. 13:1–12		☐ 27	Rom. 9–11	Ps. 46
☐ 19	Acts 13–15	Prov. 13:13–25		☐ 28	Rom. 12–13	Ps. 47
☐ 20	Acts 16–18	Prov. 14:1–18		☐ 29	*Catch Up & Reflect*	
☐ 21	*Catch Up & Reflect*			☐ 30	*Catch Up & Reflect*	
☐ 22	Acts 19–21	Prov. 14:19–35		☐ 31	*Catch Up & Reflect*	
☐ 23	Acts 22–25	Prov. 15:1–17				
☐ 24	Acts 26–28	Prov. 15:18–33		**April**		
☐ 25	Lev. 1–4	Prov. 16:1–16		☐ 1	Rom. 14–16	Ps. 48
☐ 26	Lev. 5–8	Prov. 16:17–33		☐ 2	Deut. 1–4	Ps. 49

DATE	1st PORTION	2nd PORTION	DATE	1st PORTION	2nd PORTION
☐ 3	Deut. 5–7	Ps. 50	☐ 10	Judg. 1–3	Prov. 22:17–29
☐ 4	Deut. 8–10	Ps. 51	☐ 11	Judg. 4–6	Prov. 23:1–18
☐ 5	Deut. 11–13	Ps. 52	☐ 12	Judg. 7–9	Prov. 23:19–35
☐ 6	Deut. 14–16	Ps. 53	☐ 13	Judg. 10–12	Prov. 24:1–22
☐ 7	*Catch Up & Reflect*		☐ 14	*Catch Up & Reflect*	
☐ 8	Deut. 17–19	Ps. 54	☐ 15	Judg. 13–15	Prov. 24:23–34
☐ 9	Deut. 20–22	Ps. 55	☐ 16	Judg. 16–18	Prov. 25:1–14
☐ 10	Deut. 23–26	Ps. 56	☐ 17	Judg. 19–21	Prov. 25:15–28
☐ 11	Deut. 27–30	Ps. 57	☐ 18	2 Cor. 1–3	Prov. 26:1–16
☐ 12	Deut. 31–34	Ps. 58	☐ 19	2 Cor. 4–6	Prov. 26:17–28
☐ 13	Luke 1–3	Ps. 59	☐ 20	2 Cor. 7–9	Prov. 27:1–14
☐ 14	*Catch Up & Reflect*		☐ 21	*Catch Up & Reflect*	
☐ 15	Luke 4–6	Ps. 60	☐ 22	2 Cor. 10–13	Prov. 27:15–27
☐ 16	Luke 7–9	Ps. 61	☐ 23	Ruth 1–4	Prov. 28:1–14
☐ 17	Luke 10–12	Ps. 62	☐ 24	1 Sam. 1–3	Prov. 28:15–28
☐ 18	Luke 13–15	Ps. 63	☐ 25	1 Sam. 4–6	Prov. 29:1–14
☐ 19	Luke 16–18	Ps. 64	☐ 26	1 Sam. 7–9	Prov. 29:15–27
☐ 20	Luke 19–21	Ps. 65	☐ 27	1 Sam. 10–12	Prov. 30
☐ 21	*Catch Up & Reflect*		☐ 28	1 Sam. 13–15	Prov. 31
☐ 22	Luke 22–24	Ps. 66	☐ 29	*Catch Up & Reflect*	
☐ 23	Josh. 1–3	Ps. 67	☐ 30	*Catch Up & Reflect*	
☐ 24	Josh. 4–6	Ps. 68	☐ 31	*Catch Up & Reflect*	
☐ 25	Josh. 7–9	Ps. 69:1–18			
☐ 26	Josh. 10–12	Ps. 69:19–36	**June**		
☐ 27	Josh. 13–15	Ps. 70	☐ 1	1 Sam. 16–19	Ps. 72
☐ 28	Josh. 16–18	Ps. 71	☐ 2	1 Sam. 20–22	Ps. 73
☐ 29	*Catch Up & Reflect*		☐ 3	1 Sam. 23–25	Ps. 74
☐ 30	*Catch Up & Reflect*		☐ 4	1 Sam. 26–28	Ps. 75
			☐ 5	1 Sam. 29–31	Ps. 76
May			☐ 6	2 Sam. 1–3	Ps. 77
☐ 1	Josh. 19–21	Prov. 18	☐ 7	*Catch Up & Reflect*	
☐ 2	Josh. 22–24	Prov. 19:1–14	☐ 8	2 Sam. 4–7	Ps. 78:1–39
☐ 3	I Cor. 1–2	Prov. 19:15–29	☐ 9	2 Sam. 8–10	Ps. 78:40–72
☐ 4	I Cor. 3–5	Prov. 20:1–15	☐ 10	2 Sam. 11–13	Ps. 79
☐ 5	I Cor. 6–8	Prov. 20:16–30	☐ 11	2 Sam. 14–17	Ps. 80
☐ 6	I Cor. 9–11	Prov. 21:1–16	☐ 12	2 Sam. 18–20	Ps. 81
☐ 7	*Catch Up & Reflect*		☐ 13	2 Sam. 21–24	Ps. 82
☐ 8	I Cor. 12–14	Prov. 21:17–31	☐ 14	*Catch Up & Reflect*	
☐ 9	I Cor. 15–16	Prov. 22:1–16	☐ 15	John 1–3	Ps. 83

DATE	1st PORTION	2nd PORTION
☐ 16	John 4–6	Ps. 84
☐ 17	John 7–9	Ps. 85
☐ 18	John 10–12	Ps. 86
☐ 19	John 13–15	Ps. 87
☐ 20	John 16–18	Ps. 88
☐ 21	*Catch Up & Reflect*	
☐ 22	John 19–21	Ps. 89:1–18
☐ 23	1 Kings 1–3	Ps. 89:19–52
☐ 24	1 Kings 4–6	Ps. 90
☐ 25	1 Kings 7–9	Ps. 91
☐ 26	1 Kings 10–12	Ps. 92
☐ 27	1 Kings 13–15	Ps. 93
☐ 28	1 Kings 16–19	Ps. 94
☐ 29	*Catch Up & Reflect*	
☐ 30	*Catch Up & Reflect*	

July

☐ 1	1 Kings 20–22	Eccles. 1
☐ 2	2 Kings 1–4	Eccles. 2
☐ 3	2 Kings 5–7	Eccles. 3
☐ 4	2 Kings 8–11	Eccles. 4
☐ 5	2 Kings 12–14	Eccles. 5
☐ 6	2 Kings 15–18	Eccles. 6
☐ 7	*Catch Up & Reflect*	
☐ 8	2 Kings 19–21	Eccles. 7
☐ 9	2 Kings 22–25	Eccles. 8
☐ 10	Gal. 1–3	Eccles. 9
☐ 11	Gal. 4–6	Eccles. 10
☐ 12	1 Chron. 1–4	Eccles. 11
☐ 13	1 Chron. 5–8	Eccles. 12
☐ 14	*Catch Up & Reflect*	
☐ 15	1 Chron. 9–11	Songs 1
☐ 16	1 Chron. 12–14	Songs 2
☐ 17	1 Chron. 15–17	Songs 3
☐ 18	1 Chron. 18–20	Songs 4
☐ 19	1 Chron. 21–23	Songs 5
☐ 20	1 Chron. 24–26	Songs 6
☐ 21	*Catch Up & Reflect*	
☐ 22	1 Chron. 27–29	Songs 7

DATE	1st PORTION	2nd PORTION
☐ 23	2 Chron. 1–4	Songs 8
☐ 24	2 Chron. 5–7	Ps. 95
☐ 25	2 Chron. 8–11	Ps. 96
☐ 26	2 Chron. 12–15	Ps. 97
☐ 27	2 Chron. 16–18	Ps. 98
☐ 28	2 Chron. 19–21	Ps. 99
☐ 29	*Catch Up & Reflect*	
☐ 30	*Catch Up & Reflect*	
☐ 31	*Catch Up & Reflect*	

August

☐ 1	2 Chron. 22–24	Ps. 100
☐ 2	2 Chron. 25–27	Ps. 101
☐ 3	2 Chron. 28–30	Ps. 102
☐ 4	2 Chron. 31–33	Ps. 103
☐ 5	2 Chron. 34–36	Ps. 104:1–23
☐ 6	Eph. 1–3	Ps. 104:24–35
☐ 7	*Catch Up & Reflect*	
☐ 8	Eph. 4–6	Ps. 105
☐ 9	Ezra 1–4	Ps. 106:1–23
☐ 10	Ezra 5–7	Ps. 106:24–48
☐ 11	Ezra 8–10	Ps. 107
☐ 12	Neh. 1–3	Ps. 108
☐ 13	Neh. 4–7	Ps. 109
☐ 14	*Catch Up & Reflect*	
☐ 15	Neh. 8–10	Ps. 110
☐ 16	Neh. 11–13	Ps. 111
☐ 17	Esther 1–3	Ps. 112
☐ 18	Esther 4–7	Ps. 113
☐ 19	Esther 8–10	Ps. 114
☐ 20	Phil. 1–4	Ps. 115
☐ 21	*Catch Up & Reflect*	
☐ 22	Job 1–3	Ps. 116
☐ 23	Job 4–6	Ps. 117
☐ 24	Job 7–9	Ps. 118:1–14
☐ 25	Job 10–12	Ps. 118:15–29
☐ 26	Job 13–15	Ps. 119:1–16
☐ 27	Job 16–18	Ps. 119:17–32
☐ 28	Job 19–21	Ps. 119:33–48

DATE	1st PORTION	2nd PORTION		DATE	1st PORTION	2nd PORTION
☐ 29	*Catch Up & Reflect*			☐ 3	1 Thess. 1–2	Isa. 17
☐ 30	*Catch Up & Reflect*			☐ 4	1 Thess. 3–5	Isa. 18
☐ 31	*Catch Up & Reflect*			☐ 5	Ezek. 1–4	Isa. 19
				☐ 6	Ezek. 5–7	Isa. 20

September

☐ 1	Job 22–24	Ps. 119:49–64		☐ 7	*Catch Up & Reflect*	
☐ 2	Job 25–27	Ps. 119:65–80		☐ 8	Ezek. 8–11	Isa. 21
☐ 3	Job 28–30	Ps. 119:81–96		☐ 9	Ezek. 12–15	Isa. 22
☐ 4	Job 31–33	Ps. 119:97–112		☐ 10	Ezek. 16–19	Isa. 23
☐ 5	Job 34–36	Ps. 119:113–128		☐ 11	Ezek. 20–23	Isa. 24
☐ 6	Job 37–39	Ps. 119:129–144		☐ 12	Ezek. 24–26	Isa. 25
☐ 7	*Catch Up & Reflect*			☐ 13	Ezek. 27–30	Isa. 26
☐ 8	Job 40–42	Ps. 119:145–160		☐ 14	*Catch Up & Reflect*	
☐ 9	Col. 1–4	Ps. 119:161–176		☐ 15	Ezek. 31–34	Isa. 27
☐ 10	Jer. 1–3	Ps. 120		☐ 16	Ezek. 35–38	Isa. 28
☐ 11	Jer. 4–6	Ps. 121		☐ 17	Ezek. 39–42	Isa. 29
☐ 12	Jer. 7–9	Ps. 122		☐ 18	Ezek. 43–45	Isa. 30
☐ 13	Jer. 10–12	Isa. 1		☐ 19	Ezek. 46–48	Isa. 31
☐ 14	*Catch Up & Reflect*			☐ 20	Dan. 1–3	Isa. 32
☐ 15	Jer. 13–15	Isa. 2		☐ 21	*Catch Up & Reflect*	
☐ 16	Jer. 16–18	Isa. 3		☐ 22	Dan. 4–6	Isa. 33
☐ 17	Jer. 19–21	Isa. 4		☐ 23	Dan. 7–9	Isa. 34
☐ 18	Jer. 22–24	Isa. 5		☐ 24	Dan. 10–12	Isa. 35
☐ 19	Jer. 25–27	Isa. 6		☐ 25	2 Thess. 1–3	Isa. 36
☐ 20	Jer. 28–30	Isa. 7		☐ 26	Hosea 1–4	Isa. 37
☐ 21	*Catch Up & Reflect*			☐ 27	Hosea 5–8	Isa. 38
☐ 22	Jer. 31–33	Isa. 8		☐ 28	Hosea 9–11	Isa. 39
☐ 23	Jer. 34–36	Isa. 9		☐ 29	*Catch Up & Reflect*	
☐ 24	Jer. 37–39	Isa. 10		☐ 30	*Catch Up & Reflect*	
☐ 25	Jer. 40–42	Isa. 11		☐ 31	*Catch Up & Reflect*	
☐ 26	Jer. 43–46	Isa. 12				
☐ 27	Jer. 47–49	Isa. 13				
☐ 28	Jer. 50–52	Isa. 14				
☐ 29	*Catch Up & Reflect*					
☐ 30	*Catch Up & Reflect*					

October

November

☐ 1	Lam. 1–2	Isa. 15		☐ 1	Hosea 12–14	Ps. 123–24
☐ 2	Lam. 3–5	Isa. 16		☐ 2	1 Tim. 1–3	Ps. 125–26
				☐ 3	1 Tim. 4–6	Ps. 127
				☐ 4	Joel 1–3	Ps. 128–29
				☐ 5	2 Tim. 1–4	Ps. 130–31
				☐ 6	Amos 1–3	Ps. 132
				☐ 7	*Catch Up & Reflect*	
				☐ 8	Amos 4–6	Ps. 133–34

DATE	1st PORTION	2nd PORTION		DATE	1st PORTION	2nd PORTION
☐ 9	Amos 7–9	Ps. 135		☐ 5	Hag. 1–2	Isa. 46
☐ 10	Titus 1–3	Ps. 136		☐ 6	2 & 3 John	Isa. 47
☐ 11	Obad. 1	Ps. 137		☐ 7	*Catch Up & Reflect*	
☐ 12	Philem. 1	Ps. 138		☐ 8	Zech. 1–3	Isa. 48
☐ 13	Jon. 1–4	Ps. 139		☐ 9	Zech. 4–6	Isa. 49
☐ 14	*Catch Up & Reflect*			☐ 10	Zech. 7–9	Isa. 50
☐ 15	Heb. 1–3	Ps. 140		☐ 11	Zech. 10–12	Isa. 51
☐ 16	Heb. 4–6	Ps. 141		☐ 12	Zech. 13–14	Isa. 52
☐ 17	Heb. 7–10	Ps. 142		☐ 13	Jude	Isa. 53
☐ 18	Heb. 11–13	Ps. 143		☐ 14	*Catch Up & Reflect*	
☐ 19	Mic. 1–3	Ps. 144		☐ 15	Mal. 1–2	Isa. 54
☐ 20	Mic. 4–5	Ps. 145		☐ 16	Mal. 3–4	Isa. 55
☐ 21	*Catch Up & Reflect*			☐ 17	Rev. 1–2	Isa. 56
☐ 22	Mic. 6–7	Ps. 146		☐ 18	Rev. 3–4	Isa. 57
☐ 23	James 1–2	Ps. 147		☐ 19	Rev. 5–6	Isa. 58
☐ 24	James 3–5	Ps. 148		☐ 20	Rev. 7–8	Isa. 59
☐ 25	Nah. 1–3	Ps. 149		☐ 21	*Catch Up & Reflect*	
☐ 26	1 Pet. 1–3	Ps. 150		☐ 22	Rev. 9–10	Isa. 60
☐ 27	1 Pet. 4–5	Isa. 40		☐ 23	Rev. 11–12	Isa. 61
☐ 28	Hab. 1–3	Isa. 41		☐ 24	Rev. 13–14	Isa. 62
☐ 29	*Catch Up & Reflect*			☐ 25	Rev. 15–16	Isa. 63
☐ 30	*Catch Up & Reflect*			☐ 26	Rev. 17–18	Isa. 64
				☐ 27	Rev. 19–20	Isa. 65

December

DATE	1st PORTION	2nd PORTION
☐ 1	2 Pet. 1–3	Isa. 42
☐ 2	Zeph. 1–3	Isa. 43
☐ 3	1 John 1–3	Isa. 44
☐ 4	1 John 4–5	Isa. 45

DATE	1st PORTION	2nd PORTION
☐ 28	Rev. 21–22	Isa. 66
☐ 29	*Catch Up & Reflect*	
☐ 30	*Catch Up & Reflect*	
☐ 31	*Catch Up & Reflect*	

Notes

1. Philip Yancey, *What's So Amazing About Grace?* (Grand Rapids, MI: Zondervan, 1997), 97.
2. *Steps to Peace with God* (Charlotte, NC: Billy Graham Evangelistic Association, n.d.), www.billygraham.org/specialsections/steps-to-peace/steps-to-peace.asp.
3. Adapted from a story by Rosemarie Kowalski. Used by permission.
4. Adapted from Stephen R. Covey, *First Things First* (New York: Simon & Schuster, 1994), 88–89.
5. Anna B. Warner, "Jesus Loves Me," first published in Anna B. Warner and Susan Warner, *Say and Seal* (Philadelphia: Lippincott, 1860), 115–16.
6. George H. Gallup Jr., phone interview, July 21, 2006.
7. Ray C. Stedman, "God's Strange Ways" (sermon, Peninsula Bible Church, Palo Alto, CA, September 9, 1984).
8. For an enlightening discussion of the tendency toward "will worship," see Richard J. Foster, *Celebration of Discipline: The Path to Spiritual Growth,* rev. ed. (1978; repr., San Francisco: HarperSanFrancisco, 1988), 5–6.
9. Max Lucado, *The Great House of God* (Dallas: Word, 1997), 4.
10. Francis Chan, *Crazy Love: Overwhelmed by a Relentless God* (Colorado Springs, CO: David C. Cook, 2008), 110–11.
11. Andrew Murray, quoted in Paul Lee Tan, *Encyclopedia of 7,700 Illustrations: Signs of the Times* (Garland, TX: Bible Communications, 1996), 2304.
12. Confirmed in a telephone conversation with Eugene Peterson, January 29, 2000.
13. Kent Hughes, *Liberating Ministry from the Success Syndrome* (Wheaton, IL: Tyndale, 1988), 72–73.
14. *Fried Green Tomatoes,* directed by Jon Avnet (Universal Studios, 1991), quoted in "Memorable Quotes from *Fried Green Tomatoes,*" IMDB: The Internet Movie Database, www.imdb.com/title/tt0101921/quotes.
15. Ray C. Stedman, *Authentic Christianity* (Waco, TX: Word, 1975).
16. Given all the different ages I assign Joshua in my books (due to the ridiculous amount of time it takes me to write one), you might like to know that Joshua was born in 2002.
17. Excerpted in *The Growing Disciple,* The 2:7 Series, Course 1 (Colorado Springs, CO: NavPress, 1987), 69–73.
18. Excerpted in *The Growing Disciple,* 69–73.
19. Excerpted in *The Growing Disciple,* 69–73.
20. Adapted from Peter Marshall's story told in Charles Swindoll, *Improving Your Serve: The Art of Unselfish Living,* rev. ed. (Dallas: Word, 1981), 127–28.
21. Edward Hallowell, *Worry: Controlling It and Using It Wisely* (New York: Pantheon, 1997), xi.
22. Adapted from Hallowell, *Worry,* 79–83.
23. Anabel Gillham (sermon, Glacier Bible Camp, Hungry Horse, MT, April 27, 1996).

24. Adapted from *Growing Strong in God's Family,* The 2:7 Series (Colorado Springs, CO: NavPress, 1987).

25. James Strong, *The New Strong's Exhaustive Concordance of the Bible* (Nashville: Thomas Nelson, 1996), s.v. "#1690."

26. David Giles, *Illusions of Immortality: A Psychology of Fame and Celebrity* (London: Macmillan, 2000), 95.

27. Demetrios Serfes, "St. Lazarus the Friend of Christ and First Bishop of Kition, Cyprus," Lives of the Saints, www.serfes.org/lives/stlazarus.htm.

28. From J. Sidlow Baxter's personal correspondence, September 8, 1987, quoted in Kent Hughes, *Liberating Ministry,* 78–81.

29. Baxter, as quoted in Hughes, *Liberating Ministry,* 78–81.

30. Andrea Wells Miller, *Body Care: A Proven Program for Successful Diet, Fitness and Health, Featuring Ten Weeks of Devotions to Help You Achieve God's Plan for Your Body, Mind and Spirit* (Waco, TX: Word, 1984), 86.

31. After much study I've come to believe we are three-part beings, as referred to by Paul in 1 Thessalonians 5:23: "May God himself, the God of peace, sanctify you through and through. May your whole spirit, soul and body be kept blameless at the coming of our Lord Jesus Christ." The "body" is the physical shell that houses us; the "soul" is our mind, will, and emotions; and the "spirit" is the place that comes alive when Christ takes up residence within us at salvation. For a deeper discussion on this topic and why I believe the distinction is important, see *Having a Mary Spirit: Allowing God to Change Us from the Inside Out* (beginning with chapter 2).

32. William Barclay, *The Revelation of John,* rev. ed. (Louisville, KY: Westminster/John Knox, 1976), 1:113–14.

33. Brennan Manning, *The Ragamuffin Gospel: Good News for the Bedraggled, Beat-Up, and Burnt Out* (Sisters, OR: Multnomah, 1990), 154.

34. Marla Cilley, *Sink Reflections* (New York: Bantam Books, 2001), 35.

35. Dutch Sheets, *The River of God* (Ventura, CA: Gospel Light, 1998), 195.

36. V. B. Ellis, "Let Me Touch Him," *The New National Baptist Hymnal* (Brentwood, TN: Lillenas, 1964), 357.

37. Brother Lawrence, *The Practice of the Presence of God* (Virginia Beach, VA: CBN University Press, 1978), 10.

38. Timothy Keller, *Counterfeit Gods* (New York: Dutton, 2009), 16–17.

39. W. E. Vine, *Vine's Expository Dictionary of Old and New Testament Words* (Nashville: Thomas Nelson, 1997), 845–46.

40. Adapted from William Barclay, *The Gospel of Matthew,* rev. ed. (Louisville, KY: Westminster/John Knox, 2001), 2:283–84.

41. Oswald Chambers, *The Golden Book of Oswald Chambers: My Utmost for His Highest,* Christian Library Edition (Westwood, NJ: Barbour, 1963), January 3, June 21.

42. Wendell Berry, quoted in Eugene H. Peterson, *Living the Resurrection: The Risen Christ in Everyday Life* (Colorado Springs, CO: NavPress, 2006), 13.

43. *The Passion of the Christ,* directed by Mel Gibson (20th Century Fox, 2004. Released by Newmarket Films, 2004).

44. Quoted in Dale Fincher, "A Slice of Infinity: What Do You Expect? Part 5," Ravi Zacharias International Ministries, January 30, 2004, www.rzim.org/resources/read/asliceofinfinity/todaysslice.aspx?aid=8420.

45. Adapted from Harry Pritchett Jr., "Philip's Egg," *Leadership* (Summer 1985), quoted in Charles Swindoll, *Tales of a Tardy Oxcart* (Nashville: Word, 1998), 491–92.

46. Adapted from Pritchett, *Leadership,* quoted in Swindoll, *Tales of a Tardy Oxcart,* 491–92.

47. Mrs. Charles [Lettie B.] Cowman, *Springs in the Valley,* in *Streams in the Desert and Springs in the Valley,* Zondervan Treasures (1939; repr., Grand Rapids: Zondervan, 1996), February 22.

48. Samuel Rutherford, quoted in Howard L. Rice, *Reformed Spirituality* (Louisville, KY: Westminster/John Knox, 1991), 179.

49. Charles H. Spurgeon, "A Mystery! Saints Sorrowing and Jesus Glad!" (sermon no. 585, Metropolitan Tabernacle, Newington, England, August 7, 1864), quoted in quoted in *Spurgeon's Sermons Volume 10: 1864,* Christian Classics Ethereal Library, www.ccel.org/ccel/spurgeon/sermons10.xviii_1.html.

50. C. S. Lewis, *The Voyage of the Dawn Treader* (New York: HarperTrophy, 1994), 115–16.

51. Lewis, *Voyage,* 119–20.

52. W. Ian Thomas, *The Indwelling Life of Christ* (Sisters, OR: Multnomah, 2006), 127.

53. Arthur T. Pierson, *George Müller of Bristol* (1899; repr., Grand Rapids, MI: Hendrickson, 2008), 383 (emphasis added).

54. This is actually the subtitle of Groeschel's excellent book *The Christian Atheist: Believing in God but Living as If He Doesn't Exist* (Grand Rapids, MI: Zondervan, 2010).

55. Donald Miller, *Blue Like Jazz: Nonreligious Thoughts on Christian Spirituality* (Nashville: Thomas Nelson, 2003), 79.

56. Oswald Chambers, *The Golden Book of Oswald Chambers: My Utmost for His Highest,* Christian Library Edition (Westwood, NJ: Barbour, 1963), January 31.

57. Brother Lawrence, *The Practice of the Presence of God* (Virginia Beach, VA: CBN University Press, 1978), 16–17.

58. Ann Spangler, *The Tender Words of God: A Daily Guide* (Grand Rapids, MI: Zondervan, 2008), 13.

59. Spangler, *Tender Words of God,* 15–16.

60. The Greek word *dunamis* is used in the Bible to describe God's "miraculous power." See James Strong, *The New Strong's Exhaustive Concordance of the Bible* (Nashville: Thomas Nelson, 1996), s.v. "1411, dunamis." It is also the root of our English word *dynamite.* See "Word History," *American Heritage Dictionary of the English Language,* 4th ed., s.v. "dynamite," http://dictionary.reference.com/browse/dynamite.

61. Pastor Don Burleson, "Big T-Truth" (sermon, New Covenant Fellowship, Kalispell, MT, June 8, 2008).

62. See Janet Holm McHenry, *PrayerWalk: Becoming a Woman of Prayer, Strength, and Discipline* (Colorado Springs, CO: WaterBrook, 2001).

63. Hudson Taylor, quoted in Dennis Rainey, *Planting Seeds, Pulling Weeds* (San Bernardino, CA: Here's Life, 1989), 114.

64. Selwyn Hughes, *Everyday Light* (Nashville: Broadman & Holman, 1998), day 1.

65. Robert J. Morgan, *Nelson's Complete Book of Stories, Illustrations & Quotes: The Ultimate Contemporary Resource for Speakers* (Nashville: Thomas Nelson, 2000), 16–17.

66. David Seamans, quoted in Neil T. Anderson, Mike Quarles, and Julia Quarles, *One Day at a Time: The Devotional for Overcomers* (Ventura, CA: Regal, 2000), 231.

67. Claire Cloninger, *When God Shines Through* (Dallas, TX: Word, 1994), 132.

68. This description is based on an idea found in "Lazarus (John 11)," copt.org, August 1, 2010, www.copt.org/2010/08/01/lazarus-john-11/.

69. Adapted from *Growing Strong in God's Family,* The 2:7 Series (Colorado Springs: NavPress, 1987), 13, 19–20.

70. Phyllis Diller, in "Exercise Quotes" on All the Best Quotes, http://chatna.com/theme/exercise.htm.

71. Mark Twain, quoted on *The Quotations Page,* www.quotationspage.com/quote/2164.html.

72. Special thanks to Marla Campbell, who shared this thought with me many years ago.

73. Cheryl's stories are used with her permission.

74. "J-O-Y," words and music by Bud Metzger and Sally Lewis. Copyright © 1945 by Percy B. Crawford.

75. William Barclay, *The Gospel of John,* rev. ed. (Philadelphia: Westminster, 1975), 1:249–50.

76. Beth Moore, *Further Still: A Collection of Poetry and Vignettes* (Nashville: Broadman and Holman, 2004), 99–104.

77. Warren Wiersbe, *The Wiersbe Bible Commentary: New Testament,* 2nd ed. (Colorado Springs, CO: David C. Cook, 2007), 862.

78. Mahatma Gandhi, quoted in Mother Teresa, *In My Own Words* (New York: Random House, 1996), 100.

79. Dwight L. Moody, quoted in Yancey, *What's So Amazing About Grace?,* 262.

80. First quotation is Mother Teresa, quoted in Daphne Kingsma, *Weddings from the Heart* (New York: MJF Books, 1995), 111. Second quotation is Mother Teresa, *In My Own Words,* 33.

81. George Müller, adapted from quotation in Henry Blackaby, *Experiencing God* (Nashville: LifeWay Press, 1990), 34.

82. Philip Yancey, *Disappointment with God: Three Questions No One Asks Aloud* (Grand Rapids, MI: Zondervan, 1992), 136–37.

83. Quoted in Chambers, *My Utmost for His Highest,* February 11.

84. Beth Moore, *Praying God's Word* (Nashville: B&H Publishing Group, 2009), 335.

85. Moore, *Praying God's Word,* 335.

86. Moore, *Praying God's Word,* 335.

87. Moore, *Praying God's Word,* 10.

88. Moore, *Praying God's Word,* 11.

89. Moore, *Praying God's Word,* 12.

90. Moore, *Praying God's Word,* 12–13.

91. I highly recommend attending a Basic Life Principles Seminar yourself. Check out locations and dates at Bill Gothard's website: www.iblp.org/iblp.

92. Joseph M. Scriven, "What a Friend We Have in Jesus," *The Hymnal for Worship & Celebration* (Waco, TX: Word Music, 1986), 435.

93. Barclay, *The Gospel of John,* 111.

94. Barclay, *The Gospel of John,* 112.

95. I heard this story years ago in a sermon. Source is unknown.

96. This description is taken from John Baker, *Celebrate Recovery Leader's Guide,* updated ed. (Grand Rapids, MI: Zondervan, 2005), 56.

97. Adapted with permission from author Joanie Burnside.

98. Adapted with permission from author Joanie Burnside.

99. Adapted with permission from author Joanie Burnside.

100. Adapted with permission from author Joanie Burnside.

101. The Bible Channel website, "Missions Quotes," http:// thebiblechannel.org /Missions_Quotes/missions_quotes.html.

102. Philip Yancey, *Grace Notes: Daily Readings with a Fellow Pilgrim* (Grand Rapids, MI: Zondervan, 2009), 168.

103. Henri J. M. Nouwen, *Letters to Marc About Jesus: Living a Spiritual Life in a Material World,* trans. Hubert Hoskins (San Francisco: HarperSanFrancisco, 1998), 84.

104. [Matthew] Henry and [Thomas] Scott, *A Commentary upon the Holy Bible, Matthew to Acts* (London: Religious Tract Society, 1835), 54 n. 28.

105. Spiros Zodhiates, gen. ed., *The Complete Word Study Dictionary: New Testament,* rev. ed. (Chattanooga, TN: AMG International, 1993), s.v. "#3415" and "#3418."

106. Thomas, *The Indwelling Life of Christ,* 151–52.

107. Quoted on Putting Forgiveness First website, www.forgivenessfirst.com/ ffidefiningforgiveness.htm.

108. William Plummer, "Taken by the Sea," *People,* 14 December 1992, 59–61.

109. Chip Ingram, *Holy Transformation: What It Takes for God to Make a Difference in You* (Chicago: Moody, 2003), 183.

110. Not her real name.

111. Elisabeth Elliot, *Keep a Quiet Heart* (Ann Arbor, MI: Servant, 1995), 28.

112. Herbert Lockyer Sr., ed., *Illustrated Dictionary of the Bible* (Nashville: Thomas Nelson, 1986), 1011–12.

113. Cowman, *Streams in the Desert,* February 9.

114. Cowman, *Streams in the Desert,* February 9.

115. Quoted in Mother Teresa, *Life in the Spirit* (San Francisco: Harper & Row, 1983), 76–77.

116. Kurt Richardson, *James,* vol. 36 in *The New American Commentary: An Exegetical and Theological Exposition of Holy Scripture* (Nashville: Broadman and Holman, 1997), 80 (see both text and footnote 69).

117. Dr. Donald Argue (taped sermon and interview, Billings, MT, March 1999).

118. Barclay, *The Gospel of John,* 138–39.

119. J. Oswald Sanders, *Discipleship Journal* 76 (July–August 1993): 39.

120. Kathleen Norris, *Amazing Grace: A Vocabulary of Faith* (New York: Riverhead Books, 1998), 265–66.

121. Martin Luther, "Autobiographical fragment," from E. G. Rupp and Benjamin Drewery, "Luther's Theological Breakthrough," *Martin Luther,* Documents of Modern History (London: Edward Arnold, 1970), 5–7, www.st-andrews.ac.uk /jfec/cal/reformat/theologo/rupp6218.htm.

122. *Luther,* directed by Eric Till (MGM, 2004, film released 2003).

123. Beth Moore, "Week One Viewer Guide," in *Believing God* video series (Nashville: LifeWay Christian Resources, 2002), 9.

124. Priscilla Shirer, *Discerning the Voice of God: How to Recognize When God Speaks* (Chicago: Moody, 2007), 14.

125. Chambers, *My Utmost for His Highest,* February 7.

126. Rick Renner, *Sparkling Gems from the Greek: 365 Greek Word Studies for Every Day of the Year to Sharpen Your Understanding of God's Word* (Tulsa, OK: Teach All Nations, 2003), 114.

127. Ray and Anne Ortlund, *Lord, Make My Life a Miracle* (Nashville: Broadman & Holman, 2002), 130–31.

128. Joyce Meyer, *Battlefield of the Mind: Winning the Battle in Your Mind* (New York: Warner Faith, 2002), 65.

129. Michael Tipper, "Comparisons with the Brain," *Michael Tipper's Pages on Accelerated Learning,* www.happychild.org.uk/acc/tpr/amz/0999comp.htm.

130. Tim Hansel, *Holy Sweat* (Waco, TX: Word, 1987), 103.

131. Anabel Gillham (sermon, Glacier Bible Camp, Hungry Horse, MT, April 27, 1996).

132. Anabel Gillham, *The Confident Woman: Knowing Who You Are in Christ* (Eugene, OR: Harvest House, 1993), 85.

133. Tony Evans, *No More Excuses* (Wheaton, IL: Crossway Books, 1996), 223.

134. Gary E. Gilley, "Think on These Things" newsletter 4, no. 2 (February 1998).

135. G. Ernest Wright, ed., *Great People of the Bible and How They Lived* (Pleasant-ville, NY: Reader's Digest Association, 1974), 324–25.

136. Bernard R. Youngman, *The Lands and Peoples of the Living Bible* (New York: Hawthorn, 1959), 213.

137. Youngman, *Lands and Peoples,* 213–14.

138. Strong, *The New Strong's Exhaustive Concordance,* 72, 130.

139. Wes Seeliger, *Faith at Work,* February 1972, 13, quoted in Bruce Larson, *Ask Me to Dance* (Waco, TX: Word, 1972), 11–12.

140. Jack B. Hoey Jr., "Breaking the Unplowed Ground," *Discipleship Journal* 39 (May–June 1987): 4.

141. Jerry Goebel, "Unbind Him and Let Him Go!" ONEFamily Outreach, March 13, 2005, http://onefamilyoutreach.com/bible/John/jn_11_01-45.htm.

142. Goebel, "Unbind Him."

143. Goebel, "Unbind Him."

144. C. S. Lewis, *Mere Christianity* (New York: HarperCollins, 1980), 188.

145. Lewis, *Mere Christianity,* 188. Note that actual wording is flipped. Opening phrase in my paragraph is actually the last phrase of Lewis's original.

146. Charles Swindoll, *Growing Strong in the Seasons of Life* (Portland, OR: Multnomah, 1983), 47–49.

147. R. T. Kendall, *Total Forgiveness: True Inner Peace Awaits You!* (Lake Mary, FL: Charisma House, 2002), xxix.

148. Kendall, *Total Forgiveness,* 32.

149. H. B. Macartney, quoted in V. Raymond Edman, *They Found the Secret: Twenty Transformed Lives That Reveal a Touch of Eternity* (Grand Rapids, MI: Zondervan, 1960), 20.

150. Adelaide A. Pollard, "Have Thine Own Way, Lord," in *Hymns of Glorious Praise* (Springfield, MS: Gospel Publishing, 1969), 347. First published in Northfield Hymnal with Alexander's Supplement, 1907.

151. Stedman, *Authentic Christianity,* 92.

152. A. W. Tozer, *The Pursuit of God* (Camp Hill, PA: Christian Publications, 1993), 22, 29.

153. Adapted from E. E. Shelhamer, "Traits of the Carnal Mind," first published by Shelhamer as a tract in the early 1900s, adapted by Christian Light Publications as "Traits of the Self-Life," www.anabaptists.org/tracts/ traits.html. This version has been further adapted from the Christian Light version.

154. E. E. Shelhamer, "Traits of the Carnal Mind."

155. George Frederick Graham, *A Book About Words* (London: Longman, Green and Co., 1869), 238.

156. I first heard David's story years ago on a recording from a talk he had given. I have since contacted him personally and received both his confirmation that the material is accurate and his permission to use it. For more on David Ring's Reach Out and Touch ministries, visit his website: www.davidring.org.

157. Not his real name.

158. Mark Rutland, *Holiness: The Perfect Word to Imperfect People* (Lake Mary, FL: Creation House, 2005), 72.

159. C. H. Spurgeon, "The Friend of God," *The Homiletic Review,* vol. 14, no. 1 (July–December 1887), 157.

160. George Müller to J. Hudson Taylor, in Dr. and Mrs. Howard Taylor, *Hudson Taylor's Spiritual Secret,* Moody Classics ed. (Chicago: Moody, 2009), 152–53.

161. Carol Mayhall, "Listening to God," in Judith Couchman, ed., *One Holy Passion* (Colorado Springs, CO: WaterBrook, 1998), 109–11.

162. Adapted from *The Growing Disciple,* The 2:7 Series, Course 1 (Colorado Springs, CO: NavPress, 1987), 84–85.

163. Thanks to Greg Laurie and his Harvest radio broadcast for this thought heard years ago.

164. Hughes, *Liberating Ministry from the Success Syndrome,* 139.

165. A. R. Fausset, *Fausset's Bible Dictionary,* PC Study Bible, New Reference Library (Seattle: BibleSoft, 1998–2005).

166. Philip Yancey, *Disappointment with God* (Grand Rapids, MI: Zondervan, 1988), 211.

167. Adapted from a sermon by Ed Kreiner in Whitefish, MT, date unknown.

168. Adapted from a sermon by Ed Kreiner in Whitefish, MT, date unknown.

169. "An Average Person's Anxiety Is Focused on…" quoted in John Underhill and Jack Lewis, comp., Bible Study Foundation Illustration Database, Bible Study Foundation website (www.Bible.org).

170. See Archibald D. Hart, *Overcoming Anxiety* (Dallas: Word, 1989).

171. Corrie ten Boom, quoted in *Moments—Someone Special* (Minneapolis: Heartland Samplers, 1997), n.p.

172. Johnson Oatman Jr., "Count Your Blessings," Songs for Young People (Chicago, IL: Curts & Jennings, 1897), 34, www.hymntime.com/tch/htm/c/o/u/count you.htm.

173. Bill and Kathy Peel, *Discover Your Destiny* (Colorado Springs, CO: NavPress, 1997), 202.

174. Amy Carmichael, quoted in Tim Hansel, *Holy Sweat,* 130.

175. Stedman, "God's Strange Ways."

176. CeCe Winans, *On a Positive Note* (New York: Pocket Books, 1999), 207.

177. Chambers, *My Utmost for His Highest: The Golden Book of Oswald Chambers,* March 24.

178. Frank E. Peretti, *Piercing the Darkness* (Westchester, IL: Crossway Books, 1989).

179. Renner, *Sparkling Gems from the Greek,* 74.

180. Hansel, *Holy Sweat,* 50.

181. According to the *NIV Study Bible* notes on John 9:2, "The rabbis had developed the principle that 'There is no death without sin, and there is no suffering without iniquity.' They were even capable of thinking that a child could sin in the womb or that its soul might have sinned in a preexistent state. They also held that terrible punishments came on certain people because of the sin of their parents. As the next verse [John 9:3] shows, Jesus plainly contradicted these beliefs." Kenneth L. Barker, ed., *The NIV Study Bible,* 10th anniversary ed. (Grand Rapids, MI: Zondervan, 1995).

182. Goebel, "Unbind Him and Let Him Go!"

183. Brian Jones, *Second Guessing God: Hanging On When You Can't See His Plan* (Cincinnati, OH: Standard, 2006), 13–15.

184. Beth Moore, *Get Out of That Pit* (Nashville: Thomas Nelson, 2007), chapter 6. Quotations are from 123, 128, and 131.

185. I love this definition of repentance by David K. Barnard in his book, *The New Birth,* Series in Pentecostal Theology, vol. 2 (Hazelwood, MO: Word Aflame, 1984), chapter 5, "Repentance," accessed as online edition at www.newlifeupc.org/wp-content/uploads/online-books/newbirth/new-ch5.html.

186. Joanna Weaver, "The Agony of Defeat," first appeared in *HomeLife* magazine, January 2000, 58–60.

187. The general format for this test and some of the basic ideas came from Catherine Marshall, *Beyond Our Selves* (Grand Rapids, MI: Chosen, 1961), 184–85. However, I have rewritten the items to reflect my own understanding.

188. Charles Stanley, *The Blessing of Brokenness: Why God Allows Us to Go Through Hard Times* (Grand Rapids, MI: Zondervan, 1997), 229.

189. Anderson, Quarles, and Quarles, *One Day at a Time,* 361.

190. http://precept.org/site/DocServer/PMI_IBStudyOverview_v2.pdf?docID=2921, accessed on 12/03/2011.

191. Hannah Whitall Smith, quoted in Bruce Wilkinson, *30 Days to Experiencing Spiritual Breakthroughs* (Sisters, OR: Multnomah, 1999), 62, 64–65 (emphasis added).

192. Thanks to Martha Tennison for this phrase, which I heard in a sermon delivered in Billings MT, September 24, 1999.

193. Mark Buchanan, *The Holy Wild: Trusting in the Character of God* (Sisters, OR: Multnomah, 2003), 23.

194. Zodhiates, *Complete Word Study Dictionary,* s.v. "#2083."

195. Zodhiates, *Complete Word Study Dictionary,* s.v. "#2083."

196. Donna Otto with Anne Christian Buchanan, *Finding Your Purpose as a Mom: How to Build Your Home on Holy Ground* (Eugene, OR: Harvest House, 2004), 28–29.

197. Richard J. Foster, *Prayer: Finding the Heart's True Home* (San Francisco: HarperSanFrancisco, 1992), 50.

198. This thought comes from my wise friend Alicia Britt Chole.

199. Max Lucado, *God Came Near* (Portland, OR: Multnomah, 1987), 79.

200. Frederick Buechner, *The Hungering Dark* (New York: Harper, 1985), 13.

201. www.sermoncentral.com/illustrations/stories-about-Derek.asp.

202. Mark Buchanan, *Things Unseen* (Sisters, OR: Multnomah, 2002), 43.

203. Marshall Shelley, "Two Minutes to Eternity," *Christianity Today,* May 16, 1994, 25–27, quoted in Buchanan, *Things Unseen,* 43–44.

Connect with Joanna at Facebook.com/becominghis
or by e-mail: joannaweaver@hotmail.com

Lord, whatever it takes... make me like You...

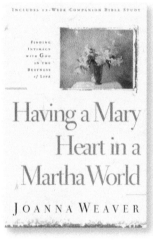

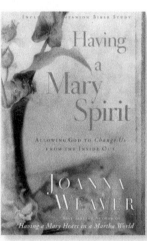

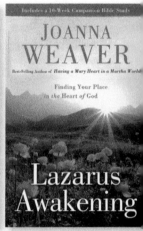

Joanna Weaver's Bethany triology is a refreshing invitation for every woman who feels she isn't godly enough...isn't loving enough ... isn't doing enough...

Each book includes a companion Bible study for group or individual discussion.

Read an excerpt from these books and more on WaterBrookMultnomah.com!

Wind, Sand and Stars

By the author of
NIGHT FLIGHT

Illustrated by
John O'H. Cosgrave, II

Illustrated Edition

Wind, Sand and Stars

by

Antoine de Saint Exupéry

Translated from the French by

Lewis Galantière

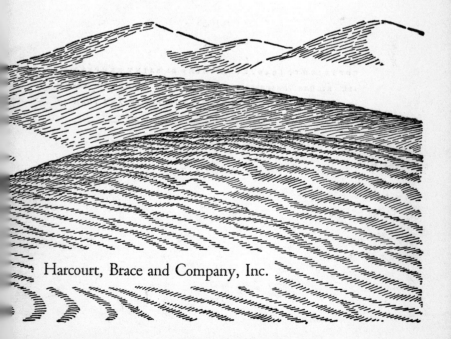

Harcourt, Brace and Company, Inc.

H.10.58

PRINTED IN THE UNITED STATES OF AMERICA

A French Aviator who followed the profession of Airline Pilot for Eight Years offers the American edition of this book in homage to the Airline Pilots of America and their Dead

Contents

· 1 ·

The Craft

IN 1926 I was enrolled as student airline pilot by the Latécoère Company, the predecessors of Aéropostale (now Air France) in the operation of the line between Toulouse, in southwestern France, and Dakar, in French West Africa. I was learning the craft, undergoing an apprenticeship served by all young pilots before they were allowed to carry the mails. We took ships up on trial spins, made meek little hops between Toulouse and Perpignan, and had dreary lessons in meteorology in a freezing hangar. We lived in fear of the mountains of Spain, over which we had yet to fly, and in awe of our elders.

These veterans were to be seen in the field restaurant—gruff, not particularly approachable, and inclined somewhat to condescension when giving us the benefit of their experience. When one of them landed, rain-soaked and behind schedule, from Alicante or Casablanca, and one of us asked humble questions about his flight, the very curtness of his replies on these tempestuous days was matter enough out of which to build a fabulous world filled with snares and pitfalls, with cliffs suddenly looming out of fog and whirling air-currents of a strength to uproot cedars. Black dragons guarded the mouths of the valleys and clusters of lightning crowned the crests—for our elders were always at some pains to feed our reverence. But from time to time one or another of them, eternally to be revered, would fail to come back.

I remember, once, a homecoming of Bury, he who was later to die in a spur of the Pyrenees. He came into the restaurant, sat down at the common table, and went stolidly at his food, shoulders still bowed by the fatigue of his recent trial. It was at the end of one of those foul days when from end to end of the line the skies are filled with dirty weather, when the mountains seem to a pilot to be wallowing in slime like exploded cannon on the decks of an antique man-o'-war.

I stared at Bury, swallowed my saliva, and ventured after a bit to ask if he had had a hard flight. Bury, bent over his plate in frowning absorption, could not hear me. In those days we flew open ships and thrust our heads out round the windshield, in bad weather, to take our bearings: the wind that whistled in our ears was a long time clearing out of our heads. Finally Bury looked up, seemed to understand me, to think back to what I was referring to, and suddenly he gave a bright laugh. This brief burst of laughter, from a man who laughed little, startled me. For a moment his weary being was bright with it. But he spoke no word, lowered his head, and went on chewing in silence. And in that dismal restaurant, surrounded by the simple government clerks who sat there repairing the wear and tear of their humble daily tasks, my broad-shouldered messmate seemed to me strangely noble; beneath his rough hide I could discern the angel who had vanquished the dragon.

The night came when it was my turn to be called to the field manager's room.

He said: "You leave tomorrow."

I stood motionless, waiting for him to dismiss me. After a moment of silence he added:

"I take it you know the regulations?"

In those days the motor was not what it is today. It would drop out, for example, without warning and with a great rattle like the crash of crockery. And one would simply throw in one's hand: there was no hope of refuge on the rocky crust of Spain. "Here," we used to say, "when your motor goes, your ship goes, too."

An airplane, of course, can be replaced. Still, the important thing was to avoid a collision with the range; and blind flying through a sea of clouds in the mountain zones was subject to the severest penalties. A pilot in trouble who buried himself in the white cotton-wool of the clouds might all unseeing run straight into a peak. This was why, that night, the deliberate voice repeated insistently its warning:

"Navigating by the compass in a sea of clouds over Spain is all very well, it is very dashing, but—"

And I was struck by the graphic image:

"But you want to remember that below the sea of clouds lies eternity."

And suddenly that tranquil cloud-world, that world so harmless and simple that one sees below on rising out of the clouds, took on in my eyes a new quality. That peaceful world became a pitfall. I imagined the immense white pitfall spread beneath me. Below it reigned not what one might think—not the agitation of men, not the living tumult and bustle of cities, but a silence even more absolute than in the clouds, a peace even more final. This viscous whiteness became in my mind the frontier between the real and the unreal, between the known and the unknowable. Already I was beginning to realize that a spectacle has no meaning except it be seen through the glass of a culture, a civilization, a craft. Mountaineers too know the sea of clouds, yet it does not seem to them the fabulous curtain it is to me.

When I left that room I was filled with a childish pride. Now it was my turn to take on at dawn the responsibility of a cargo of passengers and the African mails. But at the same time I felt very meek. I felt myself ill-prepared for this responsibility. Spain was poor in emergency fields; we had no radio; and I was troubled lest when I got into difficulty I should not know where to hunt a landing-place. Staring at the aridity of my maps, I could see no help in them; and so, with a heart full of shyness and pride, I fled to spend this night of vigil with my friend Guillaumet. Guillaumet had been over the route before me. He knew all the dodges by which one got hold of the keys to Spain. I should have to be initiated by Guillaumet.

When I walked in he looked up and smiled.

"I know all about it," he said. "How do you feel?"

He went to a cupboard and came back with glasses and a bottle of port, still smiling.

"We'll drink to it. Don't worry. It's easier than you think."

Guillaumet exuded confidence the way a lamp gives off light. He was himself later on to break the record for postal crossings in the Andes and the South Atlantic. On this night, sitting in his shirtsleeves, his arms folded in the lamplight, smiling the most heartening of smiles, he said to me simply:

"You'll be bothered from time to time by storms, fog, snow. When you are, think of those who went through it before you, and say to yourself, 'What they could do, I can do.' "

I spread out my maps and asked him hesitantly if he would mind going over the hop with me. And there, bent over in the lamplight, shoulder to shoulder with the veteran, I felt a sort of schoolboy peace.

But what a strange lesson in geography I was given! Guillaumet did not teach Spain to me, he made the country my friend. He did not talk about provinces, or peoples, or livestock. Instead of telling me about Guadix, he spoke of three orange-trees on the edge of the town: "Beware of those trees. Better mark them on the map." And those three orange-trees seemed to me thenceforth higher than the Sierra Nevada.

He did not talk about Lorca, but about a humble farm near Lorca, a living farm with its farmer and the farmer's wife. And this tiny, this remote couple, living a thousand miles from where we sat, took on a universal importance. Settled on the slope of a mountain, they watched like lighthouse-keepers beneath the stars, ever on the look-out to succor men.

The details that we drew up from oblivion, from their inconceivable remoteness, no geographer had been concerned to explore. Because it washed the banks of great cities, the Ebro River was of interest to mapmakers. But what had they to do with that brook running secretly through the water-weeds to the west of Motril, that brook nourishing a mere score or two of flowers?

"Careful of that brook: it breaks up the whole field. Mark it on your map." Ah, I was to remember that serpent in the grass near Motril! It looked like nothing at all, and its faint murmur sang to no more than a few frogs; but it slept with one eye open. Stretching its length along the grasses in the paradise of that emergency landing-field, it lay in wait for me a thousand miles from where I sat. Given the chance, it would transform me into a flaming candelabra. And those thirty valorous sheep ready to charge me on the slope of a hill! Now that I knew about them I could brace myself to meet them.

"You think the meadow empty, and suddenly bang! there are thirty sheep in your wheels." An astounded smile was all I could summon in the face of so cruel a threat.

Little by little, under the lamp, the Spain of my map became a sort of fairyland. The crosses I marked to indicate safety zones and traps were so many buoys and beacons. I charted the farmer, the thirty sheep, the brook. And, exactly where she stood, I set a buoy to mark the shepherdess forgotten by the geographers.

When I left Guillaumet on that freezing winter night, I felt the need of a brisk walk. I turned up my coat collar, and as I strode among the indifferent passers-by I was escorting a fervor as tender as if I had just fallen in love. To be brushing past these strangers with that marvelous secret in my heart filled me with pride. I seemed to myself a sentinel standing guard over a sleeping camp. These passers-by knew nothing about me, yet it was to me that, in their mail pouches, they were about to confide the weightiest cares of their hearts and their trade. Into my hands were they about to entrust their hopes. And I, muffled up in my cloak, walked among them like a shepherd, though they were unaware of my solicitude.

Nor were they receiving any of those messages now being despatched to me by the night. For this snow-storm that was gathering, and that was to burden my first flight, concerned my frail flesh, not theirs. What could they know of those stars that one by one were going out? I alone was in the confidence of the stars. To me alone news was being sent of the enemy's position before the hour of battle. My footfall rang in a universe that was not theirs.

These messages of such grave concern were reaching me as I walked between rows of lighted shop-windows, and those windows on that night seemed a display of all that was good on earth, of a paradise of sweet things. In the sight of all this happiness, I tasted the proud intoxication of renunciation. I was a warrior in danger. What meaning could they have for me, these flashing crystals meant for men's festivities, these lamps whose glow was to shelter men's meditations, these cozy furs out of which were to emerge pathetically beautiful solicitous faces? I was still wrapped in the aura of friendship, dazed a little like a child on Christmas Eve, expectant of surprise and palpitatingly prepared for happiness; and yet already I was soaked in spray; a mail pilot, I was already nibbling the bitter pulp of night flight.

It was three in the morning when they woke me. I thrust the shutters open with a dry snap, saw that rain was falling on the town, and got soberly into my harness. A half-hour later I was out on the pavement shining with rain, sitting on my little valise and waiting for the bus that was to pick me up. So many other flyers before me, on their day of ordination, had undergone this humble wait with beating heart.

Finally I saw the old-fashioned vehicle come round the corner and heard its tinny rattle. Like those who had gone before me, I squeezed in between a sleepy customs guard and a few glum government clerks. The bus smelled musty, smelled of the dust of government offices into which the life of a man sinks as into a quicksand. It stopped every five hundred yards to take on another scrivener, another guard, another inspector. Those in the bus who had already gone back to sleep responded with a vague grunt to the greeting of the newcomer, while he crowded in as well as he was able and instantly fell asleep himself. We jolted mournfully over the uneven pavements of Toulouse, I in the midst of these men who in the rain and the breaking day were about to take up again their dreary diurnal tasks, their red tape, their monotonous lives.

Morning after morning, greeted by the growl of the customs guard shaken out of sleep by his arrival, by the gruff irritability of clerk or inspector, one mail pilot or another got into this bus and was for the moment indistinguishable from these bureaucrats. But as the street lamps moved by, as the field drew nearer and nearer, the old omnibus rattling along lost little by little its reality and became a grey chrysalis from which one emerged transfigured.

Morning after morning a flyer sat here and felt of a sudden, somewhere inside the vulnerable man subjected to his neighbor's surliness, the stirring of the pilot of the Spanish and African mails, the birth of him who, three hours later, was to confront in the lightnings the dragon of the mountains; and who, four hours afterwards, having vanquished it, would be free to decide between a détour over the sea and a direct assault upon the Alcoy range, would be free to deal with storm, with mountain, with ocean.

And thus every morning each pilot before me, in his time, had been lost in the anonymity of daybreak beneath the dismal winter sky of Toulouse, and each one, transfigured by this old omnibus, had felt the birth within him of the sovereign who, five hours later, leaving behind him the rains and snows of the North, repudiating winter, had throttled down his motor and begun to drift earthward in the summer air beneath the shining sun of Alicante.

The old omnibus has vanished, but its austerity, its discomfort, still live in my memory. It was a proper symbol of the apprenticeship we had to serve before we might possess the stern joys of our craft. Everything about it was intensely serious. I remember three years later, though hardly ten words were spoken, learning in that bus of the death of Lécrivain, one of those hundred pilots who on a day or a night of fog have retired for eternity.

It was four in the morning, and the same silence was abroad when we heard the field manager, invisible in the darkness, address the inspector:

"Lécrivain didn't land at Casablanca last night."

"Ah!" said the inspector. "Ah?"

Torn from his dream he made an effort to wake up, to display his zeal, and added:

"Is that so? Couldn't he get through? Did he come back?"

And in the dead darkness of the omnibus the answer came: "No."

We waited to hear the rest, but no word sounded. And as the seconds fell it became more and more evi‹

dent that that "no" would be followed by no further word, was eternal and without appeal, that Lécrivain not only had not landed at Casablanca but would never again land anywhere.

And so, at daybreak on the morning of my first flight with the mails, I went through the sacred rites of the craft, and I felt the self-confidence oozing out of me as I stared through the windows at the macadam shining and reflecting back the street lights. Over the pools of water I could see great palms of wind running. And I thought: "My first flight with the mails! Really, this is not my lucky day."

I raised my eyes and looked at the inspector. "Would you call this bad weather?" I asked.

He threw a weary glance out of the window. "Doesn't prove anything," he growled finally.

And I wondered how one could tell bad weather. The night before, with a single smile Guillaumet had wiped out all the evil omens with which the veterans overwhelmed us, but they came back into my memory. "I feel sorry for the man who doesn't know the whole line pebble by pebble, if he runs into a snow-storm. Oh, yes, I pity the fellow." Our elders, who had their prestige to think of, had all bobbed their heads solemnly and looked at us with embarrassing sympathy, as if they were pitying a flock of condemned sheep.

For how many of us had this old omnibus served as

refuge in its day? Sixty? Eighty? I looked about me. Luminous points glowed in the darkness. Cigarettes punctuated the humble meditations of worn old clerks. How many of us had they escorted through the rain on a journey from which there was no coming back?

I heard them talking to one another in murmurs and whispers. They talked about illness, money, shabby domestic cares. Their talk painted the walls of the dismal prison in which these men had locked themselves up. And suddenly I had a vision of the face of destiny.

Old bureaucrat, my comrade, it is not you who are to blame. No one ever helped you to escape. You, like a termite, built your peace by blocking up with cement every chink and cranny through which the light might pierce. You rolled yourself up into a ball in your genteel security, in routine, in the stifling conventions of provincial life, raising a modest rampart against the winds and the tides and the stars. You have chosen not to be perturbed by great problems, having trouble enough to forget your own fate as man. You are not the dweller upon an errant planet and do not ask yourself questions to which there are no answers. You are a petty bourgeois of Toulouse. Nobody grasped you by the shoulder while there was still time. Now the clay of which you were shaped has dried and hardened, and naught in you will ever awaken the sleeping musician, the poet, the astronomer that possibly inhabited you in the beginning.

The squall has ceased to be a cause of my complaint.

The magic of the craft has opened for me a world in which I shall confront, within two hours, the black dragons and the crowned crests of a coma of blue lightnings, and when night has fallen I, delivered, shall read my course in the stars.

Thus I went through my professional baptism and I began to fly the mails. For the most part the flights were without incident. Like sea-divers, we sank peacefully into the depths of our element.

Flying, in general, seemed to us easy. When the skies are filled with black vapors, when fog and sand and sea are confounded in a brew in which they become indistinguishable, when gleaming flashes wheel treacherously in these skyey swamps, the pilot purges himself of the phantoms at a single stroke. He lights his lamps. He brings sanity into his house as into a lonely cottage on a fearsome heath. And the crew travel a sort of submarine route in a lighted chamber.

Pilot, mechanic, and radio operator are shut up in what might be a laboratory. They are obedient to the play of dial-hands, not to the unrolling of the landscape. Out of doors the mountains are immersed in tenebrous darkness; but they are no longer mountains, they are invisible powers whose approach must be computed.

The operator sits in the light of his lamp, dutifully setting down figures; the mechanic ticks off points on his chart; the pilot swerves in response to the drift of the mountains as quickly as he sees that the summits he intends to pass on the left have deployed straight ahead of him in a silence and secrecy as of military preparations. And below on the ground the watchful radio men in their shacks take down submissively in their notebooks the dictation of their comrade in the air: "12:40 a.m. En route 230. All well."

So the crew fly on with no thought that they are in motion. Like night over the sea, they are very far from the earth, from towns, from trees. The motors fill the lighted chamber with a quiver that changes its substance. The clock ticks on. The dials, the radio lamps, the various hands and needles go through their invisible alchemy. From second to second these mysterious stirrings, a few muffled words, a concentrated tenseness, contribute to the end result. And when the hour is at hand the pilot may glue his forehead to the window with perfect assurance. Out of oblivion the gold has been smelted: there it gleams in the lights of the airport.

And yet we have all known flights when of a sudden, each for himself, it has seemed to us that we have crossed the border of the world of reality; when, only a couple of hours from port, we have felt ourselves more distant from it than we should feel if we were in India; when there has come a premonition of an incursion into a forbidden world whence it was going to be infinitely difficult to return.

Thus, when Mermoz first crossed the South Atlantic in a hydroplane, as day was dying he ran foul of the Black Hole region, off Africa. Straight ahead of him were the tails of tornadoes rising minute by minute gradually higher, rising as a wall is built; and then the night came down upon these preliminaries and swallowed them up; and when, an hour later, he slipped under the clouds, he came out into a fantastic kingdom.

Great black waterspouts had reared themselves seemingly in the immobility of temple pillars. Swollen at their tops, they were supporting the squat and lowering arch of the tempest, but through the rifts in the arch there fell slabs of light and the full moon sent her radiant beams between the pillars down upon the frozen tiles of the sea. Through these uninhabited ruins Mermoz made his way, gliding slantwise from one channel of light to the next, circling round those giant pillars in which there must have rumbled the upsurge of the sea, flying for four hours through these corridors of moonlight toward the exit from the temple. And this spectacle was so overwhelming that only after he had got through the Black Hole did Mermoz awaken to the fact that he had not been afraid.

I remember, for my part, another of those hours in which a pilot finds suddenly that he has slipped beyond the confines of this world. All that night the radio messages sent from the ports in the Sahara concerning our position had been inaccurate, and my radio operator, Néri, and I had been drawn out of our course. Suddenly, seeing the gleam of water at the bottom of a crevasse of fog, I tacked sharply in the direction of the coast; but it was by then impossible for us to say how long we had been flying towards the high seas. Nor were we certain of making the coast, for our fuel was probably low. And even so, once we had reached it we would still have to make port—after the moon had set.

We had no means of angular orientation, were already deafened, and were bit by bit growing blind. The moon like a pallid ember began to go out in the banks of fog. Overhead the sky was filling with clouds, and we flew thenceforth between cloud and fog in a world voided of all substance and all light. The ports that signaled us had given up trying to tell us where we were. "No bearings, no bearings," was all their message, for our voice reached them from everywhere and nowhere. With sinking hearts Néri and I leaned out, he on his side and I on mine, to see if anything, anything at all, was distinguishable in this void. Already our tired eyes were seeing things—errant signs, delusive flashes, phantoms.

And suddenly, when already we were in despair, low on the horizon a brilliant point was unveiled on our port bow. A wave of joy went through me. Néri leaned forward, and I could hear him singing. It could not but be the beacon of an airport, for after dark the whole

Sahara goes black and forms a great dead expanse. That light twinkled for a space—and then went out! We had been steering for a star which was visible for a few minutes only, just before setting on the horizon between the layer of fog and the clouds.

Then other stars took up the game, and with a sort of dogged hope we set our course for each of them in turn. Each time that a light lingered a while, we performed the same crucial experiment. Néri would send his message to the airport at Cisneros: "Beacon in view. Put out your light and flash three times." And Cisneros would put out its beacon and flash three times while the hard light at which we gazed would not, incorruptible star, so much as wink. And despite our dwindling fuel we continued to nibble at the golden bait which each time seemed more surely the true light of a beacon, was each time a promise of a landing and of life—and we had each time to change our star.

And with that we knew ourselves to be lost in interplanetary space among a thousand inaccessible planets, we who sought only the one veritable planet, our own, that planet on which alone we should find our familiar countryside, the houses of our friends, our treasures.

On which alone we should find . . . Let me draw the picture that took shape before my eyes. It will seem to you childish; but even in the midst of danger a man retains his human concerns. I was thirsty and I was hungry. If we did find Cisneros we should re-fuel and carry on to Casablanca, and there we should come down in the cool of daybreak, free to idle the hours away. Néri and I would go into town. We would go to a little pub already open despite the early hour. Safe and sound, Néri and I would sit down at table and laugh at the night of danger as we ate our warm rolls and drank our bowls of coffee and hot milk. We would receive this matutinal gift at the hands of life. Even as an old peasant woman recognizes her God in a painted image, in a childish medal, in a chaplet, so life would speak to us in its humblest language in order that we understand. The joy of living, I say, was summed up for me in the remembered sensation of that first burning and aromatic swallow, that mixture of milk and coffee and bread by which men hold communion with tranquil pastures, exotic plantations, and golden harvests, communion with the earth. Amidst all these stars there was but one that could make itself significant for us by composing this aromatic bowl that was its daily gift at dawn. And from that earth of men, that earth docile to the reaping of grain and the harvesting of the grape, bearing its rivers asleep in their fields, its villages clinging to their hillsides, our ship was separated by astronomical distances. All the treasures of the world were summed up in a grain of dust now blown far out of our path by the very destiny itself of dust and of the orbs of night.

And Néri still prayed to the stars.

Suddenly he was pounding my shoulder. On the bit

of paper he held forth impatiently to me I read: "All well. Magnificent news." I waited with beating heart while he scribbled the half-dozen words that were to save us. At last he put this grace of heaven into my hands.

It was dated from Casablanca, which we had left the night before. Delayed in transmission, it had suddenly found us more than a thousand miles away, suspended between cloud and fog, lost at sea. It was sent by the government representative at the airport. And it said: "Monsieur de Saint Exupéry, I am obliged to recommend that you be disciplined at Paris for having flown too close to the hangars on leaving Casablanca."

It was true that I had done this. It was also true that this man was performing his duty with irritability. I should have been humiliated if this reproach had been addressed to me in an airport. But it reached me where it had no right to reach me. Among these too rare stars, on this bed of fog, in this menacing savor of the sea, it burst like a detonation. Here we were with our fate in our hands, the fate of the mails and of the ship; we had trouble enough to try to keep alive; and this man was purging his petty rancor against us.

But Néri and I were far from nettled. What we felt was a vast and sudden jubilation. Here it was we who were masters, and this man was letting us know it. The impudent little corporal! not to have looked at our stripes and seen that we had been promoted captain! To intrude into our musings when we were solemnly taking our constitutional between Sagittarius and the Great Bear! When the only thing we could be concerned with, the only thing of our order of magnitude, was this appointment we were missing with the moon!

The immediate duty, the only duty of the planet whence this man's message came, was to furnish us accurate figures for our computations among the stars. And its figures had been false. This being so, the planet had only to hold its tongue. Néri scribbled: "Instead of wasting their time with this nonsense they would do better to haul us back to Cisneros, if they can." By "they" he meant all the peoples of the globe, with their parliaments, their senates, their navies, their armies, their emperors. We re-read the message from that man mad enough to imagine that he had business with us, and tacked in the direction of Mercury.

It was by the purest chance that we were saved. I had given up all thought of making Cisneros and had set my course at right angles to the coast-line in the hope that thus we might avoid coming down at sea when our fuel ran out. Meanwhile however I was in the belly of a dense fog so that even with land below it was not going to be easy to set the ship down. The situation was so clear that already I was shrugging my shoulders ruefully when Néri passed me a second message which, an hour earlier, would have been our salvation. "Cisneros," it said, "has deigned to communicate with us. Cisneros says, '216 doubtful.'" Well, that helped. Cisneros was no longer swallowed up in space, it was actually out there on our left, almost within reach. But how far away? Néri and I talked it over briefly, decided it was too late to try for it (since that might mean missing the coast), and Néri replied: "Only one hour fuel left continuing on 93."

But the airports one by one had been waking each other up. Into our dialogue broke the voices of Agadir, Casablanca, Dakar. The radio stations at each of these towns had warned the airports and the ports had flashed the news to our comrades. Bit by bit they were gathering round us as round a sick-bed. Vain warmth, but human warmth after all. Helpless concern, but affectionate at any rate.

And suddenly into this conclave burst Toulouse, the headquarters of the Line three thousand miles away, worried along with the rest. Toulouse broke in without a word of greeting, simply to say sharply: "Your reserve tanks bigger than standard. You have two hours fuel left. Proceed to Cisneros."

There is no need of nights like the one just described to make the airline pilot find new meanings in old appearances. The scene that strikes the passenger as commonplace is from the very moment of taking off animated with a powerful magic for the crew. It is the duty of the ship's captain to make port, cost what it may. The sight of massing clouds is no mere spectacle to him: it is a matter of concern to his physical being, and to his mind it means a set of problems. Before he is off the ground he has taken its measure, and between him and it a bond is formed which is a veritable language.

There is a peak ahead, still distant. The pilot will not reach it before another hour of flight in the night. What is to be the significance of that peak? On a night of full moon it will be a useful landmark. In fainter moonglow it will be a bit of wreckage strewn in shadow, dangerous, but marked clearly enough by the lights of villages. But if the pilot flies blind, has bad luck in correcting his drift, is dubious about his position, that peak begins to stir with a strange life and its threat fills the breadth of the night sky in the same way as a single mine, drifting at the will of the current, can render the whole of the ocean a danger.

The face of the sea is as variable as that of the earth. To passengers, the storm is invisible. Seen from a great height, the waves have no relief and the packets of fog have no movement. The surface of the sea appears to be covered with great white motionless palm-trees, palms marked with ribs and seams stiff in a sort of frost. The sea is like a splintered mirror. But the hydroplane pilot knows there is no landing here.

The hours during which a man flies over this mirror are hours in which there is no assurance of the possession of anything in the world. These palms beneath the plane are so many poisoned flowers. And even when the flight is an easy one, made under a shining sun, the pilot navigating at some point on the line is not gazing upon a scene. These colors of earth and sky, these traces of wind over the face of the sea, these clouds golden in the afterglow, are not objects of the pilot's admiration, but of his cogitation. He looks to them to tell him the direction of the wind or the progress of the storm, and the quality of the night to come.

Even as the peasant strolling about his domain is able to foresee in a thousand signs the coming of the spring, the threat of frost, a promise of rain, so all that happens in the sky signals to the pilot the oncoming snow, the expectancy of fog, or the peace of a blessed night. The machine which at first blush seems a means of isolating man from the great problems of nature, actually plunges him more deeply into them. As for the peasant so for the pilot, dawn and twilight become events of consequence. His essential problems are set him by the mountain, the sea, the wind. Alone before the vast tribunal of the tempestuous sky, the pilot defends his mails and debates on terms of equality with those three elemental divinities.

The mail pouches for which he is responsible are stowed away in the after hold. They constitute the dogma of the religion of his craft, the torch which, in this aerial race, is passed from runner to runner. What matter though they hold but the scribblings of tradesmen and nondescript lovers. The interests which dictated them may very well not be worth the embrace of man and storm; but I know what they become once they have been entrusted to the crew, taken over, as the phrase is. The crew care not a rap for banker or tradesman. If, some day, the crew are hooked by a cliff it will not have been in the interest of tradespeople that they will have died, but in obedience to orders which ennoble the sacks of mail once they are on board ship.

What concerns us is not even the orders—it is the men they cast in their mould.

· 2 ·

The Men

Mermoz is one airline pilot, and Guillaumet another, of whom I shall write briefly in order that you may see clearly what I mean when I say that in the mould of this new profession a new breed of men has been cast.

I

A handful of pilots, of whom Mermoz was one, surveyed the Casablanca-Dakar line across the territory inhabited by the refractory tribes of the Sahara. Motors in those days being what they were, Mermoz was taken prisoner one day by the Moors. The tribesmen were unable to make up their minds to kill him, kept him a captive a fortnight, and he was eventually ransomed. Whereupon he continued to fly over the same territory.

When the South American line was opened up Mermoz, ever the pioneer, was given the job of surveying the division between Buenos Aires and Santiago de Chile. He who had flung a bridge over the Sahara was now to do the same over the Andes. They had given him a plane whose absolute ceiling was sixteen thousand feet and had asked him to fly it over a mountain range that rose more than twenty thousand feet into the air. His job was to search for gaps in the Cordilleras. He who had studied the face of the sands was now to learn the contours of the peaks, those crags whose scarfs of snow flutter restlessly in the winds, whose surfaces are bleached white in the storms, whose blustering gusts sweep through the narrow walls of their rocky corridors and force the pilot to a sort of hand-to-hand combat. Mermoz enrolled in this war in complete ignorance of his adversary, with no notion at all of the chances of coming forth alive from battle with this enemy. His job was to "try out" for the rest of us. And, "trying out" one day, he found himself prisoner of the Andes.

Mermoz and his mechanic had been forced down at an altitude of twelve thousand feet on a table-land at whose edges the mountain dropped sheer on all sides.

For two mortal days they hunted a way off this plateau. But they were trapped. Everywhere the same sheer drop. And so they played their last card.

Themselves still in it, they sent the plane rolling and bouncing down an incline over the rocky ground until it reached the precipice, went off into air, and dropped. In falling, the plane picked up enough speed to respond to the controls. Mermoz was able to tilt its nose in the direction of a peak, sweep over the peak, and, while the water spurted through all the pipes burst by the night frost, the ship already disabled after only seven minutes of flight, he saw beneath him like a promised land the Chilean plain.

And the next day he was at it again.

When the Andes had been thoroughly explored and the technique of the crossings perfected, Mermoz turned over this section of the line to his friend Guillaumet and set out to explore the night. The lighting of our airports had not yet been worked out. Hovering in the pitch black night, Mermoz would land by the faint glimmer of three gasoline flares lined up at one end of the field. This trick, too, he taught us, and then, having tamed the night, he tried the ocean. He was the first, in 1931, to carry the mails in four days from Toulouse to Buenos Aires. On his way home he had engine trouble over a stormy sea in mid-Atlantic. A passing steamer picked him up with his mails and his crew.

Pioneering thus, Mermoz had cleared the desert, the

mountains, the night, and the sea. He had been forced down more than once in desert, in mountain, in night, and in sea. And each time that he got safely home, it was but to start out again. Finally, after a dozen years of service, having taken off from Dakar bound for Natal, he radioed briefly that he was cutting off his rear right-hand engine. Then silence.

There was nothing particularly disturbing in this news. Nevertheless, when ten minutes had gone by without report there began for every radio station on the South Atlantic line, from Paris to Buenos Aires, a period of anxious vigil. It would be ridiculous to worry over someone ten minutes late in our day-to-day existence, but in the air-mail service ten minutes can be pregnant with meaning. At the heart of this dead slice of time an unknown event is locked up. Insignificant, it may be; a mishap, possibly: whatever it is, the event has taken place. Fate has pronounced a decision from which there is no appeal. An iron hand has guided a crew to a sea-landing that may have been safe and may have been disastrous. And long hours must go by before the decision of the gods is made known to those who wait.

We waited. We hoped. Like all men at some time in their lives we lived through that inordinate expectancy which like a fatal malady grows from minute to minute harder to bear. Even before the hour sounded, in our hearts many among us were already sitting up with the dead. All of us had the same vision before our eyes. It was a vision of a cockpit still inhabited by living men; but the pilot's hands were telling him very little now, and the world in which he groped and fumbled was a world he did not recognize. Behind him, in the glimmer of the cabin light, a shapeless uneasiness floated. The crew moved to and fro, discussed their plight, feigned sleep. A restless slumber it was, like the stirring of drowned men. The only element of sanity, of intelligibility, was the whirring of the three engines with its reassuring evidence that time still existed for them.

We were haunted for hours by this vision of a plane in distress. But the hands of the clock were going round and little by little it began to grow late. Slowly the truth was borne in upon us that our comrades would never return, that they were sleeping in that South Atlantic whose skies they had so often ploughed. Mermoz had done his job and slipped away to rest, like a gleaner who, having carefully bound his sheaf, lies down in the field to sleep.

When a pilot dies in the harness his death seems something that inheres in the craft itself, and in the beginning the hurt it brings is perhaps less than the pain sprung of a different death. Assuredly he has vanished, has undergone his ultimate mutation; but his presence is still not missed as deeply as we might miss bread. For in this craft we take it for granted that we shall meet together only rarely.

Airline pilots are widely dispersed over the face of the world. They land alone at scattered and remote airports, isolated from each other rather in the manner of sentinels between whom no words can be spoken. It needs the accident of journeyings to bring together here or there the dispersed members of this great professional family.

Round the table in the evening, at Casablanca, at Dakar, at Buenos Aires, we take up conversations interrupted by years of silence, we resume friendships to the accompaniment of buried memories. And then we are off again.

Thus is the earth at once a desert and a paradise, rich in secret hidden gardens, gardens inaccessible, but to which the craft leads us ever back, one day or another. Life may scatter us and keep us apart; it may prevent us from thinking very often of one another; but we know that our comrades are somewhere "out there"— where, one can hardly say—silent, forgotten, but deeply faithful. And when our path crosses theirs, they greet us with such manifest joy, shake us so gaily by the shoulders! Indeed we are accustomed to waiting.

Bit by bit, nevertheless, it comes over us that we shall never again hear the laughter of our friend, that this one garden is forever locked against us. And at that moment begins our true mourning, which, though it may not be rending, is yet a little bitter. For nothing, in truth, can replace that companion. Old friends cannot be created out of hand. Nothing can match the treasure of common memories, of trials endured together, of quarrels and reconciliations and generous emotions. It is idle, having planted an acorn in the morning, to expect that afternoon to sit in the shade of the oak.

So life goes on. For years we plant the seed, we feel ourselves rich; and then come other years when time does its work and our plantation is made sparse and thin. One by one, our comrades slip away, deprive us of their shade.

This, then, is the moral taught us by Mermoz and his kind. We understand better, because of him, that what constitutes the dignity of a craft is that it creates a fellowship, that it binds men together and fashions for them a common language. For there is but one veritable problem—the problem of human relations.

We forget that there is no hope of joy except in human relations. If I summon up those memories that have left with me an enduring savor, if I draw up the balance sheet of the hours in my life that have truly counted, surely I find only those that no wealth could have procured me. True riches cannot be bought. One cannot buy the friendship of a Mermoz, of a companion to whom one is bound forever by ordeals suffered in common. There is no buying the night flight with its hundred thousand stars, its serenity, its few hours of sovereignty. It is not money that can procure for us that new vision of the world won through hardship—those trees, flowers, women, those treasures made fresh by the dew and color of life which the dawn restores to us, this concert of little things that sustain us and constitute our compensation.

Nor that night we lived through in the land of the unconquered tribes of the Sahara, which now floats into my memory.

Three crews of Aéropostale men had come down at the fall of day on the Rio de Oro coast in a part of the Sahara whose denizens acknowledge no European rule. Riguelle had landed first, with a broken connecting rod. Bourgat had come along to pick up Riguelle's crew, but a minor accident had nailed him to earth. Finally, as night was beginning to fall, I arrived. We decided to salvage Bourgat's ship, but we should have to spend the night and do the job of repair by daylight.

Exactly on this spot two of our comrades, Gourp and Erable, had been murdered by the tribesmen a year earlier. We knew that a raiding party of three hundred rifles was at this very moment encamped somewhere near by, round Cape Bojador. Our three landings had been visible from a great distance and the Moors must have seen us. We began a vigil which might turn out to be our last.

Altogether, there were about ten of us, pilots and mechanics, when we made ready for the night. We unloaded five or six wooden cases of merchandise out of the hold, emptied them, and set them about in a circle. At the deep end of each case, as in a sentry-box, we set a lighted candle, its flame poorly sheltered from the wind. So in the heart of the desert, on the naked rind of the planet, in an isolation like that of the beginnings of the world, we built a village of men.

Sitting in the flickering light of the candles on this kerchief of sand, on this village square, we waited in the night. We were waiting for the rescuing dawn—or for the Moors. Something, I know not what, lent this night a savor of Christmas. We told stories, we joked, we sang songs. In the air there was that slight fever that reigns over a gaily prepared feast. And yet we were infinitely poor. Wind, sand, and stars. The austerity of Trappists. But on this badly lighted cloth, a handful of men who possessed nothing in the world but their memories were sharing invisible riches.

We had met at last. Men travel side by side for years, each locked up in his own silence or exchanging those words which carry no freight—till danger comes. Then they stand shoulder to shoulder. They discover that they belong to the same family. They wax and bloom in the recognition of fellow beings. They look at one another and smile. They are like the prisoner set free who marvels at the immensity of the sea.

Happiness! It is useless to seek it elsewhere than in this warmth of human relations. Our sordid interests imprison us within their walls. Only a comrade can grasp us by the hand and haul us free.

And these human relations must be created. One must go through an apprenticeship to learn the job. Games and risk are a help here. When we exchange manly handshakes, compete in races, join together to save one of us who is in trouble, cry aloud for help in the hour of danger—only then do we learn that we are not alone on earth.

Each man must look to himself to teach him the meaning of life. It is not something discovered: it is something moulded. These prison walls that this age of trade has built up round us, we can break down. We can still run free, call to our comrades, and marvel to hear once more, in response to our call, the pathetic chant of the human voice.

II

Guillaumet, old friend, of you too I shall say a few words. Be sure that I shall not make you squirm with any clumsy vaunting of your courage and your professional valor. In telling the story of the most marvelous of your adventures, I am after something quite different.

There exists a quality which is nameless. It may be gravity, but the word does not satisfy me, for the quality I have in mind can be accompanied by the most cheerful gaiety. It is the quality of the carpenter face to face with his block of wood. He handles it, he takes its measure. Far from treating it frivolously, he summons all his professional virtues to do it honor.

I once read, Guillaumet, a tale in which your adventure was celebrated. I have an old score to settle with the infidel who wrote it. You were described as abounding in the witty sallies of the street arab, as if courage consisted in demeaning oneself to schoolboy banter in the midst of danger and the hour of death. The man did not know you, Guillaumet. You never felt the need of cheapening your adversaries before confronting them. When you saw a foul storm you said to yourself, "Here is a foul storm." You accepted it, and you took its measure.

These pages, Guillaumet, written out of my memory, are addressed in homage to you.

It was winter and you had been gone a week over the Andes. I had come up from farthest Patagonia to join Deley at Mendoza. For five days the two of us, each in his plane, had ransacked the mountains unavailingly. Two ships! It seemed to us that a hundred squadrons navigating for a hundred years would not have been enough to explore that endless, cloud-piercing range. We had lost all hope. The very smugglers themselves, bandits who would commit a crime for a five-peso note, refused to form a rescue party out of fear of those counterforts. "We should surely die," they said; "the Andes never give up a man in winter."

And when Deley and I landed at Santiago, the Chilean officers also advised us to give you up. "It is midwinter," they said; "even if your comrade survived the landing, he cannot have survived the night. Night in those passes changes a man into ice."

And when, a second time, I slipped between the towering walls and giant pillars of the Andes, it seemed to me I was no longer seeking, but was now sitting up with, your body in the silence of a cathedral of snow.

You had been gone a week, I say, and I was lunching between flights in a restaurant in Mendoza when a man stuck his head in the door and called out:

"They've found Guillaumet!"

All the strangers in the restaurant embraced.

Ten minutes later I was off the ground, carrying two mechanics, Lefebvre and Abri. Forty minutes later I had landed alongside a road, having recognized from the air, I know not by what sign, the car in which you were being brought down from San Rafael. I remember that we cried like fools; we put our arms about a living Guillaumet, resuscitated, the author of his own miracle. And it was at that moment that you pronounced your first intelligible sentence, a speech admirable in its human pride:

"I swear that what I went through, no animal would have gone through."

Later, you told us the story. A storm that brought fifteen feet of snow in forty-eight hours down on the Chilean slope had bottled up all space and sent every other mail pilot back to his starting point. You, however, had taken off in the hope of finding a rift in the sky. You found this rift, this trap, a little to the south, and now, at twenty thousand feet, the ceiling of clouds being a couple of thousand feet below you and pierced by only the highest peaks, you set your course for Argentina.

Down currents sometimes fill pilots with a strange uneasiness. The engines run on, but the ship seems to be sinking. You jockey to hold your altitude: the ship loses speed and goes mushy. And still you sink. So you give it up, afraid that you may have jockeyed too much; and you let yourself drift to right or left, striving to put at your back a favorable peak, that is, a peak off which the winds rebound as off a springboard.

And yet you go on sinking. The whole sky seems to be coming down on you. You begin to feel like the victim of some cosmic accident. You cannot land anywhere, and you try in vain to turn round and fly back into those zones where the air, as dense and solid as a pillar, had held you up. That pillar has melted away. Everything here is rotten and you slither about in a sort of universal decomposition while the cloud-bank rises apathetically, reaches your level, and swallows you up.

"It almost had me in a corner once," you explained,

"but I still wasn't sure I was caught. When you get up above the clouds you run into those down currents that seem to be perfectly stationary for the simple reason that in that very high altitude they never stop flowing. Everything is queer in the upper range."

And what clouds!

"As soon as I felt I was caught I dropped the controls and grabbed my seat for fear of being flung out of the ship. The jolts were so terrible that my leather harness cut my shoulders and was ready to snap. And what with the frosting on the panes, my artificial horizon was invisible and the wind rolled me over and over like a hat in a road from eighteen thousand feet down to ten.

"At ten thousand I caught a glimpse of a dark horizontal blot that helped me right the ship. It was a lake, and I recognized it as what they call Laguna Diamante. I remembered that it lay at the bottom of a funnel, and that one flank of the funnel, a volcano called Maipu, ran up to about twenty thousand feet.

"There I was, safe out of the clouds; but I was still blinded by the thick whirling snow and I had to hang on to my lake if I wasn't to crash into one of the sides of the funnel. So down I went, and I flew round and round the lake, about a hundred and fifty feet above it, until I ran out of fuel. After two hours of this, I set the ship down on the snow—and over on her nose she went.

"When I dragged myself clear of her I stood up. The wind knocked me down. I stood up again. Over I went a second time. So I crawled under the cockpit and dug me out a shelter in the snow. I pulled a lot of mail sacks round me, and there I lay for two days and two nights. Then the storm blew over and I started to walk my way out. I walked for five days and four nights."

But what was there left of you, Guillaumet? We had found you again, true; but burnt to a crisp, but shriveled, but shrunken into an old woman. That same afternoon I flew you back to Mendoza, and there the cool white sheets flowed like a balm down the length of your body.

They were not enough, though. Your own foundered body was an encumbrance: you turned and twisted in your sleep, unable to find lodgment for it. I stared at your face: it was splotched and swollen, like an over-ripe fruit that has been repeatedly dropped on the ground.

You were dreadful to see, and you were in misery, for you had lost the beautiful tools of your work: your hands were numb and useless, and when you sat up on the edge of your bed to draw a free breath, your frozen feet hung down like two dead weights. You had not even finished your long walk back, you were still pant-ing; and when you turned and stirred on the pillow in search of peace, a procession of images that you could not escape, a procession waiting impatiently in the wings, moved instantly into action under your skull. Across the stage of your skull it moved, and for the twentieth time you fought once more the battle against these enemies that rose up out of their ashes.

I filled you with herb-teas.

"Drink, old fellow."

"You know . . . what amazed me . . ."

Boxer victorious, but punch-drunk and scarred with blows, you were re-living your strange adventure. You could divest yourself of it only in scraps. And as you told your dark tale, I could see you trudging without ice-axe, without ropes, without provisions, scaling cols fifteen thousand feet in the air, crawling on the faces of vertical walls, your hands and feet and knees bleeding in a temperature twenty degrees below zero.

Voided bit by bit of your blood, your strength, your reason, you went forward with the obstinacy of an ant, retracing your steps to go round an obstacle, picking yourself up after each fall to earth, climbing slopes that led to abysses, ceaselessly in motion and never asleep, for had you slept, from that bed of snow you would never have risen. When your foot slipped and you went down, you were up again in an instant, else had you been turned into stone. The cold was petrifying you by the minute, and the price you paid for taking a moment too much of rest, when you fell, was the agony of re-vivifying dead muscles in your struggle to rise to your feet.

You resisted temptation. "Amid snow," you told me, "a man loses his instinct of self-preservation. After two or three or four days of tramping, all you think about is sleep. I would long for it; but then I would say to myself, 'If my wife still believes I am alive, she must believe that I am on my feet. The boys all think I am on my feet. They have faith in me. And I am a skunk if I don't go on.' "

So you tramped on; and each day you cut out a bit more of the opening of your shoes so that your swelling and freezing feet might have room in them.

You confided to me this strange thing:

"As early as the second day, you know, the hardest job I had was to force myself not to think. The pain was too much, and I was really up against it too hard. I had to forget that, or I shouldn't have had the heart to go on walking. But I didn't seem able to control my mind. It kept working like a turbine. Still, I could more or less choose what I was to think about. I tried to stick to some film I'd seen, or book I'd read. But the film and the book would go through my mind like lightning. And I'd be back where I was, in the snow. It never failed. So I would think about other things. . . ."

There was one time, however, when, having slipped, and finding yourself stretched flat on your face in the snow, you threw in your hand. You were like a boxer emptied of all passion by a single blow, lying and listening to the seconds drop one by one into a distant universe, until the tenth second fell and there was no appeal.

"I've done my best and I can't make it. Why go on?"

All that you had to do in the world to find peace was to shut your eyes. So little was needed to blot out that world of crags and ice and snow. Let drop those miraculous eyelids and there was an end of blows, of stumbling falls, of torn muscles and burning ice, of that burden of life you were dragging along like a worn-out ox, a weight heavier than any wain or cart.

Already you were beginning to taste the relief of this snow that had now become an insidious poison, this morphia that was filling you with beatitude. Life crept out of your extremities and fled to collect round your heart while something gentle and precious snuggled in close at the centre of your being. Little by little your consciousness deserted the distant regions of your body, and your body, that beast now gorged with suffering, lay ready to participate in the indifference of marble.

Your very scruples subsided. Our cries ceased to reach you, or, more accurately, changed for you into dream-cries. You were happy now, able to respond by long confident dream-strides that carried you effortlessly towards the enchantment of the plains below. How smoothly you glided into this suddenly merciful world! Guillaumet, you miser! You had made up your mind to deny us your return, to take your pleasures selfishly without us among your white angels in the snows. And then remorse floated up from the depths of your consciousness. The dream was spoilt by the irruption of bothersome details. "I thought of my wife. She would be penniless if she couldn't collect the insurance. Yes, but the company . . ."

When a man vanishes, his legal death is postponed for four years. This awful detail was enough to blot out the other visions. You were lying face downward on a bed of snow that covered a steep mountain slope. With the coming of summer your body would be washed with this slush down into one of the thousand crevasses of the Andes. You knew that. But you also knew that some fifty yards away a rock was jutting up out of the snow. "I thought, if I get up I may be able to reach it. And if I can prop myself up against the rock, they'll find me there next summer."

Once you were on your feet again, you tramped two nights and three days. But you did not then imagine that you would go on much longer:

"I could tell by different signs that the end was coming. For instance, I had to stop every two or three hours to cut my shoes open a bit more and massage my swollen feet. Or maybe my heart would be going too fast. But I was beginning to lose my memory. I had been going on a long time when suddenly I realized that every time I stopped I forgot something. The first time it was a glove. And it was cold! I had put it down in front of me and had forgotten to pick it up. The next time it was my watch. Then my knife. Then my compass. Each time I stopped I stripped myself of something vitally important. I was becoming my own enemy! And I can't tell you how it hurt me when I found that out.

"What saves a man is to take a step. Then another step. It is always the same step, but you have to take it."

"I swear that what I went through, no animal would have gone through." This sentence, the noblest ever spoken, this sentence that defines man's place in the universe, that honors him, that re-establishes the true hierarchy, floated back into my thoughts. Finally you fell asleep. Your consciousness was abolished; but forth from this dismantled, burnt, and shattered body it was to be born again like a flower put forth gradually by the species which itself is born of the luminous pulp of the stars. The body, we may say, then, is but an honest tool, the body is but a servant. And it was in these words, Guillaumet, that you expressed your pride in the honest tool:

"With nothing to eat, after three days on my feet . . . well . . . my heart wasn't going any too well. I was crawling along the side of a sheer wall, hanging over space, digging and kicking out pockets in the ice so that I could hold on, when all of a sudden my heart conked. It hesitated. Started up again. Beat crazily. I said to myself, 'If it hesitates a moment too long, I drop.' I stayed still and listened to myself. Never, never in my life have I listened as carefully to a motor as I listened to my heart, me hanging there. I said to it: 'Come on, old boy. Go to work. Try beating a little.' That's good stuff my heart is made of. It hesitated, but it went on. You don't know how proud I was of that heart."

As I said, in that room in Mendoza where I sat with you, you fell finally into an exhausted sleep. And I thought: If we were to talk to him about his courage, Guillaumet would shrug his shoulders. But it would be just as false to extol his modesty. His place is far beyond that mediocre virtue.

If he shrugs his shoulders, it is because he is no fool. He knows that once men are caught up in an event they cease to be afraid. Only the unknown frightens men. But once a man has faced the unknown, that terror becomes the known.

Especially if it is scrutinized with Guillaumet's lucid gravity. Guillaumet's courage is in the main the product of his honesty. But even this is not his fundamental quality. His moral greatness consists in his sense of responsibility. He knew that he was responsible for himself, for the mails, for the fulfilment of the hopes of his comrades. He was holding in his hands their sorrow and their joy. He was responsible for that new element which the living were constructing and in which he was a participant. Responsible, in as much as his work contributed to it, for the fate of those men.

Guillaumet was one among those bold and generous men who had taken upon themselves the task of spreading their foliage over bold and generous horizons. To be a man is, precisely, to be responsible. It is to feel shame at the sight of what seems to be unmerited misery. It is to take pride in a victory won by one's comrades. It is to feel, when setting one's stone, that one is contributing to the building of the world.

There is a tendency to class such men with toreadors and gamblers. People extol their contempt for death. But I would not give a fig for anybody's contempt for death. If its roots are not sunk deep in an acceptance of responsibility, this contempt for death is the sign either of an impoverished soul or of youthful extravagance.

I once knew a young suicide. I cannot remember what disappointment in love it was which induced him to send a bullet carefully into his heart. I have no notion what literary temptation he had succumbed to when he drew on a pair of white gloves before the shot. But I remember having felt, on learning of this sorry show, an impression not of nobility but of lack of dignity. So! Behind that attractive face, beneath that skull which should have been a treasure chest, there had been nothing, nothing at all. Unless it was the vision of some silly little girl indistinguishable from the rest.

And when I heard of this meagre destiny, I remembered the death of a man. He was a gardener, and he was speaking on his deathbed: "You know, I used to sweat sometimes when I was digging. My rheumatism would pull at my leg, and I would damn myself for a slave. And now, do you know, I'd like to spade and spade. It's beautiful work. A man is free when he is using a spade. And besides, who is going to prune my trees when I am gone?"

That man was leaving behind him a fallow field, a fallow planet. He was bound by ties of love to all cultivable land and to all the trees of the earth. There was a generous man, a prodigal man, a nobleman! There was a man who, battling against death in the name of his Creation, could like Guillaumet be called a man of courage!

· 3 ·

The Tool

A<small>ND</small> now, having spoken of the men born of the pilot's craft, I shall say something about the tool with which they work—the airplane. Have you looked at a modern airplane? Have you followed from year to year the evolution of its lines? Have you ever thought, not only about the airplane but about whatever man builds, that all of man's industrial efforts, all his computations and calculations, all the nights spent over working draughts and blueprints, invariably culminate in the production of a thing whose sole and guiding principle is the ultimate principle of simplicity?

It is as if there were a natural law which ordained that to achieve this end, to refine the curve of a piece of furniture, or a ship's keel, or the fuselage of an airplane, until gradually it partakes of the elementary purity of the curve of a human breast or shoulder, there must be the experimentation of several generations of craftsmen. In anything at all, perfection is finally attained not when there is no longer anything to add, but when there is no longer anything to take away, when a body has been stripped down to its nakedness.

It results from this that perfection of invention touches hands with absence of invention, as if that line which the human eye will follow with effortless delight were a line that had not been invented but simply discovered, had in the beginning been hidden by nature and in the end been found by the engineer. There is an ancient myth about the image asleep in the block of marble until it is carefully disengaged by the sculptor. The sculptor must himself feel that he is not so much inventing or shaping the curve of breast or shoulder as delivering the image from its prison.

In this spirit do engineers, physicists concerned with thermodynamics, and the swarm of preoccupied draughtsmen tackle their work. In appearance, but only in appearance, they seem to be polishing surfaces and refining away angles, easing this joint or stabilizing that wing, rendering these parts invisible, so that in the end there is no longer a wing hooked to a framework but a form flawless in its perfection, completely disengaged from its matrix, a sort of spontaneous whole, its parts mysteriously fused together and resembling in their unity a poem.

Meanwhile, startling as it is that all visible evidence of invention should have been refined out of this instrument and that there should be delivered to us an object as natural as a pebble polished by the waves, it is equally wonderful that he who uses this instrument should be able to forget that it is a machine.

There was a time when a flyer sat at the centre of a complicated works. Flight set us factory problems. The indicators that oscillated on the instrument panel warned us of a thousand dangers. But in the machine of today we forget that motors are whirring: the motor, finally, has come to fulfil its function, which is to whirr as a heart beats—and we give no thought to the beating of our heart. Thus, precisely because it is perfect the machine dissembles its own existence instead of forcing itself upon our notice.

And thus, also, the realities of nature resume their pride of place. It is not with metal that the pilot is in contact. Contrary to the vulgar illusion, it is thanks to the metal, and by virtue of it, that the pilot rediscovers nature. As I have already said, the machine does not isolate man from the great problems of nature but plunges him more deeply into them.

Numerous, nevertheless, are the moralists who have

attacked the machine as the source of all the ills we bear, who, creating a fictitious dichotomy, have denounced the mechanical civilization as the enemy of the spiritual civilization.

If what they think were really so, then indeed we should have to despair of man, for it would be futile to struggle against this new advancing chaos. The machine is certainly as irresistible in its advance as those virgin forests that encroach upon equatorial domains. A congeries of motives prevents us from blowing up our spinning mills and reviving the distaff. Gandhi had a try at this sort of revolution: he was as simple-minded as a child trying to empty the sea on to the sand with the aid of a tea-cup.

It is hard for me to understand the language of these pseudo-dreamers. What is it makes them think that the ploughshare torn from the bowels of the earth by perforating machines, forged, tempered, and sharpened in the roar of modern industry, is nearer to man than any other tool of steel? By what sign do they recognize the inhumanity of the machine?

Have they ever really asked themselves this question? The central struggle of men has ever been to understand one another, to join together for the common weal. And it is this very thing that the machine helps them to do! It begins by annihilating time and space.

To me, in France, a friend speaks from America. The energy that brings me his voice is born of dammed-up waters a thousand miles from where he sits. The energy I burn up in listening to him is dispensed in the same instant by a lake formed in the River Yser which, four thousand miles from him and five hundred from me, melts like snow in the action of the turbines. Transport of the mails, transport of the human voice, transport of flickering pictures—in this century as in others our highest accomplishments still have the single aim of bringing men together. Do our dreamers hold that the invention of writing, of printing, of the sailing ship, degraded the human spirit?

It seems to me that those who complain of man's progress confuse ends with means. True, that man who struggles in the unique hope of material gain will harvest nothing worth while. But how can anyone conceive that the machine is an end? It is a tool. As much a tool as is the plough. The microscope is a tool. What disservice do we do the life of the spirit when we analyze the universe through a tool created by the science of optics, or seek to bring together those who love one another and are parted in space?

"Agreed!" my dreamers will say, "but explain to us why it is that a decline in human values has accompanied the rise of the machine?" Oh, I miss the village with its crafts and its folksongs as much as they do! The town fed by Hollywood seems to me, too, impoverished despite its electric street lamps. I quite agree that men lose their creative instincts when they are fed thus without raising a hand. And I can see that it is tempting to accuse industry of this evil.

But we lack perspective for the judgment of transformations that go so deep. What are the hundred years of the history of the machine compared with the two hundred thousand years of the history of man? It was only yesterday that we began to pitch our camp in this country of laboratories and power stations, that we took possession of this new, this still unfinished, house we live in. Everything round us is new and different—our concerns, our working habits, our relations with one another.

Our very psychology has been shaken to its foundations, to its most secret recesses. Our notions of separation, absence, distance, return, are reflections of a new set of realities, though the words themselves remain unchanged. To grasp the meaning of the world of today we use a language created to express the world of yesterday. The life of the past seems to us nearer our true natures, but only for the reason that it is nearer our language.

Every step on the road of progress takes us farther from habits which, as the life of man goes, we had only recently begun to acquire. We are in truth emigrants who have not yet founded our homeland. We Europeans have become again young peoples, without tradition or language of our own. We shall have to age somewhat before we are able to write the folksongs of a new epoch.

Young barbarians still marveling at our new toys—that is what we are. Why else should we race our planes, give prizes to those who fly highest, or fastest? We take no heed to ask ourselves why we race: the race itself is more important than the object.

And this holds true of other things than flying. For the colonial soldier who founds an empire, the meaning of life is conquest. He despises the colonist. But was not the very aim of his conquest the settling of this same colonist?

In the enthusiasm of our rapid mechanical conquests we have overlooked some things. We have perhaps driven men into the service of the machine, instead of building machinery for the service of man. But could anything be more natural? So long as we were engaged in conquest, our spirit was the spirit of conquerors. The time has now come when we must be colonists, must make this house habitable which is still without character.

Little by little the machine will become part of humanity. Read the history of the railways in France, and doubtless elsewhere too: they had all the trouble in the world to tame the people of our villages. The locomotive was an iron monster. Time had to pass before men forgot what it was made of. Mysteriously, life began to run through it, and now it is wrinkled and old. What is it today for the villager except a humble friend who calls every evening at six?

The sailing vessel itself was once a machine born of the calculations of engineers, yet it does not disturb our philosophers. The sloop took its place in the speech of men. There is a poetry of sailing as old as the world. There have always been seamen in recorded time. The man who assumes that there is an essential difference between the sloop and the airplane lacks historic perspective.

Every machine will gradually take on this patina and lose its identity in its function.

Air and water, and not machinery, are the concern of the hydroplane pilot about to take off. The motors are running free and the plane is already ploughing the surface of the sea. Under the dizzying whirl of the scythelike propellers, clusters of silvery water bloom and drown the flotation gear. The element smacks the sides of the hull with a sound like a gong, and the pilot can sense this tumult in the quivering of his body. He feels the ship charging itself with power as from second to second it picks up speed. He feels the development, in these fifteen tons of matter, of a maturity that is about to make flight possible. He closes his hands over the controls, and little by little in his bare palms he receives the gift of this power. The metal organs of the controls,

progressively as this gift is made him, become the mes-
sengers of the power in his hands. And when his power
is ripe, then, in a gesture gentler than the culling of a
flower, the pilot severs the ship from the water and establishes it in the air.

· 4 ·

The Elements

WHEN Joseph Conrad described a typhoon he said very little about towering waves, or darkness, or the whistling of the wind in the shrouds. He knew better. Instead, he took his reader down into the hold of the vessel, packed with emigrant coolies, where the rolling and the pitching of the ship had ripped up and scattered their bags and bundles, burst open their boxes, and flung their humble belongings into a crazy heap. Family treasures painfully collected in a lifetime of poverty, pitiful mementoes so alike that nobody but their owners could have told them apart, had lost their identity and lapsed into chaos, into anonymity, into an amorphous magma. It was this human drama that Conrad described when he painted a typhoon.

Every airline pilot has flown through tornadoes, has returned out of them to the fold—to the little restaurant in Toulouse where we sat in peace under the watchful eye of the waitress—and there, recognizing his powerlessness to convey what he has been through, has given up the idea of describing hell. His descriptions, his gestures, his big words would have made the rest of us smile as if we were listening to a little boy bragging. And necessarily so. The cyclone of which I am about to speak was, physically, much the most brutal and overwhelming experience I ever underwent; and yet beyond a certain point I do not know how to convey its violence except by piling one adjective on another, so that in the end I should convey no impression at all—unless perhaps that of an embarrassing taste for exaggeration.

It took me some time to grasp the fundamental reason for this powerlessness, which is simply that I should be trying to describe a catastrophe that never took place. The reason why writers fail when they attempt to evoke horror is that horror is something invented after the fact, when one is re-creating the experience over again in the memory. Horror does not manifest itself in the world of reality. And so, in beginning my story of a revolt of the elements which I myself lived through I have no feeling that I shall write something which you will find dramatic.

I had taken off from the field at Trelew and was flying down to Comodoro-Rivadavia, in the Patagonian Argentine. Here the crust of the earth is as dented as an old boiler. The high-pressure regions over the Pacific send the winds past a gap in the Andes into a corridor fifty miles wide through which they rush to the Atlantic in a strangled and accelerated buffeting that scrapes the surface of everything in their path. The sole vegetation visible in this barren landscape is a plantation of oil derricks looking like the after-effects of a forest fire. Towering over the round hills on which the winds have left a residue of stony gravel, there rises a chain of prow-shaped, saw-toothed, razor-edged mountains stripped by the elements down to the bare rock.

For three months of the year the speed of these winds at ground level is up to a hundred miles an hour. We who flew the route knew that once we had crossed the marshes of Trelew and had reached the threshold of the zone they swept, we should recognize the winds from afar by a grey-blue tint in the atmosphere at the sight of which we would tighten our belts and shoulder-straps in preparation for what was coming. From then on we had an hour of stiff fighting and of stumbling again and again into invisible ditches of air. This was manual labor, and our muscles felt it pretty much as if we had been carrying a longshoreman's load. But it lasted only an hour. Our machines stood up under it. We had no fear of wings suddenly dropping off. Visibility was generally good, and not a problem. This section of the line was a stint, yes; it was certainly not a drama.

But on this particular day I did not like the color of the sky.

The sky was blue. Pure blue. Too pure. A hard blue sky that shone over the scraped and barren world while the fleshless vertebrae of the mountain chain flashed in the sunlight. Not a cloud. The blue sky glittered like a new-honed knife. I felt in advance the vague distaste that accompanies the prospect of physical exertion. The purity of the sky upset me. Give me a good black storm in which the enemy is plainly visible. I can measure its extent and prepare myself for its attack. I can get my hands on my adversary. But when you are flying very high in clear weather the shock of a blue storm is as disturbing as if something collapsed that had been holding up your ship in the air. It is the only time when a pilot feels that there is a gulf beneath his ship.

Another thing bothered me. I could see on a level with the mountain peaks not a haze, not a mist, not a sandy fog, but a sort of ash-colored streamer in the sky. I did not like the look of that scarf of filings scraped off the surface of the earth and borne out to sea by the wind. I tightened my leather harness as far as it would go and I steered the ship with one hand while with the other I hung on to the longéron that ran alongside my seat. I was still flying in remarkably calm air.

Very soon came a slight tremor. As every pilot knows, there are secret little quiverings that foretell your real storm. No rolling, no pitching. No swing to speak of. The flight continues horizontal and rectilinear. But you have felt a warning drum on the wings of your plane, little intermittent rappings scarcely audible and infinitely brief, little cracklings from time to time as if there were traces of gunpowder in the air.

And then everything round me blew up.

Concerning the next couple of minutes I have nothing to say. All that I can find in my memory is a few rudimentary notions, fragments of thoughts, direct observations. I cannot compose them into a dramatic recital because there was no drama. The best I can do is to line them up in a kind of chronological order.

In the first place, I was standing still. Having banked right in order to correct a sudden drift, I saw the landscape freeze abruptly where it was and remain jiggling on the same spot. I was making no headway. My wings had ceased to nibble into the outline of the earth. I could see the earth buckle, pivot—but it stayed put. The plane was skidding as if on a toothless cogwheel.

Meanwhile I had the absurd feeling that I had exposed myself completely to the enemy. All those peaks, those crests, those teeth that were cutting into the wind and unleashing its gusts in my direction, seemed to me so many guns pointed straight at my defenseless person. I was slow to think, but the thought did come to me that I ought to give up altitude and make for one of the neighboring valleys where I might take shelter against a mountainside. As a matter of fact, whether I liked it or not I was being helplessly sucked down towards the earth.

Trapped this way in the first breaking waves of a cyclone about which I learned, twenty minutes later, that at sea level it was blowing at the fantastic rate of one hundred and fifty miles an hour, I certainly had no impression of tragedy. Now, as I write, if I shut my eyes, if I forget the plane and the flight and try to express the plain truth about what was happening to me, I find that I felt weighed down, I felt like a porter carrying a slippery load, grabbing one object in a jerky movement that sent another slithering down, so that, overcome by exasperation, the porter is tempted to let the whole load drop. There is a kind of law of the shortest distance to the image, a psychological law by which the event to which one is subjected is visualized in a symbol that represents its swiftest summing up: I was a man who, carrying a pile of plates, had slipped on a waxed floor and let his scaffolding of porcelain crash.

I found myself imprisoned in a valley. My discomfort was not less, it was greater. I grant you that a down current has never killed anybody, that the expression "flattened out by a down current" belongs to journalism and not to the language of flyers. How could air possibly pierce the ground? But here I was in a valley at the wheel of a ship that was three-quarters out of my control. Ahead of me a rocky prow swung to left and right, rose suddenly high in the air for a second like a wave over my head, and then plunged down below my horizon.

Horizon? There was no longer a horizon. I was in the wings of a theatre cluttered up with bits of scenery. Vertical, oblique, horizontal, all of plane geometry was awhirl. A hundred transversal valleys were muddled in a jumble of perspectives. Whenever I seemed about to take my bearings a new eruption would swing me round in a circle or send me tumbling wing over wing and I would have to try all over again to get clear of all this rubbish. Two ideas came into my mind. One was a discovery: for the first time I understood the cause of certain accidents in the mountains when no fog was present to explain them. For a single second, in a waltzing landscape like this, the flyer had been unable to distinguish between vertical mountainsides and horizontal planes. The other idea was a fixation: The sea is flat: I shall not hook anything out at sea.

I banked—or should I use that word to indicate a vague and stubborn jockeying through the east-west valleys? Still nothing pathetic to report. I was wrestling with chaos, was wearing myself out in a battle with chaos, struggling to keep in the air a gigantic house of cards that kept collapsing despite all I could do. Scarcely the faintest twinge of fear went through me when one of the walls of my prison rose suddenly like a tidal wave over my head. My heart hardly skipped a beat when I was tripped up by one of the whirling eddies of air that the sharp ridge darted into my ship. If I felt anything unmistakably in the haze of confused feelings and notions that came over me each time one of these powder magazines blew up, it was a feeling of respect. I respected that sharp-toothed ridge. I respected that peak. I respected that dome. I respected that transversal valley opening out into my valley and about to toss me God knew how violently as soon as its torrent of wind flowed into the one on which I was being borne along.

What I was struggling against, I discovered, was not the wind but the ridge itself, the crest, the rocky peak. Despite my distance from it, it was the wall of rock I was fighting with. By some trick of invisible prolongation, by the play of a secret set of muscles, this was what was pummeling me. It was against this that I was butting my head. Before me on the right I recognized the peak of Salamanca, a perfect cone which, I knew, dominated the sea. It cheered me to think I was about to escape out to sea. But first I should have to wrestle with the gale off that peak, try to avoid its down-crushing blow. The peak of Salamanca was a giant. I was filled with respect for the peak of Salamanca.

There had been granted me one second of respite. Two seconds. Something was collecting itself into a knot, coiling itself up, growing taut. I sat amazed. I opened astonished eyes. My whole plane seemed to be shivering, spreading outward, swelling up. Horizontal and stationary it was, yet lifted before I knew it fifteen hundred feet straight into the air in a kind of apotheosis. I who for forty minutes had not been able to climb higher than two hundred feet off the ground was suddenly able to look down on the enemy. The plane quivered as if in boiling water. I could see the wide waters of the ocean. The valley opened out into this ocean, this salvation.—And at that very moment, without any warning whatever, half a mile from Salamanca, I was suddenly struck straight in the midriff by the gale off that peak and sent hurtling out to sea.

There I was, throttle wide open, facing the coast. At right angles to the coast and facing it. A lot had happened in a single minute. In the first place, I had not flown out to sea. I had been spat out to sea by a monstrous cough, vomited out of my valley as from the mouth of a howitzer. When, what seemed to me instantly, I banked in order to put myself where I wanted to be in respect of the coast-line, I saw that the coast-line was a mere blur, a characterless strip of blue; and I was five miles out to sea. The mountain range stood up like a crenelated fortress against the pure sky while the cyclone crushed me down to the surface of the waters. How hard that wind was blowing I found out as soon as I tried to climb, as soon as I became conscious of my disastrous mistake: throttle wide open, engines running at my maximum, which was one hundred and fifty miles an hour, my plane hanging sixty feet over the water, I was unable to budge. When a wind like this one attacks a tropical forest it swirls through the branches like a flame, twists them into corkscrews, and uproots giant trees as if they were radishes. Here, bounding off the mountain range, it was leveling out the sea.

Hanging on with all the power in my engines, face to the coast, face to that wind where each gap in the teeth of the range sent forth a stream of air like a long reptile, I felt as if I were clinging to the tip of a monstrous whip that was cracking over the sea.

In this latitude the South American continent is narrow and the Andes are not far from the Atlantic. I was struggling not merely against the whirling winds that blew off the east-coast range, but more likely also against a whole sky blown down upon me off the peaks of the Andean chain. For the first time in four years of airline flying I began to worry about the strength of my wings. Also, I was fearful of bumping the sea—not because of the down currents which, at sea level, would necessarily provide me with a horizontal air mattress, but because of the helplessly acrobatic positions in which this wind was buffeting me. Each time that I was tossed I became afraid that I might be unable to straighten out. Besides, there was a chance that I should find myself out of fuel and simply drown. I kept expecting the gasoline pumps to stop priming, and indeed the plane was so violently shaken up that in the half-filled tanks as well as in the gas lines the gasoline was sloshing round, not coming through, and the engines, instead of their steady roar, were sputtering in a sort of dot-and-dash series of uncertain growls.

I hung on, meanwhile, to the controls of my heavy transport plane, my attention monopolized by the physical struggle and my mind occupied by the very simplest thoughts. I was feeling practically nothing as I stared down at the imprint made by the wind on the sea. I saw a series of great white puddles, each perhaps eight hundred yards in extent. They were running towards me at a speed of one hundred and fifty miles an hour where the down-surging windspouts broke against the surface of the sea in a succession of horizontal explosions. The sea was white and it was green—white with the whiteness of crushed sugar and green in puddles the color of emeralds. In this tumult one wave was indistinguishable from another. Torrents of air were pouring down upon the sea. The winds were sweeping past in giant gusts as when, before the autumn harvests, they blow a great flowing change of color over a wheatfield. Now and again the water went incongruously transparent between the white pools, and I could see a green and black sea-bottom. And then the great glass of the sea would be shattered anew into a thousand glittering fragments.

It seemed hopeless. In twenty minutes of struggle I had not moved forward a hundred yards. What was more, with flying as hard as it was out here five miles from the coast, I wondered how I could possibly buck the winds along the shore, assuming I was able to fight my way in. I was a perfect target for the enemy there on shore. Fear, however, was out of the question. I was incapable of thinking. I was emptied of everything except the vision of a very simple act. I must straighten out. Straighten out. Straighten out.

There were moments of respite, nevertheless. I dare say those moments themselves were equal to the worst storms I had hitherto met, but by comparison with the cyclone they were moments of relaxation. The urgency of fighting off the wind was not quite so great. And I could tell when these intervals were coming. It was not I who moved towards those zones of relative calm, those almost green oases clearly painted on the sea, but they that flowed towards me. I could read clearly in the waters the advertisement of a habitable province. And with each interval of repose the power to feel and to think was restored to me. Then, in those moments, I began to feel I was doomed. Then was the time that little by little I began to tremble for myself. So much so that each time I saw the unfurling of a new wave of the white offensive I was seized by a brief spasm of panic which lasted until the exact instant when, on the edge of that bubbling cauldron, I bumped into the invisible wall of wind. That restored me to numbness again.

Up! I wanted to be higher up. The next time I saw one of those green zones of calm it seemed to me deeper than before and I began to be hopeful of getting out. If I could climb high enough, I thought, I would find other currents in which I could make some headway. I took advantage of the truce to essay a swift climb. It was hard. The enemy had not weakened. Three hundred feet. Six hundred feet. If I could get up to three thousand feet I was safe, I said to myself. But there on the horizon I saw again that white pack unleashed in my direction. I gave it up. I did not want them at my throat again; I did not want to be caught off balance. But it was too late. The first blow sent me rolling over and over and the sky became a slippery dome on which I could not find a footing.

One has a pair of hands and they obey. How are one's orders transmitted to one's hands?

I had made a discovery that horrified me: my hands were numb. My hands were dead. They sent me no message. Probably they had been numb a long time and

I had not noticed it. The pity was that I had noticed it, had raised the question. That was serious.

Lashed by the wind, the wings of the plane had been dragging and jerking at the cables by which they were controlled from the wheel, and the wheel in my hands had not ceased jerking a single second. I had been gripping the wheel with all my might for forty minutes, fearful lest the strain snap the cables. So desperate had been my grip that now I could not feel my hands.

What a discovery! My hands were not my own. I looked at them and decided to lift a finger: it obeyed me. I looked away and issued the same order: now I could not feel whether the finger had obeyed or not. No message had reached me. I thought: "Suppose my hands were to open: how would I know it?" I swung my head round and looked again: my hands were still locked round the wheel. Nevertheless, I was afraid. How can a man tell the difference between the sight of a hand opening and the decision to open that hand, when there is no longer an exchange of sensations between the hand and the brain? How can one tell the difference between an image and an act of the will? Better stop thinking of the picture of open hands. Hands live a life of their own. Better not offer them this monstrous temptation. And I began to chant a silly litany which went on uninterruptedly until this flight was over. A single thought. A single image. A single phrase tirelessly chanted over and over again: "I shut my hands. I shut my hands. I shut my hands." All of me was condensed into that phrase and for me the white sea, the whirling eddies, the saw-toothed range ceased to exist. There was only "I shut my hands." There was no danger, no cyclone, no land unattained. Somewhere there was a pair of rubber hands which, once they let go the wheel, could not possibly come alive in time to recover from the tumbling drop into the sea.

I had no thoughts. I had no feelings except the feeling of being emptied out. My strength was draining out of me and so was my impulse to go on fighting. The engines continued their dot-and-dash sputterings, their little crashing noises that were like the intermittent cracklings of a ripping canvas. Whenever they were silent longer than a second I felt as if a heart had stopped beating. There! that's the end. No, they've started up again.

The thermometer on the wing, I happened to see, stood at twenty below zero, but I was bathed in sweat from head to foot. My face was running with perspiration. What a dance! Later I was to discover that my storage batteries had been jerked out of their steel flanges and hurtled up through the roof of the plane. I did not know then, either, that the ribs on my wings had come unglued and that certain of my steel cables had been sawed down to the last thread. And I continued to feel strength and will oozing out of me. Any minute now I should be overcome by the indifference born of utter weariness and by the mortal yearning to take my rest.

What can I say about this? Nothing. My shoulders ached. Very painfully. As if I had been carrying too many sacks too heavy for me. I leaned forward. Through a green transparency I saw sea-bottom so close that I could make out all the details. Then the wind's hand brushed the picture away.

In an hour and twenty minutes I had succeeded in climbing to nine hundred feet. A little to the south—that is, on my left—I could see a long trail on the surface of the sea, a sort of blue stream. I decided to let myself drift as far down as that stream. Here where I was, facing west, I was as good as motionless, unable either to advance or retreat. If I could reach that blue pathway, which must be lying in the shelter of something not the cyclone, I might be able to move in slowly to the coast. So I let myself drift to the left. I had the feeling, meanwhile, that the wind's violence had perhaps slackened.

It took me an hour to cover the five miles to shore. There in the shelter of a long cliff I was able to finish my journey south. Thereafter I succeeded in keeping enough altitude to fly inland to the field that was my destination. I was able to stay up at nine hundred feet. It was very stormy, but nothing like the cyclone I had come out of. That was over.

On the ground I saw a platoon of soldiers. They had

been sent down to watch for me. I landed near by and we were a whole hour getting the plane into the hangar. I climbed out of the cockpit and walked off. There was nothing to say. I was very sleepy. I kept moving my fingers, but they stayed numb. I could not collect my thoughts enough to decide whether or not I had been afraid. Had I been afraid? I couldn't say. I had witnessed a strange sight. What strange sight? I couldn't say. The sky was blue and the sea was white. I felt I ought to tell someone about it since I was back from so far away! But I had no grip on what I had been through. "Imagine a white sea . . . very white . . . whiter still." You cannot convey things to people by piling up adjectives, by stammering.

You cannot convey anything because there is nothing to convey. My shoulders were aching. My insides felt as if they had been crushed in by a terrible weight. You cannot make drama out of that, or out of the cone-shaped peak of Salamanca. That peak was charged like a powder magazine; but if I said so people would laugh. I would myself. I respected the peak of Salamanca. That is my story. And it is not a story.

There is nothing dramatic in the world, nothing pathetic, except in human relations. The day after I landed I might get emotional, might dress up my adventure by imagining that I who was alive and walking on earth was living through the hell of a cyclone. But that would be cheating, for the man who fought tooth and nail against that cyclone had nothing in common with the fortunate man alive the next day. He was far too busy.

I came away with very little booty indeed, with no more than this meagre discovery, this contribution: How can one tell an act of the will from a simple image when there is no transmission of sensation?

I could perhaps succeed in upsetting you if I told you some story of a child unjustly punished. As it is, I have involved you in a cyclone, probably without upsetting you in the least. This is no novel experience for any of us. Every week men sit comfortably at the cinema and look on at the bombardment of some Shanghai or other, some Guernica, and marvel without a trace of horror at the long fringes of ash and soot that twist their slow way into the sky from those man-made volcanoes. Yet we all know that together with the grain in the granaries, with the heritage of generations of men, with the treasures of families, it is the burning flesh of children and their elders that, dissipated in smoke, is slowly fertilizing those black cumuli.

The physical drama itself cannot touch us until some one points out its spiritual sense.

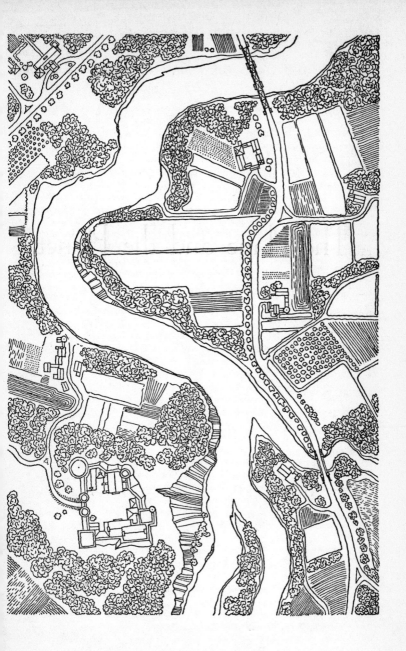

· 5 ·

The Plane and the Planet

THE airplane has unveiled for us the true face of the earth. For centuries, highways had been deceiving us. We were like that queen who determined to move among her subjects so that she might learn for herself whether or not they rejoiced in her reign. Her courtiers took advantage of her innocence to garland the road she traveled and set dancers in her path. Led forward on their halter, she saw nothing of her kingdom and could not know that over the countryside the famished were cursing her.

Even so have we been making our way along the

winding roads. Roads avoid the barren lands, the rocks, the sands. They shape themselves to man's needs and run from stream to stream. They lead the farmer from his barns to his wheatfields, receive at the thresholds of stables the sleepy cattle and pour them forth at dawn into meadows of alfalfa. They join village to village, for between villages marriages are made.

And even when a road hazards its way over the desert, you will see it make a thousand détours to take its pleasure at the oases. Thus, led astray by the divagations of roads, as by other indulgent fictions, having in the course of our travels skirted so many well-watered lands, so many orchards, so many meadows, we have from the beginning of time embellished the picture of our prison. We have elected to believe that our planet was merciful and fruitful.

But a cruel light has blazed, and our sight has been sharpened. The plane has taught us to travel as the crow flies. Scarcely have we taken off when we abandon these winding highways that slope down to watering troughs and stables or run away to towns dreaming in the shade of their trees. Freed henceforth from this happy servitude, delivered from the need of fountains, we set our course for distant destinations. And then, only, from the height of our rectilinear trajectories, do we discover the essential foundation, the fundament of rock and sand and salt in which here and there and from time to time life like a little moss in the crevices of ruins has risked its precarious existence.

We to whom humble journeyings were once permitted have now been transformed into physicists, biologists, students of the civilizations that beautify the depths of valleys and now and again, by some miracle, bloom like gardens where the climate allows. We are able to judge man in cosmic terms, scrutinize him through our portholes as through instruments of the laboratory. I remember a few of these scenes.

I

The pilot flying towards the Straits of Magellan sees below him, a little to the south of the Gallegos River, an ancient lava flow, an erupted waste of a thickness of sixty feet that crushes down the plain on which it has congealed. Farther south he meets a second flow, then a third; and thereafter every hump on the globe, every mound a few hundred feet high, carries a crater in its flank. No Vesuvius rises up to reign in the clouds; merely, flat on the plain, a succession of gaping howitzer mouths.

This day, as I fly, the lava world is calm. There is something surprising in the tranquillity of this deserted landscape where once a thousand volcanoes boomed to each other in their great subterranean organs and spat forth their fire. I fly over a world mute and abandoned, strewn with black glaciers.

South of these glaciers there are yet older volcanoes veiled with the passing of time in a golden sward. Here and there a tree rises out of a crevice like a plant out of a cracked pot. In the soft and yellow light the plain appears as luxuriant as a garden; the short grass seems to civilize it, and round its giant throats there is scarcely a swelling to be seen. A hare scampers off; a bird wheels in the air; life has taken possession of a new planet where the decent loam of our earth has at last spread over the surface of the star.

Finally, crossing the line into Chile, a little north of Punta Arenas, you come to the last of the craters, and here the mouths have been stopped with earth. A silky turf lies snug over the curves of the volcanoes, and all is suavity in the scene. Each fissure in the crust is sutured up by this tender flax. The earth is smooth, the slopes are gentle; one forgets the travail that gave them birth. This turf effaces from the flanks of the hillocks the sombre sign of their origin.

We have reached the most southerly habitation of the world, a town born of the chance presence of a little mud between the timeless lava and the austral ice. So near the black scoria, how thrilling it is to feel the miraculous nature of man! What a strange encounter! Who knows how, or why, man visits these gardens ready to hand, habitable for so short a time—a geologic age—for a single day blessed among days?

I landed in the peace of evening. Punta Arenas! I leaned against a fountain and looked at the girls in the square. Standing there within a couple of feet of their grace, I felt more poignantly than ever the human mystery.

In a world in which life so perfectly responds to life, where flowers mingle with flowers in the wind's eye, where the swan is the familiar of all swans, man alone builds his isolation. What a space between men their spiritual natures create! A girl's reverie isolates her from me, and how shall I enter into it? What can one know of a girl who passes, walking with slow steps homeward, eyes lowered, smiling to herself, filled with adorable inventions and with fables? Out of the thoughts, the voice, the silences of a lover, she can form an empire, and thereafter she sees in all the world but him a people of barbarians. More surely than if she were on another planet, I feel her to be locked up in her language, in her secret, in her habits, in the singing echoes of her memory. Born yesterday of the volcanoes, of greenswards, of brine of the sea, she walks here already half divine.

Punta Arenas! I lean against a fountain. Old women come up to draw water: of their drama I shall know nothing but these gestures of farm servants. A child, his head against a wall, weeps in silence: there will remain of him in my memory only a beautiful child forever inconsolable. I am a stranger. I know nothing. I do not enter into their empires. Man in the presence of man is as solitary as in the face of a wide winter sky in which there sweeps, never to be tamed, a flight of trumpeting geese.

How shallow is the stage on which this vast drama of human hates and joys and friendships is played! Whence do men draw this passion for eternity, flung by chance as they are upon a scarcely cooled bed of lava, threatened from the beginning by the deserts that are to be, and under the constant menace of the snows? Their civilizations are but fragile gildings: a volcano can blot them out, a new sea, a sand-storm.

This town seemed to be built upon a true humus, a soil one might imagine to be as rich as the wheatlands of the Beauce. These men live heedless of the fact that, here as elsewhere, life is a luxury; and that nowhere on the globe is the soil really rich beneath the feet of men.

Yet, ten miles from Punta Arenas there is a lake that ought to be reminding them of this. Surrounded by stunted trees and squat huts, as modest as a pool in a farm-yard, this lake is subject to the preternatural pull of the tides. Night and day, among the peaceful realities of swaying reeds and playing children, it performs its slow respiration, obedient to unearthly laws. Beneath the glassy surface, beneath the motionless ice, beneath the keel of the single dilapidated bark on the waters, the energy of the moon is at work. Ocean eddies stir in the depths of this black mass. Strange digestions take their peristaltic course there and down as far as the Straits of Magellan, under the thin layer of grasses and flowers. This lake that is a hundred yards wide, that laps the threshold of a town which seems to be built on man's own earth and where men believe themselves secure, beats with the pulse of the sea.

II

But by the grace of the airplane I have known a more extraordinary experience than this, and have been made to ponder with even more bewilderment the fact that this earth that is our home is yet in truth a wandering star.

A minor accident had forced me down in the Rio de Oro region, in Spanish Africa. Landing on one of those table-lands of the Sahara which fall away steeply at the sides, I found myself on the flat top of the frustrum of a cone, an isolated vestige of a plateau that had crumbled round the edges. In this part of the Sahara such truncated cones are visible from the air every hundred miles or so, their smooth surfaces always at about the same altitude above the desert and their geologic substance always identical. The surface sand is composed of minute and distinct shells; but progressively as you dig along a vertical section, the shells become more fragmentary, tend to cohere, and at the base of the cone form a pure calcareous deposit.

Without question, I was the first human being ever to wander over this . . . this iceberg: its sides were remarkably steep, no Arab could have climbed them, and no European had as yet ventured into this wild region.

I was thrilled by the virginity of a soil which no step of man or beast had sullied. I lingered there, startled by this silence that never had been broken. The first star began to shine, and I said to myself that this pure surface had lain here thousands of years in sight only of the stars.

But suddenly my musings on this white sheet and these shining stars were endowed with a singular significance. I had kicked against a hard, black stone, the size of a man's fist, a sort of moulded rock of lava incredibly present on the surface of a bed of shells a thousand feet deep. A sheet spread beneath an apple-tree can receive only apples; a sheet spread beneath the stars can receive only star-dust. Never had a stone fallen from the skies made known its origin so unmistakably.

And very naturally, raising my eyes, I said to myself that from the height of this celestial apple-tree there must have dropped other fruits, and that I should find them exactly where they fell, since never from the beginning of time had anything been present to displace them.

Excited by my adventure, I picked up one and then a second and then a third of these stones, finding them at about the rate of one stone to the acre. And here is where my adventure became magical, for in a striking foreshortening of time that embraced thousands of years, I had become the witness of this miserly rain from the stars. The marvel of marvels was that there on the rounded back of the planet, between this magnetic sheet and those stars, a human consciousness was present in which as in a mirror that rain could be reflected.

III

Once, in this same mineral Sahara, I was taught that a dream might partake of the miraculous. Again I had been forced down, and until day dawned I was helpless. Hillocks of sand offered up their luminous slopes to the moon, and blocks of shadow rose to share the sands with the light. Over the deserted work-yard of darkness and moonray there reigned a peace as of work suspended and a silence like a trap, in which I fell asleep.

When I opened my eyes I saw nothing but the pool of nocturnal sky, for I was lying on my back with outstretched arms, face to face with that hatchery of stars. Only half awake, still unaware that those depths were sky, having no roof between those depths and me, no branches to screen them, no root to cling to, I was seized with vertigo and felt myself as if flung forth and plunging downward like a diver.

But I did not fall. From nape to heel I discovered myself bound to earth. I felt a sort of appeasement in surrendering to it my weight. Gravitation had become as sovereign as love. The earth, I felt, was supporting my back, sustaining me, lifting me up, transporting me through the immense void of night. I was glued to our planet by a pressure like that with which one is glued to the side of a car on a curve. I leaned with joy against this admirable breast-work, this solidity, this security, feeling against my body this curving bridge of my ship.

So convinced was I that I was in motion, that I should have heard without astonishment, rising from below, a creaking of something material adjusting itself to the effort, that groaning of old sailing vessels as they heel, that long sharp cry drawn from pinnaces complaining of their handling. But silence continued in the layers of the earth, and this density that I could feel at my shoulders continued harmonious, sustained, unaltered through eternity. I was as much the inhabitant of this homeland as the bodies of dead galley-slaves, weighted with lead, were the inhabitants of the sea.

I lay there pondering my situation, lost in the desert and in danger, naked between sky and sand, withdrawn by too much silence from the poles of my life. I knew that I should wear out days and weeks returning to them if I were not sighted by some plane, or if next day the

Moors did not find and murder me. Here I possessed nothing in the world. I was no more than a mortal strayed between sand and stars, conscious of the single blessing of breathing. And yet I discovered myself filled with dreams.

They came to me soundlessly, like the waters of a spring, and in the beginning I could not understand the sweetness that was invading me. There was neither voice nor vision, but the presentiment of a presence, of a warmth very close and already half guessed. Then I began to grasp what was going on, and shutting my eyes I gave myself up to the enchantments of my memory.

Somewhere there was a park dark with firs and linden-trees and an old house that I loved. It mattered little that it was far away, that it could not warm me in my flesh, nor shelter me, reduced here to the rôle of dream. It was enough that it existed to fill my night with its presence. I was no longer this body flung up on a strand; I oriented myself; I was the child of this house, filled with the memory of its odors, with the cool breath of its vestibules, with the voices that had animated it, even to the very frogs in the pools that came here to be with me. I needed these thousand landmarks to identify myself, to discover of what absences the savor of this desert was composed, to find a meaning in this silence made of a thousand silences, where the very frogs were silent.

No, I was no longer lodged between sand and stars. I was no longer receiving from this scene its chill message. And I had found out at last the origin of the feeling of eternity that came over me in this wilderness. I had been wrong to believe it was part of sky and sand. I saw again the great stately cupboards of our house. Their doors opened to display piles of linen as white as snow. They opened on frozen stores of snow. The old housekeeper trotted like a rat from one cupboard to the next, forever counting, folding, unfolding, re-counting the white linen; exclaiming, "Oh, good Heavens, how terrible!" at each sign of wear which threatened the eternity of the house; running instantly to burn out her eyes under a lamp so that the woof of these altar cloths should be repaired, these three-master's sails be mended, in the service of something greater than herself—a god, a ship.

Ah, I owe you a page, Mademoiselle! When I came home from my first journeyings I found you needle in hand, up to the knees in your white surplices, each year a little more wrinkled, a little more round-shouldered, still preparing for our slumbers those sheets without creases, for our dinners those cloths without seams, those feasts of crystal and of snow.

I would go up to see you in your sewing-room, would sit down beside you and tell you of the dangers I had run in order that I might thrill you, open your eyes to the world, corrupt you. You would say that I hadn't changed a whit. Already as a child I had torn my shirts

—"How terrible!"—and skinned my knees, coming home as day fell to be bandaged.

No, Mademoiselle, no! I have not come back from the other end of the park but from the other end of the world! I have brought back with me the acrid smell of solitude, the tumult of sand-storms, the blazing moonlight of the tropics! "Of course!" you would say. "Boys *will* run about, break their bones and think themselves great fellows."

No, Mademoiselle, no! I have seen a good deal more than the shadows in our park. If you knew how insignificant these shadows are, how little they mean beside the sands, the granite, the virgin forests, the vast swamplands of the earth! Do you realize that there are lands on the globe where, when men meet you, they bring up their rifles to their cheeks? Do you know that there are deserts on earth where men lie down on freezing nights to sleep without roof or bed or snowy sheet? "What a wild lad!" you would say.

I could no more shake her faith than I could have shaken the faith of a candle-woman in a church. I pitied her humble destiny which had made her blind and deaf.

But that night in the Sahara, naked between the stars and the sand, I did her justice.

What is going on inside me I cannot tell. In the sky a thousand stars are magnetized, and I lie glued by the swing of the planet to the sand. A different weight brings me back to myself. I feel the weight of my body drawing me towards so many things. My dreams are more real than these dunes, than that moon, than these presences. My civilization is an empire more imperious than this empire. The marvel of a house is not that it shelters or warms a man, nor that its walls belong to him. It is that it leaves its trace on the language. Let it remain a sign. Let it form, deep in the heart, that obscure range from which, as waters from a spring, are born our dreams.

Sahara, my Sahara! You have been bewitched by an old woman at a spinning-wheel!

· 6 ·

Oasis

I HAVE already said so much about the desert that before speaking of it again I should like to describe an oasis. The oasis that comes into my mind is not, however, remote in the deep Sahara. One of the miracles of the airplane is that it plunges a man directly into the heart of mystery. You are a biologist studying, through your porthole, the human ant-hill, scrutinizing objectively those towns seated in their plain at the centre of their highways which go off like the spokes of a wheel and, like arteries, nourish them with the quintessence of the fields. A needle trembles on your manometer, and this green clump below you becomes a universe. You are the prisoner of a greensward in a slumbering park.

Space is not the measure of distance. A garden wall at home may enclose more secrets than the Great Wall of China, and the soul of a little girl is better guarded by silence than the Sahara's oases by the surrounding sands. I dropped down to earth once somewhere in the world. It was near Concordia, in the Argentine, but it might have been anywhere at all, for mystery is everywhere.

A minor mishap had forced me down in a field, and I was far from dreaming that I was about to live through a fairy-tale. The old Ford in which I was driven to town betokened nothing extraordinary, and the same was to be said for the unremarkable couple who took me in.

"We shall be glad to put you up for the night," they said.

But round a corner of the road, in the moonlight, I saw a clump of trees, and behind those trees a house. What a queer house! Squat, massive, almost a citadel guarding behind its tons of stone I knew not what treasure. From the very threshold this legendary castle promised an asylum as assured, as peaceful, as secret as a monastery.

Then two young girls appeared. They seemed astonished to see me, examined me gravely as if they had been two judges posted on the confines of a forbidden kingdom, and while the younger of them sulked and tapped the ground with a green switch, they were introduced:

"Our daughters."

The girls shook hands without a word but with a curious air of defiance, and disappeared. I was amused and I was charmed. It was all as simple and silent and furtive as the first word of a secret.

"The girls are shy," their father said, and we went into the house.

One thing that I had loved in Paraguay was the ironic grass that showed the tip of its nose between the pavements of the capital, that slipped in on behalf of the invisible but ever-present virgin forest to see if man still held the town, if the hour had not come to send all these stones tumbling.

I liked the particular kind of dilapidation which in Paraguay was the expression of an excess of wealth. But here, in Concordia, I was filled with wonder. Here everything was in a state of decay, but adorably so, like an old oak covered with moss and split in places with age, like a wooden bench on which generations of lovers had come to sit and which had grown sacred. The wainscoting was worn, the hinges rusted, the chairs rickety. And yet, though nothing had ever been repaired, everything had been scoured with zeal. Everything was clean, waxed, gleaming.

The drawing-room had about it something extraordinarily intense, like the face of a wrinkled old lady. The walls were cracked, the ceiling stripped; and most bewildering of all in this bewildering house was the floor:

it had simply caved in. Waxed, varnished and polished though it was, it swayed like a ship's gangway. A strange house, evoking no neglect, no slackness, but rather an extraordinary respect. Each passing year had added something to its charm, to the complexity of its visage and its friendly atmosphere, as well as to the dangers encountered on the journey from the drawing-room to the dining-room.

"Careful!"

There was a hole in the floor; and I was warned that if I stepped into it I might easily break a leg. This was said as simply as "Don't stroke the dog, he bites." Nobody was responsible for the hole, it was the work of time. There was something lordly about this sovereign contempt for apologies.

Nobody said, "We could have these holes repaired; we are well enough off; but . . ." And neither did they say—which was true enough—"we have taken this house from the town under a thirty-year lease. They should look after the repairs. But they won't, and we won't, so . . ." They disdained explanation, and this superiority to circumstance enchanted me. The most that was said was:

"The house is a little run down, you see."

Even this was said with such an air of satisfaction that I suspected my friends of not being saddened by the fact. Do you see a crew of bricklayers, carpenters, cabinet-workers, plasterers intruding their sacrilegious tools into so vivid a past, turning this in a week into a house you would never recognize, in which the family would feel that they were visiting strangers? A house without secrets, without recesses, without mysteries, without traps beneath the feet, or dungeons, a sort of town-hall reception room?

In a house with so many secret passages it was natural that the daughters should vanish before one's eyes. What must the attics be, when the drawing-room already contained all the wealth of an attic? When one could guess already that, the least cupboard opened, there would pour out sheaves of yellowed letters, grandpapa's receipted bills, more keys than there were locks and not one of which of course would fit any lock. Marvelously useless keys that confounded the reason and made it muse upon subterranean chambers, buried chests, treasures.

"Shall we go in to dinner?"

We went in to dinner. Moving from one room to the next I inhaled in passing that incense of an old library which is worth all the perfumes of the world. And particularly I liked the lamps being carried with us. Real lamps, heavy lamps, transported from room to room as in the time of my earliest childhood; stirring into motion as they passed great wondrous shadows on the walls. To pick one up was to displace bouquets of light and great black palms. Then, the lamps finally set down, there was a settling into motionlessness of the beaches of clarity and the vast reserves of surrounding darkness in which the wainscoting went on creaking.

As mysteriously and as silently as they had vanished, the girls reappeared. Gravely they took their places. Doubtless they had fed their dogs, their birds; had opened their windows on the bright night and breathed in the smell of the woods brought by the night wind. Now, unfolding their napkins, they were inspecting me cautiously out of the corners of their eyes, wondering whether or not they were going to make place for me among their domestic animals. For among others they had an iguana, a mongoose, a fox, a monkey, and bees. All these lived promiscuously together without quarreling in this new earthly paradise. The girls reigned over all the animals of creation, charming them with their little hands, feeding them, watering them, and telling them tales to which all, from mongoose to bees, gave ear.

I firmly expected that these alert young girls would employ all their critical faculty, all their shrewdness, in a swift, secret, and irrevocable judgment upon the male who sat opposite them.

When I was a child my sisters had a way of giving marks to guests who were honoring our table for the first time. Conversation might languish for a moment, and then in the silence we would hear the sudden impact of "Sixty!"—a word that could tickle only the family, who knew that one hundred was par. Branded by this low mark, the guest would all unknowing continue to spend himself in little courtesies while we sat screaming inwardly with delight.

Remembering that little game, I was worried. And it upset me a bit more to feel my judges so keen. Judges who knew how to distinguish between candid animals and animals that cheated; who could tell from the tracks of the fox whether he was in a good temper or not; whose instinct for inner movements was so sure and deep.

I liked the sharp eyes of these straightforward little souls, but I should so much have preferred that they play some other game. And yet, in my cowardly fear of their "sixty" I passed them the salt, poured out their wine; though each time that I raised my eyes I saw in their faces the gentle gravity of judges who were not to be bought.

Flattery itself was useless: they knew no vanity. Although they knew not it, they knew a marvelous pride, and without any help from me they thought more good of themselves than I should have dared utter. It did not even occur to me to draw any prestige from my craft, for it is extremely dangerous to clamber up to the topmost branches of a plane-tree simply to see if the nestlings are doing well or to say good morning to one's friends.

My taciturn young friends continued their inspection so imperturbably, I met so often their fleeting glances, that soon I stopped talking. Silence fell, and in that silence I heard something hiss faintly under the floor, rustle under the table, and then stop. I raised a pair of puzzled eyes. Thereupon, satisfied with her examination but applying her last touchstone, as she bit with savage young teeth into her bread the younger daughter explained to me with a candor by which she hoped to slaughter the barbarian (if that was what I was):

"It's the snakes."

And content, she said no more, as if that explanation should have sufficed for anyone in whom there remained a last glimmer of intelligence. Her sister sent a lightning glance to spy out my immediate reflex, and both bent with the gentlest and most ingenuous faces in the world over their plates.

"Ah! Snakes, are they?"

Naturally the words escaped from me against my will. This that had been gliding between my legs, had been brushing my calves, was snakes!

Fortunately for me, I smiled. Effortlessly. They would have known if it had been otherwise. I smiled because my heart was light, because each moment this house was more and more to my liking. And also because I wanted to know more about the snakes. The elder daughter came to my rescue.

"They nest in a hole under the table."

And her sister added: "They go back into their nest at about ten o'clock. During the day they hunt."

Now it was my turn to look at them out of the corner

of the eye. What shrewdness! what silent laughter behind those candid faces! And what sovereignty they exercised, these princesses guarded by snakes! Princesses for whom there existed no scorpion, no wasp, no serpent, but only little souls of animals!

As I write, I dream. All this is very far away. What has become of these two fairy princesses? Girls so fine-grained, so upright, have certainly attracted husbands. Have they changed, I wonder? What do they do in their new houses? Do they feel differently now about the jungle growth and the snakes? They had been fused with something universal, and then the day had come when the woman had awakened in the maiden, when there had surged in her a longing to find someone who deserved a "Ninety-five." The dream of a ninety-five is a weight on the heart.

And then an imbecile had come along. For the first time those sharp eyes were mistaken and they dressed him in gay colors. If the imbecile recited verse he was thought a poet. Surely he must understand the holes in the floor, must love the mongoose! The trust one put in him, the swaying of the snakes between his legs under the table—surely this must flatter him! And that heart which was a wild garden was given to him who loved only trim lawns. And the imbecile carried away the princess into slavery.

· 7 ·

Men of the Desert

THESE, then, were some of the treasures that passed us by when for weeks and months and years we, pilots of the Sahara line, were prisoners of the sands, navigating from one stockade to the next with never an excursion outside the zone of silence. Oases like these did not prosper in the desert; these memories it dismissed as belonging to the domain of legend. No doubt there did gleam in distant places scattered round the world—places to which we should return once our work was done—there did gleam lighted windows. No doubt somewhere there did sit young girls among their white lemurs or their books, patiently compounding souls as rich in delight as secret gardens. No doubt there did exist such creatures waxing in beauty. But solitude cultivates a strange mood.

I know that mood. Three years of the desert taught it to me. Something in one's heart takes fright, not at the thought of growing old, not at feeling one's youth used up in this mineral universe, but at the thought that far away the whole world is ageing. The trees have brought forth their fruit; the grain has ripened in the fields; the women have bloomed in their loveliness. But the season is advancing and one must make haste; but the season is advancing and still one cannot leave; but the season is advancing . . . and other men will glean the harvest.

Many a night have I savored this taste of the irreparable, wandering in a circle round the fort, our prison, under the burden of the trade-winds. Sometimes, worn out by a day of flight, drenched in the humidity of the tropical climate, I have felt my heart beat in me like the wheels of an express train; and suddenly, more immediately than when flying, I have felt myself on a journey. A journey through time. Time was running through my fingers like the fine sand of the dunes; the poundings of my heart were bearing me onward towards an unknown future.

Ah, those fevers at night after a day of work in the silence! We seemed to ourselves to be burning up, like flares set out in the solitude.

And yet we knew joys we could not possibly have

known elsewhere. I shall never be able to express clearly whence comes this pleasure men take from aridity, but always and everywhere I have seen men attach themselves more stubbornly to barren lands than to any other. Men will die for a calcined, leafless, stony mountain. The nomads will defend to the death their great store of sand as if it were a treasure of gold dust. And we, my comrades and I, we too have loved the desert to the point of feeling that it was there we had lived the best years of our lives. I shall describe for you our stations (Port Etienne, Villa Cisneros, Cape Juby, were some of their names) and shall narrate for you a few of our days.

I

I succumbed to the desert as soon as I saw it, and I saw it almost as soon as I had won my wings. As early as the year 1926 I was transferred out of Europe to the Dakar-Juby division, where the Sahara meets the Atlantic and where, only recently, the Arabs had murdered two of our pilots, Erable and Gourp. In those days our planes frequently fell apart in mid-air, and because of this the African divisions were always flown by two ships, one without the mails trailing and convoying the other, prepared to take over the sacks in the event the mail plane broke down.

Under orders, I flew an empty ship down to Agadir. From Agadir I was flown to Dakar as a passenger, and it was on that flight that the vast sandy void and the mystery with which my imagination could not but endow it first thrilled me. But the heat was so intense that despite my excitement I dozed off soon after we left Port Etienne. Riguelle, who was flying me down, moved out to sea a couple of miles in order to get away from the sizzling surface of sand. I woke up, saw in the distance the thin white line of the coast, and said to myself fearfully that if anything went wrong we should surely drown. Then I dozed off again.

I was startled out of my sleep by a crash, a sudden silence, and then the voice of Riguelle saying, "Damn! There goes a connecting rod!" As I half rose out of my seat to send a regretful look at that white coast-line, now more precious than ever, he shouted to me angrily to stay as I was. I knew Riguelle had been wrong to go out to sea; I had been on the point of mentioning it; and now I felt a complete and savage satisfaction in our predicament. "This," I said to myself, "will teach him a lesson."

But this gratifying sense of superiority could obviously not last very long. Riguelle sent the plane earthward in a long diagonal line that brought us within sixty feet of the sand—an altitude at which there was no question of picking out a landing-place. We lost both wheels against one sand-dune, a wing against another, and crashed with a sudden jerk into a third.

"You hurt?" Riguelle called out.

"Not a bit," I said.

"That's what I call piloting a ship!" he boasted cheerfully.

I who was busy on all fours extricating myself from what had once been a ship, was in no mood to feed his pride.

"Guillaumet will be along in a minute to pick us up," he added.

Guillaumet was flying our convoy, and very shortly we saw him come down on a stretch of smooth sand a few hundred yards away. He asked if we were all right, was told no damage had been done, and then proposed briskly that we give him a hand with the sacks. The mail transferred out of the wrecked plane, they explained to me that in this soft sand it would not be possible to lift Guillaumet's plane clear if I was in it. They would hop to the next outpost, drop the mail there, and come back for me.

Now this was my first day in Africa. I was so ignorant that I could not tell a zone of danger from a zone of safety, I mean by that, a zone where the tribes had submitted peacefully to European rule from a zone where the tribes were still in rebellion. The region in which we had landed happened to be considered safe, but I did not know that.

"You've got a gun, of course," Riguelle said.

I had no gun and said so.

"My dear chap, you'll have to have a gun," he said,

and very kindly he gave me his. "And you'll want these extra clips of cartridges," he went on. "Just bear in mind that you shoot at anything and everything you see."

They had started to walk across to the other plane when Guillaumet, as if driven by his conscience, came back and handed me his cartridge clips, too. And with this they took off.

I was alone. They knew, though I did not, that I could have sat on one of these dunes for half a year without running the least danger. What they were doing was to implant in the imagination of a recruit a proper feeling of solitude and danger and respect with regard to their desert. What I was really feeling, however, was an immense pride. Sitting on the dune, I laid out beside me my gun and my five cartridge clips. For the first time since I was born it seemed to me that my life was my own and that I was responsible for it. Bear in mind that only two nights before I had been dining in a restaurant in Toulouse.

I walked to the top of a sand-hill and looked round the horizon like a captain on his bridge. This sea of sand bowled me over. Unquestionably it was filled with mystery and with danger. The silence that reigned over it was not the silence of emptiness but of plotting, of imminent enterprise. I sat still and stared into space. The end of the day was near. Something half revealed yet wholly unknown had bewitched me. The love of the

Sahara, like love itself, is born of a face perceived and never really seen. Ever after this first sight of your new love, an indefinable bond is established between you and the veneer of gold on the sand in the late sun.

Guillaumet's perfect landing broke the charm of my musings.

"Anything turn up?" he wanted to know.

I had seen my first gazelle. Silently it had come into view. I felt that the sands had shown me the gazelle in confidence, so I said nothing about it.

"You weren't frightened?"

I said no and thought, gazelles are not frightening.

The mails had been dropped at an outpost as isolated as an island in the Pacific. There, waiting for us, stood a colonial army sergeant. With his squad of fifteen black troops he stood guard on the threshold of the immense expanse. Every six months a caravan came up out of the desert and left him supplies.

Again and again he took our hands and looked into our eyes, ready to weep at the sight of us. "By God, I'm glad to see you! You don't know what it means to me to see you!" Only twice a year he saw a French face, and that was when, at the head of the camel corps, either the captain or the lieutenant came out of the inner desert.

We had to inspect his little fort—"built it with my own hands"—and swing his doors appreciatively—"as solid as they make 'em"—and drink a glass of wine with him.

"Another glass. Please! You don't know how glad I am to have some wine to offer you. Why, last time the captain came round I didn't have any for the captain. Think of that! I couldn't clink glasses with the captain and wish him luck! I was ashamed of myself. I asked to be relieved, I did!"

Clink glasses. Call out, "Here's luck!" to a man, running with sweat, who has just jumped down from the back of a camel. Wait six months for this great moment. Polish up your equipment. Scour the post from cellar to attic. Go up on the roof day after day and scan the horizon for that dust-cloud that serves as the envelope in which will be delivered to your door the Atar Camel Corps. And after all this, to have no wine in the house! To be unable to clink glasses. To see oneself dishonored.

"I keep waiting for the captain to come back," the sergeant said.

"Where is he, sergeant?"

And the sergeant, waving his arm in an arc that took in the whole horizon, said: "Nobody knows. Captain is everywhere at once."

We spent the night on the roof of the outpost, talking about the stars. There was nothing else in sight. All the stars were present, all accounted for, the way you see them from a plane, but fixed.

When the night is very fine and you are at the stick

of your ship, you half forget yourself and bit by bit the plane begins to tilt on the left. Pretty soon, while you still imagine yourself in plumb, you see the lights of a village under your right wing. There are no villages in the desert. A fishing-fleet in mid-ocean, then? There are no fishing-fleets in mid-Sahara. What—? Of course! You smile at the way your mind has wandered and you bring the ship back to plumb again. The village slips into place. You have hooked that particular constellation back in the panoply out of which it had fallen. Village? Yes, village of stars.

The sergeant had a word to say about them. "I know the stars," he said. "Steer by that star yonder and you make Tunis."

"Are you from Tunis?"

"No. My cousin, she is."

A long silence. But the sergeant could not keep anything back.

"I'm going to Tunis one of these days."

Not, I said to myself, by making a bee-line for that star and tramping across the desert; that is, not unless in the course of some raid a dried-up well should turn the sergeant over to the poetry of delirium. If that happened, star, cousin, and Tunis would melt into one, and the sergeant would certainly be off on that inspired tramp which the ignorant would think of as torture.

He went on. "I asked the captain for leave to go to Tunis, seeing my cousin is there and all. He said . . ."

"What did the captain say, sergeant?"

"Said: 'World's full of cousins.' Said: 'Dakar's nearer' and sent me there."

"Pretty girl, your cousin?"

"In Tunis? You bet! Blonde, she is."

"No, I mean at Dakar."

Sergeant, we could have hugged you for the wistful disappointed voice in which you answered, "She was a nigger."

II

Port Etienne is situated on the edge of one of the unsubdued regions of the Sahara. It is not a town. There is a stockade, a hangar, and a wooden quarters for the French crews. The desert all round is so unrelieved that despite its feeble military strength Port Etienne is practically invincible. To attack it means crossing such a belt of sand and flaming heat that the razzias (as the bands of armed marauders are called) must arrive exhausted and waterless. And yet, in the memory of man there has always been, somewhere in the North, a razzia marching on Port Etienne. Each time that the army captain who served as commandant of the fort came to drink a cup of tea with us, he would show us its route on the map the way a man might tell the legend of a beautiful princess.

But the razzia never arrived. Like a river, it was each time dried up by the sands, and we called it the phantom razzia. The cartridges and hand grenades that the government passed out to us nightly would sleep peacefully in their boxes at the foot of our beds. Our surest protection was our poverty, our single enemy silence. Night and day, Lucas, who was chief of the airport, would wind his gramophone; and Ravel's *Bolero*, flung up here so far out of the path of life, would speak to us in a half-lost language, provoking an aimless melancholy which curiously resembled thirst.

One evening we had dined at the fort and the commandant had shown off his garden to us. Someone had sent him from France, three thousand miles away, a few boxes of real soil, and out of this soil grew three green leaves which we caressed as if they had been jewels. The commandant would say of them, "This is my park." And when there arose one of those sand-storms that shriveled everything up, he would move the park down into the cellar.

Our quarters stood about a mile from the fort, and after dinner we walked home in the moonlight. Under the moon the sands were rosy. We were conscious of our destitution, but the sands were rosy. A sentry called out, and the pathos of our world was re-established. The whole of the Sahara lay in fear of our shadows and called for the password, for a razzia was on the march. All the voices of the desert resounded in that sentry's challenge. No longer was the desert an empty prison: a Moorish caravan had magnetized the night.

We might believe ourselves secure; and yet, illness,

accident, razzia—how many dangers were afoot! Man inhabits the earth, a target for secret marksmen. The Senegalese sentry was there like a prophet of old to remind us of our destiny. We gave the password, *Français!* and passed before the black angel. Once in quarters, we breathed more freely. With what nobility that threat had endowed us! Oh, distant it still was, and so little urgent, deadened by so much sand; but yet the world was no longer the same. Once again this desert had become a sumptuous thing. A razzia that was somewhere on the march, yet never arrived, was the source of its glory.

It was now eleven at night. Lucas came back from the wireless and told me that the plane from Dakar would be in at midnight. All well on board. By ten minutes past midnight the mails would be transferred to my ship and I should take off for the North. I shaved carefully in a cracked mirror. From time to time, a Turkish towel hanging at my throat, I went to the door and looked at the naked sand. The night was fine but the wind was dropping. I went back again to the mirror. I was thoughtful.

A wind that has been running for months and then drops sometimes fouls the entire sky. I got into my harness, snapped my emergency lamps to my belt along with my altimeter and my pencils. I went over to Néri, who was to be my radio operator on this flight. He was shaving too. I said, "Everything all right?" For the moment everything was all right. But I heard something sizzling. It was a dragonfly knocking against the lamp. Why it was I cannot say, but I felt a twinge in my heart.

I went out of doors and looked round. The air was pure. A cliff on the edge of the airdrome stood in profile against the sky as if it were daylight. Over the desert reigned a vast silence as of a house in order. But here were a green butterfly and two dragonflies knocking against my lamp. And again I felt a dull ache which might as easily have been joy as fear but came up from the depths of me, so vague that it could scarcely be said to be there. Someone was calling to me from a great distance. Was it instinct?

Once again I went out. The wind had died down completely. The air was still cool. But I had received a warning. I guessed, I believed I could guess, what I was expecting. Was I right? Neither the sky nor the sand had made the least sign to me; but two dragonflies and a moth had spoken.

I climbed a dune and sat down face to the east. If I was right, the thing would not be long coming. What were they after here, those dragonflies, hundreds of miles from their oases inland? Wreckage thrown up on the strand bears witness to a storm at sea. Even so did these insects declare to me that a sand-storm was on the way, a storm out of the east that had blown them out of their oases.

Solemnly, for it was fraught with danger, the east wind rose. Already its foam had touched me. I was the extreme edge lapped by the wave. Fifty feet behind me no sail would have flapped. Its flame wrapped me round once, only once, in a caress that seemed dead. But I knew, in the seconds that followed, that the Sahara was catching its breath and would send forth a second sigh. And that before three minutes had passed the air-sock of our hangar would be whipped into action. And that before ten minutes had gone by the sand would fill the air. We should shortly be taking off in this conflagration, in this return of the flames from the desert.

But that was not what excited me. What filled me with a barbaric joy was that I had understood a murmured monosyllable of this secret language, had sniffed the air and known what was coming, like one of those primitive men to whom the future is revealed in such faint rustlings; it was that I had been able to read the anger of the desert in the beating wings of a dragonfly.

III

But we were not always in the air, and our idle hours were spent taming the Moors. They would come out of their forbidden regions (those regions we crossed in our flights and where they would shoot at us the whole length of our crossing), would venture to the stockade in the hope of buying loaves of sugar, cotton cloth, tea, and then would sink back again into their mystery. Whenever they turned up we would try to tame a few of them in order to establish little nuclei of friendship in the desert; thus if we were forced down among them there would be at any rate a few who might be persuaded to sell us into slavery rather than massacre us.

Now and then an influential chief came up, and him, with the approval of the Line, we would load into the plane and carry off to see something of the world. The aim was to soften their pride, for, repositories of the truth, defenders of Allah, the only God, it was more in contempt than in hatred that he and his kind murdered their prisoners.

When they met us in the region of Juby or Cisneros, they never troubled to shout abuse at us. They would merely turn away and spit; and this not by way of personal insult but out of sincere disgust at having crossed the path of a Christian. Their pride was born of the illusion of their power. Allah renders a believer invincible. Many a time a chief has said to me, pointing to his army of three hundred rifles, "Lucky it is for France that she lies more than a hundred days' march from here."

And so we would take them up for a little spin. Three of them even visited France in our planes. I happened to be present when they returned. I met them when they landed, went with them to their tents, and waited in infinite curiosity to hear their first words. They were of the same race as those who, having once been flown by me to the Senegal, had burst into tears at the sight of trees. What a revelation Europe must have been for them! And yet their first replies astonished me by their coolness.

"Paris? Very big."

Everything was "very big"—Paris, the Trocadéro, the automobiles.

What with everyone in Paris asking if the Louvre was not "very big" they had gradually learned that this was the answer that flattered us. And with a sort of vague contempt, as if pacifying a lot of children, they would grant that the Louvre was "very big."

These Moors took very little trouble to dissemble the freezing indifference they felt for the Eiffel Tower, the steamships, and the locomotives. They were ready to agree once and for always that we knew how to build things out of iron. We also knew how to fling a bridge from one continent to another. The plain fact was that they did not know enough to admire our technical progress. The wireless astonished them less than the telephone, since the mystery of the telephone resided in the very fact of the wire.

It took a little time for me to understand that my questions were on the wrong track. For what they thought admirable was not the locomotive, but the tree. When you think of it, a tree does possess a perfection that a locomotive cannot know. And then I remembered the Moors who had wept at the sight of trees.

Yes, France was in some sense admirable, but it was not because of those stupid things made of iron. They had seen pastures in France in which all the camels of Er-Reguibat could have grazed! There were forests in France! The French had cows, cows filled with milk! And of course my three Moors were amazed by the incredible customs of the people.

"In Paris," they said, "you walk through a crowd of a thousand people. You stare at them. And nobody carries a rifle!"

But there were better things in France than this inconceivable friendliness between men. There was the circus, for example.

"Frenchwomen," they said, "can jump standing from one galloping horse to another."

Thereupon they would stop and reflect.

"You take one Moor from each tribe," they went on. "You take him to the circus. And nevermore will the tribes of Er-Reguibat make war on the French."

I remember my chiefs sitting among the crowding tribesmen in the opening of their tents, savoring the pleasure of reciting this new series of Arabian Nights, extolling the music halls in which naked women dance on carpets of flowers.

Here were men who had never seen a tree, a river, a rose; who knew only through the Koran of the existence of gardens where streams run, which is their name for Paradise. In their desert, Paradise and its beautiful captives could be won only by bitter death from an infidel's rifle-shot, after thirty years of a miserable existence. But God had tricked them, since from the Frenchmen to whom he grants these treasures he exacts payment neither by thirst nor by death. And it was upon this that the chiefs now mused. This was why, gazing out at the Sahara surrounding their tents, at that desert with its barren promise of such thin pleasures, they let themselves go in murmured confidences.

"You know . . . the God of the French . . . He is more generous to the French than the God of the Moors is to the Moors."

Memories that moved them too deeply rose to stop their speech. Some weeks earlier they had been taken up into the French Alps. Here in Africa they were still dreaming of what they saw. Their guide had led them to a tremendous waterfall, a sort of braided column roaring over the rocks. He had said to them:

"Taste this."

It was sweet water. Water! How many days were they wont to march in the desert to reach the nearest well; and when they had arrived, how long they had to dig before there bubbled a muddy liquid mixed with camel's urine! Water! At Cape Juby, at Cisneros, at Port Etienne, the Moorish children did not beg for coins. With empty tins in their hands they begged for water.

"Give me a little water, give!"

"If you are a good lad . . ."

Water! A thing worth its weight in gold! A thing the least drop of which drew from the sand the green sparkle of a blade of grass! When rain has fallen anywhere, a great exodus animates the Sahara. The tribes ride towards that grass that will have sprung up two hundred miles away. And this water, this miserly water of which not a drop had fallen at Port Etienne in ten years, roared in the Savoie with the power of a cataclysm as if, from some burst cistern, the reserves of the world were pouring forth.

"Come, let us leave," their guide had said.

But they would not stir.

"Leave us here a little longer."

They had stood in silence. Mute, solemn, they had stood gazing at the unfolding of a ceremonial mystery. That which came roaring out of the belly of the mountain was life itself, was the life-blood of man. The flow of a single second would have resuscitated whole caravans that, mad with thirst, had pressed on into the eternity of salt lakes and mirages. Here God was manifesting Himself: it would not do to turn one's back on Him. God had opened the locks and was displaying His puissance. The three Moors had stood motionless.

"That is all there is to see," their guide had said. "Come."

"We must wait,"

"Wait for what?"

"The end."

They were awaiting the moment when God would grow weary of His madness. They knew Him to be quick to repent, knew He was miserly.

"But that water has been running for a thousand years!"

And this was why, at Port Etienne, they did not too strongly stress the matter of the waterfall. There were certain miracles about which it was better to be silent. Better, indeed, not to think too much about them, for in that case one would cease to understand anything at all. Unless one was to doubt the existence of God. . . .

"You see . . . the God of the Frenchmen . . ."

But I knew them well, my barbarians. There they sat, perplexed in their faith, disconcerted, and henceforth quite ready to acknowledge French overlordship. They were dreaming of being victualed in barley by the French administration, and assured of their security by our Saharan regiments. There was no question but that they would, by their submission, be materially better off.

But all three were of the blood of el Mammun.

I had known el Mammun when he was our vassal.

Loaded with official honors for services rendered, enriched by the French Government and respected by the tribes, he seemed to lack for nothing that belonged to the state of an Arab prince. And yet one night, without a sign of warning, he had massacred all the French officers in his train, had seized camels and rifles, and had fled to rejoin the refractory tribes in the interior.

Treason is the name given to these sudden uprisings, these flights at once heroic and despairing of a chieftain henceforth proscribed in the desert, this brief glory that will go out like a rocket against the low wall of European carbines. This sudden madness is properly a subject for amazement.

And yet the story of el Mammun was that of many other Arab chiefs. He grew old. Growing old, one begins to ponder. Pondering thus, el Mammun discovered one night that he had betrayed the God of Islam and had sullied his hand by sealing in the hand of the Christians a pact in which he had been stripped of everything.

Indeed what were barley and peace to him? A warrior disgraced and become a shepherd, he remembered a time when he had inhabited a Sahara where each fold in the sands was rich with hidden mysteries; where forward in the night the tip of the encampment was studded with sentries; where the news that spread concerning the movements of the enemy made all hearts beat faster round the night fires. He remembered a taste of the high seas which, once savored by man, is never forgotten. And because of his pact he was condemned to wander without glory through a region pacified and voided of all prestige. Then, truly and for the first time, the Sahara became a desert.

It is possible that he was fond of the officers he murdered. But love of Allah takes precedence.

"Good night, el Mammun."

"God guard thee!"

The officers rolled themselves up in their blankets and stretched out upon the sand as on a raft, face to the stars. High overhead all the heavens were wheeling slowly, a whole sky marking the hour. There was the moon, bending towards the sands, and the Frenchmen, lured by her tranquillity into oblivion, fell asleep. A few minutes more, and only the stars gleamed. And then, in order that the corrupted tribes be regenerated into their past splendor, in order that there begin again those flights without which the sands would have no radiance, it was enough that these Christians drowned in their slumber send forth a feeble wail. Still a few seconds more, and from the irreparable will come forth an empire.

And the handsome sleeping lieutenants were massacred.

IV

Today at Cape Juby, Kemal and his brother Mouyan have invited me to their tent. I sit drinking tea while Mouyan stares at me in silence. Blue sandveil drawn across his mouth, he maintains an unsociable reserve. Kemal alone speaks to me and does the honors:

"My tent, my camels, my wives, my slaves are yours."

Mouyan, his eyes still fixed on me, bends towards his brother, pronounces a few words, and lapses into silence again.

"What does he say?" I ask.

"He says that Bonnafous has stolen a thousand camels from the tribes of Er-Reguibat."

I have never met this Captain Bonnafous, but I know that he is an officer of the camel corps garrisoned at Atar and I have gathered from the Moors that to them he is a legendary figure. They speak of him with anger, but as of a sort of god. His presence lends price to the sand. Now once again, no one knows how, he has outflanked the southward marching razzias, taken them in the rear, driven off their camels by the hundred, and forced them to turn about and pursue him unless they are to lose those treasures which they had thought secure. And now, having saved Atar by this archangelic irruption and planted his camp upon a high limestone plateau, he stands there like a guerdon to be won, and such is his magnetism that the tribes are obliged to march towards his sword.

With a hard look at me, Mouyan speaks again.

"What now?" I ask.

"He says we are off tomorrow on a razzia against Bonnafous. Three hundred rifles."

I had guessed something of the sort. These camels led to the wells for three days past; these powwows; this fever running through the camp: it was as if men had been rigging an invisible ship. Already the air was filled with the wind that would take her out of port. Thanks to Bonnafous, each step to the South was to be a noble step rich in honor. It has become impossible to say whether love or hate plays the greater part in this setting forth of the warriors.

There is something magnificent in the possession of an enemy of Bonnafous' mettle. Where he turns up, the near-by tribes fold their tents, collect their camels and fly, trembling to think they might have found themselves face to face with him; while the more distant tribes are seized by a vertigo resembling love. They tear themselves from the peace of their tents, from the embraces of their women, from the happiness of slumber, for suddenly there is nothing in the world that can match in beauty, after two months of exhausting march, of burning thirst, of halts crouching under the sandstorm, the joy of falling unexpectedly at dawn upon the Atar camel corps and there, God willing, killing Captain Bonnafous.

"Bonnafous is very clever," Kemal avows.

Now I know their secret. Even as men who desire a woman dream of her indifferent footfall, toss and turn in the night, scorched and wounded by the indifference of that stroll she takes through their dream, so the distant progress of Bonnafous torments these warriors.

This Christian in Moorish dress at the head of his two hundred marauding cameleers, Moors themselves, outflanking the razzias hurled against him, has marched boldly into the country of the refractory tents where the least of his own men, freed from the constraint of the garrison, might with impunity shake off his servitude and sacrifice the captain to his God on the stony table-lands. He has gone into a world where only his prestige restrains his men, where his weakness itself is the cause of their dread. And tonight, through their raucous slumber he strolls to and fro with heedless step, and his footfall resounds in the innermost heart of the desert.

Mouyan ponders, still motionless against the back wall of the tent, like a block of blue granite cut in low relief. Only his eyes gleam, and his silver knife has ceased to be a plaything. I have the feeling that since becoming part of a razzia he has entered into a different world. To him the dunes are alive. The wind is charged with odors. He senses as never before his own nobility and crushes me beneath his contempt; for he is to ride against Bonnafous, he is to move at dawn impelled by a hatred that bears all the signs of love.

Once again he leans towards his brother, whispers, and stares at me.

"What is he saying?" I ask once again.

"That he will shoot you if he meets you outside the fort."

"Why?"

"He says you have airplanes and the wireless; you have Bonnafous; but you have not the Truth."

Motionless in the sculptured folds of his blue cloak, Mouyan has judged me.

"He says you eat greens like the goat and pork like the pigs. Your wives are shameless and show their faces —he has seen them. He says you never pray. He says, what good are your airplanes and wireless and Bonnafous, if you do not possess the Truth?"

And I am forced to admire this Moor who is not about to defend his freedom, for in the desert a man is always free; who is not about to defend his visible treasures, for the desert is bare; but who is about to defend a secret kingdom.

In the silence of the sand-waves Bonnafous leads his troop like a corsair of old; by the grace of Bonnafous the oasis of Cape Juby has ceased to be a haunt of idle shepherds and has become something as signal, as portentous, as admirable as a ship on the high seas. Bonnafous is a storm beating against the ship's side, and because of him the tent cloths are closed at night. How poignant is the southern silence! It is Bonnafous' silence. Mouyan, that old hunter, listens to his footfall in the wind.

When Bonnafous returns to France his enemies, far

from rejoicing, will bewail his absence, as if his depar-
ture had deprived the desert of one of its magnetic poles
and their existence of a part of its prestige. They will
say to me:

"Why does Bonnafous leave us?"

"I do not know."

For years he had accepted their rules as his rules. He
had staked his life against theirs. He had slept with his
head pillowed on their rocks. Like them he had known
Biblical nights of stars and wind in the course of the
ceaseless pursuit. And of a sudden he proves to them,
by the fact of leaving the desert, that he has not been
gambling for a stake he deemed essential. Unconcern-
edly, he throws in his hand and rises from the table.
And those Moors he leaves at their gambling lose confidence in the significance of a game which does not involve this man to the last drop of his blood. Still, they
try to believe in him:

"Your Bonnafous will come back."

"I do not know."

He will come back, they tell themselves. The games
of Europe will never satisfy him—garrison bridge, promotion, women, and the rest. Haunted by his lost honor
he will come back to this land where each step makes
the heart beat faster like a step towards love or towards
death. He had imagined that the Sahara was a mere adventure and that what was essential in life lay in Europe;
but he will discover with disgust that it was here in the

desert he possessed his veritable treasures—this prestige of the sand, the night, the silence, this homeland of wind and stars.

And if Bonnafous should come back one day, the news will spread in a single night throughout the country of the refractory tribes. The Moors will know that somewhere in the Sahara, at the head of his two hundred marauders, Bonnafous is again on the march. They will lead their dromedaries in silence to the wells. They will prepare their provisions of barley. They will clean and oil their breech-loaders, impelled by a hatred that partakes of love.

V

"Hide me in the Marrakech plane!"

Night after night, at Cape Juby, this slave would make his prayer to me. After which, satisfied that he had done what he could for his salvation, he would sit down upon crossed legs and brew my tea. Having put himself in the hands of the only doctor (as he believed) who could cure him, having prayed to the only god who might save him, he was at peace for another twenty-four hours.

Squatting over his kettle, he would summon up the simple vision of his past—the black earth of Marrakech, the pink houses, the rudimentary possessions of which he had been despoiled. He bore me no ill-will for my silence, nor for my delay in restoring him to life. I was not a man like himself but a power to be invoked, something like a favorable wind which one of these days might smile upon his destiny.

I, for my part, did not labor under these delusions concerning my power. What was I but a simple pilot, serving my few months as chief of the airport at Cape Juby and living in a wooden hut built over against the Spanish fort, where my worldly goods consisted of a basin, a jug of brackish water, and a cot too short for me?

"We shall see, Bark."

All slaves are called Bark, so Bark was his name. But despite four years of captivity he could not resign himself to it and remembered constantly that he had been a king.

"What did you do at Marrakech, Bark?"

At Marrakech, where his wife and three children were doubtless still living, he had plied a wonderful trade.

"I was a drover, and my name was Mohammed!"

The very magistrates themselves would send for him.

"Mohammed, I have some steers to sell. Go up into the mountains and bring them down."

Or:

"I have a thousand sheep in the plain. Lead them up into the higher pastures."

And Bark, armed with an olive-wood sceptre, governed their exodus. He and no other held sway over the nation of ewes, restrained the liveliest because of the lambkins about to be born, stirred up the laggards, strode forward in a universe of confidence and obedience. Nobody but him could say where lay the promised land towards which he led his flock. He alone could read his way in the stars, for the science he possessed was not shared by the sheep. Only he, in his wisdom, decided when they should take their rest, when they should drink at the springs. And at night while they slept, Bark, physician and prophet and king, standing in wool to the knees and swollen with tenderness for so much feeble ignorance, would pray for his people.

One day he was stopped by some Arabs.

"Come with us to fetch cattle up from the South," they said.

They had walked him a long time, and when, after three days, they found themselves deep in the mountains, on the borders of rebellion, the Arabs had quietly placed a hand on his shoulder, christened him Bark, and sold him into slavery.

He was not the only slave I knew. I used to go daily to the tents to take tea. Stretched out with naked feet on the thick woolen carpet which is the nomad's luxury and upon which for a time each day he builds his house, I would taste the happiness of the journeying hours. In the desert, as on shipboard, one is sensible of the passage of time. In that parching heat a man feels that the day is a voyage towards the goal of evening, towards the promise of a cool breeze that will bathe the limbs and wash away the sweat. Under the heat of the day beasts and men plod towards the sweet well of night as confidently as towards death. Thus, idleness here is never vain; and each day seems as comforting as the roads that lead to the sea.

I knew the slaves well. They would come in as soon as the chief had taken out the little stove, the kettle, and the glasses from his treasure chest—that chest heavy with absurd objects, with locks lacking keys, vases for non-existent flowers, threepenny mirrors, old weapons, things so disparate that they might have been salvaged from a ship cast up here in the desert.

Then the mute slave would cram the stove with twigs, blow on the embers, fill the kettle with water, and in this service that a child could perform, set into motion a play of muscles able to uproot a tree.

I would wonder what he was thinking of, and would sense that he was at peace with himself. There was no doubt that he was hypnotized by the motions he went through—brewing tea, tending the camels, eating. Under the blistering day he walked towards the night; and under the ice of the naked stars he longed for the return of day. Happy are the lands of the North whose seasons are poets, the summer composing a legend of snow, the winter a tale of sun. Sad the tropics, where in the sweating-room nothing changes very much. But happy also the Sahara where day and night swing man so evenly from one hope to the other.

Tea served, the black will squat outside the tent, relishing the evening wind. In this sluggish captive hulk, memories have ceased to swarm. Even the moment when he was carried off is faint in his mind—the blows, the shouts, the arms of men that brought him down into his present night. And since that hour he has sunk deeper and deeper into a queer slumber, divested like a blind man of his Senegalese rivers or his white Moroccan towns, like a deaf man of the sound of familiar voices.

This black is not unhappy; he is crippled. Dropped down one day into the cycle of desert life, bound to the nomadic migrations, chained for life to the orbits they describe in the sand, how could he retain any memory of a past, a home, a wife and children, all of them for him as dead as the dead?

Men who have lived for years with a great love, and have lived on in noble solitude when it was taken from them, are likely now and then to be worn out by their exaltation. Such men return humbly to a humdrum life, ready to accept contentment in a more commonplace love. They find it sweet to abdicate, to resign themselves to a kind of servility and to enter into the peace of things. This black is proud of his master's embers.

Like a ship moving into port, we of the desert come up into the night. In this hour, because it is the hour when all the weariness of day is remitted and its heats have ceased, when master and slave enter side by side into the cool of evening, the master is kind to the slave.

"Here, take this," the chief says to the captive.

He allows him a glass of tea. And the captive, overcome with gratitude for a glass of tea, would kiss his master's knees. This man before me is not weighed down with chains. How little need he has of them! How faithful he is! How submissively he forswears the deposed king within him! Truly, the man is a mere contented slave.

And yet the day will come when he will be set free. When he has grown too old to be worth his food or his cloak, he will be inconceivably free. For three days he will offer himself in vain from tent to tent, growing each day weaker; until towards the end of the third day, still uncomplaining, he will lie down on the sand.

I have seen them die naked like this at Cape Juby. The Moors jostle their long death-struggle, though without ill intent; and the children play in the vicinity of the dark wreck, running with each dawn to see if it is still stirring, yet without mocking the old servitor. It is all in the nature of things. It is as if they had said to him: "You have done a good day's work and have the right to sleep. Go to bed."

And the old slave, still outstretched, suffers hunger which is but vertigo, and not injustice which alone is torment. Bit by bit he becomes one with the earth, is shriveled up by the sun and received by the earth.

Thirty years of toil, and then this right to slumber and to the earth.

The first one I saw did not moan; but then he had no one to moan against. I felt in him an obscure acquiescence, as of a mountaineer lost and at the end of his strength who sinks to earth and wraps himself up in dreams and snow. What was painful to me was not his suffering (for I did not believe he was suffering); it was that for the first time it came on me that when a man dies, an unknown world passes away.

I could not tell what visions were vanishing in the dying slave, what Senegalese plantations or white Moroccan towns. It was impossible for me to know whether, in this black heap, there was being extinguished merely a world of petty cares in the breast of a slave— the tea to be brewed, the camels watered; or whether, revived by a surge of memories, a man lay dying in the glory of humanity. The hard bone of his skull was in a sense an old treasure chest; and I could not know what colored stuffs, what images of festivities, what vestiges, obsolete and vain in this desert, had here escaped the shipwreck.

The chest was there, locked and heavy. I could not know what bit of the world was crumbling in this man during the gigantic slumber of his ultimate days, was disintegrating in this consciousness and this flesh which little by little was reverting to night and to root.

"I was a drover, and my name was Mohammed!"

Before I met Bark I had never met a slave who offered the least resistance. That the Moors had violated his freedom, had in a single day stripped him as naked as a newborn infant, was not the point. God sometimes sends cyclones which in a single hour wipe out a man's harvests. But deeper than his belongings, these Moors had threatened him in his very essence.

Many another captive would have resigned himself to the death in him of the poor herdsman who toiled the year round for a crust of bread. Not so Bark. He refused to settle into a life of servitude, to surrender to the weariness of waiting and resign himself to a passive contentment. He rejected the slave-joys that are contingent upon the kindness of the slave-owner. Within his breast Mohammed absent held fast to the house Mohammed had lived in. That house was sad for being empty, but none other should live in it. Bark was like one of those white-haired caretakers who die of their fidelity in the weeds of the paths and the tedium of silence.

He never said, "I am Mohammed ben Lhaoussin"; he said, "My name was Mohammed," dreaming of the day when that obliterated figure would again live within him in all its glory and by the power of its resuscitation would drive out the ghost of the slave.

There were times when, in the silence of the night, all his memories swept over him with the poignancy of a song of childhood. Our Arab interpreter said to me, "In the middle of the night he woke up and talked about Marrakech; and he wept." No man in solitude can escape these recurrences. The old Mohammed awoke in him without warning, stretched himself in his limbs, sought his wife against his flank in this desert where no woman had ever approached Bark, and listened to the water purling in the fountains here where no fountain ran.

And Bark, his eyes shut, sitting every night under the same star, in a place where men live in houses of hair and follow the wind, told himself that he was living in his white house in Marrakech. His body charged with tenderness and mysteriously magnetized, as if the pole of these emotions were very near at hand, Bark would come to see me. He was trying to let me know that he was ready, that his over-full heart was quivering on the brim and needed only to find itself back in Marrakech to be poured out. And all that was wanted was a sign from me. Bark would smile, would whisper to me how it could be done—for of course I should not have thought of this dodge:

"The mails leave tomorrow. You stow me away in the Marrakech plane."

"Poor old Bark!"

We were stationed among the unsubdued tribes, and how could we help him away? God knows what massacre the Moors would have done among us that very day to avenge the insult of this theft. I had, indeed, tried

to buy him, with the help of the mechanics at the port—
Laubergue, Marchal, and Abgrall. But it was not every
day that the Moors met Europeans in quest of a slave,
and they took advantage of the occasion.

"Twenty thousand francs."

"Don't make me laugh!"

"But look at those strong arms. . . ."

Months passed before the Moors came down to a
reasonable figure and I, with the help of friends at home
to whom I had written, found myself in a position to
buy old Bark. There was a week of bargaining which
we spent, fifteen Moors and I, sitting in a circle in the
sand. A friend of Bark's master who was also my friend,
Zin Ould Rhattari, a bandit, was privately on my side.

"Sell him," he would argue in accordance with my
coaching. "You will lose him one of these days, you
know. Bark is a sick man. He is diseased. You can't see
yet, but he is sick inside. One of these days he will swell
right up. Sell him as soon as you can to the Frenchman."

I had promised fifty Spanish pesetas to another bandit,
Raggi, and Raggi would say:

"With the money you get for Bark you will be able
to buy camels and rifles and cartridges. Then you can
go off on a razzia against these French. Go down to
Atar and bring back three or four young Senegalese.
Get rid of the old carcass."

And so Bark was sold to me. I locked him up for six

days in our hut, for if he had wandered out before the arrival of a plane the Moors would surely have kidnapped him. Meanwhile, although I would not allow him out, I set him free with a flourish of ceremony in the presence of three Moorish witnesses. One was a local marabout, another was Ibrahim, the mayor of Cape Juby, and the third was his former owner. These three pirates, who would gladly have cut off Bark's head within fifty feet of the fort for the sole pleasure of doing me in the eye, embraced him warmly and signed the official act of manumission. That done, they said to him:

"You are now our son."

He was my son, too, by law. Dutifully, Bark embraced all his fathers.

He lived on in our hut in comfortable captivity until we could ship him home. Over and over again, twenty times a day, he would ask to have the simple journey described. We were flying him to Agadir. There he would be given an omnibus ticket to Marrakech. He was to be sure not to miss the bus. That was all there was to it. But Bark played at being free the way a child plays at being an explorer, going over and over this journey back to life—the bus, the crowds, the towns he would pass through.

One day Laubergue came to talk to me about Bark. He said that Marchal and Abgrall and he rather felt it would be a shame if Bark was flung into the world without a copper. They had made up a purse of a thousand francs: didn't I think that would see Bark through till he found work? I thought of all the old ladies who run charities and insist upon gratitude in exchange for every twenty francs they part with. These airplane mechanics were parting with a thousand francs, had no thought of charity, and were even less concerned about gratitude.

Nor were they acting out of pity, like those old ladies who want to believe they are spreading happiness. They were contributing simply to restore to a man his lost dignity as a human being. They knew quite as well as anybody else that once the initial intoxication of his homecoming was past, the first faithful friend to step up and take Bark's hand would be Poverty; and that before three months had gone by he would be tearing up sleepers somewhere on the railway line for a living. He was sure to be less well off there than here in the desert. But in their view he had the right to live his life among his own people.

"Good-by, old Bark. Be a man!"

The plane quivered, ready to take off. Bark took his last look at the immense desolation of Cape Juby. Round the plane two hundred Moors were finding out what a slave looked like when he stood on the threshold of life. They would make no bones about snatching him back again if a little later the ship happened to be forced down.

We stood about our fifty-year-old, new-born babe, worried a little at having launched him forth on the stream of life.

"Good-by, Bark!"

"No!"

"What do you mean?"

"No. I am Mohammed ben Lhaoussin."

The last news we had of him was brought back to us by Abdullah who at our request had looked after Bark at Agadir. The plane reached Agadir in the morning, but the bus did not leave until evening. This was how Bark spent his day.

He began by wandering through the town and remaining silent so long that his restlessness upset Abdullah.

"Anything the matter?"

"No."

This freedom had come too suddenly: Bark was finding it hard to orient himself. There was a vague happiness in him, but with this exception there was scarcely any difference between the Bark of yesterday and the Bark of today. Yet he had as much right to the sun, henceforth, as other men; as much right as they to sit in the shade of an Arab café.

He sat down and ordered tea for Abdullah and himself. This was his first lordly gesture, a manifestation of a power that ought to have transfigured him in other men's eyes. But the waiter poured his tea quite without surprise, quite unaware that in this gesture he was doing homage to a free man.

"Let us go somewhere else," Bark had said; and they had gone off to the Kasbah, the licensed quarter of the town. The little Berber prostitutes came up and greeted them, so kind and tame that here Bark felt he might be coming alive.

These girls were welcoming a man back to life, but they knew nothing of this. They took him by the hand, offered him tea, then love, very nicely; but exactly as they would have offered it to any man. Bark, preoccupied with his message, tried to tell them the story of his resurrection. They smiled most sympathetically. They were glad for him, since he was glad. And to make the wonder more wonderful he added, "I am Mohammed ben Lhaoussin."

But that was no surprise to them. All men have names, and so many return from afar! They could guess, nevertheless, that this man had suffered, and they strove to be as gentle as possible with the poor black devil. He appreciated their gentleness, this first gift that life was making him; but his restlessness was yet not stilled. He had not yet rediscovered his empire.

Back to town went Bark and Abdullah. He idled in front of the Jewish shops, stared at the sea, repeated to himself that he could walk as he pleased in any direction, that he was free. But this freedom had in it a taste of bitterness: what he learned from it with most intensity was that he had no ties with the world.

At that moment a child had come up. Bark stroked the soft cheek. The child smiled. This was not one of the master's children that one had to flatter. It was a sickly child whose cheek Bark was stroking. And the child was smiling at him. The child awoke something in Bark, and Bark felt himself more important on earth because of the sickly child whose smile was his due. He began to sense confusedly that something was stirring within him, was striding forward with swift steps.

"What are you looking for?" Abdullah had asked him.

"Nothing," was again Bark's answer.

But when, rounding a corner, he came upon a group of children at play, he stopped. This was it. He stared at them in silence. Then he went off to the Jewish shops and came back laden with treasure. Abdullah was nettled:

"Fool! Throwing away your money!"

Bark gave no heed. Solemnly he beckoned to each child in turn, and the little hands rose towards the toys and the bangles and the gold-sewn slippers. Each child, as soon as he had a firm grip on his treasure, fled like a wild thing, and Bark went back to the Jewish shops.

Other children in Agadir, hearing the news, ran after him; and these too were shod by Bark in golden slippers. The tale spread to the outskirts of Agadir, whence still other children scurried into town and clustered round the black god, clinging to his threadbare cloak and clamoring for their due. Bark, that victim of a sombre joy, spent on them his last copper.

Abdullah was sure that he had gone mad, "mad with joy," he said afterward. But I incline to believe that Bark was not sharing with others an overflow of happiness. He was free, and therefore he possessed the essential of wealth—the right to the love of Berber girls, to go north or south as he pleased, to earn his bread by his toil. What good was this money when the thing for which he was famished was to be a man in the family of men, bound by ties to other men?

The town prostitutes had been kind to old Bark, but he had been able to get away from them as easily as he had come to them: they had no need of him. The waiter in the café, the passers-by in the streets, the shopkeepers, had respected the free man he was, sharing their sun with him on terms of equality; but none of them had indicated that he needed Bark.

He was free, but too infinitely free; not striding upon the earth but floating above it. He felt the lack in him of that weight of human relations that trammels a man's progress; tears, farewells, reproaches, joys—all those things that a man caresses or rips apart each time he sketches a gesture; those thousand ties that bind him to others and lend density to his being. But already Bark was in ballast of a thousand hopes.

And so the reign of Bark began in the glory of the sun setting over Agadir, in that evening coolness that so long had been for him the single sweetness, the unique stall in which he could take his rest. And as the hour of leaving approached, Bark went forward lapped in this tide of children as once in his sea of ewes, ploughing his first furrow in the world. He would go back next day to the poverty of his family, to responsibility for more lives than perhaps his old arms would be able to sustain; but already, among these children, he felt the pull of his true weight. Like an archangel too airy to live the life of man, but who had cheated, had sewn lead into his girdle, Bark dragged himself forward, pulling against the pull of a thousand children who had such great need of golden slippers.

Such is the desert. A Koran which is but a handbook of the rules of the game transforms its sands into an empire. Deep in the seemingly empty Sahara a secret drama is being played that stirs the passions of men. The true life of the desert is not made up of the marches of tribes in search of pasture, but of the game that goes endlessly on. What a difference in substance between the sands of submission and the sands of unruliness! The dunes, the salines, change their nature according as the code changes by which they are governed.

And is not all the world like this? Gazing at this transfigured desert I remember the games of my childhood—the dark and golden park we peopled with gods; the limitless kingdom we made of this square mile never thoroughly explored, never thoroughly charted. We created a secret civilization where footfalls had a meaning and things a savor known in no other world.

And when we grow to be men and live under other laws, what remains of that park filled with the shadows of childhood, magical, freezing, burning? What do we learn when we return to it and stroll with a sort of despair along the outside of its little wall of gray stone, marveling that within a space so small we should have founded a kingdom that had seemed to us infinite—what do we learn except that in this infinity we shall never again set foot, and that it is into the game and not the park that we have lost the power to enter?

· 8 ·

Prisoner of the Sand

AFTER three years of life in the desert, I was transferred out. The fortunes of the air service sent me wandering here and there until one day I decided to attempt a long-distance flight from Paris to Saïgon. When, on December 29, 1935, I took off, I had no notion that the sands were preparing for me their ultimate and culminating ordeal.

This is the story of the Paris-Saïgon flight.

I paid my final visit to the weather bureau, where I found Monsieur Viaud stooped over his maps like a medieval alchemist over an alembic. Lucas had come with me, and we stared together at the curving lines marking the new-sprung winds. With their tiny flying arrows, they put me in mind of curving tendrils studded with thorns. All the atmospheric depressions of the world were charted on this enormous map, ochre-colored, like the earth of Asia.

"Here is a storm that we'll not hear from before Monday," Monsieur Viaud pointed out.

Over Russia and the Scandinavian peninsula the swirling lines took the form of a coiled demon. Out in Iraq, in the neighborhood of Basra, an imp was whirling.

"That fellow worries me a little," said Monsieur Viaud.

"Sand-storm, is it?"

I was not being idly curious. Day would not yet be breaking when I reached Basra and I was fearful of flying at night in one of those desert storms that turn the sky into a yellow furnace and wipe out hills, towns, and river-banks, drowning earth and sky in one great conflagration. It would be bad enough to fly in daylight through a chaos in which the very elements themselves were indistinguishable.

"Sand-storm? No, not exactly."

"So much the better," I said to myself, and I looked round the room. I liked this laboratory atmosphere. Viaud, I felt, was a man escaped from the world. When he came in here and hung up his hat and coat on the peg, he hung up with them all the confusion in which the rest of mankind lived. Family cares, thoughts of income, concerns of the heart—all that vanished on the threshold of this room as at the door of a hermit's cell, or an astronomer's tower, or a radio operator's shack. Here was one of those men who are able to lock themselves up in the secrecy of their retreat and hold discourse with the universe.

Gently, for he was reflecting, Monsieur Viaud rubbed the palms of his hands together.

"No, not a sand-storm. See here."

His finger traveled over the map and pointed out why.

At four in the morning Lucas shook me into consciousness.

"Wake up!"

And before I could so much as rub my eyes he was saying, "Look here, at this report. Look at the moon. You won't see much of her tonight. She's new, not very bright, and she'll set at ten o'clock. And here's something else for you: sunrise in Greenwich Meridian Time and in local time as well. And here: here are your maps, with your course all marked out. And here—"

"—is your bag packed for Saïgon," my wife broke in.

A razor and a change of shirt. He who would travel happily must travel light.

We got into a car and motored out to Le Bourget while Fate spying in ambush put the finishing touches to her plans. Those favorable winds that were to wheel in the heavens, that moon that was to sink at ten o'clock, were so many strategic positions at which Fate was assembling her forces.

It was cold at the airport, and dark. The *Simoon* was wheeled out of her hangar. I walked round my ship, stroking her wings with the back of my hand in a caress that I believe was love. Eight thousand miles I had flown in her, and her engines had not skipped a beat; not a bolt in her had loosened. This was the marvel that was to save our lives the next night by refusing to be ground to powder on meeting the upsurging earth.

Friends had turned up. Every long flight starts in the same atmosphere, and nobody who has experienced it once would ever have it otherwise: the wind, the drizzle at daybreak, the engines purring quietly as they are warmed up; this instrument of conquest gleaming in her fresh coat of "dope"—all of it goes straight to the heart.

Already one has a foretaste of the treasures about to be garnered on the way—the green and brown and yellow lands promised by the maps; the rosary of resounding names that make up the pilot's beads; the hours to be picked up one by one on the eastward flight into the sun.

There is a particular flavor about the tiny cabin in which, still only half awake, you stow away your thermos flasks and odd parts and over-night bag; in the fuel tanks heavy with power; and best of all, forward, in the magical instruments set like jewels in their panel and glimmering like a constellation in the dark of night. The mineral glow of the artificial horizon, these stethoscopes designed to take the heart-beat of the heavens, are things a pilot loves. The cabin of a plane is a world unto itself, and to the pilot it is home.

I took off, and though the load of fuel was heavy, I got easily away. I avoided Paris with a jerk and up the Seine, at Melun, I found myself flying very low between showers of rain. I was heading for the valley of the Loire. Nevers lay below me, and then Lyon. Over the Rhône I was shaken up a bit. Mt. Ventoux was capped in snow. There lies Marignane and here comes Marseille.

The towns slipped past as in a dream. I was going so far—or thought I was going so far—that these wretched little distances were covered before I was aware of it. The minutes were flying. So much the better. There are times when, after a quarter-hour of flight, you look at your watch and find that five minutes have gone by; other days when the hands turn a quarter of an hour in the wink of an eye. This was a day when time was flying. A good omen. I started out to sea.

Very odd, that little stream of vapor rising from the fuel gauge on my port wing! It might almost be a plume of smoke.

"Prévot!"

My mechanic leaned towards me.

"Look! Isn't that gas? Seems to me it's leaking pretty fast."

He had a look and shook his head.

"Better check our consumption," I said.

I wasn't turning back yet. My course was still set for Tunis. I looked round and could see Prévot at the gauge on the second fuel tank aft. He came forward and said:

"You've used up about fifty gallons."

Nearly twenty had leaked away in the wind! That was serious. I put back to Marignane where I drank a cup of coffee while the time lost hurt like an open wound. Flyers in the Air France service wanted to know whether I was bound for Saïgon or Madagascar and wished me luck. The tank was patched up and refilled, and I took off once more with a full load, again without mishap despite a bit of rough going over the soggy field.

As soon as I reached the sea I ran into low-hanging clouds that forced me down to sixty feet. The driving rain spattered against the windshield and the sea was churning and foaming. I strained to see ahead and keep from hooking the mast of some ship, while Prévot lit cigarettes for me.

"Coffee!"

He vanished into the stern of the cockpit and came back with the thermos flask. I drank. From time to time I flicked the throttle to keep the engines at exactly 2100 revolutions and ran my eye over the dials like a captain inspecting his troops. My company stood trim and erect: every needle was where it should be.

I glanced down at the sea and saw it bubbling under the steaming rain like a boiling cauldron. In a hydroplane this bumpy sea would have bothered me; but in this ship of mine, which could not possibly be set down here, I felt differently. It was silly, of course, but the thought gave me a sense of security. The sea was part of a world that I had nothing to do with. Engine trouble here was out of the question: there was not the least danger of such a thing. Why, I was not rigged for the sea!

After an hour and a half of this, the rain died down, and though the clouds still hung low a genial sun began to break through. I was immensely cheered by this promise of good weather. Overhead I could feel a thin layer of cotton-wool and I swerved aside to avoid a downpour. I was past the point where I had to cut through the heart of squalls. Was not that the first rift in the cloud-bank, there ahead of me?

I sensed it before I saw it, for straight ahead on the sea lay a long meadow-colored swath, a sort of oasis of deep and luminous green reminding me of those barley fields in southern Morocco that would make me catch my breath each time I sighted them on coming up from Senegal across two thousand miles of sand. Here as at such times in Morocco I felt we had reached a place a man could live in, and it bucked me up. I flung a glance backward at Prévot and called out:

"We're over the worst of it. This is fine."

"Yes," he said, "fine."

This meant that I would not need to do any stunt flying when Sardinia hove unexpectedly into view. The island would not loom up suddenly like a mass of wreckage a hundred feet ahead of me: I should be able to see it rising on the horizon in the distant play of a thousand sparkling points of light.

I moved into this region bathed by the sun. No doubt about it, I was loafing along. Loafing at the rate of one hundred and seventy miles an hour, but loafing nevertheless. I smoked a few leisurely cigarettes. I lingered over my coffee. I kept a cautious fatherly eye on my brood of instruments. These clouds, this sun, this play of light, lent to my flight the relaxation of a Sunday afternoon stroll. The sea was as variegated as a country landscape broken into fields of green and violet and blue. Off in the distance, just where a squall was blowing, I could see the fermenting spray. Once again I recognized that the sea was of all things in the world the least monotonous, was formed of an ever-changing substance. A gust of wind mantles it with light or strips it bare. I turned back to Prévot.

"Look!" I said.

There in the distance lay the shores of Sardinia that we were about to skirt to the southward.

Prévot came forward and sat down beside me. He squinted with wrinkled forehead at the mountains struggling out of their shroud of mist. The clouds had been blown away and the island was coming into view in great slabs of field and woodland. I climbed to forty-five hundred feet and drifted along the coast of this island dotted with villages. After the flower-strewn but uninhabitable sea, this was a place where I could take things easily. For a little time I clung to our great-hearted mother earth. Then, Sardinia behind me, I headed for Tunis.

I picked up the African continent at Bizerta and there I began to drop earthward. I was at home. Here was a place where I could dispense with altitude which, as every pilot knows, is our particular store of wealth. Not that we squander it when it is no longer needed: we swap it for another kind of treasure. When a flyer is within a quarter of an hour of port, he sets his controls for the down swing, throttling his motor a little—just enough to keep it from racing while the needle on his speedometer swings round from one hundred and seventy to two hundred miles an hour.

At that rate of speed the impalpable eddies of evening air drum softly on the wings and the plane seems to be drilling its way into a quivering crystal so delicate that the wake of a passing swallow would jar it to bits. I was already skirting the undulations of the hills and had given away almost the whole of my few hundred feet of altitude when I reached the airdrome, and there, shaving the roofs of the hangars, I set down my ship on the ground.

While the tanks were being re-filled I signed some papers and shook hands with a few friends. And just as I was coming out of the administration building I heard a horrible grunt, one of those muffled impacts that tell their fatal story in a single sound; one of those echoless thuds complete in themselves, without appeal, in which fatality delivers its message. Instantly there came into my mind the memory of an identical sound—an explosion in a garage. Two men had died of that hoarse bark.

I looked now across to the road that ran alongside the airdrome: there in a puff of dust two high-powered cars had crashed head-on and stood frozen into motionlessness as if imprisoned in ice. Men were running towards the cars while others ran from them to the field office.

"Get a doctor. . . . Skull crushed. . . ."

My heart sank. In the peace of the evening light Fate had taken a trick. A beauty, a mind, a life—something had been destroyed. It was as sudden as a raid in the desert. Marauding tribesmen creep up on silent feet in the night. The camp resounds briefly with the clashing tumult of a razzia. A moment later everything has sunk back into the golden silence. The same peace, the same stillness, followed this crash.

Near by, someone spoke of a fractured skull. I had no mind to be told about that crushed and bloody cranium. Turning my back to the road, I went across to my ship, in my heart a foreboding of danger. I was to recognize that sound when I heard it again very soon. When the *Simoon* scraped the black plateau at a speed of one hundred and seventy miles an hour I should recognize that hoarse grunt, that same snarl of destiny keeping its appointment with us.

Off to Benghazi! We still have two hours of daylight. Before we crossed into Tripolitana I took off my glare glasses. The sands were golden under the slanting rays of the sun. How empty of life is this planet of ours! Once again it struck me that its rivers, its woods, its human habitations were the product of chance, of fortuitous conjunctions of circumstance. What a deal of the earth's surface is given over to rock and sand!

But all this was not my affair. My world was the world of flight. Already I could feel the oncoming night within which I should be enclosed as in the precincts of a temple—enclosed in the temple of night for the accomplishment of secret rites and absorption in inviolable contemplation.

Already this profane world was beginning to fade out: soon it would vanish altogether. This landscape was still laved in golden sunlight, but already something was evaporating out of it. I know nothing, nothing in the world, equal to the wonder of nightfall in the air.

Those who have been enthralled by the witchery of flying will know what I mean—and I do not speak of the men who, among other sports, enjoy taking a turn in a plane. I speak of those who fly professionally and have sacrificed much to their craft. Mermoz said once, "It's worth it, it's worth the final smash-up."

No question about it; but the reason is hard to formulate. A novice taking orders could appreciate this ascension towards the essence of things, since his profession too is one of renunciation: he renounces the world; he renounces riches; he renounces the love of woman. And by renunciation he discovers his hidden god.

I, too, in this flight, am renouncing things. I am giving up the broad golden surfaces that would befriend me if my engines were to fail. I am giving up the landmarks by which I might be taking my bearings. I am giving up the profiles of mountains against the sky that would warn me of pitfalls. I am plunging into the night. I am navigating. I have on my side only the stars.

The diurnal death of the world is a slow death. It is only little by little that the divine beacon of daylight recedes from me. Earth and sky begin to merge into each other. The earth rises and seems to spread like a mist. The first stars tremble as if shimmering in green water. Hours must pass before their glimmer hardens into the frozen glitter of diamonds. I shall have a long wait before I witness the soundless frolic of the shooting stars. In the profound darkness of certain nights I have seen the sky streaked with so many trailing sparks that it seemed to me a great gale must be blowing through the outer heavens.

Prévot was testing the lamps in their sockets and the emergency torches. Round the bulbs he was wrapping red paper.

"Another layer."

He added another wrapping of paper and touched a switch. The dim light within the plane was still too bright. As in a photographer's dark-room, it veiled the pale picture of the external world. It hid that glowing phosphorescence which sometimes, at night, clings to the surface of things. Now night has fallen, but it is not yet true night. A crescent moon persists.

Prévot dove aft and came back with a sandwich. I nibbled a bunch of grapes. I was not hungry. I was neither hungry nor thirsty. I felt no weariness. It seemed to me that I could go on like this at the controls for ten years. I was happy.

The moon had set. It was pitch dark when we came in sight of Benghazi. The town lay at the bottom of an obscurity so dense that it was without a halo. I saw the place only when I was over it. As I was hunting for the airdrome the red obstruction lights were switched on. They cut out a black rectangle in the earth.

I banked, and at that moment the rays of a floodlight rose into the sky like a jet from a fire-hose. It pivoted and traced a golden lane over the landing-field. I circled again to get a clear view of what might be in my way. The port was equipped with everything to make a night-landing easy. I throttled down my engine and dropped like a diver into black water.

It was eleven o'clock local time when I landed and taxied across to the beacon. The most helpful ground crew in the world wove in and out of the blinding ray of a searchlight, alternately visible and invisible. They took my papers and began promptly to fill my tanks. Twenty minutes of my time was all they asked for, and I was touched by their great readiness to help. As I was taking off, one of them said:

"Better circle round and fly over us; otherwise we shan't be sure you got off all right."

I rolled down the golden lane towards an unimpeded opening. My *Simoon* lifted her overload clear of the ground well before I reached the end of the runway. The searchlight following me made it hard for me to wheel. Soon it let me go: the men on the ground had guessed that it was dazzling me. I turned right about and banked vertically, and at that moment the searchlight caught me between the eyes again; but scarcely had it touched me when it fled and sent elsewhere its long golden flute. I knew that the ground crew were being most thoughtful and I was grateful. And now I was off to the desert.

All along the line, at Paris, at Tunis, and at Benghazi, I had been told that I should have a following wind of up to twenty-five miles an hour. I was counting on a speed of 190 m.p.h. as I set my course on the middle of the stretch between Alexandria and Cairo. On this course I should avoid the danger zones along the coast, and despite any drifting I might do without knowing it, I should pick up either to port or to starboard the lights of one of those two cities. Failing them I should certainly not miss the lights of the Nile valley. With a steady wind I should reach the Nile in three hours and twenty minutes; if the wind fell, three hours and three-quarters. Calculating thus I began to eat up the six hundred and fifty miles of desert ahead of me.

There was no moon. The world was a bubble of pitch that had dilated until it reached the very stars in the heavens. I should not see a single gleam of light, should not profit by the faintest landmark. Carrying no wireless, I should receive no message from the earth until I reached the Nile. It was useless to try to look at anything other than the compass and the artificial horizon. I might blot the world out of my mind and concentrate my attention upon the slow pulsation of the narrow thread of radium paint that ran along the dark background of the dials.

Whenever Prévot stirred I brought the plane

smoothly back to plumb. I went up to six thousand feet where I had been told the winds would be favorable. At long intervals I switched on a lamp to glance at the engine dials, not all of which were phosphorescent; but most of the time I wrapped myself closely round in darkness among my miniature constellations which gave off the same mineral glow as the stars, the same mysterious and unwearied light, and spoke the same language.

Like the astronomers, I too was reading in the book of celestial mechanics. I too seemed to myself studious and uncorrupted. Everything in the world that might have lured me from my studies had gone out. The external world had ceased to exist.

There was Prévot, who, after a vain resistance, had fallen asleep and left me to the greater enjoyment of my solitude. There was the gentle purr of my beautiful little motor, and before me, on the instrument panel, there were all those tranquil stars. I was most decidedly not sleepy. If this state of quiet well-being persisted until tomorrow night, I intended to push on without a stop to Saïgon.

Now the flight was beginning to seem to me short. Benghazi, the only troublesome night-landing on the route, had banked its fires and settled down behind the horizon in that dark shuttering in which cities take their slumber.

Meanwhile I was turning things over in my mind. We were without the moon's help and we had no wireless. No slightest tenuous tie was to bind us to earth until the Nile showed its thread of light directly ahead of us. We were truly alone in the universe—a thought that caused me not the least worry. If my motor were to cough, that sound would startle me more than if my heart should skip a beat.

Into my mind came the image of Sabathier, the white-haired engineer with the clear eye. I was thinking that, from one point of view, it would be hard to draw a distinction in the matter of human values between a profession like his and that of the painter, the composer, or the poet. I could see in the mind's eye those watch-maker's hands of his that had brought into being this clockwork I was piloting. Men who have given their lives to labors of love go straight to my heart.

"Couldn't I change this?" I had asked him.

"I shouldn't advise it," he had answered.

I was remembering our last conversation. He had thought it inadvisable, and of course that had settled it. A physician, that's it! Exactly the way one puts oneself into the hands of one's doctor—when he has that look in his eye. It was by his motor that we hung suspended in air and were able to go on living with the ticking of time in this penetrable pitch. We were crossing the great dark valley of a fairy-tale, the Valley of Ordeal. Like the prince in the tale, we must meet the test without succor. Failure here would not be forgiven. We were in the lap of the inexorable gods.

A ray of light was filtering through a joint in the lamp shaft. I woke up Prévot and told him to put it out. Prévot stirred in the darkness like a bear, snorted, and came forward. He fumbled for a bit with handkerchiefs and black paper, and the ray of light vanished. That light had bothered me because it was not of my world. It swore at the pale and distant gleam of the phosphorescence and was like a night-club spotlight compared to the gleam of a star. Besides, it had dazzled me and had out-shone all else that gleamed.

We had been flying for three hours. A brightness that seemed to me a glare spurted on the starboard side. I stared. A streamer of light which I had hitherto not noticed was fluttering from a lamp at the tip of the wing. It was an intermittent glow, now brilliant, now dim. It told me that I had flown into a cloud, and it was on the cloud that the lamp was reflected.

I was nearing the landmarks upon which I had counted; a clear sky would have helped a lot. The wing shone bright under the halo. The light steadied itself, became fixed, and then began to radiate in the form of a bouquet of pink blossoms. Great eddies of air were swinging me to and fro. I was navigating somewhere in the belly of a cumulus whose thickness I could not guess. I rose to seventy-five hundred feet and was still in it. Down again to three thousand, and the bouquet of flowers was still with me, motionless and growing brighter.

Well, there it was and there was nothing to do about it. I would think of something else, and wait to get clear of it. Just the same, I did not like this sinister glitter of a one-eyed grog-shop.

"Let me think," I said to myself. "I am bouncing round a bit, but there's nothing abnormal about that. I've been bumped all the way, despite a clear sky and plenty of ceiling. The wind has not died down, and I must be doing better than the 190 m.p.h. I counted on." This was about as far as I could get. Oh, well, when I got through the cloud-bank I would try to take my bearings.

Out of it we flew. The bouquet suddenly vanished, letting me know I was in the clear again. I stared ahead and saw, if one can speak of "seeing" space, a narrow valley of sky and the wall of the next cumulus. Already the bouquet was coming to life again. I was free of that viscous mess from time to time but only for a few seconds each time. After three and a half hours of flying it began to get on my nerves. If I had made the time I imagined, we were certainly approaching the Nile. With a little luck I might be able to spot the river through the rifts, but they were getting rare. I dared not come down, for if I was actually slower than I thought, I was still over high-lying country.

Thus far I was entirely without anxiety; my only fear was that I might presently be wasting time. I decided that I would take things easy until I had flown four and a quarter hours: after that, even in a dead calm (which was highly unlikely) I should have crossed the Nile. When I reached the fringes of the cloud-bank the bouquet winked on and off more and more swiftly and then suddenly went out. Decidedly, I did not like these dot-and-dash messages from the demons of the night.

A green star appeared ahead of me, flashing like a lighthouse. Was it a lighthouse? or really a star? I took no pleasure from this supernatural gleam, this star the Magi might have seen, this dangerous decoy.

Prévot, meanwhile, had waked up and turned his electric torch on the engine dials. I waved him off, him and his torch. We had just sailed into the clear between two clouds and I was busy staring below. Prévot went back to sleep. The gap in the clouds was no help: there was nothing below.

Four hours and five minutes in the air. Prévot awoke and sat down beside me.

"I'll bet we're near Cairo," he said.

"We must be."

"What's that? A star? or is it a lighthouse?"

I had throttled the engine down a little. This, probably, was what had awakened Prévot. He is sensitive to all the variations of sound in flight.

I began a slow descent, intending to slip under the mass of clouds. Meanwhile I had had a look at my map. One thing was sure—the land below me lay at sea level, and there was no risk of conking against a hill. Down

I went, flying due north so that the lights of the cities would strike square into my windows. I must have over-flown them, and should therefore see them on my left.

Now I was flying below the cumulus. But alongside was another cloud hanging lower down on the left. I swerved so as not to be caught in its net, and headed north-northeast. This second cloud-bank certainly went down a long way, for it blocked my view of the hori-zon. I dared not give up any more altitude. My alti-meter registered 1200 feet, but I had no notion of the atmospheric pressure here. Prévot leaned towards me and I shouted to him, "I'm going out to sea. I'd rather come down on it than risk a crash here."

As a matter of fact, there was nothing to prove that we had not drifted over the sea already. Below that cloud-bank visibility was exactly nil. I hugged my win-dow, trying to read below me, to discover flares, signs of life. I was a man raking dead ashes, trying in vain to retrieve the flame of life in a hearth.

"A lighthouse!"

Both of us spied it at the same moment, that wink-ing decoy! What madness! Where was that phantom light, that invention of the night? For at the very second when Prévot and I leaned forward to pick it out of the air where it had glittered nine hundred feet below our wings, suddenly, at that very instant . . .

"Oh!"

I am quite sure that this was all I said. I am quite sure

that all I felt was a terrific crash that rocked our world to its foundations. We had crashed against the earth at a hundred and seventy miles an hour. I am quite sure that in the split second that followed, all I expected was the great flash of ruddy light of the explosion in which Prévot and I were to be blown up together. Neither he nor I had felt the least emotion of any kind. All I could observe in myself was an extraordinary tense feeling of expectancy, the expectancy of that resplendent star in which we were to vanish within the second.

But there was no ruddy star. Instead there was a sort of earthquake that splintered our cabin, ripped away the windows, blew sheets of metal hurtling through space a hundred yards away, and filled our very entrails with its roar. The ship quivered like a knife-blade thrown from a distance into a block of oak, and its anger mashed us as if we were so much pulp.

One second, two seconds passed, and the plane still quivered while I waited with a grotesque impatience for the forces within it to burst it like a bomb. But the subterranean quakings went on without a climax of eruption while I marveled uncomprehendingly at its invisible travail. I was baffled by the quaking, the anger, the interminable postponement. Five seconds passed; six seconds. And suddenly we were seized by a spinning motion, a shock that jerked our cigarettes out of the window, pulverized the starboard wing—and then nothing, nothing but a frozen immobility. I shouted to Prévot:

"Jump!"

And in that instant he cried out:

"Fire!"

We dove together through the wrecked window and found ourselves standing side by side, sixty feet from the plane. I said:

"Are you hurt?"

He answered:

"Not a bit."

But he was rubbing his knee.

"Better run your hands over yourself," I said; "move about a bit. Sure no bones are broken?"

He answered:

"I'm all right. It's that emergency pump."

Emergency pump! I was sure he was going to keel over any minute and split open from head to navel there before my eyes. But he kept repeating with a glassy stare:

"That pump, that emergency pump."

He's out of his head, I thought. He'll start dancing in a minute.

Finally he stopped staring at the plane—which had not gone up in flames—and stared at me instead. And he said again:

"I'm all right. It's that emergency pump. It got me in the knee."

Why we were not blown up, I do not know. I switched on my electric torch and went back over the furrow in the ground traced by the plane. Two hundred and fifty yards from where we stopped the ship had begun to shed the twisted iron and sheet-metal that spattered the sand the length of her traces. We were to see, when day came, that we had run almost tangentially into a gentle slope at the top of a barren plateau. At the point of impact there was a hole in the sand that looked as if it had been made by a plough. Maintaining an even keel, the plane had run its course with the fury and the tail-lashings of a reptile gliding on its belly at the rate of a hundred and seventy miles an hour. We owed our lives to the fact that this desert was surfaced with round black pebbles which had rolled over and over like ball-bearings beneath us. They must have rained upward to the heavens as we shot through them.

Prévot disconnected the batteries for fear of fire by short-circuit. I leaned against the motor and turned the situation over in my mind. I had been flying high for four hours and a quarter, possibly with a thirty-mile following wind. I had been jolted a good deal. If the wind had changed since the weather people forecast it, I was unable to say into what quarter it had veered. All I could make out was that we had crashed in an empty square two hundred and fifty miles on each side.

Prévot came up and sat down beside me.

"I can't believe that we're alive," he said.

I said nothing. Even that thought could not cheer me. A germ of an idea was at work in my mind and was already bothering me. Telling Prévot to switch on his torch as a landmark, I walked straight out, scrutinizing the ground in the light of my own torch as I went.

I went forward slowly, swung round in a wide arc, and changed direction a number of times. I kept my eyes fixed on the ground like a man hunting a lost ring.

Only a little while before I had been straining just as hard to see a gleam of light from the air. Through the darkness I went, bowed over the traveling disk of white light. "Just as I thought," I said to myself, and I went slowly back to the plane. I sat down beside the cabin and ruminated. I had been looking for a reason to hope and had failed to find it. I had been looking for a sign of life, and no sign of life had appeared.

"Prévot, I couldn't find a single blade of grass."

Prévot said nothing, and I was not sure he had understood. Well, we could talk about it again when the curtain rose at dawn. Meanwhile I was dead tired and all I could think was, "Two hundred and fifty miles more or less in the desert."

Suddenly I jumped to my feet. "Water!" I said.

Gas tanks and oil tanks were smashed in. So was our supply of drinking-water. The sand had drunk everything. We found a pint of coffee in a battered thermos flask and half a pint of white wine in another. We filtered both, and poured them into one flask. There were some grapes, too, and a single orange. Meanwhile I was computing: "All this will last us five hours of tramping in the sun."

We crawled into the cabin and waited for dawn. I stretched out, and as I settled down to sleep I took stock of our situation. We didn't know where we were; we had less than a quart of liquid between us; if we were not too far off the Benghazi-Cairo lane we should be found in a week, and that would be too late. Yet it was the best we could hope for. If, on the other hand, we had drifted off our course, we shouldn't be found in six months. One thing was sure—we could not count on being picked up by a plane; the men who came out for us would have two thousand miles to cover.

"You know, it's a shame," Prévot said suddenly.

"What's a shame?"

"That we didn't crash properly and have it over with."

It seemed pretty early to be throwing in one's hand. Prévot and I pulled ourselves together. There was still a chance, slender as it was, that we might be saved miraculously by a plane. On the other hand, we couldn't stay here and perhaps miss a near-by oasis. We would walk all day and come back to the plane before dark. And before going off we would write our plan in huge letters in the sand.

With this I curled up and settled down to sleep. I was happy to go to sleep. My weariness wrapped me round like a multiple presence. I was not alone in the desert: my drowsiness was peopled with voices and memories and whispered confidences. I was not yet thirsty; I felt strong; and I surrendered myself to sleep as to an aimless journey. Reality lost ground before the advance of dreams.

Ah, but things were different when I awoke!

In times past I have loved the Sahara. I have spent nights alone in the path of marauding tribes and have waked up with untroubled mind in the golden emptiness of the desert where the wind like a sea had raised sand-waves upon its surface. Asleep under the wing of my plane I have looked forward with confidence to being rescued next day. But this was not the Sahara!

Prévot and I walked along the slopes of rolling mounds. The ground was sand covered over with a single layer of shining black pebbles. They gleamed like metal scales and all the domes about us shone like coats of mail. We had dropped down into a mineral world and were hemmed in by iron hills.

When we reached the top of the first crest we saw in the distance another just like it, black and gleaming. As we walked we scraped the ground with our boots, marking a trail over which to return to the plane. We went forward with the sun in our eyes. It was not logical to go due east like this, for everything—the weather reports, the duration of the flight—had made it plain that we had crossed the Nile. But I had started tentatively towards the west and had felt a vague foreboding I could not explain to myself. So I had put off the west till tomorrow. In the same way, provisionally, I had given up going north, though that led to the sea.

Three days later, when scourged by thirst into abandoning the plane and walking straight on until we dropped in our tracks, it was still eastward that we tramped. More precisely, we walked east-northeast. And this too was in defiance of all reason and even of all hope. Yet after we had been rescued we discovered that if we had gone in any other direction we should have been lost.

Northward, we should never have had the endurance to reach the sea. And absurd as it may appear, it seems to me now, since I had no other motive, that I must have chosen the east simply because it was by going eastward that Guillaumet had been saved in the Andes, after I had hunted for him everywhere. In a confused way the east had become for me the direction of life.

We walked on for five hours and then the landscape changed. A river of sand seemed to be running through a valley, and we followed this river-bed, taking long strides in order to cover as much ground as possible and get back to the plane before night fell, if our march was in vain. Suddenly I stopped.

"Prévot!"

"What's up?"

"Our tracks!"

How long was it since we had forgotten to leave a wake behind us? We had to find it or die.

We went back, bearing to the right. When we had gone back far enough we would make a right angle to the left and eventually intersect our tracks where we had still remembered to mark them.

This we did and were off again. The heat rose and with it came the mirages. But these were still the commonplace kind—sheets of water that materialized and then vanished as we neared them. We decided to cross the valley of sand and climb the highest dome in order to look round the horizon. This was after six hours of march in which, striding along, we must have covered twenty miles.

When we had struggled up to the top of the black hump we sat down and looked at each other. At our feet lay our valley of sand, opening into a desert of sand whose dazzling brightness seared our eyes. As far as the eye could see lay empty space. But in that space the play of light created mirages which, this time, were of a disturbing kind, fortresses and minarets, angular geometric hulks. I could see also a black mass that pretended to be vegetation, overhung by the last of those clouds that dissolve during the day only to return at night. This mass of vegetation was the shadow of a cumulus.

It was no good going on. The experiment was a failure. We would have to go back to our plane, to that red and white beacon which, perhaps, would be picked out by a flyer. I was not staking great hopes on a rescue party, but it did seem to me our last chance of salvation. In any case, we had to get back to our few drops of liquid, for our throats were parched. We were imprisoned in this iron circle, captives of the curt dictatorship of thirst.

And yet, how hard it was to turn back when there was a chance that we might be on the road to life! Beyond the mirages the horizon was perhaps rich in veritable treasures, in meadows and runnels of sweet water. I knew I was doing the right thing by returning to the plane, and yet as I swung round and started back I was filled with portents of disaster.

We were resting on the ground beside the plane. Nearly forty miles of wandering this day. The last drop of liquid had been drained. No sign of life had appeared to the east. No plane had soared overhead. How long should we be able to hold out? Already our thirst was terrible.

We had built up a great pyre out of bits of the splintered wing. Our gasoline was ready, and we had flung on the heap sheets of metal whose magnesium coating would burn with a hard white flame. We were waiting now for night to come down before we lighted our conflagration. But where were there men to see it?

Night fell and the flames rose. Prayerfully we watched our mute and radiant fanion mount resplendent into the night. As I looked I said to myself that this message was not only a cry for help, it was fraught also with a great deal of love. We were begging water, but we were also begging the communion of human society. Only man can create fire: let another flame light up the night; let man answer man!

I was haunted by a vision of my wife's eyes under the halo of her hat. Of her face I could see only the eyes, questioning me, looking at me yearningly. I am answering, answering with all my strength! What flame could leap higher than this that darts up into the night from my heart?

What I could do, I have done. What we could do, we have done. Nearly forty miles, almost without a drop to drink. Now there was no water left. Was it our fault that we could wait no longer? Suppose we had sat quietly by the plane, taking suck at the mouths of our water-bottles? But from the moment I breathed in the moist bottom of the tin cup, a clock had started up in me. From the second when I had sucked up the last drop, I had begun to slip downhill. Could I help it if time like a river was carrying me away? Prévot was weeping. I tapped him on the shoulder and said, to console him:

"If we're done for we're done for, and that's all there is to it."

He said:

"Do you think it's me I'm bawling about?"

I might have known it. It was evident enough. Nothing is unbearable. Tomorrow, and the day after, I should learn that nothing was really unbearable. I had never really believed in torture. Reading Poe as a kid, I had already said as much to myself. Once, jammed in the cabin of a plane, I thought I was going to drown; and I had not suffered much. Several times it had seemed to me that the final smash-up was coming, and I don't remember that I thought of it as a cosmic event. And I didn't believe this was going to be agonizing either. There will be time tomorrow to find out stranger things about it. Meanwhile, God knows that despite the bonfire I had decidedly given up hope that our cries would be heard by the world.

"Do you think it's me . . ." There you have what is truly unbearable! Every time I saw those yearning eyes it was as if a flame were searing me. They were like a scream for help, like the flares of a sinking ship. I felt that I should not sit idly by: I should jump up and run— anywhere! straight ahead of me!

What a strange reversal of rôles! But I have always thought it would be like this. Still, I needed Prévot beside me to be quite sure of it. Prévot was a level-headed fellow. He loved life. And yet Prévot no more than I was wringing his hands at the sight of death the way we are told men do. But there did exist something that he could not bear any more than I could. I was perfectly ready to fall asleep, whether for a night or for eternity. If I did fall asleep, I could not even know whether it was for the one or for the other. And the peace of sleep! But that cry that would be sent up at home, that great wail of desolation—that was what I could not bear. I could not stand idly by and look on at that disaster. Each second of silence drove the knife deeper into someone I loved. At the thought, a blind rage surged up in me. Why do these chains bind me and prevent me from rescuing those who are drowning? Why does our conflagration not carry our cry to the ends of the world? Hear me, you out here! Patience. We are coming to save you.

The magnesium had been licked off and the metal was glowing red. There was left only a heap of embers round which we crouched to warm ourselves. Our flaming call had spent itself. Had it set anything in the world in motion? I knew well enough that it hadn't. Here was a prayer that had of necessity gone unheard.

That was that.

I ought to get some sleep.

At daybreak I took a rag and mopped up a little dew on the wings. The mixture of water and paint and oil yielded a spoonful of nauseating liquid which we sipped because it would at least moisten our lips. After this banquet Prévot said:

"Thank God we've got a gun."

Instantly I became furious and turned on him with an aggressiveness which I regretted directly I felt it. There was nothing I should have loathed more at that moment than a gush of sentimentality. I am so made that I have to believe that everything is simple. Birth is simple. Growing up is simple. And dying of thirst is simple. I watched Prévot out of the corner of my eye, ready to wound his feelings, if that was necessary to shut him up.

But Prévot had spoken without emotion. He had been discussing a matter of hygiene, and might have said in the same tone, "We ought to wash our hands." That being so, we were agreed. Indeed already yesterday, my eye falling by chance on the leather holster, the same thought had crossed my mind, and with me too it had been a reasonable reflex, not an emotional one. Pathos resides in social man, not in the individual; what was pathetic was our powerlessness to reassure those for whom we were responsible, not what we might do with the gun.

There was still no sign that we were being sought; or rather they were doubtless hunting for us elsewhere, probably in Arabia. We were to hear no sound of plane until the day after we had abandoned our own. And if ships did pass overhead, what could that mean to us? What could they see in us except two black dots among the thousand shadowy dots in the desert? Absurd to think of being distinguishable from them. None of the reflections that might be attributed to me on the score of this torture would be true. I should not feel in the least tortured. The aerial rescue party would seem to me, each time I sighted one, to be moving through a universe that was not mine. When searchers have to cover two thousand miles of territory, it takes them a good two weeks to spot a plane in the desert from the sky.

They were probably looking for us all along the line from Tripoli to Persia. And still, with all this, I clung to the slim chance that they might pick us out. Was that not our only chance of being saved? I changed my tactics, determining to go reconnoitering by myself. Prévot would get another bonfire together and kindle it in the event that visitors showed up. But we were to have no callers that day.

So off I went without knowing whether or not I should have the stamina to come back. I remembered what I knew about this Libyan desert. When, in the Sahara, humidity is still at forty per cent of saturation, it is only eighteen here in Libya. Life here evaporates like a vapor. Bedouins, explorers, and colonial officers all tell us that a man may go nineteen hours without water. Thereafter his eyes fill with light, and that marks the beginning of the end. The progress made by thirst is swift and terrible. But this northeast wind, this abnormal wind that had blown us out off our course and had marooned us on this plateau, was now prolonging our lives. What was the length of the reprieve it would grant us before our eyes began to fill with light? I went forward with the feeling of a man canoeing in mid-ocean.

I will admit that at daybreak this landscape seemed to me less infernal, and that I began my walk with my hands in my pockets, like a tramp on a highroad. The evening before we had set snares at the mouths of certain mysterious burrows in the ground, and the poacher in me was on the alert. I went first to have a look at our traps. They were empty.

Well, this meant that I should not be drinking blood today; and indeed I hadn't expected to. But though I was not disappointed, my curiosity was aroused. What was there in the desert for these animals to live on? These were certainly the holes of fennecs, a long-eared carnivorous sand-fox the size of a rabbit. I spotted the tracks made by one of them, and gave way to the impulse to follow them. They led to a narrow stream of sand where each footprint was plainly outlined and where I marveled at the pretty palm formed by the three toes spread fanwise on the sand.

I could imagine my little friend trotting blithely along at dawn and licking the dew off the rocks. Here the tracks were wider apart: my fennec had broken into a run. And now I see that a companion has joined him and they have trotted on side by side. These signs of a morning stroll gave me a strange thrill. They were signs of life, and I loved them for that. I almost forgot that I was thirsty.

Finally I came to the pasture-ground of my foxes. Here, every hundred yards or so, I saw sticking up out of the sand a small dry shrub, its twigs heavy with little golden snails. The fennec came here at dawn to do his marketing. And here I was able to observe another of nature's mysteries.

My fennec did not stop at all the shrubs. There were some weighed down with snails which he disdained. Obviously he avoided them with some wariness. Others he stopped at but did not strip of all they bore. He must have picked out two or three shells and then gone on to another restaurant. What was he up to? Was he nurseryman to the snails, encouraging their reproduction by refraining from exhausting the stock on a given shrub, or a given twig? Or was he amusing himself by delaying repletion, putting off satiety in order to enhance the pleasure he took from his morning stroll?

The tracks led me back to the hole in which he lived. Doubtless my fennec crouched below, listening to me and startled by the crunching of my footsteps. I said to him:

"Fox, my little fox, I'm done for; but somehow that doesn't prevent me from taking an interest in your mood."

And there I stayed a bit, ruminating and telling myself that a man was able to adapt himself to anything. The notion that he is to die in thirty years has probably never spoiled any man's fun. Thirty years . . . or thirty days: it's all a matter of perspective.

Only, you have to be able to put certain visions out of your mind.

I went on, finally, and the time came when, along with my weariness, something in me began to change. If those were not mirages, I was inventing them.

"Hi! Hi, there!"

I shouted and waved my arms, but the man I had seen waving at me turned out to be a black rock. Everything in the desert had grown animate. I stooped to waken a sleeping Bedouin and he turned into the trunk of a black tree. A tree-trunk? Here in the desert? I was amazed and bent over to lift a broken bough. It was solid marble.

Straightening up I looked round and saw more black marble. An antediluvian forest littered the ground with its broken tree-tops. How many thousand years ago, under what hurricane of the time of Genesis, had this cathedral of wood crumbled in this spot? Countless centuries had rolled these fragments of giant pillars at my feet, polished them like steel, petrified and vitrified them and indued them with the color of jet.

I could distinguish the knots in their branches, the

twistings of their once living boughs, could count the rings of life in them. This forest had rustled with birds and been filled with music that now was struck by doom and frozen into salt. And all this was hostile to me. Blacker than the chain-mail of the hummocks, these solemn derelicts rejected me. What had I, a living man, to do with this incorruptible stone? Perishable as I was, I whose body was to crumble into dust, what place had I in this eternity?

Since yesterday I had walked nearly fifty miles. This dizziness that I felt came doubtless from my thirst. Or from the sun. It glittered on these hulks until they shone as if smeared with oil. It blazed down on this universal carapace. Sand and fox had no life here. This world was a gigantic anvil upon which the sun beat down. I strode across this anvil and at my temples I could feel the hammer-strokes of the sun.

"Hi! Hi, there!" I called out.

"There is nothing there," I told myself. "Take it easy. You are delirious."

I had to talk to myself aloud, had to bring myself to reason. It was hard for me to reject what I was seeing, hard not to run towards that caravan plodding on the horizon. There! Do you see it?

"Fool! You know very well that you are inventing it."

"You mean that nothing in the world is real?"

Nothing in the world is real if that cross which I see ten miles off on the top of a hill is not real. Or is it a lighthouse? No, the sea does not lie in that direction. Then it must be a cross.

I had spent the night studying my map—but uselessly, since I did not know my position. Still, I had scrutinized all the signs that marked the marvelous presence of man. And somewhere on the map I had seen a little circle surmounted by just such a cross. I had glanced down at the legend to get an explanation of the symbol and had read: "Religious institution."

Close to the cross there had been a black dot. Again I had run my finger down the legend and had read: "Permanent well." My heart had jumped and I had repeated the legend aloud: "Permanent well, permanent well." What were all of Ali Baba's treasures compared with a permanent well? A little farther on were two white circles. "Temporary wells," the legend said. Not quite so exciting. And round about them was nothing . . . unless it was the blankness of despair.

But this must be my "religious institution"! The monks must certainly have planted a great cross on the hill expressly for men in our plight! All I had to do was to walk across to them. I should be taken in by those Dominicans. . . .

"But there are only Coptic monasteries in Libya!" I told myself.

. . . by those learned Dominicans. They have a great cool kitchen with red tiles, and out in the courtyard a marvelous rusted pump. Beneath the rusted pump; beneath the rusted pump . . . you've guessed it! . . . beneath the rusted pump is dug the permanent well! Ah, what rejoicing when I ring at their gate, when I get my hands on the rope of the great bell.

"Madman! You are describing a house in Provence; and what's more, the house has no bell!"

. . . on the rope of the great bell. The porter will raise his arms to Heaven and cry out, "You are the messenger of the Lord!" and he will call aloud to all the monks. They will pour out of the monastery. They will welcome me with a great feast, as if I were the Prodigal Son. They will lead me to the kitchen and will say to me, "One moment, my son, one moment. We'll just be off to the permanent well." And I shall be trembling with happiness.

No, no! I will *not* weep just because there happens to be no cross on the hill.

The treasures of the west turned out to be mere illusion. I have veered due north. At least the north is filled with the sound of the sea.

Over the hilltop. Look there, at the horizon! The most beautiful city in the world!

"You know perfectly well that is a mirage."

Of course I know it is a mirage! Am I the sort of man who can be fooled? But what if I *want* to go after that mirage? Suppose I enjoy indulging my hope? Suppose it suits me to love that crenelated town all beflagged with sunlight? What if I choose to walk straight ahead on light feet—for you must know that I have dropped my weariness behind me, I am happy now. . . . Prévot and his gun! Don't make me laugh! I prefer my drunkenness. I am drunk. I am dying of thirst.

It took the twilight to sober me. Suddenly I stopped, appalled to think how far I was from our base. In the twilight the mirage was dying. The horizon had stripped itself of its pomp, its palaces, its priestly vestments. It was the old desert horizon again.

"A fine day's work you've done! Night will overtake you. You won't be able to go on before daybreak, and by that time your tracks will have been blown away and you'll be properly nowhere."

In that case I may as well walk straight on. Why turn back? Why should I bring my ship round when I may find the sea straight ahead of me?

"When did you catch a glimpse of the sea? What makes you think you could walk that far? Meanwhile there's Prévot watching for you beside the *Simoon*. He may have been picked up by a caravan, for all you know."

Very good. I'll go back. But first I want to call out for help.

"Hi! Hi!"

By God! You can't tell me this planet is not inhabited. Where are its men?

"Hi! Hi!"

I was hoarse. My voice was gone. I knew it was ridiculous to croak like this, but—one more try:

"Hi! Hi!"

And I turned back.

I had been walking two hours when I saw the flames of the bonfire that Prévot, frightened by my long absence, had sent up. They mattered very little to me now.

Another hour of trudging. Five hundred yards away. A hundred yards. Fifty yards.

"Good Lord!"

Amazement stopped me in my tracks. Joy surged up and filled my heart with its violence. In the firelight stood Prévot, talking to two Arabs who were leaning against the motor. He had not noticed me, for he was too full of his own joy. If only I had sat still and waited with him! I should have been saved already. Exultantly I called out:

"Hi! Hi!"

The two Bedouins gave a start and stared at me. Prévot left them standing and came forward to meet me. I opened my arms to him. He caught me by the elbow. Did he think I was keeling over? I said:

"At last, eh?"

"What do you mean?"

"The Arabs!"

"What Arabs?"

"Those Arabs there, with you."

Prévot looked at me queerly, and when he spoke I felt as if he was very reluctantly confiding a great secret to me:

"There are no Arabs here."

This time I know I am going to cry.

A man can go nineteen hours without water, and what have we drunk since last night? A few drops of dew at dawn. But the northeast wind is still blowing, still slowing up the process of our evaporation. To it, also, we owe the continued accumulation of high clouds. If only they would drift straight overhead and break into rain! But it never rains in the desert.

"Look here, Prévot. Let's rip up one of the parachutes and spread the sections out on the ground, weighed down with stones. If the wind stays in the same quarter till morning, they'll catch the dew and we can wring them out into one of the tanks."

We spread six triangular sections of parachute under the stars, and Prévot unhooked a fuel tank. This was as much as we could do for ourselves till dawn. But, miracle of miracles! Prévot had come upon an orange while working over the tank. We shared it, and though it was little enough to men who could have used a few gallons of sweet water, still I was overcome with relief.

Stretched out beside the fire I looked at the glowing fruit and said to myself that men did not know what an orange was. "Here we are, condemned to death," I said to myself, "and still the certainty of dying cannot compare with the pleasure I am feeling. The joy I take from this half of an orange which I am holding in my hand is one of the greatest joys I have ever known."

I lay flat on my back, sucking my orange and counting the shooting stars. Here I was, for one minute infinitely happy. "Nobody can know anything of the world in which the individual moves and has his being," I reflected. "There is no guessing it. Only the man locked up in it can know what it is."

For the first time I understood the cigarette and glass of rum that are handed to the criminal about to be executed. I used to think that for a man to accept these wretched gifts at the foot of the gallows was beneath human dignity. Now I was learning that he took pleasure from them. People thought him courageous when he smiled as he smoked or drank. I knew now that he smiled because the taste gave him pleasure. People could not see that his perspective had changed, and that for him the last hour of his life was a life in itself.

We collected an enormous quantity of water—perhaps as much as two quarts. Never again would we be thirsty! We were saved; we had a liquid to drink!

I dipped my tin cup into the tank and brought up a beautifully yellow-green liquid the first mouthful of which nauseated me so that despite my thirst I had to catch my breath before swallowing it. I would have swallowed mud, I swear; but this taste of poisonous metal cut keener than thirst.

I glanced at Prévot and saw him going round and round with his eyes fixed to the ground as if looking for something. Suddenly he leaned forward and began to vomit without interrupting his spinning. Half a minute later it was my turn. I was seized by such convulsions that I went down on my knees and dug my fingers into the sand while I puked. Neither of us spoke, and for a quarter of an hour we remained thus shaken, bringing up nothing but a little bile.

After a time it passed and all I felt was a vague, distant nausea. But our last hope had fled. Whether our bad luck was due to a sizing on the parachute or to the magnesium lining of the tank, I never found out. Certain it was that we needed either another set of cloths or another receptacle.

Well, it was broad daylight and time we were on our way. This time we should strike out as fast as we could, leave this cursed plateau, and tramp till we dropped in our tracks. That was what Guillaumet had done in the Andes. I had been thinking of him all the day before and had determined to follow his example. I should do violence to the pilot's unwritten law, which is to stick by the ship; but I was sure no one would be along to look for us here.

Once again we discovered that it was not we who were shipwrecked, not we but those who were waiting for news of us, those who were alarmed by our silence, were already torn with grief by some atrocious and fantastic report. We could not but strive towards them. Guillaumet had done it, had scrambled towards his lost ones. To do so is a universal impulse.

"If I were alone in the world," Prévot said, "I'd lie down right here. Damned if I wouldn't."

East-northeast we tramped. If we had in fact crossed the Nile, each step was leading us deeper and deeper into the desert.

I don't remember anything about that day. I remember only my haste. I was hurrying desperately towards something—towards some finality. I remember also that I walked with my eyes to the ground, for the mirages were more than I could bear. From time to time we would correct our course by the compass, and now and again we would lie down to catch our breath. I remember having flung away my waterproof, which I had held on to as covering for the night. That is as much as I recall about the day. Of what happened when the chill of evening came, I remember more. But during the day I had simply turned to sand and was a being without mind.

When the sun set we decided to make camp. Oh, I knew as well as anybody that we should push on, that this one waterless night would finish us off. But we had brought along the bits of parachute, and if the poison was not in the sizing, we might get a sip of water next morning. Once again we spread our trap for the dew under the stars.

But the sky in the north was cloudless. The wind no longer had the same taste on the lip. It had moved into another quarter. Something was rustling against us, but this time it seemed to be the desert itself. The wild beast was stalking us, had us in its power. I could feel its breath in my face, could feel it lick my face and hands. Suppose I walked on: at the best I could do five or six miles more. Remember that in three days I had covered one hundred miles, practically without water.

And then, just as we stopped, Prévot said:

"I swear to you I see a lake!"

"You're crazy."

"Have you ever heard of a mirage after sunset?" he challenged.

I didn't seem able to answer him. I had long ago given up believing my own eyes. Perhaps it was not a mirage; but in that case it was a hallucination. How could Prévot go on believing? But he was stubborn about it.

"It's only twenty minutes off. I'll go have a look."

His mulishness got on my nerves.

"Go ahead!" I shouted. "Take your little constitutional. Nothing better for a man. But let me tell you, if your lake exists it is salt. And whether it's salt or not, it's a devil of a way off. And besides, there is no damned lake!"

Prévot was already on his way, his eyes glassy. I knew the strength of these irresistible obsessions. I was thinking: "There are somnambulists who walk straight into locomotives." And I knew that Prévot would not come back. He would be seized by the vertigo of empty space and would be unable to turn back. And then he would keel over. He somewhere, and I somewhere else. Not that it was important.

Thinking thus, it struck me that this mood of resignation was doing me no good. Once when I was half drowned I had let myself go like this. Lying now flat on my face on the stony ground, I took this occasion to write a letter for posthumous delivery. It gave me a chance, also, to take stock of myself again. I tried to bring up a little saliva: how long was it since I had spit? No saliva. If I kept my mouth closed, a kind of glue sealed my lips together. It dried on the outside of the lips and formed a hard crust. However, I found I was still able to swallow, and I bethought me that I was still not seeing a blinding light in my eyes. Once I was treated to that radiant spectacle I might know that the end was a couple of hours away.

Night fell. The moon had swollen since I last saw it. Prévot was still not back. I stretched out on my back and turned these few data over in my mind. A familiar impression came over me, and I tried to seize it. I was . . . I was . . . I was at sea. I was on a ship going to South America and was stretched out, exactly like this, on the boat deck. The tip of the mast was swaying to and fro, very slowly, among the stars. That mast was missing tonight, but again I was at sea, bound for a port I was to make without raising a finger. Slave-traders had flung me on this ship.

I thought of Prévot who was still not back. Not once had I heard him complain. That was a good thing. To hear him whine would have been unbearable. Prévot was a man.

What was that! Five hundred yards ahead of me I could see the light of his lamp. He had lost his way. I had no lamp with which to signal back. I stood up and shouted, but he could not hear me.

A second lamp, and then a third! God in Heaven! It was a search party and it was me they were hunting!

"Hi! Hi!" I shouted.

But they had not heard me. The three lamps were still signaling me.

"Tonight I am sane," I said to myself. "I am relaxed. I am not out of my head. Those are certainly three lamps and they are about five hundred yards off." I stared at them and shouted again, and again I gathered that they could not hear me.

Then, for the first and only time, I was really seized with panic. I could still run, I thought. "Wait! Wait!" I screamed. They seemed to be turning away from me, going off, hunting me elsewhere! And I stood tottering, tottering on the brink of life when there were arms out there ready to catch me! I shouted and screamed again and again.

They had heard me! An answering shout had come. I was strangling, suffocating, but I ran on, shouting as I ran, until I saw Prévot and keeled over.

When I could speak again I said: "Whew! When I saw all those lights . . ."

"What lights?"

God in Heaven, it was true! He was alone!

This time I was beyond despair. I was filled with a sort of dumb fury.

"What about your lake?" I rasped.

"As fast as I moved towards it, it moved back. I walked after it for about half an hour. Then it seemed still too far away, so I came back. But I am positive, now, that it is a lake."

"You're crazy. Absolutely crazy. Why did you do it? Tell me. Why?"

What had he done? Why had he done it? I was ready to weep with indignation, yet I scarcely knew why I was so indignant. Prévot mumbled his excuse:

"I felt I had to find some water. You . . . your lips were awfully pale."

Well! My anger died within me. I passed my hand over my forehead as if I were waking out of sleep. I was suddenly sad. I said:

"There was no mistake about it. I saw them as clearly

as I see you now. Three lights there were. I tell you, Prévot, I saw them!"

Prévot made no comment.

"Well," he said finally, "I guess we're in a bad way."

In this air devoid of moisture the soil is swift to give off its temperature. It was already very cold. I stood up and stamped about. But soon a violent fit of trembling came over me. My dehydrated blood was moving sluggishly and I was pierced by a freezing chill which was not merely the chill of night. My teeth were chattering and my whole body had begun to twitch. My hand shook so that I could not hold an electric torch. I who had never been sensitive to cold was about to die of cold. What a strange effect thirst can have!

Somewhere, tired of carrying it in the sun, I had let my waterproof drop. Now the wind was growing bitter and I was learning that in the desert there is no place of refuge. The desert is as smooth as marble. By day it throws no shadow; by night it hands you over naked to the wind. Not a tree, not a hedge, not a rock behind which I could seek shelter. The wind was charging me like a troop of cavalry across open country. I turned and twisted to escape it: I lay down, stood up, lay down again, and still I was exposed to its freezing lash. I had no strength to run from the assassin and under the sabre-stroke I tumbled to my knees, my head between my hands.

A little later I pieced these bits together and remembered that I had struggled to my feet and had started to walk on, shivering as I went. I had started forward wondering where I was and then I had heard Prévot. His shouting had jolted me into consciousness.

I went back towards him, still trembling from head to foot—quivering with the attack of hiccups that was convulsing my whole body. To myself I said: "It isn't the cold. It's something else. It's the end." The simple fact was that I hadn't enough water in me. I had tramped too far yesterday and the day before when I was off by myself, and I was dehydrated.

The thought of dying of the cold hurt me. I preferred the phantoms of my mind, the cross, the trees, the lamps. At least they would have killed me by enchantment. But to be whipped to death like a slave! . . .

Confound it! Down on my knees again! We had with us a little store of medicines—a hundred grammes of ninety per cent alcohol, the same of pure ether, and a small bottle of iodine. I tried to swallow a little of the ether: it was like swallowing a knife. Then I tried the alcohol: it contracted my gullet. I dug a pit in the sand, lay down in it, and flung handfuls of sand over me until all but my face was buried in it.

Prévot was able to collect a few twigs, and he lit a fire which soon burnt itself out. He wouldn't bury himself in the sand, but preferred to stamp round and round in a circle. That was foolish.

My throat stayed shut, and though I knew that was a bad sign, I felt better. I felt calm. I felt a peace that was beyond all hope. Once more, despite myself, I was journeying, trussed up on the deck of my slave-ship under the stars. It seemed to me that I was perhaps not in such a bad pass after all.

So long as I lay absolutely motionless, I no longer felt the cold. This allowed me to forget my body buried in the sand. I said to myself that I would not budge an inch, and would therefore never suffer again. As a matter of fact, we really suffer very little. Back of all these torments there is the orchestration of fatigue or of delirium, and we live on in a kind of picture-book, a slightly cruel fairy-tale.

A little while ago the wind had been after me with whip and spur, and I was running in circles like a frightened fox. After that came a time when I couldn't breathe. A great knee was crushing in my chest. A knee. I was writhing in vain to free myself from the weight of the angel who had overthrown me. There had not been a moment when I was alone in this desert. But now I have ceased to believe in my surroundings; I have withdrawn into myself, have shut my eyes, have not so much as batted an eyelid. I have the feeling that this torrent of visions is sweeping me away to a tranquil dream: so rivers cease their turbulence in the embrace of the sea.

Farewell, eyes that I loved! Do not blame me if the

human body cannot go three days without water. I should never have believed that man was so truly the prisoner of the springs and freshets. I had no notion that our self-sufficiency was so circumscribed. We take it for granted that a man is able to stride straight out into the world. We believe that man is free. We never see the cord that binds him to wells and fountains, that umbilical cord by which he is tied to the womb of the world. Let man take but one step too many . . . and the cord snaps.

Apart from your suffering, I have no regrets. All in all, it has been a good life. If I got free of this I should start right in again. A man cannot live a decent life in cities, and I need to feel myself live. I am not thinking of aviation. The airplane is a means, not an end. One doesn't risk one's life for a plane any more than a farmer ploughs for the sake of the plough. But the airplane is a means of getting away from towns and their book-keeping and coming to grips with reality.

Flying is a man's job and its worries are a man's worries. A pilot's business is with the wind, with the stars, with night, with sand, with the sea. He strives to outwit the forces of nature. He stares in expectancy for the coming of dawn the way a gardener awaits the coming of spring. He looks forward to port as to a promised land, and truth for him is what lives in the stars.

I have nothing to complain of. For three days I have tramped the desert, have known the pangs of thirst, have followed false scents in the sand, have pinned my faith on the dew. I have struggled to rejoin my kind, whose very existence on earth I had forgotten. These are the cares of men alive in every fibre, and I cannot help thinking them more important than the fretful choosing of a night-club in which to spend the evening. Compare the one life with the other, and all things considered this is luxury! I have no regrets. I have gambled and lost. It was all in the day's work. At least I have had the unforgettable taste of the sea on my lips.

I am not talking about living dangerously. Such words are meaningless to me. The toreador does not stir me to enthusiasm. It is not danger I love. I know what I love. It is life.

The sky seemed to me faintly bright. I drew up one arm through the sand. There was a bit of the torn parachute within reach, and I ran my hand over it. It was bone dry. Let's see. Dew falls at dawn. Here was dawn risen and no moisture on the cloth. My mind was befuddled and I heard myself say: "There is a dry heart here, a dry heart that cannot know the relief of tears."

I scrambled to my feet. "We're off, Prévot," I said. "Our throats are still open. Get along, man!"

The wind that shrivels up a man in nineteen hours was now blowing out of the west. My gullet was not yet shut, but it was hard and painful and I could feel that there was a rasp in it. Soon that cough would begin that

I had been told about and was now expecting. My tongue was becoming a nuisance. But most serious of all, I was beginning to see shining spots before my eyes. When those spots changed into flames, I should simply lie down.

The first morning hours were cool and we took advantage of them to get on at a good pace. We knew that once the sun was high there would be no more walking for us. We no longer had the right to sweat. Certainly not to stop and catch our breath. This coolness was merely the coolness of low humidity. The prevailing wind was coming from the desert, and under its soft and treacherous caress the blood was being dried out of us.

Our first day's nourishment had been a few grapes. In the next three days each of us ate half an orange and a bit of cake. If we had had anything left now, we couldn't have eaten it because we had no saliva with which to masticate it. But I had stopped being hungry. Thirsty I was, yes, and it seemed to me that I was suffering less from thirst itself than from the effects of thirst. Gullet hard. Tongue like plaster-of-Paris. A rasping in the throat. A horrible taste in the mouth.

All these sensations were new to me, and though I believed water could rid me of them, nothing in my memory associated them with water. Thirst had become more and more a disease and less and less a craving. I began to realize that the thought of water and fruit was now less agonizing than it had been. I was forgetting the radiance of the orange, just as I was forgetting the eyes under the hat-brim. Perhaps I was forgetting everything.

We had sat down after all, but it could not be for long. Nevertheless, it was impossible to go five hundred yards without our legs giving way. To stretch out on the sand would be marvelous—but it could not be.

The landscape had begun to change. Rocky places grew rarer and the sand was now firm beneath our feet. A mile ahead stood dunes and on those dunes we could see a scrubby vegetation. At least this sand was preferable to the steely surface over which we had been trudging. This was the golden desert. This might have been the Sahara. It was in a sense my country.

Two hundred yards had now become our limit, but we had determined to carry on until we reached the vegetation. Better than that we could not hope to do. A week later, when we went back over our traces in a car to have a look at the *Simoon*, I measured this last lap and found that it was just short of fifty miles. All told we had done one hundred and twenty-four miles.

The previous day I had tramped without hope. Today the word "hope" had grown meaningless. Today we were tramping simply because we were tramping. Probably oxen work for the same reason. Yesterday I had dreamed of a paradise of orange-trees. Today I would not give a button for paradise; I did not believe oranges existed. When I thought about myself I found in me nothing but a heart squeezed dry. I was tottering but emotionless. I felt no distress whatever, and in a way I regretted it: misery would have seemed to me as sweet as water. I might then have felt sorry for myself and commiserated with myself as with a friend. But I had not a friend left on earth.

Later, when we were rescued, seeing our burnt-out eyes men thought we must have called aloud and wept and suffered. But cries of despair, misery, sobbing grief are a kind of wealth, and we possessed no wealth. When a young girl is disappointed in love she weeps and knows sorrow. Sorrow is one of the vibrations that prove the fact of living. I felt no sorrow. I was the desert. I could no longer bring up a little saliva; neither could I any longer summon those moving visions towards which I should have loved to stretch forth arms. The sun had dried up the springs of tears in me.

And yet, what was that? A ripple of hope went through me like a faint breeze over a lake. What was this sign that had awakened my instinct before knocking on the door of my consciousness? Nothing had changed, and yet everything was changed. This sheet of sand, these low hummocks and sparse tufts of verdure that had been a landscape, were now become a stage setting. Thus far the stage was empty, but the scene was set. I looked at Prévot. The same astonishing thing had happened to him as to me, but he was as far from guessing its significance as I was.

I swear to you that something is about to happen. I swear that life has sprung in this desert. I swear that this emptiness, this stillness, has suddenly become more stirring than a tumult on a public square.

"Prévot! Footprints! We are saved!"

We had wandered from the trail of the human species; we had cast ourselves forth from the tribe; we had found ourselves alone on earth and forgotten by the universal migration; and here, imprinted in the sand, were the divine and naked feet of man!

"Look, Prévot, here two men stood together and then separated."

"Here a camel knelt."

"Here . . ."

But it was not true that we were already saved. It was not enough to squat down and wait. Before long we should be past saving. Once the cough has begun, the progress made by thirst is swift.

Still, I believed in that caravan swaying somewhere in the desert, heavy with its cargo of treasure.

We went on. Suddenly I heard a cock crow. I remembered what Guillaumet had told me: "Towards the end I heard cocks crowing in the Andes. And I heard the railway train." The instant the cock crowed I thought of Guillaumet and I said to myself: "First it was my eyes that played tricks on me. I suppose this is another of the effects of thirst. Probably my ears have merely held out longer than my eyes." But Prévot grabbed my arm:

"Did you hear that?"

"What?"

"The cock."

"Why . . . why, yes, I did."

To myself I said: "Fool! Get it through your head! This means life!"

I had one last hallucination—three dogs chasing one another. Prévot looked, but could not see them. However, both of us waved our arms at a Bedouin. Both of us shouted with all the breath in our bodies, and laughed for happiness.

But our voices could not carry thirty yards. The Bedouin on his slow-moving camel had come into view from behind a dune and now he was moving slowly out of sight. The man was probably the only Arab in this desert, sent by a demon to materialize and vanish before the eyes of us who could not run.

We saw in profile on the dune another Arab. We shouted, but our shouts were whispers. We waved our arms and it seemed to us that they must fill the sky with monstrous signals. Still the Bedouin stared with averted face away from us.

At last, slowly, slowly he began a right angle turn in our direction. At the very second when he came face to face with us, I thought, the curtain would come down.

At the very second when his eyes met ours, thirst would vanish and by this man would death and the mirages be wiped out. Let this man but make a quarter-turn left and the world is changed. Let him but bring his torso round, but sweep the scene with a glance, and like a god he can create life.

The miracle had come to pass. He was walking towards us over the sand like a god over the waves.

The Arab looked at us without a word. He placed his hands upon our shoulders and we obeyed him: we stretched out upon the sand. Race, language, religion were forgotten. There was only this humble nomad with the hands of an archangel on our shoulders.

Face to the sand, we waited. And when the water came, we drank like calves with our faces in the basin, and with a greediness which alarmed the Bedouin so that from time to time he pulled us back. But as soon as his hand fell away from us we plunged our faces anew into the water.

Water, thou hast no taste, no color, no odor; canst not be defined, art relished while ever mysterious. Not necessary to life, but rather life itself, thou fillest us with a gratification that exceeds the delight of the senses. By thy might, there return into us treasures that we had abandoned. By thy grace, there are released in us all the dried-up runnels of our heart. Of the riches that exist in the world, thou art the rarest and also the most delicate—thou so pure within the bowels of the earth! A man may die of thirst lying beside a magnesian spring. He may die within reach of a salt lake. He may die though he hold in his hand a jug of dew, if it be inhabited by evil salts. For thou, water, art a proud divinity, allowing no alteration, no foreignness in thy being. And the joy that thou spreadest is an infinitely simple joy.

You, Bedouin of Libya who saved our lives, though you will dwell for ever in my memory yet I shall never be able to recapture your features. You are Humanity and your face comes into my mind simply as man incarnate. You, our beloved fellowman, did not know who we might be, and yet you recognized us without fail. And I, in my turn, shall recognize you in the faces of all mankind. You came towards me in an aureole of charity and magnanimity bearing the gift of water. All my friends and all my enemies marched towards me in your person. It did not seem to me that you were rescuing me: rather did it seem that you were forgiving me. And I felt I had no enemy left in all the world.

This is the end of my story. Lifted on to a camel, we went on for three hours. Then, broken with weariness, we asked to be set down at a camp while the cameleers went on ahead for help. Towards six in the evening a car manned by armed Bedouins came to fetch us. A half-hour later we were set down at the house of a Swiss engineer named Raccaud who was operating a soda factory beside saline deposits in the desert. He was unforgettably kind to us. By midnight we were in Cairo.

I awoke between white sheets. Through the curtains came the rays of a sun that was no longer an enemy. I spread butter and honey on my bread. I smiled. I recaptured the savor of my childhood and all its marvels. And I read and re-read the telegram from those dearest to me in all the world whose three words had shattered me: "So terribly happy!"

· 9 ·

Barcelona and Madrid
(1936)

Once again I had found myself in the presence of a truth and had failed to recognize it. Consider what had happened to me: I had thought myself lost, had touched the very bottom of despair; and then, when the spirit of renunciation had filled me, I had known peace. I know now what I was not conscious of at the time—that in such an hour a man feels that he has finally found himself and has become his own friend. An essential inner need has been satisfied, and against that satisfaction, that self-fulfilment, no external power can prevail. Bonnafous, I imagine, he who spent his life

racing before the wind, was acquainted with this serenity of spirit. Guillaumet, too, in his snows. Never shall
I forget that, lying buried to the chin in sand, strangled
slowly to death by thirst, my heart was infinitely warm
beneath the desert stars.

What can men do to make known to themselves this
sense of deliverance? Everything about mankind is paradox. He who strives and conquers grows soft. The mag-
nanimous man grown rich becomes mean. The creative
artist for whom everything is made easy nods. Every
doctrine swears that it can breed men, but none can tell
us in advance what sort of men it will breed. Men are
not cattle to be fattened for market. In the scales of life
an indigent Newton weighs more than a parcel of pros-
perous nonentities. All of us have had the experience of
a sudden joy that came when nothing in the world had
forewarned us of its coming—a joy so thrilling that if it
was born of misery we remembered even the misery with
tenderness. All of us, on seeing old friends again, have
remembered with happiness the trials we lived through
with those friends. Of what can we be certain except
this—that we are fertilized by mysterious circumstances?
Where is man's truth to be found?

Truth is not that which can be demonstrated by the
aid of logic. If orange-trees are hardy and rich in fruit in
this bit of soil and not that, then this bit of soil is what
is truth for orange-trees. If a particular religion, or culture, or scale of values, if one form of activity rather

than another, brings self-fulfilment to a man, releases the prince asleep within him unknown to himself, then that scale of values, that culture, that form of activity, constitute his truth. Logic, you say? Let logic wangle its own explanation of life.

Because it is man and not flying that concerns me most, I shall close this book with the story of man's gropings towards self-fulfilment as I witnessed them in the early months of the civil war in Spain. One year after crashing in the desert I made a tour of the Catalan front in order to learn what happens to man when the scaffolding of his traditions suddenly collapses. To Madrid I went for an answer to another question: How does it happen that men are sometimes willing to die?

I

Flying west from Lyon, I veered left in the direction of the Pyrenees and Spain. Below me floated fleecy white clouds, summer clouds, clouds made for amateur flyers in which great gaps opened like skylights. Through one of these windows I could see Perpignan lying at the bottom of a well of light.

I was flying solo, and as I looked down on Perpignan I was day-dreaming. I had spent six months there once while serving as test pilot at a near-by airdrome. When the day's work was done I would drive into this town where every day was as peaceful as Sunday. I would sit in a wicker chair within sound of the café band, sip a glass of port, and look idly on at the provincial life of the place, reflecting that it was as innocent as a review of lead soldiers. These pretty girls, these carefree strollers, this pure sky. . . .

But here came the Pyrenees. The last happy town was left behind.

Below me lay Figueras, and Spain. This was where men killed one another. What was most astonishing here was not the sight of conflagration, ruin, and signs of man's distress—it was the absence of all these. Figueras seemed no different from Perpignan. I leaned out and stared hard.

There were no scars on that heap of white gravel, that church gleaming in the sun, which I knew had been burnt. I could not distinguish its irreparable wounds. Gone was the pale smoke that had carried off its gilding, had melted in the blue of the sky its altar screens, its prayer books, its sacerdotal treasures. Not a line of the church was altered. This town, seated at the heart of its fan-shaped roads like a spider at the centre of its silken trap, looked very much like the other.

Like other towns, this one was nourished by the fruits of the plain that rose along the white highways to meet it. All that I could discern was the slow gnawing which, through the centuries, had swallowed up the soil, driven away the forests, divided up the fields, dug out these life-giving irrigation ditches. Here was a face unlikely to change much, for it was already old. A colony of bees, I said to myself, once it was established so solidly within the boundaries of an acre of flowers, would be assured of peace. But peace is not given to a colony of men.

Human drama does not show itself on the surface of life. It is not played out in the visible world, but in the hearts of men. Even in happy Perpignan a victim of cancer walled up behind his hospital window goes round and round in a circle striving helplessly to escape the pain that hovers over him like a relentless kite. One man in misery can disrupt the peace of a city. It is another of the miraculous things about mankind that there is no pain nor passion that does not radiate to the ends of the earth. Let a man in a garret but burn with enough intensity and he will set fire to the world.

Gerona went by, Barcelona loomed into view, and I let myself glide gently down from the perch of my observatory. Even here I could see nothing out of the way, unless it was that the avenues were deserted. Again there were devastated churches which, from above, looked untouched. Faintly visible was something that I guessed to be smoke. Was that one of the signs I was seeking? Was this a scrap of evidence of that nearly soundless anger whose all-destroying wrath was so hard to measure? A whole civilization was contained in that faint golden puff so lightly dispersed by a breath of wind.

I am quite convinced of the sincerity of people who say: "Terror in Barcelona? Nonsense. That great city in ashes? A mere twenty houses wrecked. Streets heaped with the dead? A few hundred killed out of a population of a million. Where did you see a firing line running with blood and deafening with the roar of guns?"

I agree that I saw no firing line. I saw groups of tranquil men and women strolling on the Ramblas. When, on occasion, I ran against a barricade of militiamen in arms, a smile was often enough to open the way before me. I did not come at once upon the firing line. In a civil war the firing line is invisible; it passes through the hearts of men. And yet, on my very first night in Barcelona I skirted it.

I was sitting on the pavement of a café, sipping my drink surrounded by light-hearted men and women, when suddenly four armed men stopped where I sat, stared at a man at the next table, and without a word pointed their guns at his stomach. Streaming with sweat the man stood up and raised leaden arms above his head. One of the militiamen ran his hands over his clothes and his eyes over some papers he found in the man's pockets, and ordered him to come along.

The man left his half-emptied glass, the last glass of his life, and started down the road. Surrounded by the squad, his hands stuck up like the hands of a man going down for the last time.

"Fascist!" A woman behind me said it with contempt.

She was the only witness who dared betray that anything out of the ordinary had taken place. Untouched, the man's glass stood on the table, a mute witness to a mad confidence in chance, in forgiveness, in life. I sat watching the disappearance in a ring of rifles of a man who five minutes before, within two feet of me, had crossed the invisible firing line.

My guides were anarchists. They led me to the railway station where troops were being entrained. Far from the platforms built for tender farewells, we were walking in a desert of signal towers and switching points, stumbling in the rain through a labyrinthine yard filled with blackened goods wagons where tarpaulins the color of lard were spread over carloads of stiffened forms. This world had lost its human quality, had become a world of iron, and therefore uninhabitable. A ship remains a living thing only so long as man with his brushes and oils swabs an artificial layer of light over it. Leave them to themselves a couple of weeks and the life dies out of your ship, your factory, your railway; death covers their faces. After six thousand years the stones of a temple still vibrate with the passage of man; but a little rust, a night of rain, and this railway yard is eaten away to its very skeleton.

Here are our men. Cannon and machine-guns are being loaded on board with the straining muscles and the hoarse gaspings that are always drawn from men by these monstrous insects, these fleshless insects, these lumps of carapace and vertebra. What is startling here is the silence. Not a note of song, not a single shout. Only, now and then, when a gun-carriage lands, the hollow thump of a steel plate. Of human voices no sound.

No uniforms, either. These men are going off to be killed in their working garb. Wearing their dark clothes stiff with mud, the column heaving and sweating at their work look like the denizens of a night shelter. They fill me with the same uneasiness I felt when the yellow fever broke out among us at Dakar, ten years ago.

The chief of the detachment had been speaking to me in a whisper. I caught the end of his speech:

". . . and we move up to Saragossa."

Why the devil did he have to whisper! The atmosphere of this yard made me think of a hospital. But of course! That was it. A civil war is not a war, it is a disease. These men were not going up to the front in the exultation of certain victory; they were struggling blindly against infection.

And the same thing was going on in the enemy camp. The purpose of this struggle was not to rid the country of an invading foreigner but to eradicate a plague. A new faith is like a plague. It attacks from within. It propagates in the invisible. Walking in the streets, whoever belongs to a Party feels himself surrounded by secretly infected men.

This must have been why these troops were going

off in silence with their instruments of asphyxiation. There was not the slightest resemblance between them and regiments that go into battle against foreign armies and are set out on the chessboard of the fields and moved about by strategists. These men had gathered together haphazardly in a city filled with chaos.

There was not much to choose between Barcelona and its enemy, Saragossa: both were composed of the same swarm of communists, anarchists, and fascists. The very men who collected on the same side were perhaps more different from one another than from their enemies. In civil war the enemy is inward; one as good as fights against oneself.

What else can explain the particular horror of this war in which firing squads count for more than soldiers of the line? Death in this war is a sort of quarantine. Purges take place of germ-carriers. The anarchists go from house to house and load the plague-stricken into their tumbrils, while on the other side of the barricade Franco is able to utter that horrible boast: "There are no more communists among us."

The conscripts are weeded out by a kind of medical board; the officer in charge is a sort of army doctor. Men present themselves for service with pride shining in their eyes and the belief in their hearts that they have a part to play in society.

"Exempt from service for life!" is the decision.

Fields have been turned into charnel-houses and the

dead are burned in lime or petroleum. Respect for the dignity of man has been trampled under foot. Since on both sides the political parties spy upon the stirrings of man's conscience as upon the workings of a disease, why should the urn of his flesh be respected? This body that clothes the spirit, that moves with grace and boldness, that knows love, that is apt for self-sacrifice—no one now so much as thinks of giving it decent burial.

I thought of our respect for the dead. I thought of the white sanatorium where the light of a man's life goes quietly out in the presence of those who love him and who garner as if it were an inestimable treasure his last words, his ultimate smile. How right they are! Seeing that this same whole is never again to take shape in the world. Never again will be heard exactly that note of laughter, that intonation of voice, that quality of repartee. Each individual is a miracle. No wonder we go on speaking of the dead for twenty years.

Here, in Spain, a man is simply stood up against a wall and he gives up his entrails to the stones of the courtyard. You have been captured. You are shot. Reason: your ideas were not our ideas.

This entrainment in the rain is the only thing that rings true about their war. These men stand round and stare at me, and I read in their eyes a mournful sobriety. They know the fate that awaits them if they are captured. I begin to shiver with the cold and observe of a sudden that no woman has been allowed to see them off.

The absence of women seems to me right. There is no place here for mothers who bring children into the world in ignorance of the faith that will some day flare up in their sons, in ignorance of the ideologist who, according to his lights, will prop up their sons against a wall when they have come to their twenty years of life.

We went up by motor into the war zone. Barricades became more frequent, and from place to place we had to negotiate with revolutionary committees. Passes were valid only from one village to the next.

"Are you trying to get closer to the front?"

"Exactly."

The chairman of the local committee consulted a large-scale map.

"You won't be able to get through. The rebels have occupied the road four miles ahead. But you might try swinging left here. This road ought to be free. Though there was talk of rebel cavalry cutting it this morning."

It was very difficult in those early days of the revolution to know one's way about in the vicinity of the front. There were loyal villages, rebel villages, neutral villages, and they shifted their allegiance between dawn and dark. This tangle of loyal and rebel zones made me think the push must be pretty weak. It certainly bore no resemblance to a line of trenches cutting off friend from enemy as cleanly as a knife. I felt as if I were walking in a bog. Here the earth was solid beneath our feet: there we sank into it. We moved in a maze of uncertainty. Yet what space, what air between movements! These military operations are curiously lacking in density.

Once again we reached a point beyond which we were told we could not advance. Six rifles and a low wall of paving stones blocked the road. Four men and two women lay stretched on the ground behind the wall. I made a mental note that the women did not know how to hold a rifle.

"This is as far as you can go."

"Why?"

"Rebels."

We got out of the car and sat down with the militiamen upon the grass. They put down their rifles and cut a few slices of fresh bread.

"Is this your village?" we asked.

"No, we are Catalans, from Barcelona. Communist Party."

One of the girls stretched herself and sat up on the barricade, her hair blowing in the wind. She was rather thick-set, but young and healthy. Smiling happily she said:

"I am going to stay in this village when the war is over. I didn't know it, but the country beats the city all hollow."

She cast a loving glance round at the countryside, as

if stirred by a revelation. Her life had been the gray slums, days spent in a factory, and the sordid compensation afforded by the cafés. Everything that went on here seemed to her as jolly as a picnic. She jumped down and ran to the village well. Probably she believed she was drinking at the very breast of mother earth.

"Have you done any fighting here?"

"No. The rebels kick up a little dust now and then, but . . . We see a lorryload of men from time to time and hope that they will come along this road. But nothing has come by in two weeks."

They were awaiting their first enemy. In the rebel village opposite sat another half-dozen militiamen awaiting a first enemy. Twelve warriors alone in the world.

Each side was waiting for something to be born in the invisible. The rebels were waiting for the host of hesitant people in Madrid to declare themselves for Franco. Barcelona was waiting for Saragossa to waken out of an inspired dream, declare itself Socialist, and fall. It was the thought more than the soldier that was besieging the town. The thought was the great hope and the great enemy.

It seemed to me that the bombers, the shells, the militiamen under arms, by themselves had no power to conquer. On each side a single man entrenched behind his line of defense was better than a hundred besiegers. But thought might worm its way in.

From time to time there is an attack. From time to

time the tree is shaken. Not to uproot it, but merely to see if the fruit is yet ripe. And if it is, a town falls.

II

Back from the front, I found friends in Barcelona who allowed me to join in their mysterious expeditions. We went deep into the mountains and were now in one of those villages which are possessed by a mixture of peace and terror.

"Oh, yes, we shot seventeen of them."

They had shot seventeen "fascists." The parish priest, the priest's housekeeper, the sexton, and fourteen village notables. Everything is relative, you see. When they read in their provincial newspaper the story of the life of Basil Zaharoff, master of the world, they transpose it into their own language. They recognize in him the nurseryman, or the pharmacist. And when they shoot the pharmacist, in a way they are shooting Basil Zaharoff. The only one who does not understand is the pharmacist.

"Now we are all Loyalists together. Everything has calmed down."

Almost everything. The conscience of the village is tormented by one man whom I have seen at the tavern, smiling, helpful, so anxious to go on living! He comes to the pub in order to show us that, despite his few acres of vineyard, he too is part of the human race, suffers with rheumatism like it, mops his face like it with a blue handkerchief. He comes, and he plays billiards. Can one shoot a man who plays billiards? Besides, he plays badly with his great trembling hands. He is upset; he still does not know whether he is a fascist or not. He puts me in mind of those poor monkeys who dance before the boa-constrictor in the hope of softening it.

There was nothing we could do for the man. For the time being we had another job in hand. Sitting on a table and swinging my legs at committee headquarters, while my companion, Pépin, pulled a bundle of soiled papers out of his pocket, I had a good look at these terrorists. Their looks belied their name: honorable peasants with frank eyes and sober attentive faces, they were the same everywhere we went; and though we were foreigners possessing no authority, we were everywhere received with the same grave courtesy.

"Yes, here it is," said Pépin, a document in his hand. "His name is Laporte. Any of you know him?"

The paper went from hand to hand and the members of the committee shook their heads.

"No. Laporte? Never heard of him."

I started to explain something to them, but Pépin motioned me to be silent. "They won't talk," he said, "but they know him well enough."

Pépin spread his references before the chairman, saying casually:

"I am a French socialist. Here is my party card."

The card was passed round and the chairman raised his eyes to us:

"Laporte. I don't believe. . . ."

"Of course you know him. A French monk. Probably in disguise. You captured him yesterday in the woods. Laporte, his name is. The French consulate wants him."

I sat swinging my legs. What a strange session! Here we were in a mountain village sixty miles from the French frontier, asking a revolutionary committee that shot even parish priests' housekeepers to surrender to us in good shape a French monk. Whatever happened to us, we would certainly have asked for it. Nevertheless, I felt safe. There was no treachery in these people. And why, as a matter of fact, should they bother to play tricks? We had absolutely no protection; we meant no more to them than Laporte; they could do anything they pleased.

Pépin nudged me. "I've an idea we have come too late," he said.

The chairman cleared his throat and made up his mind.

"This morning," he said, "we found a dead man on the road just outside the village. He must be there still."

And he pretended to send off for the dead man's papers.

"They've already shot him," Pépin said to me. "Too

bad! They would certainly have turned him over to us. They are good kind people."

I looked straight into the eyes of these curious "good kind people." Strange: there was nothing in their eyes to upset me. There seemed nothing to fear in their set jaws and the blank smoothness of their faces. Blank, as if vaguely bored. A rather terrible blankness. I wondered why, despite our unusual mission, we were not suspect to them. What difference had they established in their minds between us and the "fascist" in the neighboring tavern who was dancing his dance of death before the unavailing indifference of these judges? A crazy notion came into my head, forced upon my attention by all the power of my instinct: If one of those men yawned I should be afraid. I should feel that all human communication had snapped between us.

After we left, I said to Pépin:

"That is the third village in which we have done this job and I still cannot make up my mind whether the job is dangerous or not."

Pépin laughed and admitted that although he had saved dozens of men on these missions, he himself did not know the answer.

"Yesterday," he confessed, "I had a narrow squeak. I snaffled a Carthusian monk away from them just as they were about to shoot the fellow. The smell of blood was in the air, and . . . Well, they growled a bit, you know."

I know the end of that story. Pépin, the socialist and notorious anti-church political worker, having staked his life to get that Carthusian, had hustled him into a motor-car and there, by way of compensation, he sought to insult the priest by the finest bit of blasphemy he could summon:

"You . . . you . . . you triple damned monk!" he had finally spluttered.

This was Pépin's triumph. But the monk, who had not been listening, flung his arms round Pépin's neck and wept with happiness.

In another village they gave up a man to us. With a great air of mystery, four militiamen dug him up out of a cellar. He was a lively bright-eyed monk whose name I have already forgotten, disguised as a peasant and carrying a long gnarled stick scarred with notches.

"I kept track of the days," he explained. "Three weeks in the woods is a long time. Mushrooms are not specially nourishing, and they grabbed me when I came near a village."

The mayor of the village, to whom we owed this gift, was very proud of him.

"We shot at him a lot and thought we had killed him," he said. And then, by way of excuse for the bad marksmanship, he added: "I must say it was at night."

The monk laughed.

"I wasn't afraid."

We put him into the car, and before we threw in the

clutch everybody had to shake hands all round with these terrible terrorists. The monk's hand was shaken hardest of all and he was repeatedly congratulated on being alive. To all these friendly sentiments he responded with a warmth of unquestionably sincere appreciation.

As for me, I wish I understood mankind.

We went over our lists. At Sitges lived a man who, we had been told, was in danger of being shot. We drove round and found his door wide open. Up a flight of stairs we ran into our skinny young man.

"It seems that these people are likely to shoot you," we told him. "Come back to Barcelona with us and you will be shipped home to France in the *Duquesne*."

The young man took a long time to think this over and then said:

"This is some trick of my sister's."

"What?"

"She lives in Barcelona. She would never pay for the child's keep and I always had to. . . ."

"Your family troubles are none of our affair. Are you in danger here, yes or no?"

"I don't know. I tell you, my sister . . ."

"Do you want to get away, yes or no?"

"I really don't know. What do you think? In Barcelona, my sister . . ."

The man was carrying on his family quarrel through

the revolution. He was going to stay here in order to do his sister in the eye.

"Do as you please," we said, finally, and we left him where he was.

We stopped the car and got out. A volley of rifle-shot had crackled in the still country air. From the top of the road we looked down upon a clump of trees out of which, a quarter of a mile away, stuck two tall chimneys. A squad of militiamen came up and loaded their guns. We asked what was going on. They looked round, pointed to the chimneys, and decided that the firing must have come from the factory.

The shooting died down almost immediately, and silence fell again. The chimneys went on smoking peacefully. A ripple of wind ran over the grass. Nothing had changed visibly, and we ourselves were unchanged. Nevertheless, in that clump of trees someone had just died.

One of the militiamen said that a girl had been killed at the factory, together with her brothers, but there was still some uncertainty about this. What excruciating simplicity! Our own peace of mind had not been invaded by those muffled sounds in the clump of greenery, by that brief partridge drive. The angelus, as it were, that had rung out in that foliage had left us calm and unrepentant.

Human events display two faces, one of drama and

the other of indifference. Everything changes according-ing as the event concerns the individual or the species. In its migrations, in its imperious impulses, the species forgets its dead. This, perhaps, explains the unperturbed faces of these peasants. One feels that they have no special taste for horror; yet they will come back from that clump of trees on the one hand content to have administered their kind of justice, and on the other hand quite indifferent to the fate of the girl who stumbled against the root of the tree of death, who was caught by death's harpoon as she fled, and who now lies in the wood, her mouth filled with blood.

Here I touch the inescapable contradiction I shall never be able to resolve. For man's greatness does not reside merely in the destiny of the species: each indi-vidual is an empire. When a mine caves in and closes over the head of a single miner, the life of the com-munity is suspended.

His comrades, their women, their children, gather in anguish at the entrance to the mine, while below them the rescue party scratch with their picks at the bowels of the earth. What are they after? Are they consciously saving one unit of society? Are they freeing a human being as one might free a horse, after computing the work he is still capable of doing? Ten other miners may be killed in the attempted rescue: what inept cost ac-counting! Of course it is not a matter of saving one ant out of the colony of ants! They are rescuing a consciousness, an empire whose significance is incommensurable with anything else.

Inside the narrow skull of the miner pinned beneath the fallen timber, there lives a world. Parents, friends, a home, the hot soup of evening, songs sung on feast days, loving kindness and anger, perhaps even a social consciousness and a great universal love, inhabit that skull. By what are we to measure the value of a man? His ancestor once drew a reindeer on the wall of a cave; and two hundred thousand years later that gesture still radiates. It stirs us, prolongs itself in us. Man's gestures are an eternal spring. Though we die for it, we shall bring up that miner from his shaft. Solitary he may be; universal he surely is.

In Spain there are crowds in movement, but the individual, that universe, calls in vain for help from the bottom of the mine.

III

Machine-gun bullets cracked against the stone above our heads as we skirted the moonlit wall. Low-flying lead thudded into the rubble of an embankment that rose on the other side of the road. Half a mile away a battle was in progress, the line of fire drawn in the shape of a horse-shoe ahead of us and on our flanks.

Walking between wall and parapet on the white highway, my guide and I were able to disregard the spatter of missiles in a feeling of perfect security. We could sing, we could laugh, we could strike matches, without drawing upon ourselves the direct fire of the enemy. We went forward like peasants on their way to market. Half a mile away the iron hand of war would have set us inescapably upon the black chessboard of battle; but here, out of the game, ignored, the Republican lieutenant and I were as free as air.

Shells filled the night with absurd parabolas during their three seconds of freedom between release and exhaustion. There were the duds that dove without bursting into the ground; there were the travelers in space that whipped straight overhead, elongated in their race to the stars. And the leaden bullets that ricocheted in our faces and tinkled curiously in our ears were like bees, dangerous for the twinkling of an eye, poisonous but ephemeral.

Walking on, we reached a point where the embankment had collapsed.

"We might follow the cross-trench from here," my guide suggested.

Things had suddenly turned serious. Not that we were in the line of machine-gun fire, or that a roving searchlight was about to spot us. It was not as bad as that. There had simply been a rustling overhead; a sort of celestial gurgle had sounded. It meant no harm to us, but the lieutenant remarked suddenly, "That is meant for Madrid," and we went down into the trench.

The trench ran along the crest of a hill a little before reaching the suburb of Carabanchel. In the direction of Madrid a part of the parapet had crumbled and we could see the city in the gap, white, strangely white, under the full moon. Hardly a mile separated us from those tall structures dominated by the tower of the Telephone Building.

Madrid was asleep—or rather Madrid was feigning sleep. Not a light; not a sound. Like clockwork, every two minutes the funereal fracas that we were henceforth to hear roared forth and was dissolved in a dead silence. It seemed to waken no sound and no stirring in the city, but was swallowed up each time like a stone in water.

Suddenly in the place of Madrid I felt that I was staring at a face with closed eyes. The hard face of an obstinate virgin taking blow after blow without a moan. Once again there sounded overhead that gurgling in the stars of a newly uncorked bottle. One second, two seconds, five seconds went by. There was an explosion and I ducked involuntarily. There goes the whole town, I thought.

But Madrid was still there. Nothing had collapsed. Not an eye had blinked. Nothing was changed. The stone face was as pure as ever.

"Meant for Madrid," the lieutenant repeated mechanically. He taught me to tell these celestial shudders apart, to follow the course of these sharks rushing upon their prey:

"No, that is one of our batteries replying. . . . That's theirs, but firing somewhere else. . . . There's one meant for Madrid."

Waiting for an explosion is the longest passage of time I know. What things go on in that interminable moment! An enormous pressure rises, rises. Will that boiler ever make up its mind to burst? At last! For some that meant death, but there are others for whom it meant escape from death. Eight hundred thousand souls, less half a score of dead, have won a last-minute reprieve. Between the gurgling and the explosion eight hundred thousand lives were in danger of death.

Each shell in the air threatened them all. I could feel the city out there, tense, compact, a solid. I saw them all in the mind's eye—men, women, children, all that humble population crouching in the sheltering cloak of stone of a motionless virgin. Again I heard the ignoble crash and was gripped and sickened by the downward course of the torpedo. . . . Torpedo? I scarcely knew what I was saying. "They . . . they are torpedoing Madrid." And the lieutenant, standing there counting the shells, said:

"Meant for Madrid. Sixteen."

I crept out of the trench, lay flat on my stomach on the parapet, and stared. A new image has wiped out the old. Madrid with its chimney-pots, its towers, its port-holes, now looks like a ship on the high seas. Madrid all white on the black waters of the night. A city outlives its inhabitants. Madrid, loaded with emigrants, is ferrying them from one shore to the other of life. It has a generation on board. Slowly it navigates through the centuries. Men, women, children fill it from garret to hold. Resigned or quaking with fear, they live only for the moment to come. A vessel loaded with humanity is being torpedoed. The purpose of the enemy is to sink Madrid as if she were a ship.

Stretched out on the parapet I do not care a curse for the rules of war. For justifications or for motives. I listen. I have learned to read the course of these gur-glings among the stars. They pass quite close to Sagit-tarius. I have learned to count slowly up to five. And I listen. But what tree has been sundered by this light-ning, what cathedral has been gutted, what poor child has just been stricken, I have no means of knowing.

That same afternoon I had witnessed a bombardment in the town itself. All the force of this thunder-clap had to burst on the Gran Via in order to uproot a human life. One single life. Passers-by had brushed rubbish off their clothes; others had scattered on the run; and when the light smoke had risen and cleared away, the be-trothed, escaped by miracle without a scratch, found at his feet his *novia*, whose golden arm a moment before had been in his, changed into a blood-filled sponge, changed into a limp packet of flesh and rags.

He had knelt down, still uncomprehending, had

nodded his head slowly, as if saying to himself, "Something very strange has happened."

This marvel spattered on the pavement bore no resemblance to what had been his beloved. Misery was excruciatingly slow to engulf him in its tidal wave. For still another second, stunned by the feat of the invisible prestidigitator, he cast a bewildered glance round him in search of the slender form, as if it at least should have survived. Nothing was there but a packet of muck.

Gone was the feeble spark of humanity. And while in the man's throat there was brewing that shriek which I know not what deferred, he had the leisure to reflect that it was not those lips he had loved but their pout, not them but their smile. Not those eyes, but their glance. Not that breast, but its gentle swell. He was free to discover at last the source of the anguish love had been storing up for him, to learn that it was the unattainable he had been pursuing. What he had yearned to embrace was not the flesh but a downy spirit, a spark, the impalpable angel that inhabits the flesh.

I do not care a curse for the rules of war and the law of reprisal. As for the military advantage of such a bombardment, I simply cannot grasp it. I have seen housewives disemboweled, children mutilated; I have seen the old itinerant market crone sponge from her treasures the brains with which they were spattered. I have seen a janitor's wife come out of her cellar and douse the sullied pavement with a bucket of water, and I am still unable to understand what part these humble slaughter-house accidents play in warfare.

A moral rôle? But a bombardment turns against the bombarder! Each shell that fell upon Madrid fortified something in the town. It persuaded the hesitant neutral to plump for the defenders. A dead child weighs heavily in the balance when it is one's own. It was clear to me that a bombardment did not disperse—it unified. Horror causes men to clench their fists, and in horror men join together.

The lieutenant and I crawled along the parapet. Face or ship, Madrid stood erect, receiving blows without a moan. But men are like this: slowly but surely, ordeal fortifies their virtues.

Because of the ordeal my companion's heart was high. He was thinking of the hardening of Madrid's will. He stood up with his fists on his hips, breathing heavily. Pity for the women and the children had gone out of him.

"That makes sixty," he counted grimly.

The blow resounded on the anvil. A giant smith was forging Madrid.

One side or the other would win. Madrid would resist or it would fall. A thousand forces were engaged in this mortal confusion of tongues from which anything might come forth. But one did not need to be a Martian, did not need to see these men dispassionately in a long perspective, in order to perceive that they were struggling against themselves, were their own enemy. Mankind perhaps was being brought to bed of something here in Spain; something perhaps was to be born of this chaos, this disruption. For indeed not all that I saw in Spain was horror, not all of it filled my mouth with a taste of ashes.

IV

On the Guadalajara front I sat at night in a dugout with a Republican squad made up of a lieutenant, a sergeant, and three men. They were about to go out on patrol duty. One of them—the night was cold—stood half in shadow with his head not quite through the neck of a sweater he was pulling on, his arms caught in the sleeves and waving slowly and awkwardly in the air like the short arms of a bear. Smothered curses, stubbles of beard, distant muffled explosions—the atmosphere was a strange compound of sleep, waking, and death. I thought of tramps on the road bestirring themselves, raising themselves up off the ground on heavy sticks. Caught in the earth, painted by the earth, their hands grubby with their gardenless gardening, these men were raising themselves painfully out of the mud in order to emerge under the stars. In these blocks of caked clay I could sense the awakening of consciousness, and as I looked at them I said to myself that across the way, at this very moment, the enemy was getting into his harness, was thickening his body with woolen sweaters; earth-crusted, he was breaking out of his mould of hardened mud. Across the way the same clay shaping the same beings was wakening in the same way into consciousness.

The patrol moved forward across fields through crackling stubble, knocking its toes against unseen rocks in the dark. We were making our way down into a narrow valley on the other side of which the enemy was entrenched. Caught in the cross-fire of artillery, the peasants had evacuated this valley, and their deserted village lay here drowned in the waters of war. Only their dogs remained, ghostly creatures that hunted their pitiful prey in the day and howled in the night. At four in the morning, when the moon rose white as a picked bone, a whole village bayed at the dead divinity.

"Go down and find out if the enemy is hiding in that village," the commanding officer had ordered. Very likely on the other side the same order had been given.

We were accompanied by a sort of political agent, a civilian, whose name I have forgotten, though not what he looked like. It seems to me he must have been rheumatic, and I remember that he leaned heavily on a knotted stick as we tramped forward in the night. His face was the face of a conscientious and elderly workman. I would have sworn that he was above politics and parties, above ideological rivalries. "Pity it is," he would say, "that as things are we cannot explain our point of view to the other fellow." He walked weighed down by his doctrine, like an evangelist. Across the way, meanwhile, was the other evangelist, a believer just as enlightened as this one, his boots just as muddy, his duty taking him on exactly the same errand.

"You'll hear them pretty soon," my commissar said. "When we get close enough we'll call out to the enemy, ask him questions; and he may answer tonight."

Although we don't yet know it, we are in search of a gospel to embrace all gospels, we are on the march towards a stormy Sinai.

And we have arrived. Here is a dazed sentry, half asleep in the shadow of a stone wall.

"Yes," says my commissar, "sometimes they answer. Sometimes they call out first and ask questions. Of course they don't answer, too, sometimes. Depends on the mood they're in."

Just like the gods.

A hundred yards behind us lie our trenches. I strike a match, intending to light a cigarette, and two powerful hands duck my head. Everybody has ducked, and I hear the whistle of bullets in the air. Then silence. The shots were fired high and the volley was not repeated— a mere reminder from the enemy of what constitutes decorum here. One does not light a cigarette in the face of the enemy.

We are joined by three or four men, wrapped in blankets, who had been posted behind neighboring walls.

"Looks as if the lads across the way were awake," one of them remarks.

"Do you think they'll talk tonight? We'd like to talk to them."

"One of them, Antonio, he talks sometimes."

"Call him."

The man in the blanket straightens up, cups his hands round his mouth, takes a deep breath, and calls out slowly and loudly: "An . . . to . . . ni . . . o!"

The call swells, unfurls, floats across the valley and echoes back.

"Better duck," my neighbor advises. "Sometimes when you call them, they let fly."

Crouched behind the stone wall, we listen. No sound of a shot. Yet we cannot say we have heard nothing at all, for the whole night is singing like a sea-shell.

"Hi! Antonio . . . o! Are you . . ."

The man in the blanket draws another deep breath and goes on:

"Are you asleep?"

"Asleep?" says the echo. "Asleep?" the valley asks. "Asleep?" the whole night wants to know. The sound fills all space. We scramble to our feet and stand erect in perfect confidence. They have not touched their guns.

I stand imagining them on their side of the valley as they listen, hear, receive this human voice, this voice that obviously has not stirred them to anger since no finger has pressed a trigger. True, they do not answer, they are silent; but how attentive must be that silent audience from which, a moment ago, a match had sufficed to draw a volley. Borne on the breeze of a human voice, invisible seeds are fertilizing that black earth across the valley. Those men thirst for our words as we for theirs. But their fingers, meanwhile, are on their triggers. They put me in mind of those wild things we would try in the desert to tame and that would stare at us, eat the food and drink the water we set out for them, and would spring at our throats when we made a move to stroke them.

We squatted well down behind the wall and held up a lighted match above it. Three bullets passed overhead. To the match they said, "You are forgetting that we are at war." To us, "We are listening, nevertheless. We can still love, though we stick to our rules."

Another giant peasant rested his gun against the wall, stood up, drew a deep breath, and let go:

"Antonio . . . o! It's me! Leo!"

The sound moved across the valley like a ship new-launched. Eight hundred yards to the far shore, eight hundred back—sixteen hundred yards. If they answered, there would be five seconds of time between our questions and their replies. Five seconds of silence, in which all war would be suspended, would go by between each question and each answer. Like an embassy on a journey, each time. What this meant was that even if they answered, we should still feel ourselves separated from them. Between them and us the inertia of an invisible world would still be there to be stirred into action. For the considerable space of five seconds we should be like men shipwrecked and fearful lest the rescue party had not heard their cries.

". . . ooo!"

A distant voice like a feeble wave has curled up to die on our shore. The phrase, the word, was lost on the way and the result is an undecipherable message. Yet it strikes me like a blow. In this impenetrable darkness a sudden flash of light has gleamed. All of us are shaken by a ridiculous hope. Something has made known to us its existence. We can be sure now that there are men across the way. It is as if in invisibility a crack had opened, as if . . . Imagine a house at night, dark and its doors all locked. You, sitting in its darkness, suddenly feel a breath of cold air on your face. A single breath. What a presence!

There it comes again! ". . . time . . . sleep!"

Torn, mutilated as a truly urgent message must be, washed by the waves and soaked in brine, here is our message. The men who fired at our cigarettes have blown up their chests with air in order to send us this motherly bit of advice:

"Quiet! Go to bed! Time to sleep!"

It excites us. You who read this will perhaps think that these men were merely playing a game. In a sense they were. I am sure that, being simple men, if you had caught them at their sport they would have denied that it was serious. But games always cover something deep and intense, else there would be no excitement in them, no pleasure, no power to stir us. Here was a game that made our hearts beat too wildly not to satisfy a real though undefined need within us. It was as if we were marrying our enemy before dying of his blow.

But so slight, so fragile was the pontoon flung between our two shores that a question too awkward, a phrase too clumsy, would certainly upset it. Words lose themselves: only essential words, only the truth of truths would leave this frail bridge whole. And I can see him now, that peasant who stirred Antonio to speech and thus made himself our pilot, our ambassador; I can see him as he stood erect, as he rested his strong hands on the low stone wall and sent forth from his great chest that question of questions:

"Antonio! What are you fighting for?"

Let me say again that he and Antonio would be ashamed to think that you took them seriously. They would insist that it was all in fun. But I was there as he stood waiting, and I know that his whole soul gaped wide to receive the answer. Here is the truncated message, the secret mutilated by five seconds of travel across the valley as an inscription in stone is defaced by the passing of the centuries:

". . . Spain!"

And then I heard:

". . . You?"

He got his answer. I heard the great reply as it was flung forth into space:

"The bread of our brothers!"

And then the amazing:

"Good night, friend!"

And the response from the other side of the world:

"Good night, friend!"

And silence.

Their words were not the same, but their truths were identical. Why has this high communion never yet prevented men from dying in battle against each other?

V

Back on the Madrid front I sat again at night in a subterranean chamber, at supper with a young captain and a few of his men. The telephone had rung and the captain was being ordered to prepare to attack before daybreak. Twenty houses in this industrial suburb, Carabanchel, constituted the objective. There would be no support: one after the other the houses were to be blown in with hand grenades and occupied.

I felt vaguely squeamish as I took something like a last look at these men who were shortly to dive into the great bowl of air, suck the blue night into their lungs, and then be blown to bits before they could reach the other side of the road. They were taking it easily enough, but the captain came back to table from the telephone shrugging his shoulders. "The first man out . . ." He started to say something, changed his mind, pushed two glasses and a bottle of brandy across the table, and said to the sergeant:

"You lead the file with me. Have a drink and go get some sleep."

The sergeant drank and went off to sleep. Round the table a dozen of us were sitting up. All the chinks in this room were caulked up; not a trickle of light could escape; the glare within was so dazzling that I blinked. The brandy was sweet, faintly nauseating, and its taste was as mournful as a drizzle at daybreak. I was in a daze, and when I had drunk I shut my eyes and saw behind my lids those ruined and ghostly houses bathed in a greenish radiance as of moonglow under water, that I had stared at a few minutes before through the sentry's loophole. Someone on my right was telling a funny story. He was talking very fast and I understood about one word in three.

A man came in half drunk, reeling gently in this half-real world. He stood rubbing a stubble of beard and looking us over with vague affectionate eyes. His glance slid across to the bottle, avoided it, came back to it, and turned pleadingly to the captain.

The captain laughed softly, and the man, suddenly hopeful, laughed too. A light gust of laughter ran over the roomful of men. The captain put out his hand and moved the bottle noiselessly out of reach. The man's glance simulated despair, and a childish game began, a sort of mute ballet which, in the fog of cigarette smoke and the weariness of the watch with its anticipation of the coming attack, was utterly dream-like. I sat hypnotized by this atmosphere of the slowly ending vigil, reading the hour in the stubbles of beard while out of doors a sea-like pounding of cannon waxed in intensity.

Soon afterwards these men were to scour themselves clean of their sweat, their brandy, the filth of their vigil, in the regal waters of the night of war. I felt in them something so near to spotless purity! Meanwhile, as long as it would last, they were dancing the ballet of the drunkard and the bottle. They were determined that this game should absorb them utterly. They were making life last as long as it possibly could. But there on a shelf stood a battered alarm clock, set to sound the zero-hour. No one so much as glanced at it but me, and my glance was furtive. They would all hear it well enough, never fear! Its ringing would shatter the stifling air.

The clock would ring out. The men would rise to their feet and stretch themselves. They would be sure to make this gesture which is instinctive in every man about to tackle the problem of survival. They would stretch themselves, I say, and they would buckle on their harness. The captain would pull his revolver out of his holster. The drunk would sober up. And all these men, without undue haste, would file into the passage. They would go as far as that rectangle of pale light which is the sky at the end of the passage, and there they would mutter something simple like "Look at that moon!" or "What a night!" And then they would fling themselves into the stars.

Scarcely had the attack been called off by telephone, scarcely had these men, most of whom had been doomed to die in the attack upon that concrete wall, begun to feel themselves safe, begun to realize that they were certain of trampling their sweet planet in their rough clogs one more day, scarcely were their minds at peace, when all in chorus began to lament their fate.

"Do they think we are a lot of women?" "Is this a war or isn't it?" A fine general staff! they grumbled sarcastically. Can't make up its mind about anything! Wants to see Madrid bombarded and kids smashed to bits. Here they were, ready to rip up those enemy batteries and fling them over the backs of mountains to save innocence imperiled, and the staff tied them hand and foot, condemned them to inaction.

It was clear enough, and the men admitted it, that none of them might have come up again after their dive into the moonlight, and that they ought in reality to be very happy to be alive and able to grouse against G. H. Q. and go on drinking their consoling brandy;— and, by the way, since the second telephone message, two curious things had happened: the brandy tasted better and the men were now drinking it cheerfully instead of moodily.

Yet at the same time I saw nothing in their vehemence that made me think it either silly or boastful. I could not but remember that all of them had been ready to die with simplicity.

Day broke. I scrubbed my face in the freezing water of the village pump. Coffee steamed in the bowls under an arbor forty yards from the enemy outpost, half-wrecked by the midnight firing but safe in the truce of dawn. Now freshly washed, the survivors gathered here to commune in life rather than in death, to share their white bread, their cigarettes, their smiles. They came in one by one, the captain, Sergeant R——, the lieutenant, and the rest, planted their elbows solidly on the table, and sat facing this treasure which they had been judicious enough to despise at a moment when it seemed it must be abandoned, but which had now recovered its price. "*Salud, amigo!*"—"Hail, friend!"— they sang out as they clapped one another on the shoulder.

I loved the freezing wind that caressed us and the

shining sun that warmed us beneath the touch of the wind. I loved the mountain air that was filling me with gladness. I rejoiced in the cheer of these men who sat in their shirtsleeves gathering fresh strength from their repast and making ready, once they had finished and risen to their feet, to knead the stuff of the world.

A ripe pod burst somewhere. From time to time a silly bullet spat against the stone wall. Death was abroad, of course, but wandering aimlessly and without ill intent. This was not death's hour. We in the arbor were celebrating life.

This whole platoon had risen up *de profundis;* and the captain sat breaking the white bread, that densely baked bread of Spain so rich in wheat, in order that each of his comrades, having stretched forth his hand, might receive a chunk as big as his fist and turn it into life.

These men had in truth risen *de profundis.* They were in very fact beginning a new life. I stared at them, and in particular at Sergeant R——, he who was to have been the first man out and who had gone to sleep in preparation for the attack. I was with them when they woke him up. Now Sergeant R—— had been well aware that he was to be the first man to step out into the line of fire of a machine-gun nest and dance in the moonlight that brief ballet at the end of which is death. His awakening had been the awakening of a prisoner in the death cell.

At Carabanchel the trenches wound among little workmen's houses whose furnishings were still in place. In one of these, a few yards from the enemy, Sergeant R—— was sleeping fully dressed on an iron cot. When we had lighted a candle and had stuck it into the neck of a bottle, and had drawn forth out of the darkness that funereal bed, the first thing that came into view was a pair of clogs. Enormous clogs, iron-shod and studded with nails, the clogs of a sewer-worker or a railway trackwalker. All the poverty of the world was in those clogs. No man ever strode with happy steps through life in clogs like these: he boarded life like a longshoreman for whom life is a ship to be unloaded.

This man was shod in his tools, and his whole body was covered with the tools of his trade—cartridge belt, gun, leather harness. His neck was bent beneath the heavy collar of the draught horse. Deep in caves, in Morocco, you can see millstones worked by blind horses. Here in the ruddy wavering light of the candle we were waking up a blind horse and sending him out to the mill.

"Hi! Sergeant!"

He sent forth a sigh as heavy as a wave and turned slowly and massively over towards us so that we saw a face still asleep and filled with anguish. His eyes were shut, and his mouth, to which clung a bubble of air, was half open like the mouth of a drowned man. We sat down on his bed and watched his laborious awaken-

ing. The man was clinging like a crab to submarine
depths, grasping in his fists I know not what dark sea-
weed. He opened and shut his hands, pulled up another
deep sigh, and escaped from us suddenly with his face
to the wall, obstinate with the stubbornness of an animal
refusing to die, turning its back on the slaughter-house.

"Hi! Sergeant!"

Once again he was drawn up from the bottom of the
sea, swam towards us, and we saw again his face in the
candle-light. This time we had hobbled our sleeper; he
would not get away from us again. He blinked with
closed eyes, moved his mouth round as if swallowing,
ran his hand over his forehead, made one great effort
to sink back into his happy dreams and reject our universe of dynamite, weariness, and glacial night, but it
was too late. Something from without was too strong
for him.

Like the punished schoolboy stirred by the insistent
bell out of his dream of a school-less world, Sergeant
R—— began to clothe himself in the weary flesh he had
so recently shed, that flesh which in the chill of awakening was soon to know the old pains in the joints, the
weight of the harness, and the stumbling race towards
death. Not so much death as the discomfort of dying,
the filth of the blood in which he would steep his hands
when he tried to rise to his feet; the stickiness of that
coagulating syrup. Not so much death as the Calvary
of a punished child.

One by one he stretched his arms and then his legs, bringing up an elbow, straightening a knee, while his straps, his gun, his cartridge belt, the three grenades hanging from his belt, all hampered the final strokes of this swimmer in the sea of sleep. At last he opened his eyes, sat up on the bed, and stared at us, mumbling:

"Huh! Oh! Are we off?"

And as he spoke, he simply stretched out his hand for his rifle.

"No," said the captain. "The attack has been called off."

Sergeant R——, let me tell you that we made you a present of your life. Just that. As much as if you had stood at the foot of the electric chair. And God knows, the world sheds ink enough on the pathos of pardon at the foot of the electric chair. We brought you your pardon *in extremis*. No question about it. In your mind there was nothing between you and death but a thickness of tissue-paper. Therefore you must forgive me my curiosity. I stared at you, and I shall never forget your face. It was a face touching and ugly, with a humped nose a little too big, high cheek-bones, and the spectacles of an intellectual. How does a man receive the gift of life? I can answer that. A man sits still, pulls a bit of tobacco out of his pocket, nods his head slowly, looks up at the ceiling, and says:

"Suits me."

Then he nods his head again and adds:

"If they'd sent us a couple of platoons the attack might have made sense. The lads would have pitched in. You'd have seen what they can do."

Sergeant, Sergeant, what will you do with this gift of life?

Now, Sergeant at peace, you are dipping your bread into your coffee. You are rolling cigarettes. You are like the lad who has been told he will not be punished after all. And yet, like the rest, you are ready to start out again tonight on that brief dash at the end of which the only thing a man can do is kneel down.

Over and over in my head there goes the question I have wanted to ask you ever since last night: "Sergeant, what is it makes you willing to die?"

But I know that it is impossible to ask such a question. It would offend a modesty in you which you yourself do not know to be there, but which would never forgive me. You could not answer with high-sounding words: they would seem false to you and in truth they would be false. What language could be chaste enough for a modest man like you? But I am determined to know, and I shall try to get round the difficulty. I shall ask you seemingly idle questions, and you will answer.

"Tell me, why did you join up?"

If I understood your answer, Sergeant, you hardly know yourself. You were a bookkeeper in Barcelona. You added up your columns of figures every day without worrying much about the struggle against the rebels. But one of your friends joined up, and then a second friend; and you were disturbed to find yourself undergoing a curious transformation: little by little your columns of figures seemed to you futile. Your pleasures, your work, your dreams, all seemed to belong to another age.

But even that was not important, until one day you heard that one of your friends had been killed on the Málaga front. He was not a friend for whom you would ever have felt you had to lay down your life. Yet that bit of news swept over you, over your narrow little life, like a wind from the sea. And that morning another friend had looked at you and said, "Do we or don't we?" And you had said, "We do."

You never really wondered about the imperious call that compelled you to join up. You accepted a truth which you could never translate into words, but whose self-evidence overpowered you. And while I sat listening to your story, an image came into my mind, and I understood.

When the wild ducks or the wild geese migrate in their season, a strange tide rises in the territories over which they sweep. As if magnetized by the great triangular flight, the barnyard fowl leap a foot or two into the air and try to fly. The call of the wild strikes them with the force of a harpoon and a vestige of savagery quickens their blood. All the ducks on the farm are transformed for an instant into migrant birds, and into those hard little heads, till now filled with humble images of pools and worms and barnyards, there swims a sense of continental expanse, of the breadth of seas and the salt taste of the ocean wind. The duck totters to right and left in its wire enclosure, gripped by a sudden passion to perform the impossible and a sudden love whose object is a mystery.

Even so is man overwhelmed by a mysterious presentiment of truth, so that he discovers the vanity of his bookkeeping and the emptiness of his domestic felicities. But he can never put a name to this sovereign truth. Men explain these brusque vocations by the need to escape or the lure of danger, as if we knew where the need to escape and the lure of danger themselves came from. They talk about the call of duty, but what is it that makes the call of duty so pressing? What can you tell me, Sergeant, about that uneasiness that seeped in to disturb your peaceful existence?

The call that stirred you must torment all men. Whether we dub it sacrifice, or poetry, or adventure, it is always the same voice that calls. But domestic security has succeeded in crushing out that part in us that is capable of heeding the call. We scarcely quiver; we beat our wings once or twice and fall back into our barnyard.

We are prudent people. We are afraid to let go of our petty reality in order to grasp at a great shadow. But you, Sergeant, did discover the sordidness of those shop-keepers' bustlings, those petty pleasures, those petty needs. You felt that men did not live like this. And you agreed to heed the great call without bothering to try to understand it. The hour had come when you must moult, when you must rise into the sky.

The barnyard duck had no notion that his little head was big enough to contain oceans, continents, skies; but of a sudden here he was beating his wings, despising corn, despising worms, battling to become a wild duck.

There is a day of the year when the eels must go down to the Sargasso Sea, and come what may, no one can prevent them. On that day they spit upon their ease, their tranquillity, their tepid waters. Off they go over ploughed fields, pricked by the hedges and skinned by the stones, in search of the river that leads to the abyss.

Even so did you feel yourself swept away by that inward migration about which no one had ever said a word to you. You were ready for a sort of bridal that was a mystery to you, but in which you had to participate. "Do we or don't we? We do." You went up to the front in a war that at bottom meant little to you. You took to the road as spontaneously as that silvery people shining in the fields on its way to the sea, or that black triangle in the sky.

What were you after? Last night you almost reached your goal. What was it you discovered in yourself that was so ready to burst from its cocoon? At daybreak your comrades were full of complaint: tell me, of what had they been defrauded? What had they discovered in themselves that was about to show itself, and that now they wept for?

What, Sergeant, were the visions that governed your destiny and justified your risking your life in this adventure? Your life, your only treasure! We have to live a long time before we become men. Very slowly do we plait the braid of friendships and affections. We learn slowly. We compose our creation slowly. And if we die too early we are in a sense cheated out of our share. We have to live a long time to fulfil ourselves.

But you, by the grace of an ordeal in the night which stripped you of all that was not intrinsic, you discovered a mysterious creature born of yourself. Great was this creature, and never shall you forget him. And he is yourself. You have had the sudden sense of fulfilling yourself in the instant of discovery, and you have learned suddenly that the future is now less necessary for the accumulation of treasures. That creature within you who opened his wings is not bound by ties to perishable things; he agrees to die for all men, to be swallowed up in something universal.

A great wind swept through you and delivered from the matrix the sleeping prince you sheltered—Man within you. You are the equal of the musician composing his music, of the physicist extending the frontier of knowledge, of all those who build the highways over which we march to deliverance. Now you are free to gamble with death. What have you now to lose?

Let us say you were happy in Barcelona: nothing more can ruin that happiness. You have reached an altitude where all loves are of the same stuff. Perhaps you suffered on earth, felt yourself alone on the planet, knew no refuge to which you might fly? What of that! Sergeant, this day you have been welcomed home by love.

VI

No man can draw a free breath who does not share with other men a common and disinterested ideal. Life has taught us that love does not consist in gazing at each other but in looking outward together in the same direction. There is no comradeship except through union in the same high effort. Even in our age of material well-being this must be so, else how should we explain the happiness we feel in sharing our last crust with others in the desert? No sociologist's textbook can prevail against this fact. Every pilot who has flown to the rescue of a comrade in distress knows that all joys are vain in comparison with this one. And this, it may be, is the reason why the world today is tumbling about our ears. It is precisely because this sort of fulfilment is promised each of us by his religion, that men are inflamed today. All of us, in words that contradict each other, express at bot-

tom the same exalted impulse. What sets us against one
another is not our aims—they all come to the same thing
—but our methods, which are the fruit of our varied
reasoning.

Let us, then, refrain from astonishment at what men
do. One man finds that his essential manhood comes
alive at the sight of self-sacrifice, cooperative effort, a
rigorous vision of justice, manifested in an anarchists'
cellar in Barcelona. For that man there will henceforth
be but one truth—the truth of the anarchists. Another,
having once mounted guard over a flock of terrified
little nuns kneeling in a Spanish nunnery, will thereafter
know a different truth—that it is sweet to die for the
Church. If, when Mermoz plunged into the Chilean
Andes with victory in his heart, you had protested to
him that no merchant's letter could possibly be worth
risking one's life for, Mermoz would have laughed in
your face. Truth is the man that was born in Mermoz
when he slipped through the Andean passes.

Consider that officer of the South Moroccan Rifles
who, during the war in the Rif, was in command of an
outpost set down between two mountains filled with
enemy tribesmen. One day, down from the mountain to
the west came a group seeking a parley. Arabs and
Frenchmen were talking over their tea when of a sudden a volley rang out. The tribesmen from the other
mountain were charging the post. When the commandant sought to dismiss his guests before fighting off their

allies, they said to him: "Today we are your guests. God will not allow us to desert you." They fought beside his men, saved the post, and then climbed back into their eyrie.

But on the eve of the day when their turn had come to pounce upon the post they sent again to the commandant.

"We came to your aid the other day," their chief said.

"True."

"We used up three hundred of our cartridges for you."

"Very likely."

"It would be only just that you replace them for us."

The commandant was an officer and a gentleman. They were given their cartridges.

Truth, for any man, is that which makes him a man. A man who has fraternized with men on this high plane, who has displayed this sportsmanship and has seen the rules of the game so nobly observed on both sides in matters of life and death, is obviously not to be mentioned in the same breath with the shabby hearty demagogue who would have expressed his fraternity with the Arabs by a great clap on the shoulders and a spate of flattering words that would have humiliated them. You might argue with the captain that all was fair in war, but if you did he would feel a certain pitying contempt for you. And he would be right.

Meanwhile, you are equally right to hate war.

If our purpose is to understand mankind and its yearnings, to grasp the essential reality of mankind, we must never set one man's truth against another's. All beliefs are demonstrably true. All men are demonstrably in the right. Anything can be demonstrated by logic. I say that that man is right who blames all the ills of the world upon hunchbacks. Let us declare war on hunchbacks—and in the twinkling of an eye all of us will hate them fanatically. All of us will join to avenge the crimes of the hunchbacks. Assuredly, hunchbacks, too, do commit crimes.

But if we are to succeed in grasping what is essential in man, we must put aside the passions that divide us and that, once they are accepted, sow in the wind a whole Koran of unassailable verities and fanaticisms. Nothing is easier than to divide men into rightists and leftists, hunchbacks and straightbacks, fascists and democrats—and these distinctions will be perfectly just. But truth, we know, is that which clarifies, not that which confuses. Truth is the language that expresses universality. Newton did not "discover" a law that lay hidden from man like the answer to a rebus. He accomplished a creative operation. He founded a human speech which could express at one and the same time the fall of an apple and the rising of the sun. Truth is not that which is demonstrable but that which is ineluctable.

There is no profit in discussing ideologies. If all of them are logically demonstrable then all of them must

contradict one other. To agree to discuss them is tanta-
mount to despairing of the salvation of mankind—
whereas everywhere about us men manifest identical
yearnings.

What all of us want is to be set free. The man who
sinks his pickaxe into the ground wants that stroke to
mean something. The convict's stroke is not the same as
the prospector's, for the obvious reason that the prospector's stroke has meaning and the convict's stroke has
none. It would be a mistake to think that the prison exists at the point where the convict's stroke is dealt.
Prison is not a mere physical horror. It is using a pickaxe
to no purpose that makes a prison; the horror resides in
the failure to enlist all those who swing the pick in the
community of mankind.

We all yearn to escape from prison.

There are two hundred million men in Europe whose
existence has no meaning and who yearn to come alive.
Industry has torn them from the idiom of their peasant lineage and has locked them up in those enormous
ghettos that are like railway yards heaped with blackened trucks. Out of the depths of their slums these
men yearn to be awakened. There are others, caught
in the wheels of a thousand trades, who are forbidden
to share in the joys known to a Mermoz, to a priest,
to a man of science. Once it was believed that to
bring these creatures to manhood it was enough to feed

them, clothe them, and look to their everyday needs; but we see now that the result of this has been to turn out petty shopkeepers, village politicians, hollow technicians devoid of an inner life. Some indeed were well taught, but no one troubled to cultivate any of them. People who believe that culture consists in the capacity to remember formulae have a paltry notion of what it is. Of course any science student can tell us more about Nature and her laws than can Descartes or Newton,—but what can he tell us about the human spirit?

With more or less awareness, all men feel the need to come alive. But most of the methods suggested for bringing this about are snares and delusions. Men can of course be stirred into life by being dressed up in uniforms and made to blare out chants of war. It must be confessed that this is one way for men to break bread with comrades and to find what they are seeking, which is a sense of something universal, of self-fulfilment. But of this bread men die.

It is easy to dig up wooden idols and revive ancient and more or less workable myths like Pan-Germanism or the Roman Empire. The Germans can intoxicate themselves with the intoxication of being Germans and compatriots of Beethoven. A stoker in the hold of a freighter can be made drunk with this drink. What is more difficult is to bring up a Beethoven out of the stoke-hold.

These idols, in sum, are carnivorous idols. The man

who dies for the progress of science or the healing of the sick serves life in his very dying. It may be glorious to die for the expansion of territory, but modern warfare destroys what it claims to foster. The day is gone when men sent life coursing through the veins of a race by the sacrifice of a little blood. War carried on by gas and bombing is no longer war, it is a kind of bloody surgery. Each side settles down behind a concrete wall and finds nothing better to do than to send forth, night after night, squadrons of planes to bomb the guts of the other side, blow up its factories, paralyze its production, and abolish its trade. Such a war is won by him who rots last —but in the end both rot together.

In a world become a desert we thirst for comradeship. It is the savor of bread broken with comrades that makes us accept the values of war. But there are other ways than war to bring us the warmth of a race, shoulder to shoulder, towards an identical goal. War has tricked us. It is not true that hatred adds anything to the exaltation of the race.

Why should we hate one another? We all live in the same cause, are borne through life on the same planet, form the crew of the same ship. Civilizations may, indeed, compete to bring forth new syntheses, but it is monstrous that they should devour one another.

To set man free it is enough that we help one another to realize that there does exist a goal towards which all

mankind is striving. Why should we not strive towards
that goal together, since it is what unites us all? The
surgeon pays no heed to the moanings of his patient:
beyond that pain it is man he is seeking to heal. That
surgeon speaks a universal language. The physicist does
the same when he ponders those almost divine equations
in which he seizes the whole physical universe from the
atom to the nebula. Even the simple shepherd modestly
watching his sheep under the stars would discover, once
he understood the part he was playing, that he was
something more than a servant, was a sentinel. And each
sentinel among men is responsible for the whole of the
empire.

It is impossible not to believe that the shepherd wants
to understand. One day, on the Madrid front, I chanced
upon a school that stood on a hill surrounded by a low
stone wall some five hundred yards behind the trenches.
A corporal was teaching botany that day. He was lectur-
ing on the fragile organs of a poppy held in his hands.
Out of the surrounding mud, and in spite of the wandering shells that dropped all about, he had drawn like a
magnet an audience of stubble-bearded soldiers who
squatted tailor fashion and listened with their chins in
their hands to a discourse of which they understood not
a word in five. Something within them had said: "You
are but brutes fresh from your caves. Go along! Catch

up with humanity!" And they had hurried on their muddy clogs to overtake it.

It is only when we become conscious of our part in life, however modest, that we shall be happy. Only then will we be able to live in peace and die in peace, for only this lends meaning to life and to death.

Death is sweet when it comes in its time and in its place, when it is part of the order of things, when the old peasant of Provence, at the end of his reign, remits into the hands of his sons his parcel of goats and olive-trees in order that they in their turn transmit them to their sons. When one is part of a peasant lineage, one's death is only half a death. Each life in turn bursts like a pod and sends forth its seed.

I stood once with three peasants in the presence of their dead mother. Sorrow filled the room. For a second time, the umbilical cord had been cut. For a second time the knot had been loosed, the knot that bound one generation to another. Of a sudden the three sons had felt themselves alone on earth with everything still to be learned. The magnetic pole round which they had lived was gone; their mother's table, where they had collected on feast days with their families, was no more. But I could see in this rupture that it was possible for life to be granted a second time. Each of these sons was now to be the head of a family, was to be a rallying point and a patriarch, until that day when each would pass on the staff of office to the brood of children now murmuring in the courtyard.

I looked at their mother, at the old peasant with the firm peaceful face, the tight lips, the human face transformed into a stone mask. I saw in it the faces of her sons. That mask had served to mould theirs. That body had served to mould the bodies of these three exemplary men who stood there as upright as trees. And now she lay broken but at rest, a vein from which the gold had been extracted. In their turn, her sons and daughters would bring forth men from their mould. One does not die on a farm: their mother is dead, long live their mother!

Sorrowful, yes, but so simple was this image of a lineage dropping one by one its white-haired members as it made its way through time and through its metamorphoses towards a truth that was its own.

That same day, when the tocsin tolled to announce to the countryside the death of this old woman, it seemed to me not a song of despair but a discreet and tender chant of joy. In that same voice the church-bell celebrated birth and death, christening and burial, the passage from one generation to the next. I was suffused with a gentle peace of soul at this sound which announced the betrothal of a poor old woman and the earth.

This was life that was handed on here from generation to generation with the slow progress of a tree's growth, but it was also fulfilment. What a mysterious ascension! From a little bubbling lava, from the vague pulp of a star, from a living cell miraculously fertilized, we have issued forth and have bit by bit raised ourselves to the writing of cantatas and the weighing of nebulae.

This peasant mother had done more than transmit life, she had taught her sons a language, had handed on to them the lot so slowly garnered through the centuries, the spiritual patrimony of traditions, concepts, and myths that make up the whole of the difference between Newton or Shakespeare and the caveman.

What we feel when we are hungry, when we feel that hunger which drew the Spanish soldiers under fire towards that botany lesson, drew Mermoz across the South Atlantic, draws a man to a poem, is that the birth of man is not yet accomplished, that we must take stock of ourselves and our universe. We must send forth pontoons into the night. There are men unaware of this, imagining themselves wise and self-regarding because they are indifferent. But everything in the world gives the lie to their wisdom.

Comrades of the air! I call upon you to bear me witness. When have we felt ourselves happy men?

· 10 ·

Conclusion

HERE, in the final pages of this book, I remember again those musty civil servants who served as our escort in the omnibus when we set out to fly our first mails, when we prepared ourselves to be transformed into men—we who had had the luck to be called. Those clerks were kneaded of the same stuff as the rest of us, but they knew not that they were hungry.

To come to man's estate it is not necessary to get oneself killed round Madrid, or to fly mail planes, or to struggle wearily in the snows out of respect for the dignity of life. The man who can see the miraculous in a poem, who can take pure joy from music, who can

301

break his bread with comrades, opens his window to the same refreshing wind off the sea. He too learns a language of men.

But too many men are left unawakened.

A few years ago, in the course of a long railway journey, I was suddenly seized by a desire to make a tour of the little country in which I was locked up for three days, cradled in that rattle that is like the sound of pebbles rolled over and over by the waves; and I got up out of my berth. At one in the morning I went through the train in all its length. The sleeping cars were empty. The first-class carriages were empty. They put me in mind of the luxurious hotels on the Riviera that open in winter for a single guest, the last representative of an extinct fauna. A sign of bitter times.

But the third-class carriages were crowded with hundreds of Polish workmen sent home from France. I made my way along those passages, stepping over sprawling bodies and peering into the carriages. In the dim glow cast by the night-lamps into these barren and comfortless compartments I saw a confused mass of people churned about by the swaying of the train, the whole thing looking and smelling like a barrack-room. A whole nation returning to its native poverty seemed to sprawl there in a sea of bad dreams. Great shaven heads rolled on the cushionless benches. Men, women, and children were stirring in their sleep, tossing from left to right and back again as if attacked by all the noises and jerkings that threatened them in their oblivion. They had not found the hospitality of a sweet slumber.

Looking at them I said to myself that they had lost half their human quality. These people had been knocked about from one end of Europe to the other by the economic currents; they had been torn from their little houses in the north of France, from their tiny garden-plots, their three pots of geranium that always stood in the windows of the Polish miners' families. I saw lying beside them pots and pans, blankets, curtains, bound into bundles badly tied and swollen with hernias.

Out of all that they had caressed or loved in France, out of everything they had succeeded in taming in their four or five years in my country—the cat, the dog, the geranium—they had been able to bring away with them only a few kitchen utensils, two or three blankets, a curtain or so.

A baby lay at the breast of a mother so weary that she seemed asleep. Life was being transmitted in the shabbiness and the disorder of this journey. I looked at the father. A powerful skull as naked as a stone. A body hunched over in uncomfortable sleep, imprisoned in working clothes, all humps and hollows. The man looked like a lump of clay, like one of those sluggish and shapeless derelicts that crumple into sleep in our public markets.

And I thought: The problem does not reside in this

poverty, in this filth, in this ugliness. But this same man and this same woman met one day. This man must have smiled at this woman. He may, after his work was done, have brought her flowers. Timid and awkward, perhaps he trembled lest she disdain him. And this woman, out of natural coquetry, this woman sure of her charms, perhaps took pleasure in teasing him. And this man, this man who is now no more than a machine for swinging a pick or a sledge-hammer, must have felt in his heart a delicious anguish. The mystery is that they should have become these lumps of clay. Into what terrible mould were they forced? What was it that marked them like this as if they had been put through a monstrous stamping machine? A deer, a gazelle, any animal grown old, preserves its grace. What is it that corrupts this wonderful clay of which man is kneaded?

I went on through these people whose slumber was as sinister as a den of evil. A vague noise floated in the air made up of raucous snores, obscure moanings, and the scraping of clogs as their wearers, broken on one side, sought comfort on the other. And always the muted accompaniment of those pebbles rolled over and over by the waves.

I sat down face to face with one couple. Between the man and the woman a child had hollowed himself out a place and fallen asleep. He turned in his slumber, and in the dim lamplight I saw his face. What an adorable face!

A golden fruit had been born of these two peasants. Forth from this sluggish scum had sprung this miracle of delight and grace.

I bent over the smooth brow, over those mildly pouting lips, and I said to myself: This is a musician's face. This is the child Mozart. This is a life full of beautiful promise. Little princes in legends are not different from this. Protected, sheltered, cultivated, what could not this child become?

When by mutation a new rose is born in a garden, all the gardeners rejoice. They isolate the rose, tend it, foster it. But there is no gardener for men. This little Mozart will be shaped like the rest by the common stamping machine. This little Mozart will love shoddy music in the stench of night dives. This little Mozart is condemned.

I went back to my sleeping car. I said to myself: Their fate causes these people no suffering. It is not an impulse to charity that has upset me like this. I am not weeping over an eternally open wound. Those who carry the wound do not feel it. It is the human race and not the individual that is wounded here, is outraged here. I do not believe in pity. What torments me tonight is the gardener's point of view. What torments me is not this poverty to which after all a man can accustom himself as easily as to sloth. Generations of Orientals live in filth and love it. What torments me is not the humps nor the hollows nor the ugliness. It is the sight, a little bit in all these men, of Mozart murdered.

Only the Spirit, if it breathe upon the clay, can create Man.

THE END